The Which? Guide to Women's Health

Dr Ann Robinson

CONSUMERS' ASSOCIATION

Which? Books are commissioned and researched by
Consumers' Association and published by
Which? Ltd, 2 Marylebone Road, London NW1 4DF
Email address: books@which.net

Distributed by The Penguin Group:
Penguin Books Ltd, 27 Wrights Lane, London W8 5TZ

First edition 1996
Second edition 1999
Copyright © 1996, 1999 Which? Ltd

British Library Cataloguing in Publication Data
A catalogue record for this book is available from the British Library

ISBN 0 85202 759 1

For a full list of *Which?* books, please write to
Which? Books, Castlemead, Gascoyne Way, Hertford X, SG14 1LH
or access our web site at http://www.which.net

Cover and text design by Kyzen Creative Consultants
Cover photograph by Tony Stone Images
Illustrations by Paul Wootton Associates and Tony Graham

Typeset by Saxon Graphics Ltd, Derby
Printed and bound in Great Britain by Clays Ltd, Bungay, Suffolk

Contents

★An asterisk next to the name of an organisation in the text indicates that the address can be found in this section

Introduction

Women have never had it so good, and they have never had it so hard. The good news is that women living at the end of the twentieth century can expect to live much longer than their mothers and grandmothers. Moreover, they enjoy better health than ever before: they are less likely to die in infancy or childbirth, and less likely to be old and infirm by the time they reach the menopause.

Progress in medicine and treatment and greater knowledge of how to prevent illness have contributed to the increased longevity. Through better education, improved health services and the media in general, women are more aware than ever of the importance of basic hygiene, exercise, a balanced diet and controlling stress. The majority of women alive today have never been threatened by killer diseases such as tuberculosis, poliomyelitis or diphtheria, thanks to childhood vaccinations and inoculations. Fifty years ago we had no drugs to treat hypertension, rheumatoid arthritis, Parkinson's or schizophrenia; back-street abortions were rife; we had no heart surgery or transplants, control of diabetes left much to be desired and there was no treatment for infertility. True, we still have cancer, stroke and heart disease to combat. But despite all we read in the press about, for example, the dangers of heart disease within the female population, the fact is that the number of women dying of heart disease has decreased since the 1980s, while screening, better drugs and more effective treatments are slowly but steadily reducing the risk from other potentially fatal conditions.

However, the use of technology and new techniques to prevent, detect and treat medical conditions and illnesses is a two-edged sword. While it is clear that they enable people to lead healthier and longer lives, they can be over-used or mis-used to the extent that they are not merely unhelpful, but positively harmful. Screening tests may help detect disease in their early stages, but they also engender a lot of anxiety: they are not always done properly, and in a few unfortunate cases the person dies from the very disease the test was supposed to pick up but did not. Moreover, we do not always prepare ourselves for the results of the tests, so when something abnormal shows up we are ill-equipped mentally, emotionally and sometimes physically to deal with the implications.

The growth in the availability of self-diagnosis kits is another case in point: women can now test not just for pregnancy but for serious conditions such as bowel cancer and diabetes in their own homes, but few know how to interpret the results properly. Thus, someone who gets a positive result may panic even though the test is not infallible, while someone whose test proves negative may be lulled into a fall sense of security and not visit the doctor to get her symptoms checked out properly.

Tests can also be done to show if women are genetically predisposed to a disease. The knowledge that we are likely to contract a serious illness in the future may help us prepare for it, but it may, on the other hand, destroy our emotional security and happiness. There is, of course, an argument to be made for giving women the choice of having a test to predict whether they will suffer from, say, Alzheimer's disease or breast cancer when they are older: they should be given the facts and be allowed to decide for themselves.

Despite all the advances in medical sciences, in many ways we do not really enjoy our good health as we might. We read and know a huge amount about illness, but often much less about how to stay well. We grow up now without expecting to encounter pain or serious illness and find we cannot cope if we are unlucky enough to experience the unexpected. We forget how far we have come, and dwell on the things that modern medicine cannot yet put right: for example, we tend to overlook the benefits of childhood immunisation when a scare story about the side-effects of a vaccine is published and are prepared to forgo the whole programme. Our expectations of the medical world are so high that we sometimes end up being disappointed.

Women have never had it so hard because we stand on the cusp of even greater medical advances, but their practical applications are tantalisingly elusive. Genetic testing can confirm diagnoses of cystic fibrosis or muscular dystrophy, but cure by genetic manipulation is still beyond our grasp. Occasionally we find that even when a treatment is available it is not provided on the National Health Service, usually for cost reasons. This could be a life-prolonging drug (for cancer, say) or a so-called 'lifestyle drug' (such as one used to treat impotence or obesity). As more becomes medically possible, the gap between what we want and what the NHS can provide is bound to widen even further.

Another gap that is growing is the one between the health of the well-off and that of the poor. The difference starts in the womb and results in a shorter lifespan. Only a combination of actions by policy-makers and self-help measures can improve this divisive situation.

Affluent and educated women going into the 21st century have an unprecedented range of choices. You can choose if and when to get pregnant, how and where to give birth, and whether to take hormone replacement therapy at the menopause. You can mix and match conventional and complementary therapies. You can acquire vast amounts of information from books, magazines, newspapers and the Internet. You may well hear about new treatments or discoveries before your doctor does. But you can drown in a surfeit of data and, for all the facts, figures and claims about different therapies and treatments, it can be very difficult to know what to do for the best, especially when new and conflicting stories are coming out all the time.

Cosmetic surgery is an interesting example of the modern woman's dilemma. Many of us are attracted to the idea of enhancing our looks and preserving our youthful face and body despite the ravages of age. Advertisements for cosmetic surgery clinics abound. They play on our insecurities about our looks, and promise quick, easy results. However, objective advice is hard to come by, with many GPs and NHS doctors uninterested or antagonistic to the whole concept of cosmetic surgery. The chapter on cosmetic surgery in this book explores the pros and cons of the main procedures such as nose re-shaping and face-lifts, and gives clear, non-judgemental advice on how to choose a cosmetic surgeon.

Women can take a proactive role in making the longer lives they can now expect to enjoy both healthy and happy. To do this, they need to make themselves as well-informed on health issues as they can: this will help them to build a better relationship with the medical professionals with whom they come into contact, so that they can become more involved in the choice of treatment they receive – which, as any doctor will confirm, is the single most positive element in their 'compliance' (in other words, their willingness to follow the treatment through and give it its best chance of working).

This book aims to address all the key health issues facing women in order that they can participate fully in this partnership. The first section considers the external factors that influence health, positive ways to maintain good health and ways of avoiding ill health. The subsequent chapters focus on the major body systems and what can be done to keep the body healthy, as well as discussing the symptoms of the disorders that can arise in each part of the body, their possible causes, what steps you may be able to take yourself to alleviate the problem and when to seek professional help; the various tests and treatments available are also described.

Above all, the book celebrates the fact that women are enjoying better health now than ever before, and stresses ways of staying healthy rather than focusing on illness.

Part 1

Mind and matter

Chapter 1

Staying well and beating illness

Most of us take good health for granted: we do not realise how well we feel normally until we experience pain or a part of our body stops functioning. As this chapter shows, it is as important to maintain good health as it is to avoid illness – and much easier.

People at the beginning of the 20th century generally did not expect to live very long lives; their lives were often marred by incurable infections and early deaths in the family. With the improvements in medical science our expectations have grown. Now that we no longer need to fear early death to the same extent as our great-grandparents, we can focus on improving the quality of our lives. We can afford to look more closely at our emotional and psychological needs and seek professional help for problems and conflicts before they become intractable.

Women nowadays have a greater level of health awareness than ever before. Most of us know the benefits of eating healthily, exercising regularly, practising safe sex, avoiding smoking and having regular screening tests. We also know how to avoid unwanted pregnancies and how best to take care of ourselves and our unborn child if we become pregnant. However, knowing what is good for us and actually putting the knowledge into practice are two different things. Ultimately it is up to each of us as individuals to adopt a healthy lifestyle, and to use health professionals, such as GPs, as the valuable sources of support and information most of them strive to be.

Many women devote almost all their physical and emotional energy to caring for others. They often find it hard to make time for themselves, but it is essential to do so. As a traditional Jewish saying

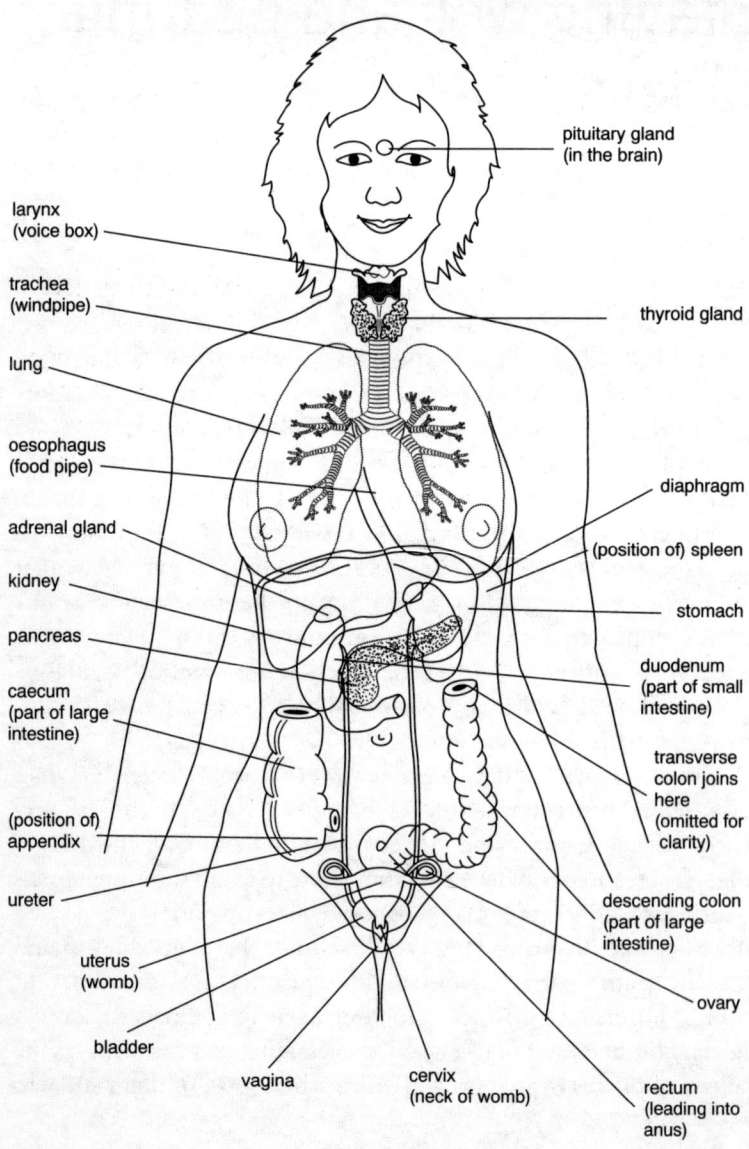

pituitary gland
(in the brain)

larynx
(voice box)

trachea
(windpipe)

thyroid gland

lung

oesophagus
(food pipe)

diaphragm

adrenal gland

(position of) spleen

kidney

stomach

pancreas

duodenum
(part of small
intestine)

caecum
(part of large
intestine)

transverse
colon joins
here
(omitted for
clarity)

(position of)
appendix

ureter

descending colon
(part of large
intestine)

uterus
(womb)

bladder

ovary

vagina

cervix
(neck of womb)

rectum
(leading into
anus)

Figure 1 Internal organs in a woman

points out, 'If I am not for myself, who will be for me? And if not now, when?'

Maintaining good health takes a certain amount of hard work and commitment: it is often easy to slide into inactivity and develop a negative attitude about oneself. But if you can acknowledge the positive aspects of your life, focus on the parts of your body that do work well and celebrate your achievements, you will be able to cope with the health problems that will, inevitably, crop up from time to time.

Factors that determine health and well-being

Being female rather than male, and being well-off rather than poor are advantages as far as health is concerned. Characteristics inherited from parents (genetics), ethnic group and where a person lives also play a part. Having an unhealthy lifestyle and breathing polluted air contribute to ill health. But these factors are also determined to a certain extent by income (see below).

Access to medical services and complementary therapies may influence how speedily health problems are addressed: medical services in some inner cities and remote rural areas are likely to be less readily available to women than in semi-rural and suburban areas. Socially disadvantaged women and members of some ethnic minorities may make less use of the medical services on offer, especially preventative services such as antenatal care or cervical screening. Treatment of established conditions may also be less effective for these disadvantaged women. For example, breast cancer is more common among better-off women, but their survival rate is better than it is for poorer women, presumably because of earlier detection and better treatment. Some complementary therapies have been available on the NHS in the last few years, principally at the surgeries of fundholding GPs. However, GPs who offer such therapies fear that as fundholding is wound down in favour of primary care groups (PCGs) they will no longer be able to manage their own budgets and that they will not receive funding for complementary medicine. Some NHS hospital speciality units offer complementary therapies – for example, pain clinics may have acupuncturists and rheumatology clinics may have osteopaths. There are also examples of charities operating in hospitals and funding extra services such as counselling, aromatherapy and massage.

Remaining in good health depends on an interaction of all these factors. The medical profession continues to work on ways of minimising health problems conferred by genetic problems. In addition, every individual woman can adopt a lifestyle which is conducive to good health.

Socio-economic factors

The single biggest determining factor for good health is wealth. Adequate income, education, housing, employment, and social support from family or friends are probably more important factors in staying healthy than what we eat or whether or not we do any exercise. The gap between the health of the well-off and the relatively poor is widening all the time. The difference in health is identifiable at every stage of life: it starts in the womb, as economically disadvantaged women have lower-birthweight babies, which may predispose their children to diabetes and heart disease in later life. The variations in health are not just due to the fact that poorer women smoke more, have poorer diets and exercise less than more affluent women. These factors probably account for only a third of the variations that are seen. It has been argued that poorer women smoke more partly as a response to the stress they experience. A

The widening gap in the health of different social classes in the UK

- On average, the most economically deprived live seven years less than the most affluent.
- Children of the most deprived are four times more likely to suffer accidental death than children of the most affluent.
- Of the 70 major causes of death in women, 64 are more common in women who are married to the most deprived men. Of all the major diseases in women, only breast cancer is more prevalent in more affluent women. This may be because more affluent women tend to have children later in life, choose not to have children, or start periods at a younger age – all of which may increase the risk of breast cancer.

---

woman who is stuck in poor accommodation, with insufficient income, dependent children and little support is unlikely to feel as healthy as she would if she were in better circumstances. Health agencies are beginning to recognise this.

While policy-makers fight over how to close the health gap, individual women can do much to improve their own health. First of all, they need to recognise how great an impact their circumstances are having on their health. A lonely, elderly woman may feel healthier if she does something stimulating socially, such as participate in a 'Fitness for the over-50s' exercise class, or visit a church-based drop-in centre, than if she visits her GP twice a week where she will, almost inevitably, be given medication which may or may not agree with her. Blaming 'the system' does not help. But recognising that your ill health may stem from your circumstances can fuel your determination to try to get a better deal for yourself and your children.

Gender factors

Many women have moments when they feel that their lot is an unhappy one compared to that of men: after all, periods, childbirth and the menopause are all exclusive to women. Even conditions like deafness, acne and arthritis are different, although not necessarily worse, in women. But, as mentioned above, although women suffer more ill health during their lifetime than men, they are the stronger sex – outliving men by five years on average.

Heart disease is the major cause of death among men and women, although the rates are falling for both sexes. Before the age of 65, women suffer relatively less heart disease than men, as the female hormone oestrogen is protective. After the menopause, oestrogen levels decline and, thereafter, female heart disease rates start to climb until they nearly catch up with men's. Hormone replacement therapy (HRT), which replaces oestrogen, can help to protect women from heart disease (and other disorders, such as osteoporosis) after the menopause.

Women under 65 suffer far fewer accidents than men, although over the age of 65 they suffer twice as many. This is because women under 65 are less likely to work in dangerous conditions and are less likely to be involved in serious car accidents. Over the age of 65, however, women live longer than men and are therefore more likely to suffer a fall or be knocked over by a car.

Ethnicity factors

There are variations in the health of women living in the UK which cannot be explained by socio-economic factors alone, and which may be attributable to ethnicity. It is likely that many of these variations start to disappear after a couple of generations, although genetic predisposition for particular conditions among certain ethnic groups may persist, e.g. sickle cell disease among Afro-Caribbeans. Some differences between ethnic groups are clearly related to lifestyle and diet and therefore subject to change. For example, as a nation the Japanese have very low rates of heart disease, but when Japanese people living in the West adopt (high-fat) Western eating habits their rates of heart disease start to increase.

There are several areas of health care where ethnicity seems to make a difference.

Visits to the GP

Women from the Indian subcontinent are more likely to consult their GPs than the population as a whole, which may reflect increased rates of illness or an inability to get effective treatment at the first visit. They may also have greater expectations of the doctor and may lack access to alternative sources of help – such as information gleaned from the media, self-help groups, or complementary therapists.

Screening for breast and cervical cancer

Despite increased attendance at a GP surgery, women from the Indian subcontinent are less likely to have breast cancer screening than other groups, and women from Pakistan and Bangladesh are less likely than the general population to have regular cervical smears. This is possibly because of poor communication about the need for the test, what it involves and how to get one done.

Skin cancer

Death rates from melanoma (a type of skin cancer) are lower among women from Asian and Afro-Caribbean countries than among the general population, probably because women from the

Indian subcontinent are less likely to expose their naked skin to the sun, and because both groups have darker skins than most Caucasian women. The pigment in dark skin protects against the sun's rays.

Stillbirth
Women born in the Indian subcontinent are 1.6 times more likely to suffer a stillbirth than women born in England or Wales. This may be related to poor maternal diet and health and to poorer antenatal care.

Inherited conditions
Afro-Caribbean women may carry the gene for sickle cell disease, and women from Mediterranean countries may carry the gene for thalassaemia, without any ill effects to themselves. If a woman who carries one of these genes has a child with a man who also carries the gene, the child may have the full-blown illness. A blood test can determine whether a woman is a carrier of these conditions, and genetic counselling is available to discuss options if the test is positive. Jewish women of East European origin (Ashkenazi) are at increased risk of carrying the gene for a fatal condition called Tay Sachs disease. A blood test is available for these women.

Heart disease and strokes
Women from India, Pakistan, Bangladesh and Sri Lanka living in the UK have particularly high rates of heart disease – 46 per cent higher than the general population. They also have an increased risk of suffering a stroke. This is probably due partly to an inherited tendency, and partly to stress, obesity, diabetes and diet. Women from African countries have fairly high rates of heart disease – higher than women from Caribbean countries, but lower than Asian women – and of strokes. Women from Caribbean countries have low rates of heart disease, but double the average risk of suffering a stroke. Death from strokes is declining among the population as a whole, including among ethnic minorities. But the risk of dying from a stroke remains disproportionately high among women born in the Caribbean. Good detection and treatment of high blood pressure are the most effective ways of further reducing strokes.

Schizophrenia

People from Afro-Caribbean countries are three to six times more likely to be diagnosed as schizophrenic than white men and women in England and Wales. This is not explained by an inherited tendency as rates of schizophrenia in the Caribbean itself are relatively low. The inability of psychiatrists in the UK to understand the cultural background of Afro-Caribbeans may be part of the reason for high rates of the diagnosis, rather than a truly higher incidence.

Depression and suicide

Asian women are more reluctant to seek medical help for mental illness such as depression than the general population. This is probably not because mental illness is less prevalent amongst Asians, but because they do not feel comfortable expressing psychological problems to a doctor. They may be more likely to present physical symptoms such as tiredness and generalised aches and pains without admitting to underlying anxiety or depression. It is unlikely that there really is less mental illness among Asian women, as their suicide rates are higher than they are within the general population, especially among young women. The suicide rate for 15–24-year-old Asian girls, especially those born in East Africa, is double that of the general population.

Regional variations in the UK

Regional variations can only partly be accounted for by differences in social class. There are health disadvantages to living in the north and north-west of England, compared to south-west England, even allowing for economic differences. Heart disease tends to be more common in the north of England than in the south-west and East Anglia, and the difference is only partly accounted for by the higher smoking rates among women in the north. The death rate from strokes is higher in the north than the south. Teenage (under-16) pregnancy rates are highest in inner-city, deprived areas where there are high rates of unemployment, such as Hull and Manchester and areas of London such as West Lambeth and Camberwell. Fatal and non-fatal accidents show little regional variation among women, although they are more common in the north among men. Most cancers occur most frequently in northern regions and least often in East Anglia and Oxford.

Breast cancer is the exception. The higher incidence in Oxford and East Anglia may be the result of a higher percentage of women in these areas choosing not to have children, or to have them at a later age.

Lung cancer, which is linked to cigarette smoking, is higher in Scotland than in the rest of the UK. In fact, Scotland has the highest lung cancer rate among women in the whole of Europe. Deaths from cervical cancer (cancer of the neck of the womb) are highest in the Mersey region and lowest in south-west Thames. More women have regular cervical smears in East Anglia (80 per cent) than in north-west and north-east Thames (60 per cent).

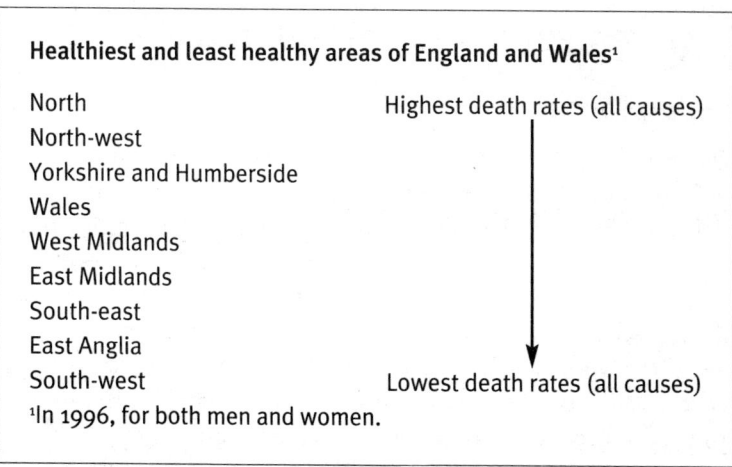

Healthiest and least healthy areas of England and Wales[1]

North   Highest death rates (all causes)
North-west
Yorkshire and Humberside
Wales
West Midlands
East Midlands
South-east
East Anglia
South-west   Lowest death rates (all causes)
[1]In 1996, for both men and women.

Workplace and environment

Conditions in the workplace and the home, and the quality of the air we breathe can all affect our health. Women may work with chemicals that can cause ill health, such as female anaesthetists who have a higher than normal rate of miscarriages, thought to be due to inhalation of anaesthetic gases. The risks from passive smoking have been widely recognised by employers in recent years, and many workplaces now ban smoking or limit it to specific areas. Environmental pollution, caused by vehicle emissions, produces increasingly poor air quality. This has been blamed for some of the present rise in cases of asthma.

Allergies

Allergies to external factors can affect health and well-being. A tendency to allergic conditions may be inherited and can result in hay fever (allergy to pollen), eczema and asthma. Coeliac disease, which is a digestive system disorder, is caused by an allergy to gluten in wheat. Conditions such as chronic sinusitis, which results in long-term or recurring inflammation of the sinuses in the face, and migraine may be caused or triggered by allergic reactions in susceptible women. There is ongoing research into whether some other conditions, such as Crohn's disease which affects the digestive system, may be the result of an allergic reaction.

Positive ways to maintain good health

Healthy eating

The way to ensure that your supermarket trolley is filled with healthy foods is to think 'low fat, low sugar, low salt, high fibre, high carbohydrate'. Eat lots of fruit and vegetables – at least five portions a day. The possible health benefits of fruit and vegetables include vitamins and minerals to maintain good health, lower heart disease (see also Chapter 8), help prevent certain cancers and prevent some types of arthritis and other diseases due to inflammation. There is still some debate about the chemicals used in producing fruit and vegetables, but at the moment it seems that any concern is more than offset by the huge health benefits. Organically farmed products are increasingly available, but unfortunately tend to be more expensive.

Try to limit high-fat foods, especially those which are high in saturated fats such as red meat and full-fat dairy products. You will also benefit from eating leaner meat such as chicken, turkey and veal in place of beef and lamb. Try low-fat yoghurts and fromage frais in place of higher-fat alternatives. Dairy foods are rich in calcium, which is good for bones and teeth, but you could have the calcium without all the fat: for example, eat low-fat hard cheeses such as Edam and Gouda in place of high-fat Cheddar, and drink skimmed or semi-skimmed milk rather than full-fat milk. Use mono- or polyunsaturated oil in place of butter or lard for cooking, and try to cook without fat if possible, by grilling instead of frying. Fill up by eating lots of bread, pasta, rice and other starches (carbohydrates), preferably the higher-fibre varieties, instead of getting most of your calories from fat-filled foods.

You should also try to eat oily fish (salmon, herring, mackerel, etc.) at least twice a week. The particular fats in oily fish can help to reduce heart disease and inflammatory diseases such as arthritis, among others. Avoid high-fat, high-sugar, low-fibre foods like bis-cuits, cakes and chocolates. It would not matter to your health if you never ate one again in your life. You could, of course, allow yourself the occasional treat, and eat fruit instead of biscuits the rest of the time. Consider alternative, lower-sugar varieties of products such as breakfast cereals, baked beans, yoghurts and drinks. Some products, especially certain breakfast cereals, may not taste sweet but contain a surprisingly large amount of sugar.

Nutritional supplements

Most women eating a well-balanced diet do not need to take extra vitamins, minerals or other supplements. Any possible deficiencies should be investigated by a doctor, as there may be a specific cause that needs treating. For example, taking iron tablets for years may mask the fact that you have a bleeding duodenal ulcer that needs treatment. It is also possible to overdose on vitamins and supple-ments: for instance, excess vitamin B6 is bad for the nervous sys-tem, and excess vitamin A is dangerous in pregnancy. Supplements can also interact with medication, which may make the medicines dangerous or ineffective. One multivitamin and mineral tablet a day will not harm anyone, but it may not contribute more to your health than eating an orange. Supplements that may be useful include:

- folic acid for women attempting to conceive. If you are trying for a baby you should take a 400 microgram tablet of folic acid every day to help prevent abnormalities of the baby's spinal cord (the cause of spina bifida). It is best to continue for the first 10–12 weeks after conception. Folic acid supplements are available free on prescription once you are pregnant, but are cheaper over the counter while you are trying to conceive
- calcium for pregnant, breast-feeding and menopausal women (45–60-year-olds). These women need 1,500mg calcium a day,

and supplements are worth considering if you do not like high-calcium foods such as dairy products and sardines
- vitamin C to help stave off colds (however, vitamin C is widely available in fruit and vegetables).

The benefits of other supplements such as royal jelly, gingko, ginseng, aloe vera juice and zinc are more questionable.

Exercise

Exercise has to be geared to the individual woman. Daily aerobic classes are not suitable – or a realistic option – for everybody. Exercise needs to be regular, varied, enjoyable and part of your daily routine. It is best to see a GP or health professional before embarking on a new exercise programme, especially if you are pregnant, elderly, have diabetes or any other long-term medical condition, or have recently had a heart attack. If you have not been used to exercising and would like to start, it is best to start with an activity that you have done in the past, and work at a level which is only slightly more active than the level you normally operate at, increasing the duration of the exercise gradually.

Exercise programme for previously inactive women

Activity: brisk walking

| Week | Distance (miles) | Age of woman | | | | No. of times a week |
| | | <30 | 30–39 | 40–49 | 50+ | |
		(target time for each group in minutes)				
1	1.0	15.0	15.5	16.0	16.5	2–3
2	1.0	14.0	14.5	15.0	15.5	2–3
3	1.5	21.0	21.5	22.5	23.5	2–3
4	2.0	28.0	29.0	30.0	31.0	2–3

A mixture of brisk walking, swimming, cycling and jogging provides the ideal mix of exercise for health. Fitness and stamina in each of these can be gradually built up in the same way as for walking.

Avoiding stress

Being psychologically fit and well is as important as being physically fit and well, and the two are inextricably linked. Physical illness is depressing, and depression induces physical illnesses. There are ways in which you can try to maintain your mental health, in the same way that you watch your diet and exercise to maintain your physical health.

Adequate sleep is essential if you are to cope with the day ahead. You may not be sleeping well if you have a young baby who will not settle, your partner snores or you are too tense or depressed. But no-one who is always tired can function properly, and you need to seek expert help to break the cycle and get back to a refreshing sleep pattern.

A balanced diet is also important in keeping mentally well. Under-nourishment, excessive dieting or binge-eating carbo-hydrates may contribute to a lack of energy that saps your spirit. Physical exercise such as 20–30 minutes a day of brisk walking helps to enhance your sense of well-being.

Loneliness and social isolation make mental stress much harder to deal with, and lonely women are more likely to be unhappy. Women who are at home with three children or more under the age of 14, women who have lost their mother in child-hood, those who have no supportive partner and those who do not work outside the home are most at risk of depression. Social support from groups, such as postnatal ones organised by the National Childbirth Trust,★ can provide much-needed friend-ship as well as being a source of advice and support.

There are some lucky women who have the capacity to see a pos-itive side to even the most gloomy events, who are happy and con-tent with their lot, and who view the future optimistically. Women who are blessed with that kind of temperament have a head start in weathering life's ups and downs. Other women become very stressed by change and uncertainty, and always fear the worst out-come of any event. It is possible to have counselling which is specif-ically geared to examining your reaction to events, and modifying that reaction. It is not a question of changing your personality, but counselling can help to make some women more resilient and hap-pier. Evidence exists to show that attitude affects the outcome of conditions such as breast cancer. The inference is that by modifying your attitude you can affect the progress of the disease. Needless to say, it would be completely wrong to suggest that a woman's atti-tude is responsible for her disease, merely that learning to adopt a slightly different attitude may help the outcome. Numerous relaxation techniques are available which can be helpful in controlling stress, including massage, reflexology, laughter therapy, yoga and transcendental meditation. If a woman says she needs some 'time out' for relaxation, sets aside the time, finds a therapist or therapy, values the therapy enough to pay for it, and completes a course of therapy, she is almost certain to feel better for it, whatever the therapy involved.

Self-help for relaxing

- Value times for relaxation. Put aside some 'good' time: do not just slot it in. Consider it 'essential', not just 'desirable'.
- Build relaxing activities into your daily routine. Take your time, do not rush and do not try too hard.
- Learn a relaxation routine, but remember that it will take practice. Options include an audio tape which guides you through exercises to release muscle tension, a yoga routine or a meditation ritual.
- Do not worry about the physical signs of tension, e.g. aches, palpitations, sweating and stomach churning – although you should see a doctor if you get any new, unexplained symptoms.
- Keep physically fit. Brisk walking or swimming may help to release tension.

Dental health

Caring for your mouth, tongue, gums and teeth is essential to avoid bad breath, bleeding gums and dental decay which may result in expensive and painful dental work, and early loss of teeth. Dental care includes cutting down the frequency with which you eat or drink sugary products. It is better for your teeth to eat the week's ration of sweets in one go than to space them out throughout the week. Acidic food and drinks including sugar-free fizzy drinks are largely responsible for dental erosion, whereby the enamel and dentine are dissolved. Even fizzy mineral water may be harmful in excess because of its acidity.

Cleaning teeth and gums thoroughly every day using a fluoride toothpaste is also essential. It takes three minutes to brush your teeth properly, going round each tooth in turn. It is better to brush once really thoroughly than to brush frequently but inadequately. Use a soft-to-medium toothbrush and buy a new one every three months. Your dentist or hygienist will advise you how to brush properly, using a circular scrubbing action from the top of the tooth downwards to where it meets the gum. They will also tell you whether you need to use dental floss. Everyone should have regular (usually six-monthly) dental check-ups, even if you no longer have teeth. Professional cleaning helps prevent decay. Dentists can detect teeth that have started to decay and prevent further damage by exploring the cavity and, if necessary, filling it with metal. Examination by a dentist also allows early detection of oral cancers such as cancer of the tongue which tends to start as a small abnormal patch, many years before it develops into cancer. Biopsy (taking a small sample) and early treatment can prevent the development of a very nasty type of cancer.

Dentists believe that water fluoridation can reduce the incidence of tooth decay by a third. At present only 10 per cent of the population in the UK drinks fluoridated water, whereas in the USA the figure is 60 per cent. Concerns that too much fluoride can be bad, especially for children's teeth, can be addressed by using less fluoridated toothpaste. Women are more susceptible to gum disease and dental decay during pregnancy because of high hormone levels. It is particularly important to have a dental check-up as early as possible in pregnancy. Dental checks are free in pregnancy and for a year after the birth of the baby, so you could fit in four free dental check-ups in that time. Having plaque removed by a hygienist or dentist, in addition to careful, regular flossing and brushing, prevents the build-up of plaque, which is responsible for a swelling that can appear in pregnancy between two teeth. It is an old wives' tale that pregnant women need to drink extra milk or take calcium to protect their developing baby's teeth, or their own. In fact, so long as a woman has a normal, well-balanced diet, the baby's teeth will develop without having any effect on the mother's teeth or calcium levels. Local anaesthetic injections, dental X-rays and dental work are all perfectly safe during pregnancy. Many dentists advise patients to have major dental work done in the second third of pregnancy, when most women feel particularly well.

Smokers have more dental problems than non-smokers and their teeth are often rendered unsightly by yellow or brown staining. Stopping smoking will prevent further staining; bleaching of teeth is not recommended.

After the menopause, women's bones start to thin; if the bones become too thin, they become brittle and prone to breaks (osteoporosis). Osteoporosis can affect the jawbone, and may contribute to teeth becoming looser. Treatments for osteoporosis such as HRT or a drug called etidronate may halt the progress of this condition and prevent further damage.

Avoiding ill health

Avoiding smoking

Smoking is the single biggest preventable cause of premature death among men and women, and the message that smoking is bad for health has been having an impact. Fewer women and men smoke now than was the case in the 1970s. But whereas most smokers used to be men, they are now almost equally divided between the sexes. In 1996, about 29 per cent of men and 28 per cent of women were smokers. It may soon be the case that there will be more women smokers than men, as statistics show that men are more likely to quit. Younger women are more likely to smoke than older women, and often start between the ages of 12 and 13. Among school-leavers, girls are more likely to smoke than boys, although the boys who do smoke tend to smoke more heavily. Between the ages of 16 and 20, girls who smoked occasionally while at school often become heavy, regular smokers who are never going to quit. Lung cancer among women has risen in tandem with smoking. Heart disease and lung conditions such as bronchitis and emphysema can cause long-term health problems to women as well as premature death. Women who smoke while they are pregnant are at increased risk of having low-birthweight babies who are predisposed to illness while they are very small and to health problems in later life.

Young children who breathe in cigarette smoke are more prone to ear and chest infections and are possibly at increased risk of lung cancer themselves because of passive smoking at an early age. They are also far more likely to become smokers than the children of non-smokers.

A European study under the aegis of the World Health Organisation (WHO) reported in 1998 that the risk of lung cancer rose by 16 per cent among non-smoking partners of smokers. The estimated increased risk for non-smokers who work in smoky workplaces was 17 per cent. However, the study did not show an increased risk of lung cancer among adults who had been exposed to passive smoking as children.

A group of independent scientific advisers in the UK produced a report in March 1998 stating categorically that passive smoking does cause lung cancer and heart disease. The report called for smoking in public places to be restricted on the grounds of public health.

Women may smoke as a response to stress, because they believe it helps them to stay slim, or because they believe that smoking enhances their image and (for younger women) makes them seem older and more sophisticated. It is true that women who quit put on an average of 3kg (about half a stone), but this is mostly because they eat more as a distraction from smoking. Women who are concerned about gaining weight must be careful not to overeat. For some women, having a cigarette is an escape from reality – an activity which is just for themselves and which they associate with relaxing. It can be very hard to give up smoking, although there are many success stories. Nicotine is addictive and women who stop smoking can minimise withdrawal symptoms by using nicotine replacement in the form of patches, gum or sprays. Support and encouragement are vital. A nurse or GP at a local surgery can provide advice. Information and support are also available from self-help groups (see address list).

Avoiding excess alcohol

Although alcohol is socially acceptable – and may even be good for us in small quantities – it is an addictive and potentially dangerous drug. The death rate from alcohol-related disease in England and Wales has more than doubled in both men and women since the 1950s. The latest (1995) guidelines on sensible drinking compiled by the Department of Health says that 1–2 units of alcohol a day is the best amount for good health – even better than no alcohol at all. Drinking 2–3 units a day will not do you any harm, but drinking more than 3 units a day on a regular basis may well lead to health problems such as liver damage. A daily, moderate amount of alcohol is better than occasional binge drinking. If you do drink more than is good for you one day, it is best to avoid alcohol altogether for 48 hours.

Around 12 per cent of women drink more than the equivalent of two glasses of wine a night (14 units a week). About 5 per cent of women are 'problem drinkers' compared with 9 per cent of men. Younger women (aged 18–24) and more affluent women are more likely to exceed the guidelines for sensible drinking. What constitutes 'sensible drinking' depends on your gender, weight and shape, and your capacity to clear alcohol from your body. Women are far less likely than men to be heavy, regular drinkers, and are more likely to be teetotal. But if a woman has a pint of beer alongside a man who weighs the same as her, she will have higher levels of alcohol in her blood as alcohol is diluted in body water, and women have less water and more fat than men. The less you weigh, the higher the alcohol levels will rise for a given measure of drink. This is why women get alcohol-related physical problems such as heart and liver disease even if they drink only half to two-thirds as much as men. Drinking alcohol to excess can also produce a higher risk of breast cancer and gastric problems, as well as eventual dementia, and may of course lead to accidents.

Heavy drinking during pregnancy can cause a spectrum of problems for the baby, ranging from low birthweight, feeding and sleeping difficulties, and irritability, through to a syndrome known as fetal alcohol syndrome, which could result in the baby having certain physical characteristics, delayed development and permanent intellectual impairment. Women who are either pregnant or trying to get pregnant are advised either to abstain from alcohol or to limit themselves to no more than two small glasses of wine or a pint of beer once or twice a week. Research done in Denmark in 1998 found that women drinking five or fewer units a week were twice as likely to conceive within six months as women drinking double that amount. Some experts claim that a glass or two of (especially red) wine a day confers health benefits – in certain countries the chemicals in red wine appear to help reduce heart disease. Debate about the health benefits of beer and spirits relative to wine continues: it has been said that beer is of no particular benefit to health, and spirits are harmful.

Women who find it hard to control their alcohol intake, or feel they are drinking to excess, need expert help. GPs have access to specialist help, and may be able to offer support and advice. Alcoholics Anonymous★ and other self-help groups are mentioned in the address list.

Avoiding drug abuse

Drug misuse and dependence is a serious and growing problem in the UK. The main risks of drug misuse are infection with HIV and hepatitis as a result of sharing injection needles, increasing dependence on the drugs and accidental overdose or accidents which occur while you are 'high'.

Cannabis is a relatively harmless substance, especially compared to nicotine. But women who roll joints using tobacco are exposing themselves to the same risks as cigarette-smokers. Smoking cannabis during pregnancy has not been shown to be particularly harmful to the baby, although it can hardly be recommended. Cannabis, like alcohol and nicotine, is potentially addictive. Regular users can become both physically and psychologically dependent on it. Unlike alcohol and nicotine, however, cannabis is illegal except in exceptional cases: for example, for multiple sclerosis patients who find it relieves muscle spasm.

The British Medical Association (BMA) has called for cannabis to be available for limited medical use in trials. The only cannabis-like drug currently licensed for legal use is the drug nabilone, used to relieve nausea and vomiting after chemotherapy. Cannabis may also be useful to stimulate the appetite, relieve nausea, help pain and counter depression in people with AIDS. However, the BMA does not advocate recreational use of cannabis because smoking it can cause heart and lung disease, have other side-effects and become addictive.

A group of mood-altering drugs known as 'recreational' or 'designer' drugs, such as Ecstasy, has received a great deal of publicity because they can cause potentially fatal reactions in susceptible individuals. The tablets may also be contaminated with more harmful chemicals, since they are not subject to the usual strict controls or quality assurance. It is the duty of all parents to tell their children that all drugs, whether illegal, bought over the counter or prescribed by a doctor, should be treated with great caution. No-one should take any tablet unless he or she has a valid reason for doing so, and any drug that affects mood or mental faculties should be treated with great suspicion.

Cocaine and heroin are highly addictive drugs that may lead users into a remorseless downward spiral. Women who inject themselves with heroin are at risk of HIV infection and AIDS if they use contaminated needles. Using heroin during pregnancy leads to the birth of a baby who is dependent on heroin, having been exposed to it in the womb. Heroin-addicted babies get withdrawal symptoms soon after birth and need specialised care. Addicted women soon forget the highs they once achieved on these drugs, as their lives are destroyed by the constant craving and the physical, mental and social decline that inevitably sets in. Specialised help is essential and is available (see address list).

Heroin use has risen among young people under the age of 19 in England and Wales throughout the 1990s. Although the users are primarily amongst the young who feel excluded from society, young people from affluent families are also taking it as a recreational drug.

Avoiding obesity

The proportion of overweight men and women is increasing all the time in the UK. This is because, as a nation, we eat too much and take too little exercise. Women take less regular exercise than men, and poorer women exercise less than more affluent women. Obesity is usually measured using the body mass index (BMI) which is weight in kilograms divided by height in metres squared. In 1993, around 46 per cent of women aged 16–64 were in the right weight range for their height (BMI 20–25); 30 per cent were overweight (BMI 25–30), and 16 per cent were obese (BMI more than 30). A smaller 8 per cent were underweight (BMI less than 20). By 1996, 17 per cent of women and 16 per cent of men aged 16–64 in England were obese.

However, it is now apparent that it does not matter just how fat you are, but where you carry the fat. The typical British pear-shaped woman, with a smallish waist and more ample hips and thighs, is better off from a health point of view than a woman who carries her extra fat round her stomach. Some experts say that a simple waist measurement can determine which women need to lose weight (those whose waists measure more than 80cm).

ARE YOU A HEALTHY WEIGHT?

Take a straight line across from your height (without shoes) and a line up from your weight (without clothes). Put a mark where the two lines meet.

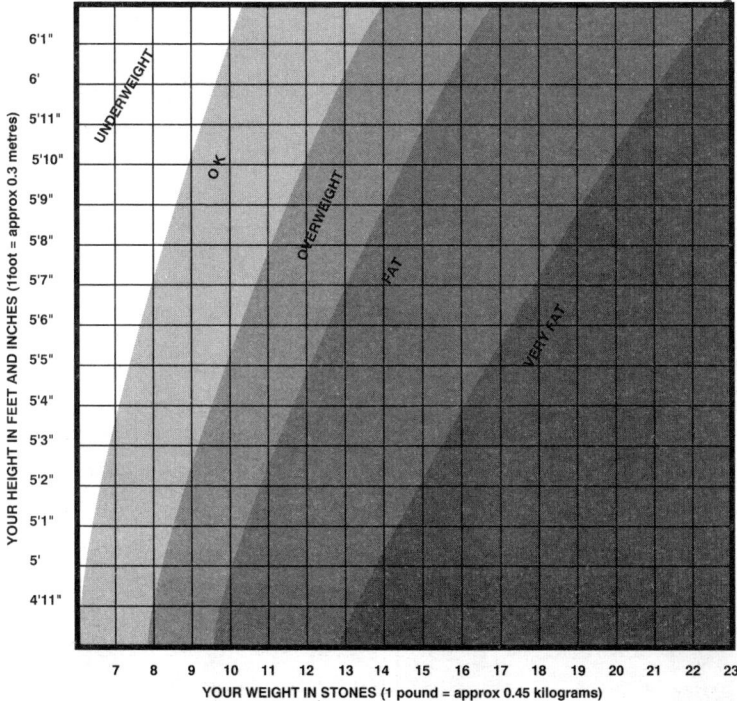

UNDERWEIGHT?   Maybe you need to eat a bit more. But for for well-balanced nutritious foods, and don't just fill up on fatty and sugary foods. If you are very underweight, see your doctor about it.

OK?   You're eating right *quantities* of food but you need to be sure that you're getting a healthy balance in your diet.

OVERWEIGHT?   You should try to lose weight.

FAT?   You need to lose weight.

VERY FAT?   You urgently need to lose weight. You would do well to see your doctor, who might refer you to a dietician.

Obesity increases the risk of high blood pressure and diabetes. Both of these conditions may cause ill health and premature death from heart disease or strokes. Carrying excess weight also puts pressure on joints and the spine, so that joints get worn out (osteoarthritis) and may become painful, stiff and swollen. Backache also becomes common. The risk of blood clots in the leg veins (thrombosis) increases if you are obese, partly because you are more likely to remain immobile for longer periods: for example, after a back injury or operation. There are few health risks associated with being slightly overweight, but weight tends to increase as women get older, and many women who are a bit overweight in their thirties have become seriously overweight by the time they reach their fifties. Women who are slightly overweight should not become obsessive about dieting, but they should try to ensure that their weight does not gradually creep up over the years.

Six tips for changing your eating behaviour

1. Keep a food diary for two weeks, recording where, when and what you ate and how you felt at the time: e.g. '11am – chocolate bar – by the fridge – feeling fed-up'.

2. Try to identify circumstances associated with eating when you are not really hungry, and write down ways to avoid them: e.g. 'chocolate – from newsagent mid-afternoon. Will avoid going to the shop'.

3. Eat at mealtimes only, and make each meal an occasion. Always sit down at a table, take your time, do not do anything else while you eat, and eat slowly, savouring your food.

4. Shop from a list. Do not shop when you are hungry. Avoid last-minute purchases not on the list, e.g. chocolate at the checkout. Put the food away on returning home, do not 'try' the items you have bought.

5. If you know you turn to food when you are upset, angry or stressed, try to develop other strategies, e.g. a relaxation tape, yoga exercises or listening to soothing music. Do not use cigarettes as a substitute.

6. Cook only what you need. Serve yourself a normal-sized portion, as you would serve to any other adult. Put the rest of the food away. Do not finish off leftovers, scrape out the bowl, 'tidy up the edges' or 'have a nibble'.

In contrast, about 1 per cent of teenage girls and young adult women are anorexic and at least twice as many have an eating disorder of one kind or another (see Chapter 2). There is tremendous pressure on young girls to be thin, emanating from images of underweight models in magazines and advertising, and a diet industry that feeds off women's insecurities about their bodies. Huge numbers of women are not overweight enough for their health to be at risk, but because of poor self-image subject themselves to unrealistic food restriction. They usually find they cannot maintain such a regime, which results in weight going up and down ('yo-yo dieting'). This is more dangerous to health than remaining at a constant weight, so long as you are not obese. A healthy lifestyle with moderate amounts of a balanced variety of foods, plus adequate exercise, is the best way to avoid obesity. See Chapter 2 for more information.

Avoiding sexually transmitted infections

Human immunodeficiency virus (HIV) is a virus that can be contracted in several different ways:

- unprotected penetrative vaginal or anal intercourse with an infected person
- sharing a needle or syringe with an infected person
- mother-to-baby transmission during childbirth and breast-feeding
- blood transfusions in countries which do not screen blood (blood is always screened in the UK)
- donor insemination from an infected man (donor clinics screen all donors in the UK but some women make private arrangements with unscreened men).

Note that the virus *cannot* be caught from kissing, cuddling, toilets, towels, shaking hands or sharing cups. Some people have HIV infection for years without any consequences to their health. Some will develop relatively minor symptoms but others will go on to develop acquired immune deficiency syndrome (AIDS). AIDS leaves the body's defence system weakened and makes the body vulnerable to infections and some cancers.

The total number of cases of AIDS that had been reported in the UK by the end of March 1996 was 12,565. Over twice this number of people were reported as being infected with HIV at the same time. The vast majority of cases of AIDS and HIV infection have been among men, and are presumed to have been caused by sexual intercourse between men. Of the 1,206 recorded cases of women who have contracted AIDS, 144 had done so by having sexual intercourse with an infected man, 224 as a result of intravenous drug abuse and 73 from infected blood transfusions. As many as 338 were children who had contracted HIV from their mother during childbirth or breast-feeding, and a further 20 were due to other or unexplained factors. A total of 3,950 women in England were reported to have been infected with HIV by the end of March 1996. That means that they are carrying the virus that can cause AIDS, although how many of them will go on to develop the disease is uncertain. An anonymous survey of HIV infection in England and Wales in 1996 showed either static or declining rates among most groups of people with the greatest risk of catching the virus. However, one of the most worrying aspects of these figures is the low awareness of HIV status among pregnant women. Less than a fifth of pregnant women who are infected with HIV know their status. Testing for HIV status in antenatal clinics remains patchy and voluntary. Ideally, most women would want to know their HIV status before getting pregnant in order to make an informed choice about whether or not to have a child. Progress in the treatment of AIDS has continued with the use of combinations of powerful anti-AIDS drugs. Unfortunately, an AIDS vaccine appears to be some way off. Prevention is the key to stopping the spread of this virus.

- Be aware of your sexual partner's history and habits.
- Use barrier methods of contraception (e.g. condom).
- Avoid intravenous drug use.
- Seek expert travel advice before visiting countries where HIV is endemic, e.g. Uganda.
- Accept HIV screening in antenatal clinics – caesarean section and bottle-feeding can protect babies born to HIV-positive mothers.
- Check that any blood products or donated tissues, including donor sperm, have been checked for HIV status before you accept them. All such products are now carefully screened in the UK.

For information on other sexually transmitted diseases, see Chapter 11.

Most common conditions seen among women at genito-urinary clinics in England in 1995

Candidiasis (thrush)
Chlamydial infection
Bacterial vaginosis
Genital warts
Herpes simplex (genital herpes)
Gonorrhoea
Trichomonas
Scabies and pubic lice
Syphilis

Preventing specific illnesses

Staying healthy in the ways described above is the key to good health. Preventing specific illnesses is also important in staving off ill health. Good hygiene in the home and at work helps to prevent ill health. Responsible parents who keep children off school when they have a sticky eye (conjunctivitis) are helping to prevent spread of the infection. Similarly, parents who promptly treat their child's worms or nits are also helping to prevent the problem spreading to others. Public health departments monitor trends in diseases throughout the UK, offering advice to all of us, usually via GPs, if any action needs to be taken. Environmental health officers must be notified by GPs or hospital doctors if there is an outbreak of food poisoning which appears to originate from one particular restaurant or food source. Investigation may result in measures to prevent further cases.

Most organised preventative health care in the UK is provided by GPs. Prevention of ill health may involve a nationwide screening programme, such as childhood immunisations, cervical smears and mammography (breast X-ray) screening. Alternatively, the screening may be offered on an ad hoc basis when you go to the GP for some reason, such as a blood pressure check. Some forms of preventative health care are suitable only for certain individuals. Women who are at risk of an inherited condition (genetic disease) may be offered a screening blood test when they are pregnant to ensure that the unborn child is not affected. Some screening tests induce anxiety in the woman having it, but the potential benefits of preventing ill health before it develops (e.g. immunising against measles) or catching it early enough to be able to halt its progress (e.g. cervical smears) or minimise its complications (e.g. diabetes) should far outweigh any short-term stress. It should be remembered, however, that not all conditions screened for can be cured (e.g. antenatal screening for certain abnormalities in the foetus), and also that some women with abnormal screening results are eventually found to have no disease.

Major causes of death in women of all ages in England and Wales 1995

Heart disease and strokes	34%
Cancers (all types)	23%
Lung disease (e.g. pneumonia)	17%
Other circulatory problems	10%
Digestive disorders	4%
Mental disorders	2%
Injury and poisoning	2%
Other	7%

Chance and cause of dying prematurely in England and Wales in the 1990s

Cause	Before age 50	Before age 75
Breast cancer	1 in 200	1 in 30
Lung cancer	1 in 800	1 in 40
Heart attack	1 in 700	1 in 14
Stroke	1 in 500	1 in 35
Accidental death	1 in 200	1 in 100

Avoiding heart disease and strokes

The risk of heart disease and strokes is greater if you have a family history of heart disease or strokes; it also increases as you get older. These are not factors within your control. But the following factors can and should be checked and controlled to minimise your risk.

- Do not smoke.
- Avoid obesity.
- Have an annual blood pressure check, and aim for good control if your blood pressure is high (see Chapter 8).
- Have an annual check for diabetes, and aim for good control if you are diabetic (see Chapter 7).
- Have a blood test for cholesterol, and aim for good control if the result is high.
- Eat healthily (see above).
- Exercise regularly (see above).
- Do not drink excess alcohol (see above).

Avoiding cancer

Cancers are the second biggest killers after heart disease and strokes, and the major cause of premature death in men and women over the age of 35. At least 50 per cent of cancers could be prevented because they are strongly related to lifestyle. Smoking contributes to 30 per cent of all deaths from cancer and to at least 85 per cent of deaths due to lung cancer. A committee of cancer experts has devised the following European Code Against Cancer which, they claim, could reduce deaths from cancer in the European Union by as much as 15 per cent by the year 2000, if it were widely practised.

These tips could help you avoid certain cancers or increase the chances of their being cured.

- Do not smoke. Smokers should not smoke in the presence of others and should stop smoking as soon as possible.
- Moderate your consumption of alcoholic drinks, beers, wines or spirits.
- Avoid excessive exposure to the sun.

- Follow health and safety instructions, especially in the working environment, relating to the production, handling or use of any substance that may cause cancer.
- Eat fresh fruits and vegetables and cereals with a high fibre content on a regular basis.
- Avoid being overweight and limit your intake of fatty foods.
- See a doctor if you notice a lump or a change in a mole, or have any abnormal bleeding.
- See a doctor if you have persistent problems, such as persistent cough, persistent hoarseness, a change in bowel habits or unexplained weight loss.
- Have a cervical smear test regularly.
- Check your breasts regularly and undergo mammography at regular intervals once you are over the age of 50.

Timetable for check-ups

All the check-ups listed below are available at a GP surgery or health centre, unless otherwise stated.

Screening for high blood pressure

Every woman should have her blood pressure checked once every three years from the age of 20, or more regularly if she is pregnant, on the contraceptive pill, on HRT, or if high blood pressure has been detected in the past or runs in the family.

Screening for high cholesterol

Any woman who has a parent, sibling or child who developed heart disease before the age of 50 should have a blood test for cholesterol levels, preferably while she is in her twenties. If the test result is normal, no further tests are necessary. If it is abnormally high, advice about ways to reduce cholesterol in the diet will be offered by the GP and/or the dietician. Treatment with cholesterol-lowering drugs, e.g. simvastatin, may be advised if the levels remain high. Drug treatment is usually for life.

Screening for diabetes

Any woman who joins a GP surgery or is pregnant will be offered a urine or blood test for diabetes. Women who have a parent, sibling or child with diabetes should request a test. If the result is normal, it need not be repeated while you remain in good health.

Screening for colorectal (bowel) cancer
Any woman with a family history of bowel cancer should be referred to a specialist unit by her GP and have annual screening from the age of 50. This usually involves examination of the stool for blood and examination of the bowel with a telescope (colonoscopy).

Screening for breast cancer
All women should have a mammogram (X-ray of the breasts) every three years after the age of 50. Women with a family history of breast cancer should be referred to a specialist unit by their GP in case screening is recommended more frequently or from a younger age.

Screening for cervical cancer
All women should have a smear test every three years from the age of 20, or younger if they are sexually active.

Screening for ovarian cancer
All women with a family history of ovarian cancer should be referred to a specialist unit for advice about screening. There is not one test, but a combination of vaginal examination, ultrasound scanning and blood tests.

Screening for gynaecological conditions
Vaginal examination by a trained doctor or nurse may be offered when you have a smear, when you attend for contraception or HRT advice, or in early pregnancy. This is to screen for a variety of gynae-cological conditions including ovarian cysts and fibroids.

Screening for eye disease
All women with a family history of glaucoma (increased pressure in the eyes) should have annual eye tests to check vision and pressure. Women without a family history should have an eye check every two years from the age of 40. People whose jobs cannot be done without the use of visual display units (VDUs) are entitled to an annual eye check, paid for by their employer. However, using a VDU does not put your eyes at increased risk of eye disease or dete-rioration of vision. If the examination shows that you need to wear spectacles solely for VDU use, your employer has to contribute to

the cost of the glasses. Contact the Eye Care Information Service★ for more information.

Screening for osteoporosis

All women at risk of osteoporosis (see Chapters 3 and 14) should have bone density screening after the menopause. This can be arranged by your GP.

Screening for dental decay

All women should have six-monthly dental check-ups from early childhood, and especially while they are pregnant.

Complementary therapies

There is a large and growing number of different complementary therapies, some of which are described below. As with conventional medicine, much of the effectiveness of any treatment lies in the skill of the practitioner. The bottom line for any therapy, conventional or complementary, is that it should do no harm. Some of the therapies and disciplines are easier to explain in conventional medical terms than others which require completely different models of how the body works and why illness occurs.

Complementary therapies can be difficult to assess and compare to conventional therapies because controlled scientific experiments to prove or disprove their worth may not have been done, partly because funding for research into complementary therapies is limited. The therapies that have most conventional medical credibility and acceptance are osteopathy and acupuncture. The most credible scientific research has been carried out in the fields of acupuncture, biofeedback, chiropractic, homeopathy, hypnotherapy, meditation, osteopathy and yoga.

One in three GPs now has some skills in complementary therapies, such as homeopathy or acupuncture, and many GPs now recommend these therapies, especially for conditions which conventional medicine cannot cure.

Acupressure

This therapy combines massage and acupuncture (see below). Instead of inserting needles, firm massage is used on pressure points. Acupressure aims to improve the body's own healing powers by balancing a flow of energy called *Qi* which is believed to run through invisible channels in the body known as meridians. Acupressure is used to treat a wide variety of problems including allergies, arthritis, back pain, depression and migraine.

Acupuncture
Needles are stuck into the skin along energy channels (meridians) to release or block the *Qi* (see *Acupressure*, above). The aim is to restore internal balance between two opposing yet complementary forces called yin and yang. Acupuncture is used to control pain and also to treat tiredness, addictions, anxiety, allergy, eczema and other conditions.

Alexander Technique
This technique was developed in 1894 by an Australian actor, Frederick Matthias Alexander. It teaches correct posture so that the body can work in a more relaxed, natural and efficient way. Gentle manipulation is combined with exercise to retrain the body's postures and movements, thereby reducing stress and pains. Alexander Technique is used for backache, headaches, high blood pressure and many stress-related conditions and forms of arthritis.

Aromatherapy
Highly concentrated oils extracted from plants are used to treat a variety of conditions. They can be massaged into the skin, inhaled, added to baths or put on to compresses. Aromatherapy is used for long-term or recurring conditions as well as stress-related and painful conditions.

Autogenic training
This is a relaxation therapy based on simple mental exercises intended to relieve stress and allow the body to heal itself. The premise is that the cure comes from within. Autogenic training is used for stress management, especially by people trying to give up tranquillisers or alcohol, and to control headaches, high blood pressure, indigestion and a wide variety of other complaints.

Ayurvedic medicine
This is an all-embracing system of medicine which originated in India. It means 'life' and 'knowledge' and encompasses physical,

mental and spiritual well-being. It emphasises the prevention of illness and patients are advised on all aspects of lifestyle by a practitioner. Medicines are given if considered necessary.

Bach flower remedies

These are a series of 38 preparations made from wild flowers and plants, named after an English doctor, Edward Bach (pronounced 'batch'), who believed that all ailments could be cured by natural remedies which restore the body's natural balance. The flower remedies are designed to be diluted with spring water before they are swallowed. Bach flower remedies are used for a wide range of conditions.

The Bates Method

This is a set of simple eye exercises designed to keep eyes healthy. The method was created by a New York eye specialist called Dr William Bates. The exercises are taught by Bates practitioners. They can be used by people with normal or failing sight, but they are not a substitute for conventional treatment of eye conditions such as cataracts or glaucoma.

Bioenergetics

This therapy aims to make people aware of their posture and body movements and the emotions that accompany these stances. Exercises are taught to correct some of the stances, which are thought to relieve underlying emotional problems. Bioenergetics focuses primarily on personal growth rather than the treatment of illnesses.

Biofeedback

Biofeedback therapists use machines to let the patient observe how certain bodily functions, e.g. blood pressure, are measured. The patient is then taught to control or alter the function by using techniques such as relaxation and meditation. In this way, patients can voluntarily control bodily functions and may be able to avoid medication for, e.g., high blood pressure or irritable bowel syndrome or avoid the physical effects of anxiety such as palpitations.

Chiropractic

Chiropractic is a system of manipulation of the spine to relieve back pain and a variety of other problems which chiropractors believe stem from spinal problems. Chiropractors usually take and interpret X-rays of the spine themselves, unlike osteopaths (see below), but the main skills of the two kinds of therapists are similar.

Clinical ecology

Clinical ecologists aim to identify foods or chemicals which may be causing ill health. They use conventional techniques to detect allergies, such as putting a person on an elimination diet, and introducing tiny amounts of the suspect food or chemical to provoke a reaction in the person. Avoiding the foods or chemicals identified in this way is the usual treatment. An alternative approach – desensitisation – is also used, whereby tiny amounts of the food or chemical are swallowed by the patient to build up resistance to it.

Colonic irrigation

The purpose of colonic irrigation is to remove toxins from the body by inserting a tube into the back passage and flooding the large intestine (colon) with fluid which washes out faecal material. It is used to relieve digestive and stress-related conditions as well as a wide range of other conditions which are said to be related to toxin build-up.

Colour therapy

Colour therapists believe that the body absorbs light and gives out its own aura in a pattern of vibrations that the therapist can pick up. An unhealthy body is said to give out an unbalanced pattern. A colour therapy instrument is used that beams coloured lights on to the patient to restore the balance. Colour therapy is used to treat a wide range of conditions including migraine, irritable bowel syndrome and depression.

Dowsing

Divining rods and forked hazel twigs or a pendulum on a silk thread are held over a sample of hair or urine, or over the whole person, to determine whether there is any imbalance in any organ or gland of the body. The swinging of the pendulum is interpreted as either 'yes' or 'no'. The practitioner may then give treatment or, having made a diagnosis, suggest a different specialist for treatment.

Herbalism

Herbalists treat a wide variety of conditions with the aim of restoring overall vitality and health as well as treating specific illnesses. Around 15 per cent of all conventional medicines are plant-based, although drug companies extract the active ingredients from plants and make medicines from the active ingredient alone. Herbalists believe that using the whole plant is safer and better. Herbal remedies are natural but not invariably free of side-effects.

Homeopathy

Homeopathy uses highly diluted forms of natural remedies to boost the body's natural healing powers and restore balance to the whole person, rather than just treating specific symptoms.

Hypnotherapy

Hypnosis is used to induce a trance-like state which brings about a sense of calm and tranquillity. While the patient is in this state, the therapist tries to bring about physical and mental change. Hypnotherapy is used to treat anxiety, stress-related problems, digestive problems and smoking and other addictions.

Iridology

Iridology therapists study the markings on the coloured part of the eye (iris) and observe changes in them. Most iridologists diagnose problems but then refer patients to other specialists such as homeopaths if treatment is necessary.

Meditation

Meditation is a way of reaching a tranquil state in order to refresh the mind and body. There are a variety of techniques and disciplines such as yoga. Meditation can help a wide variety of physical and mental conditions.

Osteopathy

Osteopaths aim to diagnose and treat mechanical problems which originate in the bones, ligaments and muscles, using massage and manipulation. Osteopathy is used for backache, arthritis, whiplash and sports injuries and also in a variety of conditions such as colic, period pains and headaches. Cranial osteopathy uses these techniques on the scalp.

Reflexology

This is massage of 'reflex areas' on the feet and aims to relieve illness in all parts of the body. It is based on a belief in energy channels similar to the philosophy underlying acupuncture.

Rolfing

This therapy is based on a premise similar to that underpinning the Alexander Technique, i.e. that many of the body's problems are due to poor posture. Rolfing uses massage of the limbs, muscles and backbone to correct this.

Chapter 2

Emotional and mental well-being

Psychological and physical well-being are inextricably linked. It has been shown, for example, that the incidence of physical illnesses, cancers and death increases in the year after a bereavement. There is also some evidence that a woman's state of mind can affect how well her body fights diseases such as breast cancer. Many women will be familiar with the 'winter blues': feeling psychologically below par seems to make it more difficult to shrug off coughs and colds, while having repeated physical illnesses makes you sink further down in the dumps. But whereas it is relatively easy to discuss physical illness with your partner, friends or a doctor, it is much more difficult to admit to psychological distress.

Psychological problems can range from minor inconveniences, like mild phobias, to major and life-threatening illnesses such as severe depression and suicide. The same spectrum exists for physical illnesses, but without the stigma that psychological problems still carry among some people. Women readily seek help for physical ailments and should feel just as free to seek help for psychological problems. A GP can carry out simple tests to exclude a physical cause for a psychological problem. For example, tiredness may be due to anaemia or an under-active thyroid, or it could be a side-effect of medication. Once a physical cause has been excluded, the underlying psychological problem needs to be precisely defined so you and your doctor can decide on the ideal course of action. Counselling and a variety of other complementary therapies may be appropriate to restore a woman's equilibrium and psychological well-being. Many women who would not tolerate being in physical pain for years on end put up with being depressed or anxious, believing that there is no alternative. But mental pain is as debilitating as physical pain, and it is worth exploring every avenue in the attempt to find a solution.

The main psychological problems that women experience are:

- tiredness and lethargy
- sexual problems
- premenstrual tension
- eating disorders
- depression – including bereavement, anxiety, phobias, postnatal depression and depression associated with physical problems
- memory loss or dementia
- confusion, disturbed perceptions and loss of sense of reality.

Tiredness and lack of energy

The saying 'If you want to get something done, ask a busy person' is true to a certain extent: the body gradually adapts to whatever is required of it. A woman who has been intensively training for a marathon will find that her body and mind become used to a certain level of exercise, without which she may feel irritable and even unwell. After the marathon, she will need to wind down gradually, reducing her level of exercise to one that feels comfortable. A woman who has been off her feet for a while with a prolonged bout of 'flu will not be able to resume her normal level of activity immediately, but will have to build up gradually, increasing what she does by a little every day.

The body is a machine which thrives on consistency and moderation. Yo-yo dieting, with periods of relative starvation followed by binges, is far worse for the body than eating around the same number of calories every day of your life, even if it means being slightly overweight. Many people treat their cars better than their own bodies. The car gets regular servicing, the engine is turned over every day, fuel levels are kept topped up but not overflowing and a mechanic carries out an annual MOT. Women get tired because they often demand a lot of themselves. Juggling the responsibilities of wage-earner, homemaker, shopper, mother, wife, lover, carer and friend – not to mention all the other roles that so many women take on – is no mean feat.

In a study done in 1996 of over 15,000 men and women living in southern England, 18.3 per cent reported that they had suffered from 'substantial fatigue' for six months or longer. Of these, 40 per cent attributed the fatigue to stress or lifestyle. But tiredness and lethargy may be more than just the result of a hectic lifestyle. There may be an underlying reason for tiredness that can be cured.

Symptoms associated with tiredness that may suggest an underlying medical cause

Symptoms	Condition
Anxious, stressed and depressed	Anxiety or depression
Tiredness associated with starting new medication, and no other symptoms	Side-effect of drug treatment, e.g. an antihistamine for hay fever
Fatigue preceded by viral illness	Post-viral fatigue syndrome (ME)
Weight loss, sweating, racing heart	Over-active thyroid
Weight gain, dry skin, feeling cold	Under-active thyroid
Missed periods, nausea	Pregnancy
Dizzy and giddy, especially after a hot bath; low mood	Low blood pressure – rarely diagnosed in the UK
Heavy blood loss, e.g. after labour; feeling faint, dizzy and breathless	Anaemia
Very overweight; poor-quality sleep	Obesity and/or sleep disturbance
Aching limbs, 'flu-like illness, dry throat and blocked nose	Work-associated illness, e.g. 'sick building syndrome', possibly due to work-related stress as well as the working environment
Pain and/or swelling joints	Rheumatoid arthritis, lupus or fibromyalgia (see Chapter 3)

Short of breath, weight loss, cough, coughing up blood	Tuberculosis or lung cancer; rare (see Chapter 8)
Thirsty; passing more water, sudden weight loss	Diabetes (see Chapter 7)

Post-viral fatigue syndrome

This condition is also known as myalgic encephalomyelitis (ME) or chronic fatigue syndrome. It particularly affects women in their twenties. Post-viral fatigue syndrome is usually preceded by a 'flu-like illness. In itself it is a very protracted condition. It lasts for at least six months, but may involve symptoms which come and go for years. Fatigue is the worst problem, however. It is made worse by exertion and is not improved by resting or a good night's sleep. Initially women with ME sleep for up to 14 hours a day, but never feel refreshed. Later on sleep patterns become even more disturbed: some women become insomniacs, and others, especially children, cannot sleep at night, but sleep all day. Other symptoms include muscle aches, abdominal bloating, feeling sick and becoming easily full up, sore throats, sweating, palpitations, cold hands and feet, headaches, dizziness, occasional fever and fluid retention.

Many women with ME are told they are just depressed. But depression causes low self-esteem and a loss of pleasure in the good things of life. Post-viral fatigue syndrome does not tend to affect people's perceptions of themselves in this way. Before diagnosing this condition the doctor must ensure that there is no other underlying condition requiring specific treatment. A general physical examination, chest X-ray and blood tests may be required. There is no one treatment that works reliably. Anti-viral drugs, steroids, diets to combat candida infection, and evening primrose oil have all been tried, but have not been proved to help. Magnesium supplements, the antidepressant drug sertaline, and a rehabilitation programme with graded exercise and psychological training have all been useful in some cases. Unfortunately, however, until more is understood about this condition, treatment options will remain limited.

Sexual problems

Acknowledging that you have a sexual problem is difficult. Seeking help is even more daunting. Of course, the problem often goes away on its own. For many women with young children, for example, sex drive returns as soon as they can get a decent night's sleep. Simple solutions may also solve the problem, such as using a little K-Y jelly as lubrication if the vagina is sore and dry after the menopause. But persistent sexual problems that are starting to affect your relationship warrant expert advice from a psychosexual counsellor – GPs and family planning clinics can arrange referrals.

Many women have worries about their sexuality. It is very common to worry about low sex drive, and wonder whether you are 'normal' in not having a great desire for sex. Although women generally find it easier to talk about sex nowadays, it may not be easy for a woman to tell her partner exactly what she needs to feel sexually satisfied. Some women worry that they enjoy sex too much or feel that one partner cannot satisfy their sexual appetites. Women who find that they are attracted to other women rather than men may find it hard to come to terms with being gay, and even if they do form satisfying relationships, they may encounter a great deal of prejudice from family and friends. The same applies to women who believe they are men trapped in a woman's body. They need expert counselling and advice.

Some women have little or no interest in sex – no thoughts about sex, no erotic fantasies and no desire for sexual pleasure. This is a problem only if you are concerned about it. Alternatively, you may just lose interest in having sex with your partner: you have no desire for your partner but you still have sexual thoughts and erotic fantasies, and you enjoy sex with other partners. Problems can also arise if sex is painful, or if you experience spasm in the vagina (vaginismus, see Chapter 11), if you are not sexually aroused, or if you are unable to have an orgasm. Some women even develop a total aversion to sex.

Lack of interest in sex

Lack of interest in sex is a problem only if the other half of the partnership is interested and becomes frustrated – or looks elsewhere –

as a result. Wives of much older husbands may be disappointed as the man's sex drive fades with age, while men may be upset when a woman cannot face sex for some time after painful childbirth or while she is exhausted from caring for a young baby. The problem may coincide with an unhappy event, such as the redundancy of either partner, or may have been triggered by physical but unrelated causes (such as diabetes) or a new medication. It is worth asking yourself the following questions:

- Are my expectations realistic?
- Has this always been a problem, or has it just started?
- How is it affecting my relationship?
- Do I want help?

If a woman loses all interest in sex it could be the result of poor general health; physical factors such as a vaginal infection or pain after childbirth or an operation; or hormonal factors such as pre-menstrual tension, postnatal depression or the menopause. Some drugs, especially some of those used to treat high blood pressure, anxiety and fluid retention, can also produce this effect, as can the contraceptive pill on occasions. Alternatively, psychological factors could be to blame, such as a deteriorating relationship with a partner which is producing deep-seated anger and resentment; bereavement; stress; depression; and sexual abuse in the past. Alcohol may help you lose your inhibitions and increase your interest in sex, but it reduces your ability to respond and reach orgasm.

Lack of arousal or orgasm

Women do not necessarily have to have an orgasm to feel sexually satisfied. There are several reasons why a woman may not be completely aroused, including inadequate stimulation – most women need direct clitoral stimulation for orgasm; premature ejaculation by the male partner; negative emotions about the partner, e.g. anxiety, guilt or resentment; or damaged nerves in conditions such as multiple sclerosis.

Aversion to sex

Women may fear specific sexual acts or aspects of sex, e.g. fear of being suffocated by the man, fear of vaginal penetration, fear of having breasts fondled, aversion to semen or vaginal secretions. As with any type of phobia, women may go to extreme measures to avoid the activities or situations to which they have an aversion – becoming obsessed with doing the ironing every night when it is time to go to bed, for example. Recognising the problem is half the battle. Sex therapy can be very effective, allowing a woman to confront her phobia in stages, and gradually overcome it. Antidepressants used in the treatment of phobias (serotonin reuptake inhibitors, e.g. fluoxetine – Prozac) may be helpful.

Premenstrual syndrome (PMS)

Most women have some premenstrual symptoms. Up to 40 per cent feel bad enough to mention it to a doctor, and 2–6 per cent are incapacitated by their symptoms, i.e. they need to take a day or two off work most months owing to the condition, or are otherwise unable to cope with their normal routine. PMS is distressing but it is not dangerous, and it does not affect fertility. The symptoms of PMS include:

- depression, irritability, anxiety, mood swings and loss of self-control
- poor concentration, loss of sex drive, aggression, tiredness and food cravings
- headache, breast swelling and breast tenderness, backache, weight gain, bloating
- swollen ankles and fingers, stomach upsets and acne.

PMS symptoms can start at any time up to 14 days before a period, and improve as soon as the period starts. The first week after a period should be completely free of symptoms. Keeping a careful record of symptoms for at least two months is a good way to be sure you have PMS. It seems certain that PMS is caused by hormonal changes, but no consistent link has been shown between the condition and levels of any particular hormone. The hormonal changes that occur after ovulation (two weeks before a period) until the period starts are probably responsible, but the exact mechanism is not fully understood yet. This explains why there is no single reliable cure for PMS. It is possible that women could inherit a tendency to PMS, although no direct genetic link has been identified. It is also possible that personality type may be a factor – for example, women who are more anxious suffer more from PMS, but the link has not been proven.

Self-help for PMS

The following may help in the two weeks before a period.

- Walk, swim or cycle daily.
- Practise stress management skills, e.g. yoga or meditation.
- Eat starchy foods every three hours to maintain steady blood sugar levels.
- Try taking evening primrose oil. This can restore fatty acid levels that may be low in women with PMS. It is helpful for some women, but not for others. In particular it may help breast tenderness.
- Take paracetamol or aspirin for headache and other aches.

You could also try reducing your caffeine intake by cutting back on tea, coffee and cola; cutting down your fluid and salt intake; and taking vitamin B6 supplements. These are all measures that have been suggested but lack consistent supporting evidence as to their efficacy. Vitamin B6 in doses of over 2gm a day may cause nerve damage.

PMS treatments available on prescription

There are several different approaches that your GP might recommend. Hormone treatment often involves oestrogens which are used to suppress the normal cycle. Oestrogen patches are commonly prescribed, but progestogen must be given with it to protect the womb lining. The combination of oestrogen and progestogen in the contraceptive pill helps some women, and you can try different combinations if necessary. The side-effects of hormone treatment include rare but serious complications, such as thrombosis, and more common but less dangerous ones, such as breast tenderness and headaches.

Other drug treatments include antidepressants such as fluoxetine (Prozac) if depression is a major problem, mefenamic acid (Ponstan) for pains, fatigue and low mood, and diuretics (water pills) for fluid retention. However, long-term use of diuretics may cause kidney damage. Only one trial has shown an improvement in mood with the diuretic, spironolactone, compared to a placebo (sugar pill). A drug called danazol can also be used to suppress the normal cycle. It may relieve PMS but can cause weight gain, acne and facial hair if used at higher doses. Lower doses of 200mg a day do not usually cause problems. A slightly unusual treatment is goserelin injections, or buserelin nasal spray. These stop the ovaries functioning by inducing an early, temporary, menopause. They are an effective treatment for PMS but are not widely used because of the menopausal side-effects that may occur, such as hot flushes, a dry vagina and a risk of bone-thinning (osteoporosis).

Eating disorders

The most common eating disorders are obesity, obsessive dieting, bulimia and anorexia nervosa. Half of British women are on long-term weight-reducing 'diets'. By no means all of these women are overweight, though they all believe they are. The diets rarely result in lasting weight loss: they just make women feel guilty about the food they are eating. Yo-yo dieting is more harmful than constantly being slightly overweight.

Obesity

Being very overweight – or obese – is a serious medical problem. In the vast majority of cases, obesity is due to many years of over-eating and under-exercising. Very occasionally it is due to an under-active thyroid, or is a side-effect of drugs. Doctors define obesity using a formula involving your weight and your height. A woman of 5'4" would be considered severely obese if she weighed more than 105kg (16.5 stone). This level of obesity affects about 1 in 100 women and results in a 50 per cent increased risk of strokes, 150 per cent increased risk of diabetes, 33 per cent increased risk of heart disease and a generally increased risk of gall stones, arthritis, varicose veins and hernias. Women who are overweight for their height should reduce their calorie intake by 500 calories a day, to lose 0.5kg (roughly 1lb) a week (see Chapter 8 for more details). More drastic weight loss is unlikely to be lasting. Comfort eating, bingeing, refusing to eat in public or in company and constant snacking without sitting down to a prepared meal are all habits which need to be broken. Expert help (see below) is needed for women who are severely overweight because the task of losing weight will seem very daunting without help and support.

Treatment for obesity

Obesity can be treated with drugs and, very occasionally, surgery.

Orlistat (Xenical), licensed in the UK in August 1998, is a drug that results in 30 per cent of the fat content of what is eaten being excreted in the stool without being digested. Women on the drug could lose about 10kg, but this is possibly partly because the unpleasantness of the side-effects – the undigested fat comes out as a fatty stool that tends to float in the toilet, and there could be an oily leakage from the back passage – makes some women eat less fat anyway. A person can lose similar amounts of weight by cutting out about 150 calories a day from her normal diet for six months, without needing to take any drugs.

Other existing drug treatments for obesity include bulk-forming drugs (e.g. Celevac), which expand in the stomach to give a feeling of fullness, and appetite-suppressants (e.g. Duromine), which work on the brain to suppress the urge to eat. Duromine is recommended for no longer than 12 weeks, and other drugs of the same type, e. g. dexfenfluramine and fenfluramine, have been withdrawn because of reports of heart disease associated with their use.

Surgery for obesity is rarely performed in the UK because of the high incidence of potentially dangerous side-effects, the inherent risks of operating on very obese people and the fact that many obese people regain weight over a period of time even if they have had most of their stomach removed or stapled. Newer techniques such as banding, in which the stomach is made smaller by placing a tight rubber band over part of it, are not substantially safer or more successful than older treatments.

Anorexia nervosa and bulimia

Anorexia nervosa and bulimia affect as many as one in ten women and are relatively rare among men. They occur because of an inter-

Facts about anorexia nervosa

- Anorexia lasts on average for five years.
- Anorexic women may feel deeply insecure.
- Anorexics may be obsessional, studious and over-controlled.
- Anorexia is often about control: denying yourself food is a way of trying to gain control of your own life.
- Anorexics starve themselves. As their weight drops, their periods stop, their bones thin, their ovaries develop cysts, and eventually they may have epileptic fits and kidney failure.
- Anorexia affects about 1 per cent of girls aged 16–18.
- Anorexia often starts at about the age of 15, and takes a couple of years to be detected.
- Nine out of ten anorexics are women.
- Families of anorexics may be very strict and controlling, and an anorexic may be expressing abnormal family dynamics.
- Three-quarters of anorexics recover after 12 years.
- Anorexics are six times more likely than the general population to commit suicide or die as a result of the physical effects of mal-nourishment and starvation.

Facts about bulimia

- Bulimia is far more common than anorexia: it affects about 5.4 per cent of the UK population to some degree.
- Bulimics may be impulsive, emotionally uncontrolled and prone to hysteria.
- Family life may be unstable, with absent, alcoholic or sexually abusive parents.
- Bulimia may be triggered by the first sexual relationship.
- Bulimics may have a chaotic lifestyle.
- Bulimics are not usually under- or overweight.
- Bulimics will binge on food, then abuse laxatives or make themselves vomit.
- Bulimia may go undetected for years.
- About half of all bulimics recover.
- Bulimics are six times more likely than the general population to commit suicide or die as a result of complications of repeated vomiting, laxative, alcohol and drug abuse.

action of many factors which are not yet fully understood. Emotional factors such as fear of sexual maturity and an inability to feel lovable, pressure by peers to diet, pressures by society that being thin is desirable, personal stress such as exams, unhappy family life, and possibly an inherited tendency to an eating disorder, may all contribute.

Anorexia usually starts in the mid-teens, although occasionally it can start in girls as young as eight, or in women in their thirties. It affects about one 15-year-old girl in every 150, and seems to be more prevalent among girls whose parents are professional or affluent people, especially if other members of the family have suffered from the same problem. Anorexia usually starts when a teenager goes on a diet to lose weight and does not return to normal eating habits. Weight loss continues as the girl eats only low-calorie foods like salads, exercises a great deal and still regards herself as 'fat' even when she is seriously underweight. As time goes on, she may also start to abuse laxatives and make herself vomit in the same way as women with bulimia. Periods almost always stop, as her weight continues to fall. A young woman with anorexia needs expert help, rather than parental confrontation which can be counter-productive. She needs to know what weight she should be, and be given specific advice about what to eat to reach that weight. Reassurance that it is possible to eat normally and well without becoming overweight, and counselling to explore underlying fears, worries and insecurities are needed. Along with continuing support from her family, this could enable a young woman to overcome her anorexia, re-establish normal eating habits and attain a normal weight. Occasionally, hospital admission is needed to remove her from her home, and offer counselling and regular meals in a structured environment. Treatment with antidepressant drugs is also sometimes advised. Publicity is often given to the most dramatic and tragic cases of women with anorexia, but many women can and do recover from this challenging condition.

Bulimia tends to affect women in their twenties, especially those who may have been overweight as children. It results in an exaggerated fear of becoming fat, although most women with bulimia are around normal weight. Bulimic women tend to 'binge', consuming several packets of biscuits and bars of chocolate within a couple of hours, and then trying to compensate by starvation, using laxatives or making themselves vomit to prevent weight gain. This chaotic way of eating can dominate a woman's life. Expert help is advisable for anyone with bulimia. Experts aim to help a woman achieve a steady and regular way of eating, and explore the underlying worries that may have contributed to her eating disorder. In this way, bulimic women can learn that eating three regular, nutritious meals a day, without vomiting or laxative abuse, need not result in excessive weight gain. Counselling, and the use of antidepressant drugs, can help many bulimic women regain control of their lives and recover from this eating disorder.

Treating anorexia and bulimia

The first challenge for the sufferer is to recognise that there is a problem. Ideally, anyone suffering from anorexia or bulimia should be referred to a team of professionals who specialise in eating disorders, although GPs are the first port of call. The aim of any treatment is to help the anorexic or bulimic to regain normal weight and establish normal eating patterns. The treatment involves counselling, support and information. Behaviour therapy, psychotherapy and intensive counselling are useful for bulimics.

The first step for the sufferer is to keep an accurate food diary that records incidents of vomiting and taking laxatives. The second step is a supervised regular diet which allows weight to be maintained at a normal level, without the cycle of semi-starvation and bingeing. Anorexics who are very weak from starvation need to gain weight before they can embark on psychotherapy or intensive counselling. Admission to a specialised unit or hospital may be necessary. Drugs are rarely helpful for anorexics, although antidepressants and tranquillisers may be advised in the short term. Antidepressants such as fluoxetine (Prozac) may help bulimics since they help to restore normal appetite.

Depression and anxiety

Every woman has times when she loses her zest for life and feels sad, negative or lethargic. This may be a perfectly normal response to stressful events such as money worries, children leaving home, bereavement, or major changes at work. Sometimes the sadness wells up without an obvious cause. Hormonal fluctuations before a period, after childbirth or around the menopause may be partly responsible. Personalities differ: some women are naturally blessed with a positive temperament while others are more pessimistic by nature. Most women weather the ups and downs of life without succumbing to a depressive illness. But one in five of all women seeing a GP is depressed enough for it to affect her life significantly. Anxiety is a form of depression which causes physical symptoms such as sweating.

It can be hard to know whether you are just fed-up, or seriously depressed and in need of expert help. Depression puts you in a low mood and makes you feel sad, with no optimism about the future. It is hard to enjoy anything or gain pleasure even from people or events that would normally make you happy. You feel tired and lethargic, with poor concentration and feelings of guilt and unworthiness. Your self-esteem suffers badly and whenever you think about the future it is with a sense of foreboding. Some depressed women sleep very little and fitfully; others find they sleep a great deal and are reluctant to get out of bed in the morning. Some women eat erratically and many lose their appetite. More profound depression can make you think about harming or even killing yourself.

Some women are naturally more anxious than others. A certain level of anxiety can enhance performance in an exam or job interview, and being too laid back may mean you let others walk all over you and never achieve your goals. There is obviously a happy medium. But some women find that their anxiety levels become so high that they feel stressed and on edge and cannot function normally in their daily life. Anxiety makes you feel worried, tense and nervous. It makes you snappy, irritable and unable to concentrate. Physical symptoms are common in anxiety because anxiety triggers the sympathetic nervous system and prepares the body for emergencies. Being anxious makes your brain think that even minor upsets are major crises, and the sympathetic nervous system goes into overdrive. The results are headaches, restlessness, shaky hands, palpitations, sweatiness, stomach cramps, diarrhoea, dizziness and a dry mouth.

Causes of depression and anxiety

Depression and anxiety are illnesses. People are often reluctant to seek help for depression and anxiety, seeing it as an admission of inadequacy and failure, but it is quite normal to feel depressed or anxious – particularly after a distressing event such as a bereavement. And it is an emotional necessity to have a period of mourning after the death of a loved one, the loss of a baby after an abortion, miscarriage or stillbirth, or the loss of part of your own body such as after a mastectomy for breast cancer.

We all need to grieve for lost individuals and opportunities. Parents of a child born with special needs will mourn for the baby they might have had, and for the problems that their child is likely to encounter. As individuals with special needs grow up into adulthood, they may need to express their sense of lost opportunities and acknowledge the special challenges that life holds for them.

Circumstances play a large part in how well we can cope with life's challenges. Women who are well supported by a network of friends and family may find it easier to cope with ups and downs than women who are lonely, have pressing financial or social worries or are already burdened by a physical illness or disability. Depression may follow a viral illness and make recovery take longer than usual. Painful and long-term conditions such as some forms of arthritis, heart disease, strokes and cancers will make many women feel depressed and anxious about their future. Hormones undoubtedly play a part in depression. Premenstrual tension is a common problem which, by definition, improves after each period. Some women find that they become irritable and depressed as they go through the menopause.

As many as one in ten women suffers from postnatal depression. Postnatal depression can cast a shadow on the most eagerly awaited birth. It causes tearfulness, irritability, utter exhaustion, an inability to get to sleep even when you have the chance, loss of appetite, loss of enjoyment in anything (including the new baby), a feeling of being unable to cope, and terrible anxiety about the baby. Almost all women experience these problems to a certain extent: most feel weepy, deflated and a little anxious about three or four days after the baby is born, but then start to recover (this is known as the 'baby blues').

Postnatal depression is more profound and longer-lasting than the baby blues. It usually starts in the first month after the birth, and may last for several months. An even rarer and more serious form of extreme postnatal depression is puerperal psychosis, which occurs in only 1 in 500 births but may occasionally be serious enough to result in a mother harming her baby.

Postnatal depression is more common among women who have had a similar problem after previous pregnancies, who have been depressed in the past, whose baby is premature or ill, whose own mother died prematurely, or who have a number of difficult circumstances to cope with such as financial and housing worries.

Another trigger for postnatal depression is the hormone levels that fall rapidly after childbirth: some women are probably more sensitive to these hormonal changes than others.

Recognising that you are suffering from postnatal depression, rather than feeling guilty for being a 'bad' mother, can be helpful in itself. It is important to share how you feel with a partner or close friend, and speak to a trained, impartial professional such as a health visitor. Antidepressant drugs or hormone treatment such as oestrogen patches may be useful additions to counselling. Postnatal depression can be a frightening and disappointing start to parenthood. But this common and distressing condition passes, usually leaving no psychological scars on either the mother or the baby.

Personality also plays a part in depression and anxiety. No-one is immune to either condition, but some women are more prone to depression than others. Early childhood experiences, life events, your underlying personality type and chemicals in the brain all play a part in determining mood. Women seem to be more prone to depression than men. This may be because of the complex juggling act that many women achieve involving work both inside and outside the home with very little time or space for themselves. It may also be because traditionally men have been encouraged to bottle up or suppress their feelings, or may express their frustrations and upsets in drinking sessions or physical fighting.

Alcohol and some prescribed drugs may cause depression and are a likely cause if the depression dates from the time of starting new medication or starting to drink more heavily. Heavy drinking may, in itself, be a sign rather than a cause of depression. A particular form of depression – manic depression – results in periods of elation or overactivity between bouts of serious depression. This condition affects men and women equally and may run in families. It tends to be treated with counselling and the drug lithium.

When to see a doctor

Whenever you feel depressed or anxious you should seek professional help, but especially if you experience the following:

- a persistent inability to enjoy things that used to give you pleasure
- ideas about suicide or self-harm
- concern about a possible underlying physical illness
- an inability to cope with day-to-day life.

Self-help for depression or anxiety

There are many ways of helping yourself if you are suffering from depression or anxiety. It is important not to bottle things up, but to share upsetting events or news with others. Physical activity is also useful as it can improve your appetite, sleep and mood. You may not feel up to working or strenuous exercise, but a daily walk and a daily routine involving a task like walking to the newsagent for a paper and doing some housework can be valuable. Eating well helps to prevent weight loss and physical weakness, which can only contribute to the depression. Drowning your sorrows in alcohol may be tempting, but may in itself make the depression worse and create another problem of alcohol dependence in addition to those you have already. Taking each day as it comes, celebrating small achievements and trying not to dwell on setbacks are important steps to recovery.

There are three elements to recovery: problem-solving, involving others and coping with day-to-day life.

Problem-solving

- Draw up a list of specific problems.
- Try to write down options for dealing with each problem.
- Divide the options into the ideal and alternative solutions.
- Choose a solution for each problem.
- Decide how you can implement the solution.

Involving others

Share your problems with a partner or friend, join a self-help group for company and support, or seek professional help if the depression is affecting your life (see below).

Coping with day-to-day life

- Break work into small tasks, e.g. some washing or local shopping.
- Attempt only one task at a time.
- Have a break at the end of each completed task.
- Plan a small reward for yourself for completing the task.
- Set aside time each day to do something enjoyable.
- Take some physical exercise every day, e.g. a short walk.
- Tell someone you trust when you have completed a task.

Treating depression and anxiety

It is important to seek professional help in addition to enlisting the support of family and friends. Social workers or housing officers may be able to help with specific problems like inadequate housing that may be contributing to your depression. Counselling is available from your GP, local branches of MIND* or private agencies such as Relate* which specialise in relationship problems. Women who are depressed may gain relief and a sense of calm and well-being from various complementary therapies such as massage, reflexology or hypnotherapy. Homeopaths may be able to restore a sense of physical and mental equilibrium. Self-help groups can offer information, support and the experiences of fellow sufferers. Underlying medical problems which are contributing to depression or anxiety should be addressed by your GP. You may need special help in pain control, or further investigations to rule out any physical cause of your state of mind. Antidepressant drugs such as fluoxetine (Prozac) and lofepramine (Gamanil) can be a very useful addition to counselling. Referral to a psychiatrist may also be helpful for an expert opinion and advice.

Phobias and panic attacks

These are two particular types of anxiety. Phobias are irrational fears. Some women with a phobia are generally anxious but others are fine so long as they can avoid the situation which frightens them. Phobias may arise from a previous bad experience, but are usually impossible to explain. Social phobias could include becoming very anxious in certain social situations, such as eating in a restaurant, or being at a party. Other common phobias are fear of spiders or the Underground.

'Anxiety management' by a trained therapist such as a clinical psychologist can help. Treatment usually occupies about nine sessions lasting an hour each. The aim is to have help in overcoming the fears of anxiety, to learn how to relax and to be eased into taking part in activities that have previously caused the anxiety. The therapist helps the woman to confront her fears and change the irrational ideas. The therapist may also accompany the woman in her first encounters with the phobic situation, until she is confident to go on her own.

Agoraphobia is the name given to the severe anxiety or panic that some women feel when they leave the house or find themselves in a crowded place that would be difficult to get out of quickly, such as a rush-hour train or busy shopping centre. Sufferers become so frightened of being in the situation that they avoid it altogether. The extreme form of this is refusing to leave the house at all. The treatment is similar to that described above. Anxiety management and gradual exposure to the feared situation, with the support of a skilled therapist, offer the best hope of a lasting recovery.

Panic attacks are severe and unpredictable bouts of extreme anxiety. Unlike phobias they are not usually related to any particular situation. The physical effects can make a panic attack a physically uncomfortable experience. Palpitations, dizziness and trembling are common. Fifteen weekly sessions of therapy aimed at reducing the specific fears that contribute to the panic attacks have been shown to be more effective than drug treatment with the tranquilliser alprazolam. Drug treatment with tranquillisers is best avoided if possible as the drugs are potentially addictive and can cause drowsiness and memory loss. Antidepressant drugs such as imipramine are sometimes prescribed for panic attacks, but all these drugs have potential side-effects and recurrence is more likely after drug treatment than after psychological help.

Dementia and memory loss

Mild forgetfulness and the inability to recall facts and figures as fast as you used to are irritating and may be worrying. But being scatter-brained or a bit slower on the uptake than you were as a youngster does not mean you are demented. Most people can get round age-related forgetfulness by writing themselves reminder notes, or developing little tricks like putting spectacles on a string around the neck, or leaving spare keys with the neighbours. There is some evidence, however, that the brain is like the rest of the body: if you do not use it, you lose it. Exercising the mind by continuing personal education helps to keep the brain active. Women who have been educated to a high standard are less prone to dementia, or can cope with it better, than women who have not been given the opportunity to stretch themselves intellectually.

Dementia means progressive memory loss over months or years. It makes it increasingly difficult for the sufferer to carry out normal day-to-day tasks such as shopping and cooking. Personality changes such as uncharacteristic rudeness or aggression are also common. Dementia is part of the ageing progress. It is very rare under the age of 55, affects 5–10 per cent of those over 65, and 20 per cent of those over 80. The causes of dementia are Alzheimer's disease, multi-infarct, alcohol abuse, Huntington's disease, Creutzfeldt-Jakob disease (CJD), Parkinson's and several other physical conditions such as an under-active thyroid.

A test for dementia

Try this test. Each correct answer scores one mark. A total score below seven may suggest dementia.

- What is your age?
- What is the time (to the nearest hour)?
- Note this address: 42 West Street.
- What year is it?
- Where are you at the moment?
- Do you recognise two people around you (if there are old friends or family in the room)?
- What is your date of birth?
- In what year did the First World War start?
- What is the name of the present monarch?
- Count backwards from 20 to 1.
- What was that address?

Alzheimer's disease

This is the most common cause of dementia and is more prevalent among women than among men. The type that affects younger women may be inherited. Alzheimer's comes on gradually and gets progressively worse. There are no specific physical problems, but women with Alzheimer's find it increasingly difficult to cope with daily tasks and activities. The problem seems to be a gradual loss in the chemicals released by nerves in the brain (neurotransmitters), which are responsible for passing messages between the nerves. The neurotransmitter acetylcholine seems to be particularly important. Drug treatments such as tacrine aim to increase the production of neurotransmitters, but they can cause liver damage and any improvement in the dementia is only temporary. There is as yet no definitive treatment for Alzheimer's disease.

Multi-infarct dementia

In this case the dementia is caused by a series of mini strokes which restrict blood supply to the brain. Sufferers often have high blood pressure and may have suffered from a stroke in the past. The deterioration is often less gradual than for Alzheimer's disease. The dementia may develop rapidly – deterioration may occur in a series of steps, each step marking a further deterioration. There is no specific treatment for this form of dementia, although controlling high blood pressure and thinning the blood with aspirin or other blood-thinning drugs (anticoagulants) is sometimes advised to try to prevent further damage.

Huntington's disease

This is an inherited form of dementia that starts in middle age. The gene that determines this condition has been isolated so that children of affected people can be tested to see whether they too carry the gene and are likely to develop the disease. There is as yet no cure. The child of an affected parent has a 50:50 chance of getting the condition. It develops slowly but progressively, producing jerky limb movements, personality changes, increasing irritability, dementia, fits and then death. Loss of nerves in the central part of the brain is responsible for these terrible symptoms.

Creutzfeldt-Jakob disease (CJD)

The classical or sporadic form of CJD (spCJD), which affects about one person in a million in the UK (mainly among the elderly), is thought to be caused by a 'prion' (an altered form of a protein) or a 'slow virus' – one that starts to cause signs of disease only months or years after the original infection. It has been linked to infected brains from corpses, which have been used as a source of growth hormone injections in the past, as well as to infected cornea transplants. The prion is thought to accumulate in the nervous system, causing damage that has a 'spongy' appearance.

In addition to a progressive deterioration in intellectual function and personality, the victim develops sudden muscle contractions and loses the ability to co-ordinate movements. In an advanced stage of the disease, she may go blind and be unable to speak. There is no cure, and death usually occurs within 12 months.

A government advisory body announced in March 1996 that cases had been reported of a new variant of CJD (nvCJD). The committee said that the most likely explanation for this new disease pattern was exposure to bovine spongiform encephalopathy (BSE) in cattle before offal controls were put in place in 1989. So far, relatively few cases of this new form of CJD have been identified.

The symptoms of nvCJD are similar to those of spCJD, but usually begin with unsteadiness when walking and a difficulty with speech before dementia becomes apparent. No cure is available as yet, and death usually occurs within two years.

Various measures have been taken to minimise the risks of nvCJD spreading: a ban is in place on feeding cattle with meat and bone meal from any farm animal; cattle thought to be already infected with BSE are compulsorily slaughtered; the brain, spinal cord, retinas and offal are removed from animals that have been slaughtered for food; and a ban has been imposed on the consumption of beef on the bone and the use of beef bones in stock cubes.

Although no cases of nvCJD are thought to have been caused by contaminated blood or blood products, the government is taking steps to reduce any theoretical risks associated with them.

With the recent discovery of nvCJD in the appendix of a patient who later developed the disease, research is now under way to test anonymously several thousand specimens kept from previous appendix removals to establish how many other people in the population might be expected to develop nvCJD.

For more information on CJD, or to talk to others who have looked after someone with this condition, contact the National CJD Support Network★ or the Human BSE Foundation.★

Parkinson's disease

This usually starts in people aged 60–70. It causes shaking hands (tremor), which is most noticeable when the hands are resting and tends to improve when you are trying to lift or hold something; slow movements with slow speech and a slow and shuffling gait, and stiff limb movements (see also Chapter 9). The cause of Parkinson's disease is not fully understood but is due to a loss of nerve cells in the part of the brain that controls movement. Treatment includes aids to help mobility, physiotherapy, and drug treatment to try to replace the chemicals (e.g. dopamine) which are released by the nerves depleted in this condition. The symptoms of Parkinson's disease may also be caused by drugs which are used in the treatment of schizophrenia. Stopping the drugs, or adding an additional drug called procyclidine, may improve the symptoms.

Physical conditions that can cause memory loss

There are several physical conditions that can result in memory loss. An under-active thyroid, for example, also causes weight gain, dry skin, puffy ankles and a low voice. It is diagnosed with a blood test and treated with thyroid tablets (see Chapter 8). Certain vitamin deficiencies – namely folic acid and vitamin B12 – can occur in a variety of conditions and produce dementia. They are diagnosed by means of a blood test. More seriously, brain tumours and HIV – the virus that causes AIDS – can cause dementia.

Caring for people with dementia

Caring for people with dementia can be a soul-destroying task. The dementia can make the sufferer aggressive and even violent, and he or she is most likely to turn against the one who takes greatest responsibility for caring. It is vital that carers recognise their own needs, can take regular breaks, and can meet other carers who understand the day-to-day stresses of coping with a demented person. If the condition is suspected, the first action to take is to seek medical help to exclude potentially treatable causes of memory loss such as an under-active thyroid. At the same time you can discuss with the GP whether any prescribed drugs may be causing or exacerbating memory loss. Sometimes drugs can be stopped or substituted. It is also important to ensure that concurrent illnesses such as diabetes are being fully treated since they may be adding to the problem. Then compile, with the help of an occupational therapist who can visit at home, a list of specific disabilities. Whether the person has independent control of bowels, bladder, grooming, toilet use, feeding, moving from bed to chair, mobility, dressing, climbing stairs and bathing needs to be assessed. The aim is to agree a set of goals with professionals and carers for improving ability and to work out how best to achieve the goals. You can discuss your eligibility for allowances and benefits with a social worker.

Confusion

Everyone gets confused from time to time. You may momentarily be unsure where you are after waking from a deep sleep. Or you may not be able to remember what time of day it is after you start taking a new drug. For most of us, the moment of confusion passes and we know exactly where we are, what we are supposed to be doing, and roughly what time of day it is. A true confused state develops much more rarely. The person becomes increasingly disoriented and this leads to sustained unusual behaviour. Some confused people become drowsy, others agitated. Either way, relatives and close friends notice a personality change over a few hours or days. Confused people may have hallucinations, seeing or hearing things that are not really there, or develop mistaken beliefs that people are plotting against them or want to harm them. Confused people get worse at night or if they are moved to unfamiliar surroundings, such as a hospital ward. The confusion develops fairly rapidly in a person who has not had psychological problems in the past. Urgent medical attention is essential because the underlying cause is often treatable, whereas the confusion often gets worse if it is left untreated.

Most physical conditions can cause confusion, especially in elderly people. An elderly person who suddenly becomes confused may well have an easily treated urinary tract or chest infection. Drugs such as antidepressants, sedatives, general anaesthetics and strong painkillers are also a common cause of confusion, and stopping the drug normally solves the problem. Diabetes causes high levels of glucose in the blood, which can lead to confusion. But so too can the dramatically low blood sugar levels which occur if the diabetic has been vomiting or is unable to eat. Anyone who becomes confused should be tested for diabetes. Any known diabetic who suddenly becomes confused should be given a sugary drink or something to eat to help to correct low blood sugar.

Other conditions which cause confusion include the following.

Alcohol withdrawal or over-consumption of alcohol Most people who are drunk are confused. Alcoholics who are dependent on alcohol may become confused two to five days after they stop drinking alcohol.

Loss of sodium from the blood The most common reason for this is excess use of water pills (diuretics) and various conditions such as kidney failure. A blood test can readily check this.

Lack of oxygen People who have severe breathing problems such as emphysema or chronic bronchitis may be unable to get enough oxygen into their blood. Treatment with oxygen can help.

Lack of blood to the brain This could occur during a stroke or severe heart attack. Chest pain is the main sign of a heart attack, and loss of power down one side of the body is the usual sign of a stroke. An elderly person who becomes confused may well have had a stroke, and the paralysis may not be immediately apparent. Aspirin to thin the blood, treating high blood pressure or other risk factors for further strokes, physiotherapy and speech therapy are the main treatments for stroke sufferers.

Head injuries The person may not even remember falling or banging the head. Headache, personality change and periods of disorientation which come and go are signs of bleeding veins in the brain known as a subdural haematoma. Elderly people whose veins are more delicate, epileptics and alcoholics (more prone than others to banging their heads), are most at risk of this problem. The clot can be drained during an operation which usually leads to full recovery.

Schizophrenia

Schizophrenia is a distressing mental illness which has a major impact on not only the people who suffer from it, but also their families, friends and carers. It is a condition that arouses many fears and prejudices which make the individual's sense of alienation from society even deeper. The vast majority of women and men with schizophrenia are not dangerous. Some are a danger to themselves as the risk of suicide among schizophrenics is higher than among the population at large, but isolated cases of violence against others have enhanced the public perception that people with schizophrenia are 'mad and bad'. It is a debilitating illness, and sufferers deserve accurate diagnosis, expert help, appropriate treatment and sympathy and compassion.

The signs of schizophrenia include:

* progressive withdrawal from society – an inability to hold down a job, maintain relationships, keep clean and tidy or look after oneself
* hallucinations – seeing or hearing things that are not there, e.g. hearing voices talking about you or telling you to do things
* delusions – e.g. believing that people on the television are talking about you
* an inability to respond emotionally either with sadness or happiness
* an inability to communicate by speaking to people.

Like many illnesses and conditions, there does not appear to be one specific cause of schizophrenia. It is almost certainly a combination of factors: an inherited predisposition, possible triggers such as viral illness, a certain type of upbringing and personality type, and an underlying fault in the chemical receptors of the brain.

The pattern of schizophrenia is that there are episodes of disturbed thought and behaviour, which may be severe. Between 10 and 15 per cent of people will have no further problems after an initial attack, but it is hard to predict who they will be. The majority will have relapses, and it is for this reason that medication is normally advised except if the symptoms are mild, relapse is thought to be unlikely and the sufferer lives with a supportive partner or friends. Various drugs are used, either as daily tablets or as injections every one to five weeks. Drug treatment halves the relapse rate. The drugs tend to be effective in curing the hallucinations and delusions that are so distressing for people with schizophrenia. The drugs are less effective in improving the isolation and emotional apathy that can make schizophrenic people depressed and lonely. The drug clozapine is helpful for some people who are resistant to other conventional drugs. Its major drawback is that it can destroy white blood cells which are needed to fight infection. This can be potentially life-threatening. Ongoing psychological support and therapy to prevent isolation and long-term unemployment are essential. This can be arranged by a GP or psychiatrist. Self-help groups for people with schizophrenia and their families provide very useful support.

Many people who have experienced schizophrenia recover sufficiently to work, have families, sustain relationships and function successfully in society. However, there is understandable concern that community care is failing some mentally ill people and is also failing to protect society adequately. A tiny minority of mentally ill people are responsible for a percentage of violent crimes although, as mentioned above, people with severe schizophrenia are far more likely to harm themselves by committing suicide than to harm others. Better psychiatric care, improved understanding of how and why schizophrenia occurs, and more effective drug and psychological treatments should help improve the outlook for schizophrenia sufferers themselves and for those who care for them.

Part 2

Your body and how to care for it

Chapter 3

Bones and joints

It is all too easy to take for granted the ability to move freely and pain-lessly. However, backache and joint pains affect most of us at one time or another and give an inkling of the pain and frustration that afflict the thousands of people who suffer these problems on a long-term basis.

This chapter covers the main causes of back and joint problems, with an emphasis on prevention. It also looks at self-help, and con-ventional and complementary therapies for these conditions.

The structure of the skeleton and joints

The body contains 206 bones, all of them moved around by mus-cles. Bones protect internal organs and give the body form. Some contain bone marrow, which makes red blood cells. The skull and spinal column provide the basic frame of the body. The skull pro-tects the brain, and the messages to and from the brain pass down the spinal cord, which runs through the middle of the spinal col-umn. The spinal column is made up of blocks of bone called verte-brae and ends in the tailbone (sacrum and coccyx). Nerves extend from the spinal cord and pass between the vertebrae to the rest of the body to control voluntary and involuntary movements.

It is the muscles attached to the bones of the skeleton (called skeletal or voluntary muscles) that allow movement because they are attached to two or more bones, either directly or by a fibrous attachment called a tendon. In response to a message from the brain, muscle fibres shorten, moving the bones into a new position.

Other muscles work all the time, without a specific message from the brain. These involuntary muscles keep digestion, breath-ing, circulation and heartbeat going.

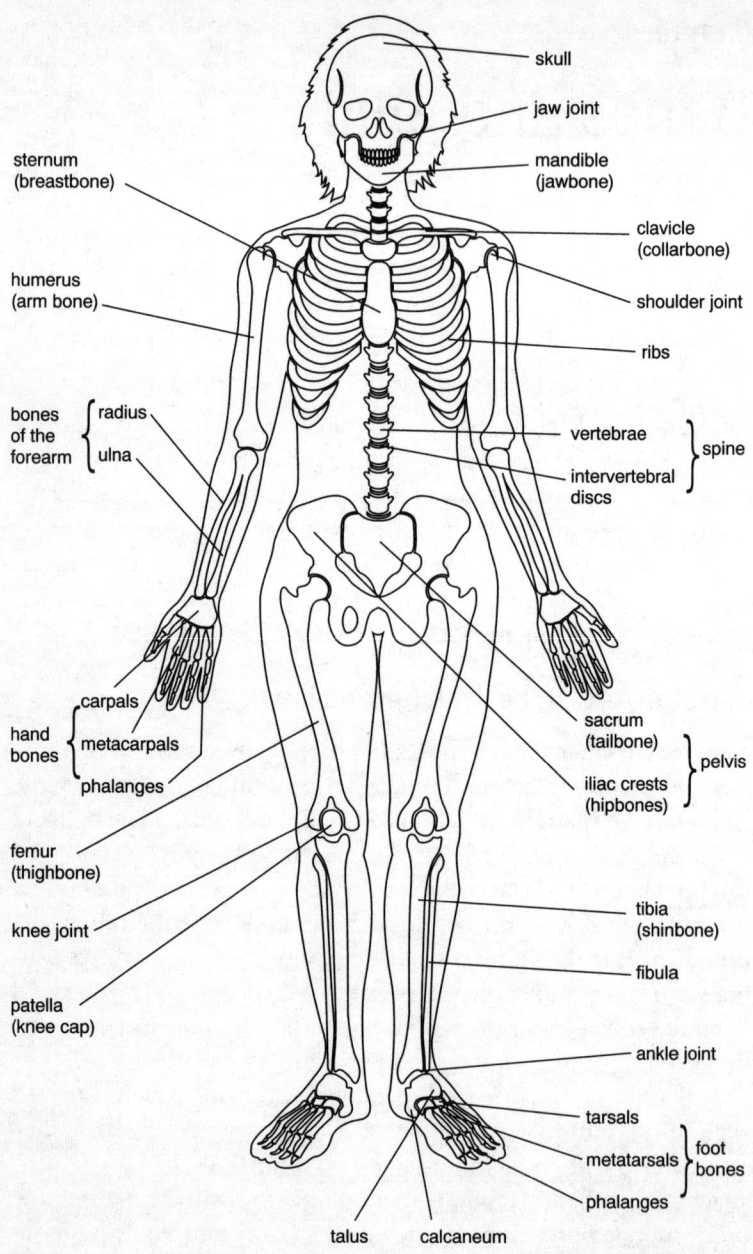

Figure 2 Structure of the skeleton

The bones of the skeleton are connected by joints. Some joints allow no movement at all, but hold bones tightly together, like the bones of the skull. Joints in the wrists and thumbs allow a small amount of movement. Elbows, knees, fingers and toes work like hinges. The two bones that meet at the hinge joint are held together by tough ligaments and the joint has lubricating fluid to ease movement. Inflammation, for whatever reason, such as injury or overuse, causes a build-up of protective lubricating fluid, so knees and elbows often swell after an injury. Cartilage, which is a tough, elastic material, contributes to the flexibility and strength of the joint. Worn or torn cartilage can make a joint lock or give way on certain movements.

The large joints in the body are the hip and shoulder joints and they allow a wide range of movement. They are ball-and-socket joints, the end of the arm (or leg) being shaped like a ball which fits into the socket of the shoulder (or pelvis). There are other small joints between bones that allow relatively little movement. These include joints between the tail- and hipbones (sacroiliac joints), which can move apart a little in pregnancy, to allow more room for childbirth.

Symptoms of joint and back problems

Joints can become inflamed by wear and tear (osteoarthritis); an inflammatory disease process (e.g. rheumatoid arthritis or lupus); injury due to a fall or sports injury (fractured bone, dislocated joint, torn cartilage or sprain); or crystals deposited in the joint (e.g. gout). Inflamed joints tend to swell up and cause pain and stiffness, which restricts movement of that joint. Some diseases that cause joint inflammation can also cause inflammation and damage to other organs of the body. Rheumatoid arthritis, for example, can affect the eyes, heart and lungs.

Most back problems are mechanical and are caused by household tasks, poor seating, a poor mattress, incorrect bending, high-heeled shoes or having one leg longer than the other. The disc which lies between two bones of the backbone (the intervertebral disc) becomes worn. The two facet joints, which lie at the back of the vertebrae, and the ligaments that hold the vertebrae together become strained as the disc becomes worn. Pain comes from the disc itself, the facet joints, the ligaments, or all three. If the disc actually bulges outwards at the back and sides of the vertebrae, it may squash the nerves which are exiting at that point. This can cause pain and numbness in the area of the body which is served by that nerve. For example, in sciatica, the sciatic nerve is squashed by a protruding disc and causes pain down the back of the leg and numbness on the foot.

Causes of joint and back problems

In developed countries, joint and bone problems (musculoskeletal disease) are the most common cause of disability and the most common reason for time taken off work. The biggest single joint problem is osteoarthritis, which tends to affect the knee, spine and hip. Since osteoarthritis is mostly due to wear and tear of the joints, it is likely to affect most men and women who live to a good age. But since women tend to live longer than men, osteoarthritis is two to three times more common among women. Excessive loads on the joints, either from repeated exercise or, more commonly, from being overweight, may speed up the development of osteoarthritis. There is some new evidence that we can inherit a tendency to it, and the search for a gene is under way.

The second greatest musculoskeletal problem is osteoporosis, sometimes referred to as 'brittle bones', which is a thinning of the bones due to an acceleration of bone deterioration through loss of bone cells. Osteoporotic bones are thin, weak and prone to fractures. More than a third of all women are likely to have an osteoporotic fracture of the wrist, hip or spine at some time. Women are affected more than men, especially after the menopause, when levels of the hormone oestrogen fall.

Rheumatoid arthritis is a condition that causes widespread inflammation, destruction of joints and inflammation of a range of other organs. It affects less than one-seventh of the number of people who get osteoarthritis but is a major cause of disability, although the incidence appears to be falling. It affects three times as many women as men. The cause is unknown, although it can run in families: you have a threefold increase in your risk of having it if one of your first-degree relatives is affected. Being on the contraceptive pill, having babies and breast-feeding all appear to reduce the chances of having rheumatoid arthritis.

There are several other, rarer, conditions that can cause joint problems. These include lupus, which affects nine times as many women as men. It may run in families, tends to start between the ages of 35 and 45, and causes inflammation of joints as well as rashes, mouth ulcers, sensitivity to sunshine, and blood and kidney disorders. Like rheumatoid arthritis, the underlying problem is that the body is reacting against itself (i.e. it is a so-called auto-immune disease) but the cause is not yet understood.

Men are generally less prone to joint problems than women. But two conditions are more common among men than women: gout, which usually causes inflammation of the big toe, and ankylosing spondylitis, which causes stiffness and pain in the back.

Mechanical back pain is extremely common, affecting about 80 per cent of men and women alike at one time or another. Back pain is not inherited but may be related to a recent pregnancy, height, weight and occupation. Back pain is more common among people who are depressed, dislike their job and who feel pessimistic about their future. Rare causes of back pain include spread from cancers such as ovarian cancer. Back and leg pain in people over 60 may be due to a narrowing of the spinal canal, where the spinal cord lies.

Conditions such as osteoarthritis, osteoporosis, rheumatoid arthritis and lupus can affect a variety of joints and are discussed first below. Some joints and parts of the body are more prone to certain conditions than others owing to their position and function. The likely causes of pain and the resulting limitation of movement in the major joints, limbs and back are examined in detail.

Common conditions that cause joint problems

Osteoarthritis

Osteoarthritis is the most common cause of knee and hip pain. It is related to age and obesity. Only 5 per cent of 40-year-old men and women have osteoarthritis of the knees, but by the age of 75 over 70 per cent are affected. Women are two to three times more likely than men to develop disability due to osteoarthritis, and for many the first signs appear between the ages of 45 and 55. Osteoarthritis is more common among white women than in Afro-Caribbean and Asian women. Recent evidence suggests that there may be a genetic factor in up to half of all cases.

Carrying extra weight is the main reason women develop osteoarthritis in their knees. For every 5kg increase in weight, the risk of developing osteoarthritis increases by 30 per cent. Women who have to bend their knees repeatedly (e.g. playgroup assistants and others dealing with young children), and those who have had knee surgery to remove damaged cartilage, are also at increased risk. It is possible, though unproven, that high-impact sports like jogging increase the incidence of osteoarthritis.

Osteoarthritis in the hips is less common than it is in the knee and is not related to overweight to the same extent. Osteoarthritis of the hands, which may result in nodules at the ends of the fingers, often runs in families.

The main symptoms of osteoarthritis are pain, swelling and disability, which may result in loss of movement, stiffness and pain in the joint. Rest helps when the pain is particularly bad, but it is very important to keep as mobile as possible, otherwise increasing stiffness prevents recovery. The more excess weight carried, the worse the problem becomes. When every step hurts, it is a strong incentive to lose weight.

Dietary supplements such as evening primrose oil do not appear to help osteoarthritis. Physiotherapy to strengthen surrounding muscles and ease the stiffness of the inflamed joint is often very helpful, and acupuncture is useful for pain. Therapies which encourage a positive attitude, such as hypnotherapy or counselling, may help to stave off depression and despair. Relaxation therapies such as massage and aromatherapy can also help. Anti-inflammatory drugs such as the prescription-only tablet diclofenac (Voltarol) are useful, but can cause indigestion. Injection of anti-inflammatory drugs into the inflamed joint is an effective short-term measure. Strong painkillers such as coproxamol can be taken with anti-inflammatory drugs if necessary. Practical help in fitting aids to help mobility and everyday functioning in the home is available from an occupational therapist. If requested by a GP, hospital doctor or social worker, he or she can visit sufferers at home. GPs and social workers should be able to help patients claim benefits as well. Surgery may offer the best hope for anyone with severe osteoarthritis. Loose bits of bone and cartilage which are making the joint lock in position can be washed out using a telescope (arthroscope). Operations to replace the osteoarthritic knee or hip with an artificial one are usually very successful, offering patients a new lease of life.

Osteoporosis

Osteoporosis already constitutes a major health problem and appears to be on the increase worldwide. It is due to loss of bone mass, resulting in thin, weak bones which break easily after even relatively minor falls. Bones are strongest in men and women at the age of 30. Thereafter, both men and women lose about 1 per cent of their bone mass every year, but for women, this loss speeds up for 5–10 years after the menopause. Men are comparatively well protected from rapid bone loss by their male hormones. Women who have an early menopause, are very skinny, or who stop having periods because of hormonal imbalance or anorexia are at increased risk of osteoporosis because of a shortage of oestrogen, which helps to drive calcium into the bones to keep them strong. Women who have a close relative with osteoporosis are also at increased risk. Caucasian and Asian women are more susceptible than Afro-Caribbean women.

Osteoporosis often causes no symptoms until a fall results in a serious fracture. After a hip fracture, one-fifth of women die within a year due to the immobility and general deterioration that tends to follow. Osteoporosis can cause deformities such as the 'dowager's hump' or rounded back, loss of height and protruding abdomen which are commonly seen among elderly women.

Risk factors for osteoporosis

The following factors could predispose a woman to osteoporosis:

- menopause before the age of 45
- lack of periods due to an eating disorder, excessive exercise or polycystic ovaries
- smoking
- high alcohol intake
- physical inactivity
- thinness
- osteoporosis in the family.

Detecting osteoporosis

The best way to detect osteoporosis is to have a scan to measure bone density. The most sophisticated way of doing this at present uses a technique called DEXA (dual energy X-ray absorptiometry). Two X-ray beams of different energies scan the spine, hips and other relevant bones for about 2–7 minutes. The total amount of calcium in the skeleton can be estimated from these scans. Ultrasound, which uses sound waves, is being evaluated as a potential way of detecting and monitoring osteoporosis in the future.

Preventing osteoporosis

There is nothing you can do about increasing age, but there are several steps you can take to reduce your risk of developing osteoporosis. Start by taking regular, weight-bearing exercise, e.g. brisk walking or aerobics. Make sure that you have enough calcium in your diet. Adult women need about 800mg of calcium a day, which is provided by one pint of milk. Skimmed milk has as much calcium as full-fat milk. If a bone scan shows you are at risk of osteoporosis or that you already have it, you should consider taking HRT. In addition, stop smoking and modify your alcohol intake.

Bone scans

Women who ideally should have bone scans are those:

- who had an early menopause (before the age of 45)
- trying to decide whether to take hormone replacement therapy (HRT)
- who have a deformity of the spine suggestive of osteoporosis, e.g. a hump
- whose X-rays suggest osteoporosis
- who have been treated for osteoporosis, as a follow-up.

Bone scans are not widely available on the NHS and it is usually necessary to be referred by a GP to a rheumatologist, who can recommend a scan if appropriate.

Treating established osteoporosis

The most effective treatment is HRT, which also helps to protect you from heart disease. It needs to be taken for a minimum of five years to halt the natural tendency of your bones to become thinner and prone to fracture. There is a possible increased risk of breast cancer after five years of HRT (see Chapter 10). HRT should not be taken by women with breast cancer (or a history of it) and some other cancers; or women who have a history of thrombosis, undiagnosed abnormal vaginal bleeding or severe liver and kidney disease (see Chapter 14).

Women suffering from osteoporosis are usually offered a three-year course of a drug, cyclical etidronate (e.g. Didronel PMO), which slows bone loss. The drug is effective at slowing vertebral osteoporosis but does not help the pain at all. An alternative – Calcitonin – is a hormone treatment available only in injection form at present, although a nasal spray is also being developed. This does help with the pain. Calcium supplements – 1,000mg daily – are no help to women before the menopause (because diets usually contain adequate calcium) but may be helpful in elderly women, and do not cause any side-effects at the recommended doses. If you are getting enough calcium in your diet (see above), there is little evidence that extra calcium strengthens bones further. Elderly women should also make sure they are getting enough vitamin D from foods such as margarine, other fats and sunlight. Fluoride increases bone mass but there is little evidence yet that it helps to prevent fractures. In any case, it is difficult to get the dose right and overdose may be dangerous.

If you suffer a fracture you may benefit from pain relief in the form of drugs, injections, acupuncture, or a TENS machine which stimulates the small nerve endings in the skin (see Chapter 13). It is important to prevent further falls by removing hazards in your home, using a stick or frame to aid walking, wearing hip protectors to protect your hips during a fall, and asking a doctor whether medication is necessary or could be changed if it is making you dizzy or confused.

Rheumatoid arthritis

This condition affects three times more women than men. Up to three in every hundred women are affected by it. It can be very mild, or severe and debilitating. It is most common among women of child-bearing age. Pregnancy tends to improve it, but it often flares up again after childbirth. Being on the contraceptive pill makes you less prone to developing rheumatoid arthritis.

No one is sure why rheumatoid arthritis occurs. It may run in the family. What we do know is that infection does not play a part. Rheumatoid arthritis usually comes on gradually. Joints in the hands or elsewhere in the body, such as the knees, may become hot, painful, swollen and tender to touch. The initial attacks often settle down and no further damage may occur. If the inflammation does progress, however, damage to the joints can result in deformity and loss of useful function.

Other problems with rheumatoid arthritis include thinning of the bones because of decreased mobility, increased risk of infections because immobility makes urinary and chest infections more common, and depression. You may also have dry and gritty eyes, eye inflammation, skin ulcers or lung and heart problems, as rheumatoid arthritis can cause inflammation of many organs and parts of the body. Anaemia is also common and can cause additional tiredness and lethargy.

The diagnosis is made on the basis of the symptoms, X-rays and blood tests. Treatment aims to relieve symptoms, preserve use in the joints, prevent deformity and help you maintain as normal a lifestyle as possible. Physiotherapy is vital, and physiotherapists can design splints, teach exercises and relieve pain with manipulations and other therapies. Occupational therapists can visit the patient at home and provide useful aids in and around the house, from handrails to specially adapted tin-openers.

Drug treatment involves anti-inflammatory drugs, simple painkillers such as paracetamol, steroids by injection or by mouth, and drugs such as gold, penicillamine, sulphasalazine, azathioprine, methotrexate and cyclosporin to damp down the whole process of inflammation and joint destruction. All these drugs have benefits, but they also all have side-effects, the most common of which is irritation of the stomach from anti-inflammatory drugs, possibly leading to ulcers (see Chapter 7).

It is not clear whether dietary changes or supplements help rheumatoid arthritis. Evening primrose oil and fish oils may be of benefit. Elimination diets that cut out all but a few basic foods such as rice, carrots and fish are sometimes advocated but there is little evidence of their value.

Complementary therapies

Acupuncture may be useful for pain relief. Osteopathy and chiropractic may help relieve pain and improve mobility. Massage and other relaxation therapies are good for your general well-being, even if they do not influence the actual disease. Homeopathy can also give good results in some cases, and homeopathic preparations do not have side-effects, unlike more conventional drugs.

Lupus

Lupus is also known as systemic lupus erythematosus (SLE). It is one of several conditions called auto-immune diseases that can cause joint pains and damage as a result of the body reacting against itself. Lupus is rare, affecting only three or four people in every 10,000. Women are nine times more likely to get it than men, and it is nine times more common among Asian and Afro-Caribbean women than among white women.

The symptoms of lupus come and go. Some or all of these symptoms may be present at some stage in the disease:

- joint pains and stiffness, especially in the morning, although the joints may look normal
- mood changes, including depression
- rapid hair loss, with regrowth as the disease wanes
- skin rashes which may be precipitated by sunlight, e.g. a butterfly-shaped rash over the face
- mouth ulcers
- Raynaud's syndrome in which fingers, and sometimes toes, turn white, then blue, then bright red when they get cold
- severe tiredness
- inflammation of the kidneys, which would not cause any specific symptoms but which would be detected in a urine test. This occurs in only a minority of people but it can be serious. Inflammation around the heart and lungs may also occur, leading to chest pain and shortness of breath
- a small group of sufferers are at increased risk of blood clots in the lung (pulmonary embolism) and recurrent miscarriages.

Diagnosis and treatment

The diagnosis of lupus is based on the pattern of symptoms and the result of blood tests. Because it is a long-term condition which waxes and wanes unpredictably, maintaining a positive approach is essential. Preventing flare-ups of the skin rashes involves avoiding bright sunshine, using sunscreens and wearing protective clothing. The oral contraceptive pill which contains oestrogen is usually not advisable because of the increased risk of pulmonary embolism. The mini pill, which contains only progestogen, may be suitable. Most of the individual symptoms can be treated as and when necessary.

There is no overall cure for lupus, or for the other forms of arthritis. Pregnancy is normally safe for mother and baby, although there is a higher rate of miscarriage then normal, and both kidney disease and high blood pressure caused by lupus may get worse during pregnancy.

The drugs that help to control flare-ups all work by reducing inflammation. They include steroids, the anti-malarial drug chloroquine and powerful drugs such as azathioprine. All these can cause side-effects and other problems, such as fluid retention (steroids), eye damage (chloroquine) and damage to blood cells resulting in easy bruising (azathioprine). The specialist who prescribes any of these drugs will arrange for check-ups and discontinue the treatment if serious side-effects occur.

Pain in different joints and parts of the body

Temporomandibular joint pain

A disorder of the joint that connects either side of the jawbone to the skull, temporomandibular joint pain (TMJ) is a common cause of pain around the jaw joint. It is often mistaken for other conditions such as rheumatoid arthritis, trigeminal neuralgia (see Chapter 9) and earache.

The main cause of TMJ is the clenching or grinding of teeth, which many women do in their sleep, especially when stressed. The second most common cause is derangement or misalignment of the jaw joint, and the third reason is wear and tear (osteoarthritis) of the jaw joint.

The symptoms are pain around the jaw joint which often spreads up and across the cheek, clicking jaw noises and restricted jaw movements. The pain may come and go and does not usually get progressively worse. TMJ causes great anxiety, but as it is made worse by anxiety patients find that they get into a vicious circle which is hard to break.

Self-help for TMJ

Resting the jaw by avoiding yawning, singing and chewing gum may help. Eating soft foods, laying a warm wet flannel on the jaw and massage are also soothing. Stress avoidance and management may be the key to long-term relief, and relaxation therapies such as yoga can be very helpful.

Treatment for TMJ

Anti-inflammatory drugs such as ibuprofen can relieve pain and anti-depressants can help reduce depression and anxiety. Dentists or oral surgeons can make splints for a patient to wear in her mouth at night: this helps over 70 per cent of jaw-pain sufferers. Physiotherapy by an expert therapist helps some people, and a tiny minority of sufferers have surgery on their jaw joint, usually only when all else has failed.

The neck

The neck is made up of seven vertebrae including the first vertebra (atlas) and second vertebra (axis) – the two bones on which the base of the skull rests. Nerves which extend from the spinal cord in the neck run across the scalp and along to the shoulders. Neck pain after a whiplash injury, in which the head is jerked back or thrown forward, can spread across the scalp and shoulders. Tension and stress make many people tense up the muscles of the shoulders and neck, which can cause traction or pulling on the same nerves and similarly cause pains in the head, scalp and shoulders.

Neck pain is so common that up to half of the population experience it at one time or another. Most people put up with the problem and see a doctor only as a last resort. There are many possible causes.

Mechanical causes of pain

The vast majority of neck pain is caused by spasm of the muscles which support the neck. Sitting badly and craning forward to peer at a computer screen; sitting on poorly supporting chairs; sleeping in awkward positions; and driving without a headrest are all common scenarios that contribute to the problem. Carrying a heavy shopping bag in one hand and nothing in the other also puts uneven strain on the neck muscles. This kind of neck pain comes and goes. It may be possible to link the pain to one event, such as neck pain that develops only after carrying a child on the shoulders. Identifying the cause and avoiding it are the keys to cure. Dividing the shopping into two bags of equal weight may be the only treatment necessary.

Self-help for mechanical neck pain

- Do exercises to encourage neck movements. Start as soon as possible after the pain starts. Lean your head gently on one shoulder. Slowly roll your head to the other shoulder, then back again. Repeat every 2–3 hours.
- Wear a support collar for activities that exacerbate the neck pain, such as driving. But do not wear one all the time: constant use makes the neck stiffer. Do not use a collar for longer than 2–3 weeks at a time. Support collars are available from chemists or can be tailor-made for you by a physiotherapist or occupational therapist.
- Stretch your neck by pulling your head upwards. This practice is popular in the USA and Scandinavia, although it seems to be much less popular in the UK. No firm evidence exists that it is beneficial although many individuals say that it helps them.
- Improve your posture and positions at work. This can help to prevent recurrences. The Alexander Technique teaches correct posture.
- Anti-inflammatory drugs, e.g. ibuprofen, are available over the counter and are good for relieving pain.

Wear and tear or osteoarthritis

General wear and tear is less common than mechanical causes of neck pain. But if the neck pain is accompanied by pain and weakness in the arm, the small nerves that extend from the spinal cord in the neck may be trapped or irritated by wear and tear on the vertebrae in the neck and the discs between them. Anti-inflammatory drugs, physiotherapy or manipulation by a chiropractor or osteopath plus occasional use of a collar are the treatments advised.

Whiplash

Car accidents often result in a whiplash injury where the head jerks forward and then flops back, usually when a car is rammed from behind or has to stop very suddenly. The pain may not start until the following day, but can be felt in the neck, shoulders, arms and head. The neck becomes very stiff and it can be hard to move the head. Treatment is the same as for wear and tear damage.

Fibromyalgia

Fibromyalgia is the name given to pain in the neck and elsewhere in the body. The main symptoms are pain, mainly in the neck and back, marked tiredness after even minimal exertion, poor sleep from which one wakes unrefreshed, headaches, abdominal pains, period pains and an urgent, frequent need to urinate. There may be numerous highly tender spots on the body which are painful when touched. The underlying cause remains unclear. Treatment aims at improving the quality of sleep (often with the help of a sedative, antidepressant drug, e.g. amitriptyline), building up physical fitness with a structured exercise programme and teaching the person coping strategies such as meditational yoga.

Meningitis

Meningitis (see Chapter 9) is a rare cause of a stiff neck and it is important to recognise that the vast majority of people with a stiff neck do not have meningitis. The other signs of meningitis include fever, severe headache, nausea or vomiting, dislike of bright lights, confusion or drowsiness. If you are concerned, insist on prompt medical attention: either get your GP to visit or go to a casualty department.

Spinal cord damage

Spinal cord damage may, rarely, follow a severe jolt or injury to the neck. The signs are loss of bladder or bowel control, difficulty moving limbs, and numbness or tingling in any limb. If you think there is any possibility you have damaged your spine, seek urgent medical help and stay still until help arrives.

Other underlying disease

Very rarely, a serious disease is the cause underlying neck pain. Rheumatoid arthritis, for example, can cause pain and swelling of the joints in the neck; cancer can spread to the bones, including those in the neck; and infection of the bones (osteomyelitis) or tuberculosis can cause neck pain. Your neck may also feel stiff and painful due to the enlarged glands associated with tonsillitis or an ear infection.

When to see a doctor
See your GP if:

- pain is continuous, with no let-ups
- pain spreads down both arms
- pain is worse while you are resting and interferes with your sleep
- you have limited neck movements in all directions
- there is a possibility of meningitis
- there is a possibility of spinal damage
- you are concerned or have severe pain.

Tests and treatments for neck pain
X-rays of the neck are of very limited value. It may be wise to have an X-ray after a serious injury to rule out a fracture, and after a whiplash injury an X-ray may be useful if there is likely to be legal action. But anyone over the age of 40 who has a neck X-ray is likely to be told there is some 'degenerative change'. This means wear and tear, and is perfectly normal. It is unlikely to be the cause of any pain.

Magnetic resonance imaging (MRI), which produces an image of internal organs using a magnetic field rather than X-rays, is useful if more serious underlying disease is suspected.

Self-help measures are likely to be effective in most cases of neck pain (see above). Anti-inflammatory drugs, e.g. ibuprofen, can be prescribed. Physiotherapy to relax neck muscles may also be helpful, and acupuncture is a good form of pain relief. Osteopathy and chiropractic can also ease mechanical neck pain. Specific treatment of other forms of neck pain will depend on the underlying cause.

The shoulder

The shoulder joint is made up of the bone of the upper arm (humerus) and the shoulder blade (scapula). The most mobile joint in the body, it comprises a ball and socket, which means it can swivel around in its socket, being held in place by a band of muscles and tendons that surround the joint (the rotator cuff). The problem with the shoulder joint is that it is not very stable and has a tendency to dislocate (slip out of position) or become painful and stiff as its surrounding cuff of muscles and tendons becomes damaged by excessive or over-ambitious movement.

The shoulder joint allows the arms to swing in a full circle. This is very useful for tennis players and golfers, and is also handy for mundane tasks like brushing your hair and scratching your back.

Rotator cuff problems ('frozen shoulder')

The cuff of muscles that keeps the shoulder joint in place can become strained and inflamed, leading to pain in the upper arm, difficulty lying on the painful side, and pain on trying to raise the arm. This is the most common shoulder problem in men and women under the age of 40. Excessive use of the shoulder, for instance by playing a lot of tennis or squash and serving the ball a great deal, tends to bring on the pain. Apart from advising you to rest and recommending anti-inflammatory drugs, your doctor might offer you an injection of steroid and local anaesthetic into the shoulder with a rotator cuff injury. If there is severe damage you will need to have it repaired with surgery, but results from such surgery can be mixed. Sometimes the condition cures itself over time, while the exercise which causes the problem is being avoided.

Referred pain

Pain in the shoulder tip may actually be coming from the diaphragm, which separates the chest from the abdomen. Acid reflux from the stomach (heartburn) is the most common cause of this. Pain from gall stones, just under the ribs on the right, or from a clot in the lungs are also possible causes. The reason pain is felt in the shoulder tip is that the diaphragm develops high in the chest in the fetus, and moves down to its permanent spot before birth, taking its nerve supply with it. The brain simply misinterprets where the pain is coming from. These conditions have other symptoms, e.g. nausea after fatty foods (gall stones), belching and pain behind the breastbone (acid reflux), and shortness of breath (clot on a lung).

Osteoarthritis (wear and tear)
Pain at the junction of the clavicle (collarbone) and shoulder is either due to excessive sport, such as tennis, or wear and tear (osteoarthritis). Pain is worse when you try to pull your arm across your chest. This is a common problem among older men and women. Steroid injections sometimes work for osteoarthritis in the shoulder.

Capsulitis
If the capsule that surrounds the shoulder joint becomes inflamed, any shoulder movements will cause pain. The problem may last a year or two and then clear up on its own. The cause is unknown. If you have capsulitis, your doctor will recommend stretching exercises.

Unstable shoulder joint
An aching and 'dead' feeling in the arm after throwing a ball may be due to an unstable shoulder joint. It is very rare for the shoulder to actually slip out of its joint altogether. Exercises to strengthen the joint are all that is necessary and can be demonstrated by a physio-therapist.

Polymyalgia rheumatica
This condition, affecting elderly people, results in profound weakness of the shoulder muscles, making it very hard to push yourself out of a chair. The muscle weakness can be linked with inflammation of blood vessels in the temples which can lead to blindness if it is not detected and treated. Polymyalgia rheumatica can be treated with steroids.

Self-help for shoulder pain
It is important to rest any shoulder injuries for 24–48 hours. Then you can:

- lift your arm above your head slowly, then lower it, and repeat several times a day
- take anti-inflammatory drugs such as ibuprofen to help the pain
- refrain from any activity which may have caused the injury, e.g. tennis, until you are fully healed. If the injury is sports-related,

check your technique and your warm-up and cool-down routines to prevent it happening again.

When to see a doctor

See your GP immediately if the pain affects both your shoulders, you are over 60, and have pain in your temples. If all three symptoms are present, you may have polymyalgia rheumatica (see above). You should also see a doctor if a stiff shoulder does not improve within a week because starting physiotherapy soon after a rotator cuff injury improves the result. Other symptoms such as shortness of breath suggest that the source of the pain may be from elsewhere in the body, so you need to see your GP to get a diagnosis.

The elbow

The elbow is a hinge joint which allows the forearm to flex (bend upwards) and extend (stretch out again). The two bones of the forearm (the radius and the ulna) rotate slightly around one another to allow the forearm to turn from side to side. If the elbow becomes stiff or immobilised, it is hard to control hand movements such as opening a tin. The bone of the upper arm (humerus) is joined to the radius and ulna at the elbow joint. Ligaments at the sides, front and back help to hold the bones of the elbow joint in place.

Golfers and tennis players are particularly prone to pain at the inner and outer sides of the elbow, respectively. Any gripping and twisting, for instance trying to unscrew a tight jar lid, becomes very painful as a result.

An injection of steroid and local anaesthetic into the elbow joint is often very painful for a couple of days, and may then help the problem. Supporting the elbow on a splint, and having ultrasound treatment from a physiotherapist are also useful.

Pain in the upper arms

Pain in the upper arms may be due to a shoulder or elbow problem, or it could be the result of polymyalgia rheumatica (see above) or repetitive strain injury (RSI). RSI is also known as 'over-use syndrome' or 'work-related upper limb disorder'. It causes pain, inability to use the hand or arm properly, swelling, redness, crackling of the joints and muscle-wasting. These symptoms are all brought on by doing a particular repetitive set of movements, such as typing. Factors that make it worse are having too much work, insufficient rest periods while at work, lack of variety in the tasks done at work and poorly designed office equipment, such as desks and chairs which are placed badly or at the wrong height. Employers have a responsibility to protect employees against work-related damage and you must take any rest periods you are offered. Self-employed people should have a short rest every 20–30 minutes, ensure as far as possible that their working day is restricted to a few, specific, hours everyday and take a lunch break of at least 30 minutes. Picking up the signs of RSI early is vital. Physiotherapy is more successful if it is started as soon as the trouble starts. Adjustments to both workload and office design can help.

Hand and wrist problems

The wrist is a vital joint which enables us to use our hands effectively. It allows movement up, down and from side to side. Hand movements are also helped by movement at the elbow joint (see above). The wrist is where one of the bones of the forearm (the radius) is joined to three bones in the hand. It is strengthened by ligaments on either side. Beyond the three hand bones that form part of the wrist joint, there is a further row of four bones. These form small joints with the long bones of the hand (the metacarpals) which in turn form small joints with the smaller bones of the individual fingers. A small amount of gliding can occur in these joints, but it would not be an advantage to have highly mobile joints within the fingers, otherwise different parts of the fingers would veer off at different angles. The thumb is a more complex joint, with a wider range of movement to allow it to touch the other fingers so that we can grip.

Pain in the hands can be very worrying, as well as making activities such as opening a can, peeling a potato or playing an instrument impossible. Knowing the cause of the pain, and whether it is likely to progress, can dispel the worst fears. The chart below should help you to work out what has gone wrong.

Swollen wrists and fingers
Swollen wrists and fingers are uncomfortable, unsightly and make hand movements awkward. If the swelling is restricted to the wrist,

Pain in the wrist and hand: symptoms, causes and treatment

Nature of the pain	Cause	Treatment
Tingling in fingers; pain in neck or shoulder	Wear and tear on the neck joint; whiplash	Physiotherapy and painkillers, e.g. ibuprofen
Stiffness and pain in fingers which is worse in the morning; the affected finger cannot be straightened	Inflammation of the sheath around the tendon which moves the finger	Injection into the sheath by a joint specialist (rheumatologist)
Swelling around the wrist which feels firm. Usually painless	Ganglion – a bulge in the sheath around the tendon	Ganglions get better on their own, but they tend to recur. They can be emptied with a needle by a GP or removed by a surgeon, although they may then recur
Hand pain at night. Numb hand, with pins and needles and a sense of swelling. The pain is worse premenstrually, during pregnancy, or if you have rheumatoid arthritis	Carpal tunnel syndrome – the nerve is trapped as it passes into the wrist	Splint the wrist at night. Lose weight if you need to. A steroid injection or an operation may be necessary

Bony swellings at the ends of the fingers which are usually painless. Hands are red and swollen at times	Osteoarthritis	No specific treatment is necessary
Both hands and the bases of the fingers are painful, red and swollen. The wrists are often affected too	Rheumatoid arthritis	Anti-inflammatory drugs, physiotherapy and splints
Fingers turn pale when cold, then blue, then painful red. This usually affects women in their early twenties	Raynaud's phenomenon, which is harmless	Keep your hands warm. Drugs can be given to keep the blood vessels open
Pain, swelling and tenderness at the base of the thumb after a fall on to an outstretched hand	Fracture of a small bone in the hand (scaphoid)	A plaster cast for six weeks. You may need to have repeat X-rays because this fracture is easily missed

it is likely to be due to inflammation which may be caused by a sprain or fracture, transient arthritis linked to a viral infection, or osteo- or rheumatoid arthritis. More commonly, swollen wrists and fingers are part of generalised swelling due to fluid retention (oedema). It is often most noticeable as puffiness round the ankles after a day on your feet, and puffiness under the eyes after lying down all night. Wrists and fingers commonly look and feel swollen too if there is generalised oedema.

Female sex hormones can cause mild oedema, which is why women who are premenstrual, pregnant, on the contraceptive pill or taking HRT may feel bloated and swollen. Oedema in pregnancy is usually normal but may be part of pre-eclampsia, a condition in which blood pressure rises with potentially dangerous consequences. Some drugs cause fluid retention and oedema, such as ibuprofen, which is a commonly used anti-inflammatory drug. An under-active thyroid can also cause oedema, as can various kidney and liver diseases. It is best to seek medical advice if oedema develops in any part of the body.

The hips

The hip joint is a mobile and stable joint which allows us to walk, swing our legs over a bike, jump and cross our legs. Like the shoulder, it is a ball and socket joint. The rounded head of the thighbone (femur) fits into the socket in the hipbone. Strong ligaments keep the hip joint in place. It is the strong ligaments and neat way that the bones fit in to one another that makes the joint so stable.

Pain in the hips and legs can have devastating consequences because it can limit mobility. Without the ability to walk, independence is jeopardised. For many elderly people, being unable to get around on their own marks the point at which they give up the will to live. Women are 8–10 times more likely than men to suffer a fractured hip (which is actually a fracture of the upper part of the thighbone or femur). And up to half of all women will have a fractured hip or vertebra because of osteoporosis during their lifetime. Pain in the hips, buttocks, groin and thighs has many possible causes.

Possible causes of pain in the hip area

Hip: osteoarthritis, avascular necrosis (loss of blood supply to the top of the thighbone), Paget's disease (bone thickening which traps nerves), osteomalacia (vitamin D deficiency), cancer deposits, rheumatoid arthritis, snapping and infection

Buttock: low back pain, sacroilitis (inflammation where the hip bones join the tailbone, to the side of the backbone), polymyalgia rheumatica (see above) and poor blood supply

Groin: osteoarthritis of the hip, a fractured hip

Outer thigh: bursitis (inflammation caused by straining muscles).

When to see a doctor
See your GP if you have:

- severe, constant pain which is not relieved by resting or losing weight. There may be cancer deposits in the bone
- weight loss, sweats at night and fever. You may have an infection in the joint, especially if there is an artificial hip or the joint is weakened by rheumatoid arthritis
- a sudden inability to walk. You may have fractured your hip, especially if the joint is already weakened by osteoporosis (thin bones)
- hip pain when you are pregnant, if you are an alcoholic, if you are on steroids, or if you have lupus or sickle cell disease. You may have avascular necrosis – a loss of blood supply to the head of the thighbone
- severe stiffness in the morning, and you are over 60 years old. You may have polymyalgia rheumatica, which is inflammation of the muscles of the thighs and upper arms (see above).

Tests to find the cause of hip pain
X-rays will show a fracture clearly, and may also pick up signs of osteoarthritis, osteoporosis, Paget's disease and osteomalacia (see below). They are no longer the most accurate way of detecting the other problems mentioned above, but they are often done as a first step. Bone scans involve injecting a radioactive substance into a vein. The substance is then taken up by the bones, which are scanned a few hours after the injection. This is the best way of detecting cancer deposits and osteoporosis. If you need an MRI scan you will have to lie in a tunnel – large enough to pass over your body while you lie on a couch – which emits a magnetic field. A computerised picture is built up from the way the body's tissues bounce back the magnetic waves. This is the most accurate way of detecting infection and avascular necrosis. Blood tests can be used to help make a diagnosis in the case of rheumatoid arthritis, polymyalgia rheumatica, osteomalacia and Paget's disease.

Treatment for hip pain
Hip fractures If you have a hip fracture you will have to go into hospital, where the broken hip will be fixed under a general anaes-

thetic. Because most women who fracture a hip are elderly, recovery may be slow and complicated by wound infection, chest infections and blood clots. Fewer than a quarter of women who fracture a hip ever regain full mobility. This is why the prevention of osteoporosis is such a major health challenge.

Paget's disease This is often diagnosed from an X-ray, and can co-exist with osteoarthritis. It can be hard for specialists to know whether the Paget's is just a chance finding, or is a cause of pain. The condition may run in the family, but its cause is unknown. It results in softening and weakness of the bones, then thickening of the bone which can compress surrounding nerves and cause pain. Paget's is often picked up on a routine X-ray: it may cause no symptoms at all. Treatment is with the hormones calcitonin or etidronate if doctors think it is causing your pain.

Osteomalacia Vegetarian Asian women are most at risk of this adult form of rickets, which is caused by too little vitamin D. The vitamin is made in the skin when it is exposed to sunshine, and it is added to margarines, but not to *ghee* (clarified butter). To make things worse, the flour that *chapattis* (an unleavened bread) are made from contain phytates which interfere with vitamin D absorption. Osteomalacia causes bone pain, muscle weakness and a tendency to fractures. Treatment is with vitamin D supplements.

The knee

The knee joint is made up of the thighbone (femur) above and the shinbone (tibia) below. The kneecap (patella) lies in front of the joint. It is a hinge joint which allows the lower leg and foot to move up and down as the knee bends and straightens. The joint also allows a bit of twisting at the knee – but not as much as some sportsmen and women subject it to. Two strong ligaments either side of the knee joint and two internal ligaments (cruciates), help to hold it in place. Two C-shaped pieces of cartilage lie within the joint and their purpose is to make the knee more stable by allowing the bones to fit smoothly on one another. Cartilage may become worn and torn, and if pieces become detached and float around inside the joint, the knee may become swollen, painful and lock or give way under you. There are various spaces (bursae) around the knee joint wherever skin, tendon or muscle may rub against bone. These spaces fill up with fluid if the knee is subjected to abnormal pressure (bursitis). Stiffness and swelling often accompany the pain.

Knee pain can also be caused by osteoarthritis, arthritis (rheumatoid or psoriatic), a fall or other injury, infection or gout. The most common cause of knee pain among women in their forties and onwards is osteoarthritis. The outcome of this is very unpredictable. It may flare up for a while and then settle down on its own. Exercise, losing weight if you are overweight and taking anti-inflammatory drugs such as ibuprofen are the first line of attack. An operation to replace the knee is much more successful now than when it was first introduced and is worth considering for severe osteoarthritis.

Bursitis, the build-up of fluid in spaces surrounding a joint, may result from repeated kneeling. If your knee swells up and feels tight and painful after you have spent several hours on your knees, say, laying a new floor, it is almost certainly due to bursitis, or what some people call 'housemaid's knee'. You can prevent it by kneeling on a foam pad, or by giving up 'housemaid's' tasks. Resting the knee allows the swelling to go down on its own. A cyst can develop as part of bursitis: there will be a swelling at the back of the knee and pain down the calf if the cyst bursts. Another form of bursitis causes pain on the inner side of the knee. Steroid injections into the tender area can be helpful.

Knee injury

A heavy fall on to the knee can cause bleeding into the knee joint, which produces a swollen and painful knee. Sometimes the damage occurs more gradually after a fall and the knee may swell, lock or buckle for a while, then improve and then hurt again. An orthopaedic surgeon may suggest looking into the knee with a telescope (arthroscope) to see if there is any damage that can be repaired. MRI scans are beginning to replace arthroscopy, as they give an accurate view of the inside of the joint without the need to penetrate the joint. However, arthroscopy has the advantage that treatment such as washing out the joint to remove debris can be carried out at the same time.

Knee infection

A red, hot, swollen knee may be a sign of infection in the joint. Bacteria can get into the joint through cuts in the overlying skin, or from an internal infection. A GP or specialist will put a needle into the swollen joint to draw off some fluid which can be examined under a microscope to make a firm diagnosis. A confirmed joint infection is treated with antibiotics, usually given through a drip. Gout and rheumatoid arthritis can also cause a red, painful and swollen knee, as can arthritis linked with the skin condition psoriasis. There are normally other signs of these conditions too (see above and Chapter 6).

Pain in the lower leg

Pain and swelling of the lower leg is usually due to a muscle strain or bruise following exercise, an injury or varicose veins. Varicose veins are more common among women than men, tend to run in families and are more likely if you are on your feet all day or if there is pressure on the veins during pregnancy. They are swollen leg veins which occur because of damage to the valves that normally keep blood flowing efficiently. Pregnancy often triggers their development or exacerbates existing varicose veins because the pregnant womb presses on pelvic veins into which the veins of the leg flow. The veins on the back of the calves and the inside of the leg are most often affected. They become engorged, may make the leg ache, and cause puffy ankles. Self-help measures include putting your feet up whenever possible, wearing support stockings, which can be prescribed by your GP, and using moisturising cream to prevent dry skin around the ankles, which can eventually lead to ulcers. A surgeon can inject varicose veins or strip out the veins in an operation under general anaesthetic.

Thrombophlebitis is inflammation of the veins which lie near the surface of the legs, the same veins that may be varicose. A small area on the calf becomes red and very tender to the touch. It may occur as part of a generalised condition causing inflammation, such as lupus, or happen out of the blue. Anti-inflammatory drugs are usually prescribed. A thrombosis (blood clot) in the deep veins of the leg (deep-vein thrombosis or DVT) is a rarer cause of pain and swelling but needs urgent treatment to thin the blood and minimise the risk of the clot dislodging and travelling to the lungs (pulmonary embolus, see Chapter 8). Thrombosis is more likely after long periods of immobility or major surgery. It is also more common among women taking oestrogens in the oral contraceptive pill or HRT. Any woman who develops sudden pain and swelling in one calf should seek immediate medical advice.

Muscle cramps are common, especially in bed at night, and are often worse during pregnancy. Cramps can be brought on by unaccustomed exercise: the best thing to do if you get cramp in the calf is to stretch the leg muscles by pulling your foot backwards and forwards. Muscle-relaxant drugs can be prescribed by a GP if cramps are particularly troublesome.

The ankle

The ankle joint consists of the lower end of the shinbone (the tibia), the other smaller bone of the lower leg (the fibula) and a bone in the foot called the talus. It is a hinge joint which allows the foot to move up and down. Ligaments hold the joint in place, although they are very prone to injuries (sprains). This is by far the most common cause of ankle problems. A sprain causes pain and swelling, especially on the outer side of the ankle. It may happen after a twisting injury – if you go over on your foot, for example – or it may recur after a previous injury. The RICE regime is recommended for all sprained joints, especially the wrists and ankles: Rest, Ice (cold compress), Compression (Tubigrip bandage) and Elevation (e.g. putting your ankle up on a footstool). Physiotherapy may speed up recovery.

If you fracture your ankle after a fall or injury, the joint will swell immediately. You will be in excruciating pain, and you will not be able to bear your own weight or move your ankle. There is often bruising as well with a fracture.

Ankle pain can also be caused by osteoarthritis and rheumatoid arthritis.

The foot

The feet are made up of the talus bone which forms part of the ankle joint, the calcaneum to which the talus is joined by ligaments, and several smaller bones. There are small joints between all these bones which allow little movements. The foot supports your body weight and acts as a lever to propel you forward when you are walking. Because the foot has an arch, the main points of contact with the ground when you walk or stand are the heel and the ball of the foot. These are the most common sites of foot pain.

Inflamed heel pad

Women who suddenly become more active and take up walking several miles a day, having done no exercise for years, may experience heel pain. Inflammation of the heel pad can cause burning, aching and a throbbing pain on the heel. The heel may feel warm to the touch. Any direct pressure on the heel, such as walking, will hurt. Heel cushions can be bought from chemists. Anti-inflammatory gels and creams available over the counter can be rubbed into the painful heel. Physiotherapists can provide ultrasound treatment, which also eases the pain. Occasionally, an injection of steroid and local anaesthetic into the painful spot can reduce the inflammation. This is done by a GP or a joint specialist, a rheumatologist.

Osteoarthritis

Osteoarthritis (see above) in the foot can cause pain and stiffness, especially in the big toe. Tight shoes, injuries to the feet and repeated attacks of gout all make osteoarthritis more likely.

Rheumatoid arthritis

Rheumatoid arthritis (see above) often starts in the foot. The soles of the feet may become sore and it can feel like walking on pebbles. The foot can become very distorted as rheumatoid arthritis progresses, making walking more difficult and painful. Podiatrists (chiropodists) can design insoles for shoes and advise about foot care. Anti-inflammatories and other drug treatment can help to control the arthritis.

Psoriasis

Psoriasis (see Chapter 6) is a skin condition that causes scaly plaques on the skin and scalp. It can also cause skin changes on the feet, and a form of arthritis can be linked to the skin condition.

Gout

Gout causes a painful, throbbing big toe which is excruciatingly tender to touch. It is caused by the build-up of uric acid in the bloodstream, which forms crystals in joints – especially the big toe.

It is less common among women than men. Excess alcohol and diuretic (water) pills predispose people to gout. Anti-inflammatory drugs help in the short term, and long-term prevention with the drug allopurinol reduces the blood levels of uric acid.

Metatarsalgia

Metatarsalgia is inflammation in the ball of the foot. It can cause sudden attacks of severe pain or pins and needles on walking, often in the third and fourth toes. It is more common in women who wear high-heeled shoes and is due to trapping of the nerve and artery that supply the toes. Swapping the high heels for some 'sensible' flatties is the best solution. A podiatrist can make inserts for shoes so your feet get into the right position, and a joint specialist (rheumatologist) can inject steroid and local anaesthetic into the sore point.

Stress fracture

A stress fracture is a small fracture in one of the long foot bones (the metatarsals). It occurs if women suddenly subject their feet to more pressure than normal, either by taking up long-distance jogging, or gaining a lot of weight rapidly. Exercise makes the pain worse. X-rays or a bone scan can detect it. Rest and padding in the shoe allow the fracture to heal naturally.

Plantar fasciitis

Pain on the inner side of the arch of the foot may be due to inflammation. This can be the result of flat or turned-in feet, or it may be due to little nodules in the tissue of the foot (fascia). Shoe inserts can be used to correct abnormal foot positions, and rest and treatment with ultrasound may be helpful.

Bunions, corns, calluses and chilblains

A bunion is a tender, bony lump on the outer surface of the big toe. It can become red, hot and painful if it is rubbed by shoes. Bunions are due to a misalignment of the bones in the big toe, which means that the toe joint has a tendency to stick out. Narrow shoes cause rubbing and pain. Wide shoes, padding and treatment by a surgeon or chiropodist are necessary.

Corns or calluses are lumps of hard skin on the surface of the toes. They are caused by ill-fitting shoes. Women with toes that stick out at an angle and do not lie flat are more prone to corns. To pare away the corn, first use a corn solvent to soften it, then rub with a corn file. Small spongy rings (corn plasters) will protect the corn. All these products are available from chemists or from chiropodists (podiatrists).

Verrucas are small patches of thickened skin, with a black dot in the centre, and are infectious. They appear on the soles of the feet and may be tender to walk on, or may cause no problems at all. They are caused by a wart virus and disappear on their own in time. Remedies from the chemist can be painted on the verruca, or a doctor can freeze or burn it off.

For more information on bunions, corns and verrucas see Chapter 6.

Chilblains are painful red patches that occasionally cause ulcers on the hands and feet if they have been exposed to the cold and inadequately covered or protected.

Back pain

The spine is made up of individual blocks of bone called vertebrae. The top seven are in the neck (cervical spine), the next twelve down are chest vertebrae (thoracic spine), then come five in the lower back (lumbar spine) and the last five vertebrae are fused together to make up the sacrum. The coccyx, a vestigial tail composed of four tiny vertebrae fused together, forms the thin end of the wedge. The lower back (lumbar spine) bears the most weight and is subjected to more twisting and straining than other parts of the back. That is why low back pain is such a common problem. The vertebrae are joined to each other at small facet joints which can be strained. These are the joints on which chiropractors concentrate their attentions.

Discs lie between the vertebrae. They are made up of a web of tough tissue and a central jelly-like substance and act as shock absorbers. If the tough web is torn, the jelly-like substance can protrude. This is what is known as a 'slipped disc', which is not a very good name for it, as the disc does not actually slip. The spinal cord runs through a canal in the middle of the vertebrae. Nerves come off the spinal cord and emerge at the sides of the vertebrae, to travel to all parts of the body. The nerves can easily be squashed by a damaged disc, facet joint, or if there is arthritis in the spine. The part of the body supplied by the squashed nerve may feel numb, tingly or painful, and you may be unable to move it properly.

The sciatic nerve which emerges from the lower back is often squashed and causes pain right down the back of the leg – the area of the body that the nerve supplies. This is known as sciatica.

The scale and nature of the problem

Human beings are rather badly designed. The spine has to support the pull of gravity and our own, often excessive, weight on top. Backs are subjected to horrendous twists and strains, carrying loads like shopping, children and bags of compost. Chairs are often badly designed and desks are even worse. The wonder is not that back pain is so common, but that it is not universal. In fact, at least 60 per cent of the population does suffer back problems each year. Back pain is a major health concern, both for the individuals who suffer, and for the nation as a whole. The bill for sickness and invalidity benefits due to back problems is steadily increasing. The annual cost to the NHS of treating back pain in the UK is £480 million.

When to see a doctor

Most people with low back pain will get better within six weeks. If the pain is bearable, and improving with home remedies and exercises, there is no need to see a doctor. But the following warning signs mean that there is pressure on the nerves of the spinal cord, or an underlying disease. It is important to see a doctor if you experience any of the following along with back pain:

- difficulty passing urine or opening your bowels. This is a potential emergency and requires urgent medical attention (see below)
- numbness around the back passage
- fever or weight loss
- continuous pain and pain at night
- marked stiffness first thing in the morning
- a numb, woolly feeling in your legs when you walk, which improves when you stop and bend forwards.

The first two symptoms may suggest pressure on the lowest nerves of the spine (cauda equina); the next three symptoms may be

Preventing mechanical back pain

Chairs At home, choose high-backed chairs – high enough to allow easy rising and sitting. You should be able to sit in the chair with your knees at right angles and your feet flat on the floor. The chair should ideally have padded arms for comfort, with wooden ends to grip when rising.

At work, chairs should have adaptable seat height and a back rest. They should not be too deep, otherwise the edge can cut into the back of the knees. They should allow you to swivel from one work surface to another without any strain, and to look slightly down on to a computer screen. Sit with your feet flat on the floor or on a small stool. Check the chair height in relation to your work surface, and consider sloping the work surface if possible.

Repetitive tasks Take small, regular breaks to allow a change of position and posture. Gardeners also need to take breaks.

Clothing Avoid restrictive clothing such as tight jeans, and high heels if possible.

Washing hair Kneel at the side of the bath and use a shower attachment or shampoo hair under a shower, instead of leaning over a sink.

Bath Buy a non-slip mat and consider a handrail: many back injuries occur as a result of slipping in the bath.

Diet Avoid constipation, as straining to pass a motion can cause low back pain. Losing weight if you are overweight may help, as obesity is a major cause of strain on the back. There is no evidence that specific diets or supplements help the common type of mechanical back pain.

Shopping Divide heavy loads between two bags and carry equal weights in both hands. Use trolleys and ask for someone to pack your bags and wheel your trolley to the car, if you have one.

Picking up children Bend from the knees, do not stoop, and hold the child closely in front of you. Try not to sling the child on to one hip.

Work Know your rights. Employers have a statutory responsibility to avoid asking employees to carry out hazardous manual tasks, to identify and assess risks to staff, and to take preventative measures to try to overcome these.

Exercise classes Avoid touching your toes, doing sit-ups and making full circles with your neck, all of which can strain your back.

signs of arthritis or a tumour on the spine; and the next symptom may be due to narrowing of the vertebral canal through which the spinal cord runs (spinal stenosis).

Posture problems: mechanical back pain

The vast majority of women who develop back pain have a perfectly normal spine but subject it to abnormal stresses, putting strain on the muscles which support the vertebral column. The muscles go into spasm which results in stiffness and pain on moving. The common causes of this kind of back pain are:

- working for long periods in a fixed position. Varying tasks, activities and position throughout the day will reduce the risk
- prolonged driving. Car seat design is sometimes very poor and drivers can suffer as a result
- poorly designed office equipment and seating
- sagging mattresses and poorly designed seating at home.

Complementary therapies for back pain

Osteopathy and chiropractic involve manipulation of the spine. Physiotherapy, osteopathy or chiropractic are encouraged by conventional practitioners, especially within four weeks of the pain starting. In one study, people who had a course of chiropractic reported more benefit and long-term satisfaction than a comparable group treated in a hospital outpatient department. Alexander Technique is a discipline which teaches correct posture and which you might expect would help to prevent if not treat back pain, but no formal, controlled trials have yet been done using it. Acupuncture and TENS machines both provide counter-stimulation to nerves to distract you from the pain. Homeopathy takes a holistic approach to pain by treating the whole person, and aims to relieve symptoms by restoring balance in the body. It is not harmful, but there is no reliable evidence for its effectiveness in treating low back pain.

One study has looked at the benefits of supervised fitness programmes. The researchers found that those who had twice-weekly exercise classes for a month as well as exercises to do at home had less disability, pain and restriction on walking than a similar group who were just shown exercises to do at home.

Conventional medical treatment

There has recently been a change in the way doctors are encouraged to help people suffering from back pain. The new thinking is that treatment must take place within three months if it is to be effective. GPs need to refer patients with back pain to a physiotherapist, osteopath or chiropractor quickly. Delays in referral make treatment less likely to succeed. Once back pain has gone on for more than six weeks, it is likely to become a long-term (chronic) problem. This is true for whichever therapy or treatment you choose. Having ruled out serious disease, the doctor should encourage sufferers to exercise rather than rest. Anyone who is off work for six months because of back pain has only a 50 per cent chance of ever returning to work. So do not be alarmed if your doctor encourages you to return to work as soon as possible: it is in your interests to do so.

Back pain in pregnancy

Back pain is common in pregnancy. It is usually a dull ache with stiffness in the lower back, and it tends to get worse as the pregnancy progresses. In the first three months of pregnancy backache is usually due to relaxation of the ligaments that help to support the spine. Backache accompanied by vaginal bleeding may mean a miscarriage. In the middle of pregnancy, backache is due to relaxation of the ligaments, an exaggerated curvature of the mother's spine to allow room for the baby, and pressure from the growing baby. Towards the end of pregnancy, persistent backache may mean the start of labour. Yoga, gentle swimming and good posture can all help to relieve the discomfort of low back pain in pregnancy.

Internal disease (spondyloarthropathy or spondylitis)

Back pain is occasionally part of an underlying condition which causes inflammation in internal organs and other joints. These conditions – such as psoriasis, Reiter's syndrome, reactive arthritis, Crohn's disease, ulcerative colitis and ankylosing spondylitis – often run in the family and usually start in early adult life. Women are slightly less likely to develop these conditions than men. The back pain that is associated with these conditions may be felt at the sides of the lower part of the spine, which is where the tailbone meets the hipbones at the back (sacroiliac joints). Pain is often felt in the buttocks and is worse after sitting for a long time. The eyes are often affected too, due to inflammation which affects many organs in addition to the joints, with grittiness, soreness and redness flaring up when the joint and back pains are bad. The other features that can occur in association with these conditions are shown below.

A joint specialist (rheumatologist) usually oversees the care of women with these conditions. The objectives of treatment are the same as for mechanical low back pain: to relieve the pain and keep the individual active and mobile. Anti-inflammatory drugs, physiotherapy and daily exercises to do at home are the most helpful aspects of treatment. Acupuncture for pain relief, osteopathy or chiropractic to aid mobility, and homeopathy to boost general well-being may all be worth trying.

Other causes of back pain

- Spinal tumours. These are very rare. They cause weight loss, fevers, general tiredness, weakness, and severe pain which disturbs sleep and is worse at night. Tumours can arise in the spine, or they may be due to the spread of cancerous cells from cancers elsewhere, such as the breast or ovary.
- Spinal stenosis. This is fairly common in men and women over the age of 60. It is caused by a narrowing in the spinal canal through which the spinal cord runs and is due to wear and tear. It causes leg pain on walking and is eased when you lean forward or sit, relieving compression on the spinal cord. Surgery can help this condition.
- Inflammation or infection in other organs of the body. Indigestion with acid reflux can irritate the diaphragm and cause pain round to the back beneath the shoulder blades, and up to the shoulder tips. Gall bladder inflammation due to stones can cause pain round to the right-hand side of the back, just below the shoulder blade. Inflammation of the lining of the lungs (pleurisy) can cause back pain which is worse on taking a deep breath.
- An aortic aneurysm. This is a potentially dangerous widening of the body's major blood vessel (the aorta), which can cause back pain.
- Kidney stones. These cause pain on either side of the small of the back.

Conditions which may be associated with back pain

Condition	Features (may not all be present)
Psoriasis	Scaly plaques on skin; scaly scalp; painful joints; swollen fingers; pitted nails
Reiter's syndrome	Pain or swelling in a joint for more than a month; pain on passing urine; inflammation of the cervix leading to vaginal bleeding
Reactive arthritis	Pain or swelling in a joint after a recent infection, e.g. dysentery which causes bloody diarrhoea
Crohn's disease and ulcerative colitis	Pain or swelling in joints; bloody diarrhoea and slimy stools
Ankylosing spondylitis	Stiff, painful spine and difficulty moving. Most common in young men

Chapter 4

Eyes

Most of us enjoy a lifetime of reliable service from our eyes with minimal disturbance. They repair themselves well and are not as prone to disease as are some other organs. However, when eye-related problems occur, they are often the first indicators of under-lying disease elsewhere in the body, such as high blood pressure, diabetes or multiple sclerosis. Regular check-ups and prompt, expert care when an eye problem arises can help to avoid visual impairment in many cases.

This chapter looks at the structure of the eye and how it works; care of the eyes; discomfort in the eye and problems with vision, outlining the treatments available.

Structure of the eye: how we see

The eye is like an extremely well-designed camera.

1. Light bounces off objects and surfaces. The light rays enter our eyes through a round, transparent window (cornea) which bends the rays so they eventually form a sharp image. The cornea is surrounded by the white of the eye (sclera), which does not let light through.
2. Rays pass through the cornea via a chamber filled with watery fluid (aqueous). Raised pressure in this chamber causes glaucoma, which impairs vision.
3. The rays pass through a hole (pupil) in the middle of a band of coloured, muscular tissue (iris). The iris, which gives the eye its characteristic colour, can alter the pupil size depending on the amount of light entering the eye.

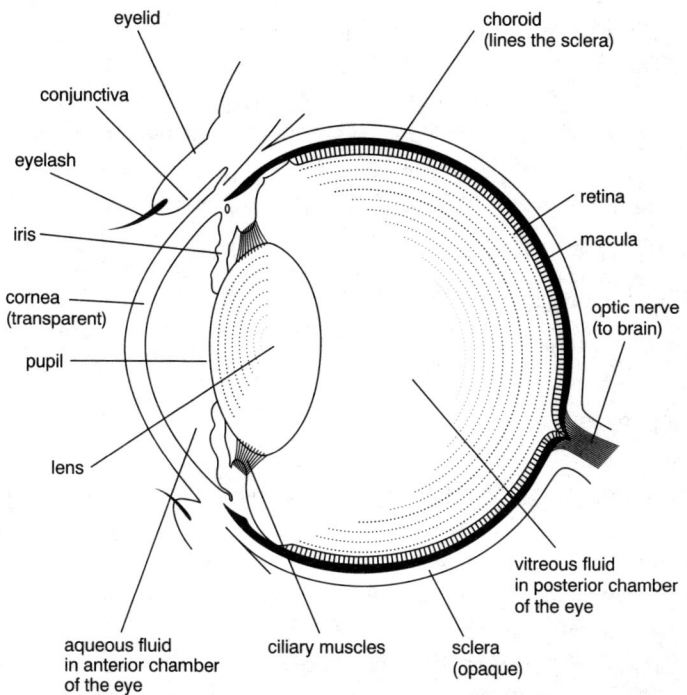

Figure 3 Cross-section of the eye

4. Just behind the iris lies the lens, which is moved by muscles on either side to allow for clear vision in different light conditions. If the lens becomes hazy, the condition is called a cataract, and light is less well focused, making vision blurred.

5. Behind the lens is the main chamber of the eye, filled with a jelly-like substance (vitreous) which gives the eye its shape.

6. The curved screen at the back of the eye is lined by a light-sensitive layer (retina). The light-sensitive cells (rods and cones) of the retina convert the pattern of light that falls on them into an electrical message which is transmitted to the brain along the optic nerves. The image is transmitted in full colour and detail. The retina is like a photographic film, and the image is 'developed' by the brain. If the retina becomes detached, vision is impaired. Inflammation of the optic nerve can cause pain and visual loss too.

Red eyes

Five out of every 100 visits to a GP are about eye problems, and of these nearly half are about red and uncomfortable eyes caused by conjunctivitis, an inflammation of the layer of the eye that covers the eyeball and the inside of the eyelids. Conjunctivitis could be bacterial, viral or allergic.

Bacteria account for the majority of infections, and in such cases the GP will usually prescribe antibiotic eye drops or eye ointment (chloramphenicol or Fucithalmic), which kill the bacteria and stop the inflammation. Viral conjunctivitis produces similar symptoms to the bacterial variety, but does not require specific treatment. Rarely, conjunctivitis is caused by the chlamydia bacteria which can also lead to a vaginal discharge (see Chapter 11); it is usually treated with oral antibiotics and eye drops.

Allergic reactions, especially hay fever, are a common cause of conjunctivitis. In such cases of conjunctivitis, unlike the bacterial kind, no pus collects as crusts in the corners of the eye. The treatment for allergy-triggered conjunctivitis is to avoid the source of the allergy, wear dark glasses, use anti-allergic eye drops (e.g. Opticrom, which is available over the counter) and take antihistamine tablets by mouth (e.g. Triludan, also available over the counter).

Eye care

- Wear spectacles or contact lenses to correct short-sightedness, long-sightedness and some cases of crooked images caused by a slightly abnormally shaped eye (astigmatism).
- Avoid heavy, oil-based cosmetics. Always remove eye make-up each night, preferably with hypoallergenic make-up remover pads. Stop using cosmetics if eyes become irritated.
- Have an eye check every two years if you are over the age of 40, especially if you have a family history of glaucoma, by a qualified and registered ophthalmic optician. Look for the letters MBCO or DO after the optician's name. Women under the age of 40 are unlikely to suffer from glaucoma, but they should have any visual disturbance checked.
- An eye check should test vision, measure pressure in the eyes (for glaucoma) and examine the back of the eyes (by fundoscopy) for early signs of disorders such as diabetes and high blood pressure.
- Those working on computers are entitled to an annual eye check. For employees, this should be paid for by the employer (see Chapter 1).
- Those who wear contact lenses must follow the supplier's instructions for removal and cleaning to avoid eye problems. If irritation occurs, take the lenses out, wear glasses and see an ophthalmic optician or doctor.
- Women with mild to moderate short-sightedness who are considering laser surgery (see below) should note that it is generally not available on the NHS, may result in some loss of vision and could lead to impaired night vision.

The following table lists the main symptoms and causes of a red eye, and outlines the various treatments.

Main causes of and treatment for red eyes

Symptoms and diagnosis	Treatment
Inflammation and crusting of lid (blepharitis); may accompany other skin problems, e.g. dry, flaky scalp and skin on face (seborrhoeic dermatitis)	Clean eyelids with cotton-wool buds dipped in warm water. See GP for antibiotic ointment. Treating the skin problem can prevent further flare-ups
Eyelid turned in or out, which means it does not protect eye properly (entropion or ectropion)	See GP. A small operation can help both conditions. It is common among elderly women and stroke-sufferers
'Boil' on eyelid around an eyelash, head of pus (stye)	Use a towel soaked in warm water and hold to eye as a compress. Get an antibiotic ointment from GP
Small, hard lump on eyelid (chalazion)	Use a warm compress as above. Get an antibiotic ointment from GP. If it is persistent or troublesome, it can be surgically removed
Gritty eye, no pus, occurring as a result of a foreign body in the eye	See GP/go to casualty without delay
Red, gritty eye with crusting or pus (conjunctivitis – bacterial)	See GP. Get antibiotic eye drops/ointment. Very contagious (use own towel)
Pink, gritty eyes, runny nose, clear discharge from eyes (conjunctivitis – viral)	See GP if the problem is persistent for more than a few days. Extremely contagious
Red, gritty eyes, long-standing, pus, vaginal	See GP. May need to see specialist. Antibiotic eye drops

discharge (conjunctivitis – chlamydia)
Itchy, red eyes, runny nose, sneezing, seasonal (conjunctivitis – pollen allergy)

and oral antibiotics will be prescribed
Get antihistamines and eye drops from the chemist. See GP if symptoms persist

Red, gritty eyes after using new eye make-up (conjunctivitis – contact allergy)

Stop using the product. Get sodium cromoglycate (Opticrom) eye drops and antihistamines from chemist. See GP if symptoms persist

Painless blood-red eye after coughing/sneezing/straining (subconjunctival haemorrhage)

See GP to check blood pressure. There is no specific treatment: it resolves on its own

Pain followed by red eyes and light sensitivity (iritis)

See GP. Referral to a specialist likely. Steroid drops will be prescribed. Sometimes related to certain types of arthritis

Painful, bloodshot eye, blisters around eye (shingles – reactivation of dormant chickenpox)

See GP, who may refer you to a specialist. Anti-shingles drug (acyclovir) will be prescribed

Bloodshot and very painful eyes in a contact lens wearer (ulcer of cornea)

Remove contact lenses. See GP or go to casualty without delay. Drops (fluorescein) in eye show up any damage

Severe, sudden pain in one eye, generally in women over 50, vomiting, haloes around lights, hazy vision, eye feels hard (acute glaucoma)

See specialist urgently. Pressure in eye is reduced with drugs and by surgery

Sudden visual loss

Floaters and retinal detachment

Everyone gets occasional specks (floaters) in front of their eyes, especially when looking at a light background: they are nothing to worry about. But if they are visible in any light, suddenly increase in number or are associated with any loss of vision, seek urgent help. Floaters which occur without any loss of vision are usually harmless. They occur because, as one gets older, the jelly (vitreous) which fills the back of the eye can become detached from the retina which it usually backs on to. No treatment is required for this condition.

A more serious, and less common, problem is that as the vitreous detaches from the retina, it can tear a hole in the retina and even cause the retina itself to detach from its moorings. If this happens, you will experience flashing lights, be aware of numerous floaters and start to lose vision. Retinal detachment is more likely in very short-sighted women, diabetics or women who have had surgery for cataracts in the past. Surgery is required to seal the holes in the retina.

Migraine

A migraine is a violent headache, often over one eye, which may be accompanied by nausea, vomiting, slurred speech, visual disturbance and loss of sensation on one side of the body. It is thought to be caused by blood vessels in the brain narrowing down and then expanding again.

Migraine often runs in families. It may be set off by a particular trigger such as red wine, chocolate, cheese or fatigue, or be related to periods. Women who suffer from migraine may know they are about to get an attack, and may feel sick or get a characteristic headache over one eye. Zigzag, shimmering lines and multi-coloured flashing lights are often seen during a migraine. A sufferer may find it hard to see properly for a few hours but vision returns to normal after that. Identifying and avoiding triggers and having specific anti-migraine treatment such as sumitrapan (Imigran) may help. Referral to a specialist may be necessary (see Chapter 9 for more details).

Optic neuritis

An optic nerve runs from the back of each eye into the brain, taking information from the retina to the part of the brain that interprets images. Women aged between 20 and 40 may experience visual loss due to inflammation of this nerve (optic neuritis).

In this condition, there is pain in one eye which worsens on moving the eye. Red objects may look faded through the bad eye, and normally bright through the normal eye. Vision is usually impaired in the bad eye. Often the inflammation improves without specific treatment. If other problems such as pins and needles in limbs, incontinence or weakness of various muscles are experienced, they may be a sign of multiple sclerosis. However, many cases of optic neuritis are isolated events and are not linked to any other conditions. Referral to a specialist is likely to confirm the diagnosis.

Blockage of the artery

A blood vessel (retinal artery) enters the eye next to the optic nerve and supplies the eye with its vital blood supply. If this artery becomes blocked, the sufferer will feel as if a curtain has descended over one eye. This condition is very rare in young women. Smoking, diabetes and raised cholesterol levels all predispose women to this problem. Although the blockage can sometimes clear and vision may be restored, immediate referral to hospital is essential if the sight in the affected eye is to be saved.

Blockage of the vein

A blood vessel (retinal vein) takes blood from the eye and back to the heart. If this vein becomes blocked, thus putting pressure on the retina, there may be only vague visual disturbance such as blurring, or more marked loss of vision, depending on which part of the vein is blocked. High blood pressure, diabetes and raised pressure in the eye (glaucoma) can all predispose women to this problem. Laser treatment (see below) can help.

Macular degeneration

The macula is the area of the retina where vision is sharpest. Light-sensitive cells (cones) responsible for clarity of vision are most concentrated here. The macula may start to degenerate, leading to a condition known as 'macular degeneration'.

Macular degeneration increases with age and is rare in women under 60. Very short-sighted women are more prone to it. The condition may come on gradually or suddenly: straight lines will begin to look wavy, and objects will seem distorted and may look bigger or smaller than usual. Referral to a specialist is necessary. The specialist will show a woman with macular degeneration a piece of paper with a grid pattern on it. Because of her condition, the sufferer will be able to see the pattern at the edges of the paper but will miss the grid in the centre of the page, or the lines will look distorted to her. Drawing the area where she can see the changes on the grid allows the specialist to chart the progress of the condition. Treatment with laser is possible in a few cases.

Laser treatment for eye conditions

Laser beams can be directed at parts of the eye to treat a wide variety of conditions including short-sightedness, retinal disease (especially that caused by diabetes), macular degeneration, glaucoma and blockage of the retinal vein.

The laser used for short-sightedness reshapes the cornea. To treat retinal damage caused by diabetes a laser is used to seal off abnormal blood vessels, thus clearing the retina.

Laser treatment is painless and no anaesthetic is needed. The patient sits on a seat and the laser beam is directed into her eye by sensitive machines controlled by an ophthalmologist. Treatment time varies but rarely exceeds half an hour; 5–10 minutes is more typical. Some women find that their eyes ache after treatment, but paracetamol usually overcomes this. Others experience no discomfort at all. Vision may be blurred for a few hours afterwards because drops are put into the eyes to open up the pupils to allow treatment. The blurring wears off on its own.

The advent of lasers has revolutionised the treatment of potentially sight-threatening conditions, and has allowed some men and women the chance to throw away their spectacles.

Gradual visual loss

Short-sightedness

Short-sightedness (myopia) occurs when the eyeball is so long that light rays form an image in front of the retina instead of on it, which makes the image unclear. A lens which curves inwards (concave) corrects this so that the image will form on the retina.

Short-sighted people can see objects that are nearby and may be able to read a book without glasses, but more distant objects, like a cinema screen viewed from the back row, will be blurred. Women who are short-sighted are more prone to the gradual type of glaucoma, retinal detachment and macular degeneration (see above).

Correcting short-sightedness

Lenses to focus the rays correctly on to the retina are available as contact lenses or spectacles. Contact lenses are preferable to many women for cosmetic reasons, and because they are safer in certain occupations and sports in which glasses may get smashed. Moreover, contact lenses may give a much clearer image if a cataract has been removed from one eye but not the other. The disadvantages of contact lenses are that they can cause allergies and infections and are fiddly to use, especially for women with arthritis.

Surgery for short-sightedness has been available in the USA for around ten years and is gaining popularity in the UK. Correction of the myopia is achieved using computer-controlled laser destruction of the central part of the cornea (see above). It is best for women over 25, by which time the eye is fully developed. Ironically, the best results are achieved in women whose short-sightedness is mild or moderate. But the operation is available on the NHS only for people with severe short-sightedness, and even then its availability is very limited. Most people who have the surgery are very pleased with it. However, around 5 per cent have some loss of vision, and over 38 per cent will not be able to see so well at night. Five per cent will find that they cannot drive at all at night.

Long-sightedness

Long-sightedness (hypermetropia) occurs when the eyeball is so short that light rays form an image behind the retina, or when the lens is too weak to bring the rays together at the right spot on the retina. A lens which curves outwards (convex) corrects this so the image forms on the retina. A long-sighted person can read better than normal at a distance: for example, she will be able to read the route number of a bus when it is still far away, but will find it hard to focus on objects nearby, such as print. Reading glasses may become necessary by the age of 30, whereas normal-sighted people usually need reading glasses only later in life. As the eye ages further, glasses for both near and distance vision may become necessary. Long-sighted women are more prone to the sudden type of glaucoma (see below).

Cataracts

The lens of the eye becomes cloudy with age. This is an inevitable part of ageing, so everyone over 80 has some clouding of the lens. An operation is necessary only if the cataract interferes with vision. Women with cataracts have difficulty reading, recognising faces, watching television, seeing in bright lights and driving. Cataracts are more common among diabetic women; those who have taken steroids over a long period of time for any reason are also prone to them.

Surgery to treat cataracts is remarkably successful. An artificial lens is generally implanted in the eye during the operation. The eyes are normally left slightly short-sighted so that the woman can read without glasses and is still able to see fairly well at a distance. After the operation, the use of steroid and antibiotic eye drops for several weeks is advised, and bending and strenuous exercise should be avoided for at least a week.

Glaucoma

Glaucoma is a disease caused by raised pressure in the eye, which impairs vision. Fluid called aqueous is produced in the eye, flows around inside it and then drains away. Any obstruction to the flow or drainage causes glaucoma. The treatment for this condition is with eye drops, which are used for life. Drops include timolol, which reduces the amount of fluid in the eye, pilocarpine which closes the pupil to allow better drainage of the fluid, and adrenaline, which improves drainage. Surgery, sometimes using a laser, will be necessary if the drops do not work.

Chronic glaucoma

This, the most common type of glaucoma, develops gradually and painlessly. The periphery of vision is affected until eventually only the central part of vision remains. This means that everything looks as if it were being viewed down a tunnel.

This type of glaucoma is very rare in women under 50, but increases to 10 per cent of all those over 80. Anyone with a close relative with this type of glaucoma has a one in ten chance of developing it themselves. Diabetics and short-sighted people are also at increased risk.

Brothers, sisters, parents and children of glaucoma sufferers are entitled to free eye tests annually over the age of 40. It is important to ask the optician to perform all three tests for glaucoma. These are measurement of pressure in the eye, examination of the back of the eye and a test of the fields of vision.

Prevention is vital because treatment cannot reverse visual loss – it can only prevent further deterioration. Apart from eye drops, oral tablets such as acetazolamide are sometimes prescribed. Careful monitoring will be needed for the rest of the sufferer's life. Laser treatment or more extensive surgery to relieve the obstruction may be necessary.

Acute glaucoma

This type of glaucoma is much less common but more dramatic than the chronic glaucoma described above. Elderly and long-sighted women are especially prone to it. It occurs because the angle near the lens of the eye narrows. The condition is more likely to come on at night because the pupil opens up to allow more light through. This tends to constrict the angle so much that fluid cannot drain, and the pressure builds up quickly.

In this type of glaucoma the eye becomes red and very painful, with no obvious cause. The eyeball will feel tender to touch and may feel harder than the other eye. Vision will be blurred and lights may appear to have haloes around them. The sufferer may have had similar warning attacks in the past which improved after sleep.

This type of glaucoma requires emergency treatment if sight in that eye is to be saved. It is best to go straight to a casualty department, rather than wait at home for a GP to visit. A drug (acetazolamide) may be injected into a vein and pilocarpine drops will be put in both eyes to close the pupil and control the problem. Laser treatment or surgery will then be required for both eyes to prevent further attacks.

Other eye conditions needing treatment

Watering eyes

Eyes would water constantly if it were not for the excellent drainage system that sweeps tears across the eye and allows them to drain down a tube which starts at the inner corner of each eye (punctum) near the nose and ends in the nose itself.

Tears will not drain properly if the eyelid is turned outwards such that the punctum is not in the right position to catch the tears. This happens frequently as women get older and the skin around the eyes becomes loose. It can also happen as a result of a stroke or weakness of the facial muscles. An antibiotic ointment (chloramphenicol) helps to prevent infection. A minor operation under local anaesthetic can correct the problem.

The drainage system can become blocked, although this is relatively rare in adults. A major operation to relieve the obstruction is occasionally necessary.

Dry eyes

Dry eyes are common among elderly women because tear production decreases. Diuretics (water pills), which are prescribed for fluid retention, high blood pressure and heart disease, can make the problem worse.

Dry, gritty and sore eyes may be a feature of rheumatoid arthritis, in which there is widespread inflammation of joints and other organs of the body because the body reacts against itself. Inflammation of the tear glands makes the tears dry up. Artificial tear drops, which lubricate the eye, are very useful. Inflammation of other parts of the eye can cause a red, painful eye which requires oral or injected treatment with steroids or other drugs which damp down the inflammatory process.

Rosacea (see Chapter 6), a skin condition which causes a red face, can cause inflammation of the eyelids, which in turn can result in recurrent styes and cysts and reduced tear production. Artificial tears and treatment with oral antibiotics (tetracycline) can improve the skin and eyes. A simple ointment which lubricates the eyes is useful at night but has limited use during the day because it blurs vision.

Puffy eyes

The skin around the eyes is very loose and fluid can easily accumulate there. Eyes tend to look most puffy after a night's sleep because lying down allows fluid to collect. Sitting up and standing during the day usually allows the puffiness to go down.

The most common causes of puffy eyes are allergy to cosmetics or soaps and mild fluid retention just before a period. It is a good idea to get a GP to check that there is no protein in the urine, as puffy eyes can sometimes be a sign of fluid retention caused by kidney disease. An under-active thyroid gland can also cause fluid to be retained; a blood test can be done to check thyroid function.

The following self-help measures are useful once a GP has confirmed that there is no underlying disease.

- Sleep with an extra pillow: raising your head can help drain the fluid.
- Avoid excess salt in the diet because too much salt can increase overall fluid retention.
- Check eye make-up to see whether it is the cause: stop using it for two weeks and see whether there is an improvement.

It is not advisable to use diuretics (water pills) or to restrict fluid intake as this is unlikely to help and may cause kidney damage.

Bulging eyes

Swollen eyelids, bulging eyes and reduced blinking may all be due to an over-active thyroid gland. Your GP will do a blood test to check. Referral to a specialist is likely (see Chapter 8 for details).

Chapter 5

Ear, nose and throat

The reason ear, nose and throat are frequently treated together as one entity (ENT) is that the three organs are joined to one another and conditions that affect one often cause problems in another. For instance, a cold may make your nose feel stuffy and blocked with mucus. The mucus runs down the back of your throat, causing a sore throat and irritating cough. The tube which drains your middle ear into your nose may then become blocked because your nose is 'bunged up', causing earache and temporary deafness.

This chapter describes the structure of each of these three organs, showing how they interconnect; looks at what can go wrong with them; and outlines the treatments available.

Structure of the ear, nose and throat

The ear

The ear is made up of three parts. The outer part includes the part of the ear that you can see and it collects sound waves. The sound waves are funnelled down the hair-lined ear canal, which is kept clean by wax produced in the canal and shed on to our pillows while we sleep, taking dirt and debris with it. The ear canal ends at the eardrum, which vibrates when sound waves hit it.

The middle ear is a closed chamber on the other side of the eardrum. When the eardrum vibrates, it sets off vibrations in a chain of three small bones in the middle ear which carry the sound across the middle ear to the inner ear. With the eardrum on one side and the inner ear on the other, the middle ear has only one link with the nose – the eustachian tube. If the eustachian tube becomes blocked owing to a cold or in the pressurised cabin

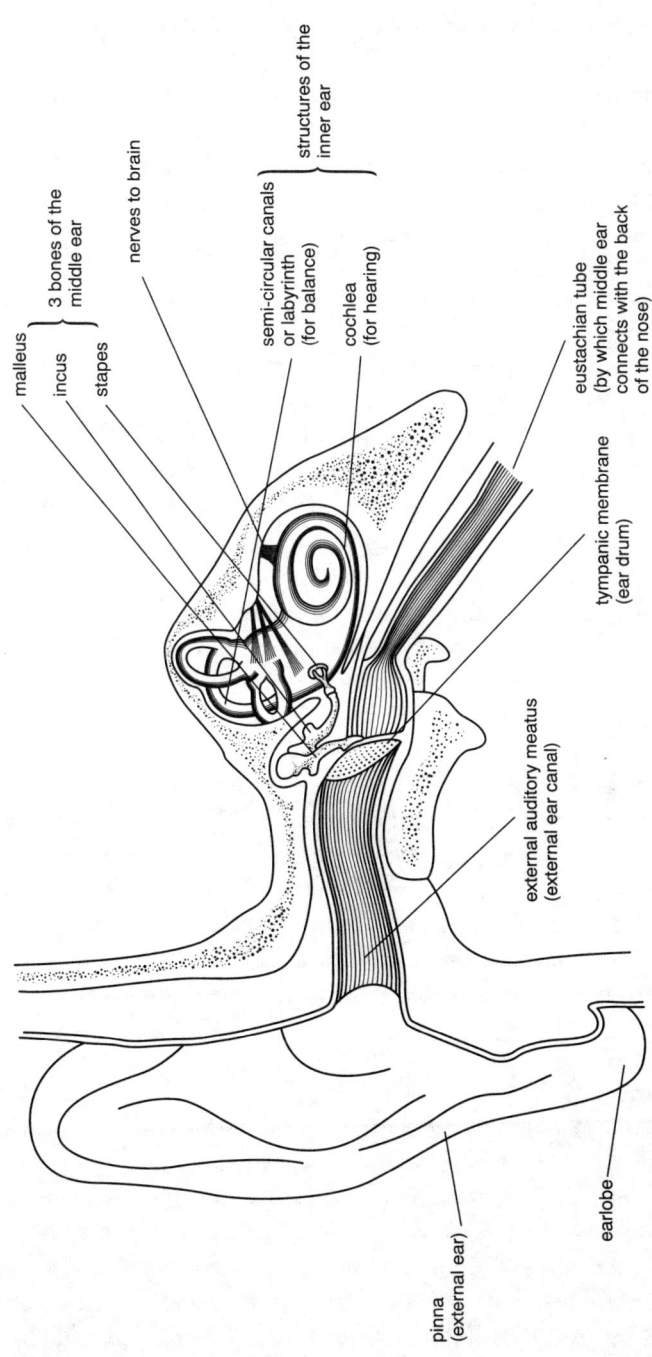

malleus
incus } 3 bones of the middle ear
stapes

nerves to brain

semi-circular canals or labyrinth (for balance)
cochlea (for hearing) } structures of the inner ear

eustachian tube (by which middle ear connects with the back of the nose)

tympanic membrane (ear drum)

external auditory meatus (external ear canal)

pinna (external ear)

earlobe

Figure 4 Structure of the ear

of an aeroplane, it can cause pressure on the middle ear which results in earache.

The inner ear picks up the sound that has been transmitted across the middle ear and converts it into an electrical message which it sends to the brain. The brain interprets the sound and makes sense of it. The inner ear is also partly responsible for balance. Inner-ear conditions commonly cause hearing loss and/or loss of balance and dizziness.

The nose

The nose has three main functions.

Breathing We breathe in air through our nose and mouth. Hairs in our nose filter out dirt particles, and mucus produced by the nose helps to flush out the dirt and debris. When we breathe in (inhale), air passes up the nose or through the mouth, down the windpipe (trachea) and into the lungs, where oxygen is absorbed into the bloodstream to be taken to all the cells of the body. When we breathe out (exhale), the oxygen-depleted air is pushed out of the lungs, up the windpipe and out of the nose and mouth.

Smell Air that passes up the nose carries odours. The nose contains specially designed cells that pick up smells and send a message to a part of the brain that interprets the smell. If the nose is blocked because of a cold, the sense of smell may be impaired.

Drainage The middle ear drains into the back of the nose by the eustachian tube (see above), tears from the eyes drain into an opening inside the nose by the lachrymal duct and the network of spaces (sinuses) in the skull drains into the nose. It is no wonder that a blocked-up nose can cause a great deal of pressure which makes your ears ache, your face throb owing to congested sinuses and your eyes water.

The throat

The throat (pharynx) is the back of the mouth. The back of the nose is joined to the back of the mouth, which is why if your nose is full of mucus from a cold and you lie down, the mucus runs down your throat, making you cough. There are two collections of tissue that help to fight infections when one is very young – the tonsils in the throat, and adenoids at the back of the nose. Adenoids normally shrink to nothing by the age of seven, but tonsils do not shrink in the same way and can become infected (tonsillitis, see below).

The throat can easily become inflamed by inhaled smoke, hot and spicy foods, alcohol or a cold virus, causing a condition called pharyngitis. The same irritants can inflame the voice box (larynx), which is a continuation of the nasal passages leading into the lungs. This inflammation is sometimes called laryngitis. The vocal cords which produce sound by opening and closing as we breathe out lie in the larynx, which is why laryngitis makes the voice sound hoarse.

Ears

What can go wrong with ears

Ears are vital for hearing and balance. They serve us efficiently and need hardly any maintenance. However, things can go wrong with them; indeed, earache can be an extremely painful condition.

Hearing loss, which is an almost inevitable consequence of getting older and which could affect women at a young age too, can be a very isolating and debilitating problem. It can be made even more distressing by tinnitus ('ringing' in the ears). Fortunately, hearing aids and operations can help many women with hearing problems; help is also available for tinnitus sufferers.

Dizziness and loss of balance are very unpleasant sensations which can result from ear complaints. The dizziness can make one feel very nauseous, like being constantly seasick, and it is comforting to know that the most common cause is a viral infection which affects the inner ear and clears up on its own within a few weeks.

Earache

Earache can be dull and throbbing or sharp and needle-like. Either way it is a rather dreadful sensation. The inner ear has no pain fibres, so earache is usually a result of problems with the outer and middle sections of the ear.

Outer ear

The outer ear is a hair-lined tunnel which is prone to boils and inflammation. A boil or severe inflammation can block off the

Ear care

- Wash outer part of ears regularly with soap and water and dab dry with a soft towel. Do not try to wash or clean the ear canals.
- If water gets in your ears during swimming, a shower or a hair wash, hold earlobe and shake it gently while turning head on that side. The water will drain out.
- Water sometimes gets trapped in ears and makes the wax there swell so the ear feels very 'bunged up'. Never stick hard objects like hairclips into your ears to try to get wax out – you may perforate your eardrum. Put olive oil or almond oil drops, available from a chemist, into your ears every night for five nights, and lie with the blocked ear uppermost for 5–10 minutes. Then ask your GP to syringe your ears to remove the wax.
- If your ears feel sensitive, itchy or inflamed, do not be tempted to push cotton buds in to clean them. Avoid getting water in your ears by putting a plug of cotton wool covered in Vaseline into your ear while washing your hair or swimming, and seek medical advice.
- Sensitive, itchy ears may be caused by dry, flaky skin and severe dandruff. Olive oil drops once a week can help prevent irritation; it is also worth asking your GP for advice about treating the underlying problem of flaking skin and scalp.
- If your ears have just been pierced, keep gold sleepers in the holes as advised, clean holes daily with surgical spirit and go back to wearing sleepers if the ear holes start getting sore or red or ooze pus. See a doctor if the earlobes swell: this could be caused by an infection or an allergy to earrings.

whole tunnel and cause hearing loss in that ear. Glands just in front of or behind the ear usually become enlarged to try to fight the infection. The glands could become tender to touch, and any movement of the earlobe could be painful. There is not usually much discharge from the ear.

If the inflammation has been brought on by a great deal of swimming, it may settle on its own if the ears are kept dry. Pain can be relieved with painkillers such as paracetamol and by holding a warm hot-water bottle to the ear. Most people will want to see their GP if the earache persists more than a day or two because it is so uncomfortable. The ear drops usually prescribed contain aluminium acetate to toughen the skin, antibiotics to treat the infection and steroids to treat the inflammation.

A test for diabetes is a good idea if a woman gets recurrent boils in the ear, so the GP may request a urine or blood test. Antibiotics by mouth are prescribed if there is fever and very large, tender glands or if a woman has had a spate of boils. Sometimes, a long ribbon of gauze soaked in a paste to relieve inflammation is packed into the swollen outer ear and changed daily until the swelling subsides. Very occasionally, a large, stubborn boil will need to be lanced by a specialist in a minor operation.

Middle ear

As described above, the middle ear is separated from the outer ear by the eardrum. It contains the bones that transmit sound and is a closed chamber. The only conduit from the middle ear is the eustachian tube, which connects it with the nose. This part of the ear can easily become infected as bugs travel up the nose. This is common in children, who have smaller faces and shorter eustachian tubes, and it also happens to some unlucky adults. Glands in the neck may swell and ache as they try to fight off the middle-ear infection. Bugs, pus and general debris build up in the middle ear causing pressure, a throbbing earache and the consequent temporary loss of hearing in the affected ear. Either the debris eventually gets absorbed or the eardrum bursts to release the pressure. The eardrum then gradually heals up on its own over a few weeks. If the eardrum bursts, there might be some yellowish 'gunge' on the pillow in the morning. The pain subsides when the eardrum bursts. Antibiotics speed up the process a little but there is no harm in allowing nature to take its course, so long as the pain or accompanying fever are bearable. A hearing test is important if hearing loss persists after the pain has settled.

A stuffy or 'bunged-up' pain in the ears may occur after flying because of the pressure changes that occur during ascent and descent when the plane is flying at a height of over 8,000 feet. It is best not to fly if there is already increased pressure in the middle ear from fluid or infection. Hay fever and colds which tend to make the nose blocked also raise the risk of earache when flying. To relieve the pressure in the ears, you can make your ear 'pop' by tightly pinching the nose with finger and thumb and blowing hard down on the nose. To prevent earache, you need to start 'popping' the ears as soon as descent starts and keep doing it every few minutes. Other ways to prevent flight-related earache are to take an oral antihistamine (e.g. Triludan, available over the counter), which unblocks the nose and relieves pressure in the middle ear, the day before and the day of the flight, or to use a nasal spray (e.g. Otrivine), which works in a similar way to the antihistamine, before and during the flight. Sometimes earache and a blocked feeling in the ear can persist after a flight. This usually settles with no treatment. If the symptoms remain after a few days, consult your GP.

Other sources of earache

Factors causing earache apart from the ones discussed above include tonsillitis; tooth decay, abscess in the gums or impacted wisdom teeth; pain in the jaw; and neck pain resulting from a whiplash injury or arthritis.

When to see a doctor

You should consult your GP if you have:

- earache and hearing loss for more than ten days
- earache and blood-stained discharge from the ear
- earache which worsens over a few days with high fever
- heavy discharge from the ear for more than ten days
- earache and/or hearing loss persisting more than a few days after a flight.

Hearing loss

Hearing loss affects about 6 in every 100 adults in the UK. Some degree of hearing loss, often more profound in one ear, is an almost inevitable consequence of living to a ripe old age. Given that women tend to live longer than men, they are more likely to develop age-related hearing loss.

Severe hearing loss in both ears is a terrible burden for anyone to bear. It cuts one off from the world and presents great hurdles. A woman who is hearing-impaired from childhood generally has great difficulty mastering speech, and a woman who becomes

Main causes of and treatments for hearing loss

Pattern of deafness	Possible cause	Treatment
Develops suddenly, ear feels bunged up, often only one affected	Wax, debris or a foreign body, e.g. cotton wool, in ear canal	Use olive oil drops; see GP to have ear syringed
Develops suddenly, no sound at all in one ear, follows ear infection or blow with flat hand	Perforated eardrum	Usually heals on its own
Develops gradually, runs in the family, one/both ears affected. May worsen during pregnancy	One of the bones in the middle ear becomes fixed (otosclerosis)	A hearing aid or an operation may be needed
Develops after a flight, cold or hay fever. Both ears feel bunged up	Fluid in the middle ear	Clears on its own. See GP if it persists more than three days
Develops gradually in both ears, affects the elderly and occasionally women in their 50s	Inner-ear damage due to age (presbyacusis)	A hearing aid may be needed
Develops fairly gradually in both ears, after exposure to excessive noise. Rare in women	Inner-ear damage due to noise	Avoid the noise; ear plugs or a hearing aid may be needed
Develops gradually in one ear, bouts of dizziness, most common between ages of 30 and 50	Build-up of fluid in the inner ear (Ménière's disease; see Chapter 9); tumour in the inner ear	Drugs may be prescribed to relieve the dizziness; an operation may be needed

severely hearing-impaired in adult life develops a flat, monotonic, harsh voice because she cannot hear the sound of her own voice. Tinnitus (ringing in the ears) often accompanies hearing loss and can be very distressing.

If your ears feel blocked and you cannot hear properly, the chances are that you have excess wax in your ears. Use olive oil ear drops, available with a special dropper from any chemist, every night for five nights. Then ask a GP to check your ears and syringe out the wax and debris if necessary. More stubborn wax, or foreign bodies such as dead flies which have become trapped in the ear, can be fished out by a specialist using a microscope and long tweezers. An ear infection which may be part of a bad cold causes earache and a fever. Sometimes, the eardrum bursts due to the pressure of infected debris in the middle ear, especially if this section of the ear cannot drain into the nose because the eustachian tube is blocked. If the eardrum bursts, it develops a hole through which middle-ear debris can drain out of the ear, usually on to your pillow. The pressure on the middle ear is instantly relieved when the eardrum bursts so any earache usually clears up, but the sight of a blood-stained discharge on the pillow can be alarming. It is important to see a doctor to confirm what has happened. Perforated eardrums heal on their own. But eardrums that fail to heal can have a graft of tissue to seal up the hole and restore hearing.

Occasionally the middle ear remains blocked after an infection. It may feel stuffy and hearing may be impaired. The GP may recommend referral to a specialist, who may suggest a small operation to insert grommets, which are small tubes pushed through the eardrum into the middle ear to drain middle-ear fluid and prevent it building up again. Grommets are used for children with persistent middle-ear fluid ('glue ear') but are occasionally recommended for adults.

Although both women and men can suffer from hearing loss, women are more prone to one particular cause of it than men – otosclerosis. This condition, which tends to run in families, may start in early adulthood. Hearing loss results from one of the small bones in the middle ear becoming so fixed and rigid that it cannot transmit sound. The problem may start or worsen during pregnancy. If only one ear is affected, a hearing aid could help. But if hearing loss is severe, an operation (stapedectomy) to replace the bone may be recommended.

There may not always be a readily treatable cause for hearing loss. The only way of improving hearing in some cases may be to amplify sound using a hearing aid. Hearing aids are available on the NHS or from commercial hearing aid dispensers who are controlled by the Hearing Aid Council.★ The NHS should be able to provide for most people's needs, although private dispensers may carry a wider range. If hearing is poor in both ears, the aid will be fitted in the better ear to give maximum benefit, otherwise it will be put in the poorer ear.

Hearing-impaired people may also need to be taught other ways around their disability. Advice about lip reading and other specialised help is available from the Royal National Institute for Deaf People.★

Some unfortunate women who have no hearing at all in either ear as a result of inner ear damage may benefit from a cochlear implant. This provides direct electrical stimulation of the cochlea (inner ear).

When to see a doctor
You should consult your GP if your hearing loss:

- is severe and develops suddenly
- is associated with earache, dizziness, ringing in the ears or discharge/blood from the ear
- worsens in pregnancy and runs in the family
- is severe enough to cause distress.

The GP will organise hearing tests to confirm the diagnosis. Further investigations and treatment will depend on the results of these tests.

Hearing tests
Doctors use tuning forks to determine a patient's type and extent of deafness. They hold the fork in front of the ear and on the bone behind the ear and ask the woman at which position the sound seems louder. The fork is then put on the patient's forehead and she is asked which ear the sound is loudest in. Her answers can tell the doctor whether the hearing loss is due to a middle ear or an inner ear problem.

Audiometry, another hearing test, is available in some GPs' surgeries or can be done at a local hospital or clinic. The patient wears a pair of headphones and a series of sounds is played by a tester. The volume of the sounds is increased until the woman indicates that she has heard it. This is repeated with a different headset which rests on the bones behind the ears. Audiometry (which produces an audiogram) determines the extent of hearing loss and the range of sounds that cannot be heard.

Acoustic impedance testing is often done at the same time as audiometry. The tester puts a small probe into the ear canal. Air is pumped through the probe on to the eardrum. The ability of the eardrum to bounce sound back at different air pressure levels is tested. This shows whether the eardrum and middle ear are functioning normally.

Ringing in the ears

Ringing in the ears (tinnitus) is an awareness of noise in the ears. Normally, background noises from the environment and from one's own body are shut out by the brain. But when, for instance, one is in a soundproofed room or when one suffers from hearing loss (which tinnitus often accompanies), because other noises cannot be heard, the body's own natural noises become more intrusive. The condition can be infuriating and sometimes frightening, but it helps to know that it is not a sign of brain disease or of an imminent stroke or fit.

See a GP if tinnitus disturbs your sleep or affects your moods. Increasing background noise can distract the brain from the tinnitus. A radio can be tuned to between stations at night to produce the kind of low-grade crackle needed to do this. (During the day there is usually enough ambient noise to help.) Tinnitus maskers, which look just like hearing aids, are available commercially and sometimes on the NHS, and can help some sufferers.

Constant tinnitus can make anyone low. The more depressed one is, the harder it is to shrug off the tinnitus and focus on other, more positive, things. Treating the depression with counselling and antidepressant drugs can be helpful.

Nose

What can go wrong with the nose

Most conditions affecting the nose are short-lived and minor. One of the most common of these is a blocked nose caused by a cold, which is uncomfortable and interferes with the sense of smell. Runny noses are also annoying but short-lived, and get better without any special treatment. When pollen counts are high, hay fever could result in a blocked and/or runny nose.

Nose bleeds are also usually minor, one-off events that require no special treatment. However, occasionally they may be a sign of an underlying condition, such as high blood pressure. A severe nose bleed can be alarming and sometimes even life-threatening.

Some women are born with a nose that they feel is misshapen and mars their looks. Others develop a misshapen nose after accidents or injuries. Most women come to terms with the shape of their nose, but for those who do not or for those who have breathing problems or discomfort, cosmetic nose surgery ('rhinoplasty') is a possibility. See Chapter 15 for details.

Runny nose

A runny nose is usually caused by an infection – the most common of which is a cold – or an allergy.

Infective sinusitis Mucus accumulates during a cold, and the hairs in the nose that normally waft particles away become less efficient. If the mucus builds up and becomes infected it turns from clear and thin to thick and green. It could then spread to the sinuses, which are connected to the nasal passages, causing a condition known as sinusitis. The symptoms are a persistent fever after a recent cold, pain in the face or head that worsens on bending down or straining, and occasionally even toothache.

The condition usually gets better as the nose starts to clear itself, but some people suffer from chronic sinusitis. Signs of this are a blocked and runny nose which lingers for 3–6 weeks, a dull feeling of pressure in the face, often behind the eyes, and sometimes a sore throat and hoarseness because of the mucus which drips down the back of the throat.

Allergic rhinitis Characterised by a blocked, runny nose accompanied by itchy eyes and sneezing, this form of sinusitis usually occurs as part of hay fever. House dust mites and pets' fur are other fairly common triggers of allergic rhinitis. As a result of this condition, the lining of the nose becomes swollen and little swellings (polyps) may form. These are harmless but make breathing through the nose difficult.

Nose care

- Avoid a chapped, sore nose in cold weather or when you have a cold by rubbing Vaseline on the end of your nose, round your nostrils.
- Consider wearing a balaclava or a muffler in winter if you suffer from a bright red nose in the cold.
- Relieve a congested nose by inhaling steam. Adding inhalants does not help greatly: it is the steam that helps to unblock the nose. Be careful not to scald yourself. Taking a sauna bath is also very helpful.
- Sodium chloride nose drops available from a chemist may also help a blocked nose. Decongestant sprays and drops may give short-term relief but the problem may rebound when you stop using them.
- A constant runny nose and sneezing may be due to an allergy. Keep a record of when the symptoms are worst to try to identify the source of the allergy. For example, if the condition started when you got a new cat and clears up whenever you are away from the cat, you may have your answer.
- Seasonal nasal congestion is usually due to hay fever. Avoid being outdoors when pollen counts are high. Use oral antihistamines (e.g. Triludan, available over the counter) and/or a nasal spray (e.g. Rynacrom). The latter should be started 2–3 weeks before the hay fever season starts.
- If you have your nose pierced, follow the instruction for pierced ears.

Self-help for sinusitis

For infective sinusitis, take paracetamol or aspirin to control the fever, inhale steam to help unblock the nose and take as much rest as you can, especially in the early stages of the infection. If you have the allergic variety, try to avoid the triggers and take oral antihistamines (e.g. Triludan) to ease the symptoms.

When to see a doctor
Infective sinusitis See your GP if you have:

- a fever for longer than 48 hours
- symptoms of thick, green mucus and a blocked nose
- persistent, severe, sinusitis. He or she may refer you to a specialist, who may require some investigations to be done. Surgical treatment to drain the sinuses is sometimes needed.

Allergic rhinitis See your GP if the symptoms interfere with your daily life.

Blocked nose

In addition to sinusitis and allergic rhinitis, nasal blockage may result from a deviated nasal septum, which may be present from birth or may follow an injury to the nose. The condition is sometimes associated with a crooked appearance of the external nose, but usually the nose is straight to look at. It can be corrected by an operation.

Nasal polyps typically occur in association with allergic rhinitis. They can cause severe blockage of the nose, but they are nothing to worry about. You cannot usually see them yourself. Your doctor may give you a spray or drops for your nose. If that does not help, the polyps can be removed by an operation.

Pregnant women sometimes suffer from nasal blockage as a result of the effect of hormones on the nasal lining. This is known as 'rhinitis of pregnancy'. The problem disappears after the baby is born, and no specific treatment is necessary or recommended.

Nasal decongestant sprays and drops (e.g. Otrivine and Vicks) can be bought over the counter. These are helpful for short periods only: you should not use them for longer than one week. If you do, your nose will react to them and the nasal blockage may become much worse.

Misshapen nose

The nose could be fractured by being punched or by its owner walking into something. If that happens, the nose will be swollen for about a week, after which time it is possible to see whether it is distorted and misshapen.

It is not always necessary to have an X-ray done to check on the damage. Occasionally the nose may have a small fracture, but if there are no symptoms (such as breathing difficulties) or the nose is not misshapen, it may heal on its own.

Around one week after a fracture, the nose is reset if it is mis-shapen. It should not be left for longer than three weeks after the injury as the nasal bones become set after that time. Urgent medical attention is required if rapid swelling of the cheeks and a haemorrhage in the eye occur soon after a blow to the face. This may mean that one of the other facial bones has been fractured too.

Nose bleeds

Nose bleeds can seem alarming. The blood loss often looks greater than it is, and bleeds may happen without any warning or obvious cause. The blood vessels that tend to bleed are a group that come together on the lining of the nose, near the tip and at a spot called Little's Area. Sneezing or blowing the nose may set off a bleed in anyone. High blood pressure makes spontaneous nose bleeds more likely. Someone whose blood does not clot properly could find it hard to staunch the flow once it starts.

Self-help for nose bleeds

- Lean forwards.
- Pinch nostril between finger and thumb.
- Apply ice packs (or a pack of frozen peas from the freezer) to bridge of nose.
- Let any excess blood drip into a bowl; do not swallow the blood.
- If feeling faint at any time, lie down.

When to see a doctor

It is best to see a doctor for all but the most minor of nose bleeds. Urgent medical attention is required for elderly or debilitated women, for whom the blood loss may have drastic consequences, and for any nose bleeds which do not stop on their own within a few minutes.

Making sure that the loss of blood is not excessive is a priority for a doctor treating nose bleeds. The usual treatment consists of the nose being sprayed with chemicals to numb it, stop the flow of blood and allow a closer inspection to find the spot that is bleeding.

Blood is then sucked out of the nose. A stick coated with silver nitrate may be placed briefly on to the bleeding spot to cauterise it. If the bleeding continues, the nose is packed with a ribbon of gauze for 1–2 days to absorb the blood. A short stay in hospital is necessary in some cases. For severe bleeds, a blood transfusion may be required.

Throat

Sore throat

The majority of sore throats are the result of an infection caused by the common-cold virus. The rest are largely caused by bacterial infections. The best way to deal with a sore throat is to drink plenty of fluids and take soluble paracetamol or aspirin regularly. It also helps to take it easy, but it is not necessary to stay indoors. Vitamin supplements such as extra vitamin C may make one feel healthier but will not help the sore throat. Antibiotics work against bacteria only, not viruses, and are not advisable unless a woman has a high temperature, severe tonsillitis (inflammation of the patches of tissue at the back of the throat) and enlarged glands in the neck, so the popular belief that antibiotics help a sore throat is not always true.

Sore throats normally come and go fairly quickly. But constantly recurring sore throats are usually due to continuing irritation of the throat. Cigarette smoke, air-conditioning, spirits, shouting, singing, coughing and repeated vomiting are the usual culprits. If these irritants are avoided, the soreness could clear up without medication.

Tonsillitis is particularly common in children, but also often affects adults. If recurrent tonsillitis is causing disruption to a woman's life, an operation to remove the tonsils (tonsillectomy) is likely to help.

Occasionally when someone swallows a small bone from a fish or a chicken, the throat could receive a scratch and therefore feel sore. The bone itself usually passes straight down the throat, into the stomach and guts and out in the faeces without causing any damage. But there could be some swelling around the scratch which makes it feel as if the bone is still there. This sensation usu-

Mouth and throat care

- Avoid chapped lips in winter by using Vaseline or a moisturising lipstick. Always use a sunblocking lipscreen when skiing or sun-bathing.
- Keep some Zovirax cream handy at all times if you suffer from cold sores (herpes simplex). Start using the cream as soon as your lip starts tingling because this usually heralds the start of a new cold sore and the quicker you start using the cream the faster it will heal.
- Mouth ulcers can be relieved by dissolving a tablespoon of salt in a cup of warm water and using it as a mouthwash. Carmellose gelatin paste (Orabase, Orahesive) may help to protect the ulcers from further erosion by the digestive chemicals in saliva and to relieve the pain. Any ulcer which lasts more than three weeks requires medical attention.
- White patches in the mouth are usually caused by thrush, but require medical attention to confirm that and to exclude other conditions.
- Bad breath is often due to gum disease. Visit a dentist for a check-up and have a scale and polish by an oral hygienist.
- A sore throat, caused usually by a viral infection such as a cold, will get better on its own. Keeping the throat moist by sipping drinks or sucking boiled sweets may provide some relief. Gargling with soluble paracetamol or aspirin in water helps some people. Lozenges, throat pastilles and syrups are not particularly useful. Antibiotics are not usually necessary for sore throats but are occasionally prescribed.
- If you lose your voice, try to speak in a whisper rather than force your voice, and speak only when you have to. Anyone who has a hoarse voice for more than three weeks should see a doctor to check on whether she has any serious underlying disease.

ally gets gradually better over a day or two; if after that period it has not disappeared, it is best to seek medical help. An X-ray will show up the presence of any bone lodged in the throat; the bone can be retrieved by a specialist if necessary.

Complications that can arise from tonsillitis

Glandular fever Most sore throats get better within a week. A persistent sore throat, swollen glands and lethargy may be the result of a virus, infectious mononucleosis, which causes glandular fever. Because it is a viral infection, there is no specific treatment for the condition.

Earache During tonsillitis the middle ear may become infected and give rise to earache.

Quinsy This is an abscess that develops when pus accumulates behind the tonsil after a bout of tonsillitis. If a woman with tonsillitis finds it increasingly hard to swallow, a quinsy might be developing. In severe cases, it is impossible to swallow even saliva. Hospital admission is necessary. Antibiotics are given in the early stages, and the abscess has to be drained if it develops further. Tonsillectomy (an operation to remove the tonsils) is sometimes recommended as a quinsy can recur.

Streptococcal allergy The bacteria responsible for many sore throats are called streptococci. The body sometimes reacts against these bacteria in such a way as to cause damage to the kidneys, the heart or the nervous system. However, the widespread use of antibiotics has made such complications very rare nowadays.

Difficulty in swallowing

Probably the most common cause of difficulty in swallowing is acid refluxing up the gullet (oesophagus) from the stomach and causing heartburn (a burning sensation felt behind the breastbone, see Chapter 7). Heartburn worsens when one lies down and may cause burping or pain behind the breastbone, round to the back and up to the shoulder tips. In hiatus hernia – a condition characterised by the same symptoms – the whole stomach rolls up towards the oesophagus. The way to treat heartburn is to cut down on dietary acid (e.g. restricting the intake of spicy or acidic foods including citric fruits), avoid stooping, prop oneself up on more pillows when in bed and take medication (antacids such as Rennies) to neutralise or eliminate acid. Because acid production is increased by stress, some counselling or stress management techniques like yoga can help a great deal.

Other reasons why a person may have difficulty in swallowing include:

- tonsillitis or pharyngitis – the problem comes on suddenly and is usually accompanied by other symptoms of a cold, e.g. fever, runny nose, cough, etc.
- the presence of a foreign body in the throat, e.g. a swallowed chicken bone
- narrowing of the oesophagus – this causes progressive difficulty in swallowing and may result in weight loss and vomiting. Narrowings (strictures) may be benign, owing to acid reflux or, rarely, malignant, caused by cancer of the oesophagus
- psychological factors – some people have a sensation of something being stuck in their throat although no physical cause can be found even after detailed investigations. Psychological interventions such as psychotherapy are needed to tackle the underlying problems
- neurological conditions such as multiple sclerosis may cause progressive difficulty in swallowing owing to a lack of co-ordination of the muscles involved.

When to see a doctor
Difficulty in swallowing always requires medical attention, especially if it is progressive; there is weight loss; food regurgitates into the mouth; it is associated with anaemia (a web of tissue may develop behind the gullet and eventually develop into a cancer, in a condition most common in middle-aged women but rare over-all); or accompanied by a sharp pain on swallowing and in the ear, tenderness in the neck or fever, all of which may point to a foreign body trapped in the gullet. Investigations and treatment depend on the underlying cause. A GP will refer to the appropriate specialist any woman whose condition suggests a serious cause.

Hoarseness

Teachers, singers and harassed mothers of children with selective deafness are all prone to hoarseness. Voices, like their owners, may become strained. Hoarseness is usually a short-lived nuisance with no serious health implications. Straining the voice and viral laryngitis are the most common causes.

Causes of hoarseness

- Laryngitis – inflammation of the vocal cords, associated with smoking, voice abuse, i.e. shouting, and colds
- Non-cancerous lumps (nodules) on the vocal cords – common among singers
- Growths on the vocal cords – may be pre-cancerous or cancerous and are associated with smoking
- Paralysis of the vocal cords – may occur as a result of nerve damage caused by lung cancer (again, far more common among smokers) or other cancers of the head and neck.

Self-help for hoarseness

See a doctor if hoarseness persists longer than six weeks. Do not smoke or drink alcohol, rest your voice as much as possible and speak in a normal, but quiet voice. Taking fluids and paracetamol or soluble aspirin for the cold symptoms may help too. Homeopaths recommend phosphorus for hoarseness and herbalists recommend garlic to fight infections.

When to see a doctor

See your GP if the hoarseness:

- lasts more than six weeks
- has no obvious cause, especially if you are a smoker
- affects your livelihood
- is accompanied by fever and a severe cough – you may need antibiotics.

Seeing a specialist

A GP should refer anyone whose hoarseness persists longer than six weeks, especially if she is a smoker. This is to allow the ENT specialist to look carefully for any cancer around the vocal cords (cancer of the larynx). Cancer is very rarely a cause of hoarseness, but if it is caught early it can be treated, with excellent results (see below).

Treatment of hoarseness

Hoarseness resulting from smoking, straining the voice or a cold will get better on its own. Many women stop smoking while they are hoarse, only to resume when their voice recovers, which is unwise.

Psychological stress can make some women adopt a hoarse voice even in the absence of any physical problem. Counselling about underlying problems and speech therapy to retrain the voice are both helpful.

Singers who have harmless nodules on their vocal cords causing hoarseness can be treated by voice therapy so that they do not strain their voice. Occasionally the nodules need to be removed surgically. Cancer of the larynx is treated with laser in its early stages. Some 90 per cent of people whose cancer has been caught and treated early will be alive five years later. Ignoring persistent hoarseness delays treatment and allows the cancer to grow and spread. Treatment then has to be far more drastic and is much less successful.

Chapter 6
Skin

Skin is a wonderful material. It is waterproof, stretchy and constantly replaces itself as it wears out. It can mend itself to a remarkable degree. It comes in a range of colours and it fits all sizes. Women's skin is made of the same components as men's skin, but that is where the similarity ends. Women's skin is often affected by the hormonal ups and downs that occur in every menstrual cycle, during pregnancy and at the menopause. In addition, there are certain medical conditions that can cause rashes or skin changes, such as an under-active thyroid and a condition called lupus, that are far more common among women than men.

Both women and men can have inflamed skin as a result of acne, eczema or psoriasis. But only women find that their acne flares up before a period, or that their eczema improves while they are pregnant.

Skin complaints can be alarming, upsetting, irritating and embarrassing, but they are very rarely dangerous. Even the majority of skin cancers are treatable, although malignant melanoma can be fatal. Skin problems such as psoriasis and lichen planus may also affect your hair and nails. For example, psoriasis can cause a scaly scalp, scaly skin patches and pitted nails. Hair and nail problems may also be due to damage that we do to them: hair that falls out because of tight braiding or years of bleaching, or nails that become flaky and fragile because of repeated washing-up without rubber gloves. Hair and nail changes may also be a sign of an underlying illness or medical condition, such as an under- or over-active thyroid. Treating the condition will not only restore hair and nails to their former glory, but may also prevent further medical problems.

Knowing what causes hair, skin and nail problems, how to help yourself and when to seek professional advice may serve to reduce the anxiety they cause.

The structure of skin

Skin consists of two layers: the epidermis (on the surface) and the dermis (underneath). Skin cells are continually shed from the surface of the skin and are replaced by new skin cells that are produced at the bottom of the epidermis. The number of cells produced should be just enough to replace the cells that are being shed. But in conditions such as psoriasis, too many cells are produced and the skin becomes heaped up in plaques.

The deeper layer (the dermis) contains sweat glands that produce sweat to cool the body down by evaporation when you get hot. Hair follicles are also embedded in the dermis and play a part in temperature regulation. Sebaceous glands around the hair follicles produce waxy sebum which oozes on to the surface of the skin to keep it supple. Cysts can form in these sebaceous glands and excess sebum contributes to acne. Blood vessels in the skin open up if you are hot (making you look red), to allow you to cool down, and close up if you are cold (making you look pale), to conserve heat. If the blood vessels in the skin are damaged, blood leaks into the dermis and a bruise forms.

Changes in women's skin

A woman may find that her skin changes with every monthly cycle, during pregnancy, while taking the contraceptive pill and after the menopause.

Skin during the menstrual cycle The level of the hormone progesterone is higher in the second half of the menstrual cycle and falls again after a period. This accounts for the spottiness that some women get just before a period.

Skin during pregnancy Areas of the body that are already pigmented, such as the areola (the dark area surrounding the nipple), tend to become darker during pregnancy. The skin on the inner side of the thighs, under the eyes, in the armpits and on the genitals may all become darker too. A dark line commonly appears down your abdomen. Stretch marks often appear across the abdomen and pos-

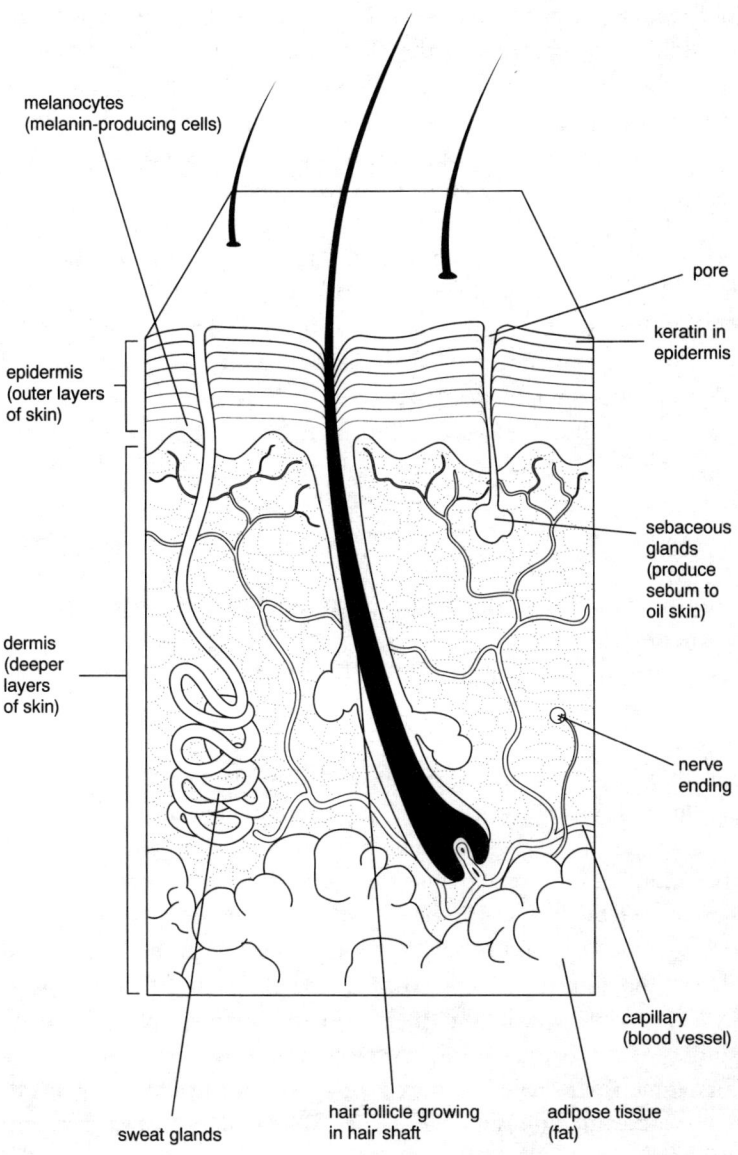

melanocytes
(melanin-producing cells)

pore

keratin in
epidermis

epidermis
(outer layers
of skin)

sebaceous
glands
(produce
sebum to
oil skin)

dermis
(deeper
layers
of skin)

nerve
ending

sweat glands

hair follicle growing
in hair shaft

adipose tissue
(fat)

capillary
(blood vessel)

Figure 5 Structure of skin

sibly the upper arms, thighs, hips and breasts. They are due to the breakdown of proteins in the skin because of the high levels of pregnancy hormones. No creams or special diets will affect these stretch marks, though they tend to fade in the year after the baby is born. Many women find that pre-existing skin conditions such as eczema and psoriasis tend to improve while they are pregnant, as the naturally occurring pregnancy hormones act as steroids to damp down inflammation. Some women are disappointed to find that instead of blooming during pregnancy they not only wilt but become spotty. This is probably because they are sensitive to the high levels of hormones needed to keep the pregnancy going.

Skin when on the contraceptive pill Many women do not notice any difference to their skin when they start the contraceptive pill. However, if acne and greasy skin develop for the first time when you start the pill, it may be because it has too much progestogen relative to its oestrogen content. Changing to a different pill with a relatively higher oestrogen content may help, or you could use a pill which is both contraceptive and helpful for acne, such as Dianette.

Skin after the menopause The fall in the hormone oestrogen that occurs after the menopause can contribute to skin becoming dry and lifeless. The natural ageing process means that skin becomes more wrinkled as time goes on, and this ageing process may be accelerated among women who have spent many years in the sun or who smoke. However, women who notice a dramatic change in their skin after the menopause may find that hormone replacement therapy (HRT) helps. Anti-ageing creams tend not to be very effective because they add moisture to the surface of the skin only for a short time, although some women find that using them helps to iron out some wrinkles as their skin regains moisture. Cosmetic surgery (see Chapter 15) to reverse the signs of ageing is available for women who feel that they cannot tolerate the ageing process. Techniques include removal of bags under the eyes, face-lifts and chin tucks.

Rashes

A rash is an eruption of spots on the skin. It is often the result of an allergy to a drug, food, cosmetics or a soap powder. If you are unwell

Skin care

- Wash face thoroughly twice a day to avoid spots and black-heads.
- Don't squeeze blackheads or spots, as they may get infected and take longer to heal.
- Seek help if you have a skin sore that has not healed within three weeks; a lump that is growing; a change in the colour or size of a mole or a new pigmented spot or patch, to ensure it is not an early skin cancer.
- Avoid prolonged exposure to bright sunshine, wear a hat and use sunblocking creams or lotions to avoid skin cancer.
- Use a moisturising cream that does not block pores (non-come-dogenic) daily if you have a tendency to dry skin. Re-apply the cream before going outdoors in windy or sunny weather. Note that some skin cleansers can dry out the skin. If your skin becomes dry after the menopause, HRT may help. Dry skin can also be a sign of an under-active thyroid (together with weight gain, fatigue and sensitivity to cold weather). Medication to restore thyroid levels to normal will help the dry skin.
- Greasy skin can be a natural tendency or it may be a sign of excessive male hormones (androgens) which can occur with polycystic ovaries (see Chapter 11). Using cleansers which dry the skin and avoiding greasy cosmetics will help. The oral contraceptive pill Dianette contains an anti-androgen and may help women with greasy skin who want to take the pill for contraception.

with a rash, it is most likely due to a viral infection. Most women have been exposed to the main viral infections that cause rashes (e.g. rubella, measles, chickenpox) in childhood, either by catching the virus, or being immunised against it. Most of the rashes caused by infection are relatively harmless unless you are pregnant, in which case you need expert medical advice about whether there is any risk to your baby. The most potentially serious infection that can cause a rash is meningitis, and if meningitis is a possibility, you need immediate medical attention. Since rashes due to infections are fairly rare among adult women, they are not covered in great detail in the text.

Most skin rashes are relatively painless, but shingles, which is the reactivation of a dormant chickenpox virus, can cause very painful blisters. The pain may persist even after the rash has cleared. Early antiviral treatment may lessen the extent and duration of the pain, so expert diagnosis and advice is important.

A skin rash may also be a pointer to an underlying condition such as lupus, which can cause inflammation of many of the body's internal organs (see Chapter 3).

Guide to diagnosing a rash

If there is a fever

Raised, itchy spots that then blister	Chickenpox
Dull red blotches; cough; sore eyes; runny nose	Measles
Pink spots; swollen glands at the back of the neck	Rubella (German measles)
Small purple spots or blotches; vomiting; headache; pain on bending head; pain in the eyes in strong light	Meningitis

If there is no fever

Ring-shaped patch (or patches) of reddened skin which is (or are) flaky, scaly and distinct from the surrounding skin	Ringworm
Itchy, red patches that merge into the surrounding skin	Eczema
Red, greasy flakes, non-itchy patches, especially around the nose, eyebrows and scalp	Seborrhoeic dermatitis
Thick, red, scaly patches usually on knees, elbows and scalp	Psoriasis
Bright red, transient, slightly raised itchy rash; occasional swelling of the face and mouth	Urticaria (hives)
Painful, blistery rash on one side of the body	Shingles

Area of itchy, slightly raised spots	Insect bites
Widespread, very itchy rash with spots between fingers and toes	Scabies
Widespread blotchy rash; use of new medication	Allergic reaction

Eczema

Eczema is itchy, dry skin. It is also known as dermatitis. Eczema starts off as red skin and small red blisters. Dryness and scaling follow. It can be caused by external irritants which are in contact with the skin, such as a new washing powder, or an allergic reaction to, say, a nickel watch strap, or it can be the result of an internal process, as in atopic eczema. The latter is a tendency which is often inherited and is the most common cause of eczema in children. Sufferers are more prone to hay fever and asthma as well.

What it looks like

Eczema often ends up as patches of red skin, tiny blisters and scratch marks because it is itchy. It is commonly found behind the knees and in elbow creases in atopic eczema, and on the face, trunk and hands in other types of eczema. If there are yellow pustules as well, it is because scratching has introduced an infection. Long-term scratching can make the skin thick, dry and scaly.

There are several different types of eczema: each with distinctive features. Coin-shaped, red, itchy patches on the legs and trunk are a type of eczema called discoid eczema. They are often mistaken for ringworm, but the difference is that they do not improve with an antifungal cream. Severe dandruff, and a red, itchy rash on the face, chest, armpits, under the breasts and in the groin are signs of seborrhoeic dermatitis. This can also cause crusting around the eyebrows and eyelashes. Dry skin with brown staining around the lower legs may be varicose eczema if there are varicose veins or a previous thrombosis. The skin is itchy and tends to become thin and prone to ulcers. Red, itchy, scaly skin on one nipple is called Paget's disease of the breast and may suggest underlying cancer. It needs urgent medical attention. Eczema on both nipples or breasts is not a sign of cancer. Itchy blisters on the palms or soles is a type of eczema called pompholyx. Red, itchy skin in areas exposed to sunlight may be due to excessive sensitivity to the sun (photodermatitis). Covering up and sunblocking cream are the answer. Cracked, painful, red hands are a common and debilitating form of contact eczema. This occurs if the hands are in contact with any substance to which they are sensitive, such as washing-up liquid.

What makes eczema worse

Heat Avoid overheating. Use layers of pure cotton next to the skin, avoid synthetics and switch off central heating in the bedroom if possible.

Allergies Eczema on the hands alone is often due to contact with substances which cause an allergic reaction in susceptible women. Rubber gloves used for washing-up are a common culprit. Using polythene gloves or wearing cotton gloves inside rubber ones can help. Washing hands after wearing gloves gets rid of the latex and minimises the risk of eczema. Latex allergy is linked to allergies caused by avocados and bananas.

Sunblock Eczema that gets worse in sunshine may be caused by an allergy to sunblocks. Fortunately, hypoallergenic sunblocking creams are available, but any new preparations should be tried out first on a small patch of skin.

Steroid creams and ointments These are often used to treat eczema, but occasionally they induce eczema themselves.

Certain emollients Women who are allergic to lanolin should avoid emollient products like E45.

Self-help for eczema

There are several things you can do to fight eczema. Preventing the skin from getting too dry is essential. The best thing is to have a bath with the addition of a bath oil such as Oilatum Plus which contains a moisturiser and an antiseptic. Use a moisturiser such as Unguentum Merck, E45 or aqueous cream at least twice a day: this is probably the most important thing you can do. A cheap alternative to the commercially available moisturisers (emollients) is to put two tablespoons of Emulsifying Ointment BP into a kitchen blender with a pint of water to make a creamy mixture that can be used in the bath. Otherwise put the emollient on to wet skin straight after a bath.

If you have eczema on your hands it is important to:

- avoid using soap
- dry your hands carefully after washing
- wear cotton gloves under rubber ones for washing-up (or plastic if you are allergic to rubber)
- wear gloves in cold weather to avoid chapping
- avoid contact with shampoo, polishes, detergents and fruit peel – especially citrus fruit
- use moisturisers recommended by your GP
- continue using moisturisers even after your skin seems to have healed, to stop the eczema coming back.

If you have varicose veins, wearing support stockings may help to prevent varicose eczema (see above). It is essential to moisturise the skin once varicose eczema does develop, and to try to protect your lower legs from knocks which might lead to ulcers.

Evening primrose oil (see Chapter 10) is of debatable value in treating or preventing eczema. It may help about one in three women by making skin less dry and itchy. It needs to be taken in adequate doses (8–12 500mg capsules a day) and for at least eight weeks before you can see whether it is going to help or not. Sunshine often helps atopic eczema, but too much exposure to either natural sunshine or sunbeds can cause premature skin ageing and increase the risk of skin cancer. Pregnancy often improves eczema because of the naturally occurring steroid hormones that circulate. The problem is that it lasts only nine months.

Complementary therapies

Chinese herbal medicines are traditionally used to treat eczema. They are made up for individual patients and vary according to their needs. But recent collaboration between dermatologists and Chinese practitioners has led to the production of a standardised preparation which you can get from reputable practitioners. Details are available from the National Eczema Society.* However, the medicines can potentially cause liver damage and it is advisable to have blood tests at intervals to check your liver.

Homeopathic remedies include graphites for weeping eczema, sulphur for itch and petroleum for chapped skin. A consultation with a homeopath to tailor treatment to your individual needs is more likely to be effective than buying the preparations at a chemist.

When to see a doctor
You need to see your GP if your eczema is:

- causing unbearable itching which is affecting your sleep
- infected (yellow pustules) or failing to heal
- probably caused by an allergy
- widespread or troublesome, and not responding to your own treatment (see above).

Treatments available from a GP
Your GP may recommend one or more of the following:

Avoidance Avoiding something that is causing eczema may be all the treatment that is needed. A GP may be able to point out likely causes of a localised patch of eczema, e.g. a nickel stud on a pair of jeans.

Moisturisers Most creams, ointments and bath oils are available over the counter, but if large quantities are needed it may be cheaper to get them on prescription. Some moisturisers contain lanolin, a derivative of sheep's wool, to which some women are allergic. Your GP can advise you about lanolin-free moisturisers.

Steroid creams and ointments Steroids suppress the inflammation and itching associated with eczema. The most effective way to use them is to apply a strong steroid (such as Betnovate or Dermovate) frequently for just a few days, then change to a milder steroid (such as Eumovate or Hydrocortisone) used less frequently. Oily ointments are best for dry skin, and creams for more inflamed skin. Combining steroids with antibiotic creams (Fucibet) is good for infected eczema. Strong steroids should never be used on the face. Long-term use of strong steroids can thin the skin, make darker skin lose colour and cause acne and small broken blood vessels on the face.

Antibiotics Eczema often gets infected because scratching introduces bacteria into the damaged skin. Yellow pustules (impetigo) or eczema that is failing to heal despite treatment are both signs of possible infection. A course of oral antibiotics is often necessary and the eczema sometimes heals rapidly after antibiotics are started.

Antihistamines Eczema cannot heal if it is being scratched incessantly. A night-time dose of an antihistamine can help to reduce the itchiness. Some antihistamines like Piriton and Phenergan also cause sleepiness, which is a useful side-effect if the itching is interfering with sleep.

Bandages Your GP can also write a prescription for zinc paste and icthammol bandages. These can be wound around your arms and legs at night. They are soothing and have the additional benefit that they prevent scratching.

Anti-fungal creams, ointments and shampoos Seborrhoeic dermatitis (see above) is caused by an excess of yeasts or high sensitivity to yeasts in the skin. Anti-yeast treatments such as ketoconazole (Nizoral) help this condition enormously.

Treatments available from a dermatologist

Dermatologists can arrange patch testing to try to identify the causes of contact eczema (see above). This involves putting a wide range of test substances on your back, leaving them in place for 48 hours and then removing them and noting any positive reactions. Another examination takes place two days later in case there have been any delayed reactions. You will then be told which specific trigger substances to avoid.

Dermatologists may also recommend you have a course of psoralens ultraviolet A (PUVA). This is a combination of sunbed treatment, which provides a safe dose of UVA rays (see *Skin cancer,* below), and a drug called psoralens, which increases the sensitivity of the skin to the UVA, thus enhancing the healing properties of the rays. PUVA produces an improvement in six out of ten women with atopic eczema. However, worries about premature ageing and skin cancer limit the use of this treatment. An alternative is the drug cyclosporin which was previously used in kidney transplant patients to prevent them rejecting the kidney. It can be used in severe atopic eczema which has not responded to more conventional treatment. The problems are that it frequently causes side-effects such as headache and nausea, occasionally leads to high blood pressure and kidney damage, interacts with many commonly used drugs, and can be used only for eight weeks at a time.

Psoriasis

Psoriasis is a condition in which the outer layer of skin cells are produced too rapidly. Skin gets heaped up into scaly, thickened patches, the scalp can become flaky, nails become pitted and a form of arthritis can make joints painful and swollen. Dennis Potter's television play *The Singing Detective* portrayed psoriasis in its severest form. His tortured hero had debilitating arthritis and extensive skin disease. But for most women with psoriasis, the condition is limited to a scaly scalp and occasional flare-ups of skin patches (plaques). As with so many long-term conditions that cannot be cured, a positive attitude and refusal to let the condition rule your life are vital.

What psoriasis looks like

Psoriasis appears as pink or red patches which are distinct from the surrounding skin. They have a scaly surface like small fish scales. Scratching the surface exposes further scaling. Patches are called plaques and may vary a great deal in size. Plaques can be round and may be mistaken for eczema, but psoriasis is more scaly and tends to be less itchy. Plaques most commonly appear on elbows, knees and scalp. The scalp becomes flaky, which can look like bad dandruff, and there is often redness at the hairline which can extend on to the forehead, nape of the neck and round the ears. Small deep pustules can appear on the soles of the feet and sometimes on the palms. Finger nails and toe nails may develop small pits and can become thickened.

What makes it worse

Most women with psoriasis find that flare-ups are triggered by specific events or when they are generally run-down. Identifying triggers helps us to understand, and even anticipate, flare-ups. Triggers include stress, certain drugs such as anti-malarials, beta blockers and lithium, and infection. Guttate psoriasis is small, round, red patches which appear all over the trunk of adolescents after a sore throat caused by streptococcal bacterial infection. The patches become scaly then the rash clears over the next few months. Psoriasis may develop later or there may never be another sign of it. Steroid tablets or creams may help psoriasis but the condition can get worse when they are stopped.

Self-help for psoriasis

Psoriasis comes and goes. It may flare up severely after a pregnancy or bereavement and then clear up completely. If stress is clearly the

---

Facts about psoriasis

- Psoriasis is most common among white-skinned people. It affects about 1–3 per cent of the total population of the UK.
- It usually starts in early adult life (commonly 15–40).
- The condition may run in the family (a child of an affected parent has a 25 per cent chance of developing psoriasis).
- It may appear in a cut or some other injury to the skin.
- Psoriasis tends to clear up in the sun, although one in ten people finds it gets worse in the sun.
- Fingers, toes or another joint may hurt, as arthritis develops in about 5 per cent of people with psoriasis.

---

major trigger for flare-ups, it makes more sense to tackle the sources of stress or find ways to counteract stress than to concentrate on the skin itself. Special anti-psoriasis diets are advertised, many making extravagant claims, but there is no evidence that diet has any impact on psoriasis. It is important to keep your skin moist, so shower quickly instead of soaking in a hot bath: repeated washing dries the skin. Hot skin also irritates and itches more. Wearing cotton clothes instead of synthetics allows air to circulate and prevents overheating. Several layers of cotton are better than one thick woolly jumper. Creams which keep your skin from getting too dry are also very useful and should be applied regularly. You can use Vaseline for very dry and cracked lips, or on the soles of your feet, commercial hand creams for your palms, and general moisturising creams such as E45 or aqueous cream all over. Usually people try a few different creams to find out which suits them best.

Complementary therapies

Several branches of complementary therapy claim to be able to help treat psoriasis. Hypnotherapists aim to induce a more relaxed state of mind which can help to prevent further flare-ups in some people, while homeopaths prescribe sulphur for dry, red, itchy patches and petroleum for cracked, rough skin. Aromatherapists recommend pure essential oils of bergamot and lavender used in the bath and as an oil or lotion, but check they are appropriate for you before trying them out. Herbalists prescribe blood-cleansing infusions such as dandelion root, red clover flowers and burdock. Among the Bach remedies are preparations such as Rescue Remedy cream for itching. Scientific trials have not yet been conducted into the effectiveness of these treatments but they are unlikely to do any harm. Chinese herbal remedies have been used to good effect with psoriasis although they are more commonly used for eczema. The Dead Sea in Israel has a well-developed tourist resort which offers treatments for psoriasis sufferers, and both the Dead Sea and the Blue Lagoon in Iceland have mineral-rich mud and salty water to bathe in. Cosmetic products derived from Dead Sea minerals are available at some chemists.

When to see a doctor
See your GP if you have:

- skin patches or a scaly scalp which worry or upset you
- disturbed sleep because of itching
- joint pains
- depression.

Treatments available from a GP
Some GPs have specialist training in dermatology, while others have an arrangement with a dermatologist to visit the surgery at regular intervals (outreach clinics). Referral to a hospital dermatologist will be necessary only if there is any doubt about the diagnosis or if the usual treatments available on prescription are not helping. A new system on trial in a few surgeries allows GPs to beam pictures of patients' skin conditions to dermatologists in hospital clinics. If you are not satisfied that your GP has sufficient skill in treating your condition, you can request referral to a specialist.

Skin psoriasis Your GP may offer you one or more of the following treatments:

- calcipotriol (Dovonex) cream/ointment – a vitamin D derivative used to treat mild to moderate psoriasis. Its use is limited to 100gm a week because it can increase blood calcium levels. One in five users finds the ointment irritates, but the cream causes fewer problems. Tacalcitol (Zorac), which is similar to Dovonex, is a new gel that needs to be applied only once a day.
- moisturisers, e.g. E45, to prevent dryness and itching

- dithranol – this is a very effective treatment but it can irritate the skin. It has to be started at very low doses which are gradually increased. Normal skin near treated areas has to be protected with Vaseline. Dithranol is usually left on for an hour. It can stain the skin and clothes
- steroid creams and ointments – these should be used only for short periods with GP or specialist advice. They help psoriasis but they become less effective after a time. They can also thin the skin and cause loss of colour in darker skins.

Scalp psoriasis Your GP may offer you one or more of the following treatments:

- calcipotriol (Dovonex) scalp lotion. It is effective and easy to use, therefore worth trying
- Psorin scalp gel (a combination of dithranol and salicylic acid) – dithranol scalp applications are fairly effective but can stain blonde hair orange and peroxided hair purple
- Polytar or T gel shampoo – these contain tar and have a distinctive smell that not everybody likes, but can be effective, especially in mild cases of psoriasis
- steroid scalp applications such as Betnovate scalp application – these relieve itch but are not much help long term in controlling scales. Doctors can direct chemists to make up a concoction containing sulphur and salicylic acid, which help scaling and inflammation; this is added to an oily base such as emulsifying ointment and can be put on the scalp twice a week, left on for at least four hours, then washed out with Polytar shampoo.

Nail psoriasis Treatment may not be wholly successful. Dovonex cream is sometimes advised.

Treatments available from a dermatologist

When psoriasis is not responding to the range of treatments described above, a GP may suggest you see a skin specialist (a dermatologist). You can have the PUVA sunbed treatment described above as an outpatient. There are several possible side-effects including skin ageing, skin cancer and cataracts on the eyes. But with proper eye protection using goggles, and with supervision of the amount of radiation, these should not be a problem.

Dermatologists can also prescribe a range of powerful drugs including the anti-cancer drug methotrexate, which stops cells dividing at an abnormal rate. This can be useful in severe psoriasis. People taking methotrexate need regular blood tests to ensure that it is not affecting the liver or the production of blood cells. The drug cyclosporin can also help in psoriasis since it stops the body reacting against its own cells. Again, blood tests are essential to ensure the kidneys are not damaged. A third drug, acitretin, is derived from vitamin A found in carrots. It is very effective but often causes cracked lips and dry itchy skin. It is so damaging to unborn babies that women taking it need to use safe contraception for two years after the treatment finishes to ensure there are no traces left in their bodies.

Acne

Although adolescence is the peak time for acne, one in 20 women in their mid-thirties has acne that is bad enough for her to seek treatment. In fact, so far as acne is concerned, doctors see more people in their late teens and early twenties than they do 14- and 15-year-olds. Acne is caused by skin that is particularly sensitive to the male hormones that circulate in both men and women after puberty. This sensitivity of the skin usually calms down a few years after puberty. Among the unlucky 5 per cent of women who carry on suffering from acne well into their thirties, about half have raised levels of the male hormone, testosterone. The other half have normal levels of testosterone but have skin that remains very sensitive to its effects.

What acne looks like

Acne is usually a combination of greasy skin, especially on the face; blackheads (comedones) on the face, back and chest; small, red, inflamed spots or pimples; infected spots or pustules which have a yellow head (the bacteria *Propionibacterium acnes* are the main culprit); cysts which are tender lumps caused by swelling of the underlying gland which produces sebum, the natural grease which oils skin; and pits in the skin caused by scarring as spots heal.

What makes it worse

The cosmetics you use, the time of the month, your job and even exercising can all make acne worse. Cosmetics which block the pores can cause blackheads and pustules, and cheap, greasy lotions and creams may be particularly bad for the skin. Expensive cosmetics are not always better, but products which are 'non-comedogenic' are marketed as being less likely to block pores and may be preferable for acne sufferers. Occupations which expose your skin to cooking oils, tars and some chemicals may also induce acne. If your acne is caused by drugs then you will notice you have spots but not blackheads – because the drugs do not block the pores. Progestogens which make up the mini pill and are part of all combined oral contraceptives can cause acne. Many women also find that their skin flares up just before a period. This is probably caused by fluid retention (due, in turn, to high levels of progesterone) which can swell ducts in the skin and block the pores. There has also been a suggestion that pre-menstrual acne is exacerbated if the diet is deficient in the essential fatty acids found in nuts, seeds and wholegrain cereals. Women who find that their acne gets worse when they start working out in the gym may be sweating more than usual, which can also block the pores.

Acne can also be part of a condition called polycystic ovaries (see Chapter 11) in which the ovaries have multiple small cysts and there is too much male hormone circulating. It is the male hormones that cause acne and excess facial hair. The oral contraceptive Dianette contains a drug that blocks the male hormone and is effective against acne of this type.

Self-help for acne

Above all else, avoid squeezing, picking or touching spots: this delays healing and can cause scarring. Obsessive cleaning of the skin can make the skin dry and more irritated. Acne is not caused by dirt, and there is no evidence that diet affects it. However, some women do find that chocolate, nuts, coffee or fizzy drinks seem to bring them out in spots. If you think that is the case with you, then it is obviously worthwhile avoiding the offending food to see if your skin improves. Non-greasy cosmetics are obviously preferable to greasy make-up.

Sunshine can make acne temporarily better, but too much exposure to ultraviolet rays can cause premature ageing and skin cancer, so it is not a good idea to use sunbeds.

Adolescent acne may clear up on its own, is not infectious and is usually much more obvious to the sufferer than to other people. Keeping the problem in perspective is essential, and reassurance may be all that a teenager needs. (Treatment is readily available for those who want it.)

If you want to try treating acne yourself you can buy benzoyl peroxide gel from chemists without a prescription. Benzoyl peroxide dries the skin and can clear acne if there are just a few spots. It is best to start with the lowest strength available (1 per cent) to avoid skin irritation. A strength of 2.5 per cent is often needed to be effective. Other acne preparations that contain salicylic acid, e.g. Acnisal (available over the counter), can also be helpful.

Complementary therapies

Herbalists recommend a home-made facial wash made by soaking a camomile tea bag in a cup of water for ten minutes. This can be dabbed on to spots with cotton wool to soothe the skin. Homeopaths recommend Kali bichromicum for long-term acne, and sulphur for infected spots.

When to see a doctor

See your GP if:

- acne starts for the first time in later adult life (say, after the age of 45)
- adolescent acne is interfering with your self-esteem
- acne fails to respond to self-help
- acne may be linked to your occupation (compensation may be available)
- you have excessive body or facial hair as well as acne – your GP will check for polycystic ovaries
- acne is uncomfortable, getting worse, causing depression or not responding to self-help measures.

Treatments available from a GP

Your GP can offer advice about preparations you can put on your skin, such as benzoyl peroxide, or prescribe a course of oral antibiotics. A larger dose is often given at first to get the acne under control, then a lower maintenance dose is continued for several weeks. Minocin MR is a once-daily antibiotic which does not need to be taken on an empty stomach, rarely causes side-effects and needs to be taken for a minimum of six months. It cannot be taken while you are pregnant or while breast-feeding. Women who are taking the contraceptive pill should continue to take it, but use additional precautions such as a condom for the first week when starting an antibiotic. This is because the gut needs to adjust to the antibiotic and may not absorb the contraceptive pill properly at first. Minocin should be stopped immediately if unexplained pain in the joints occurs for the first time, as there have been some reports of it causing arthritis in a few cases. Alternatives to Minocin are erythromycin, oxytetracycline and doxycycline.

Your GP can also prescribe topical vitamin A acid as a cream or gel, and topical antibiotics, which are lotions or creams applied directly to the skin. Topical antibiotics, e.g. Benzamycin, may be as effective as oral antibiotics with fewer side-effects. The contraceptive Dianette may be advised for women who want to take an oral contraceptive anyway and have trouble with acne.

Treatments available from a dermatologist
Only dermatologists are allowed to prescribe the most powerful treatment for acne, a drug called Isotretinoin, which is a derivative of vitamin A. It clears the severest of acne in 80 per cent of cases. But it invariably causes dry, peeling skin and cracked lips. Regular blood tests are needed to check that it is not causing liver damage or affecting the fats in the blood. Isotretinoin causes serious damage to developing fetuses, so contraception is vital while using it.

Rosacea

Rosacea is a common problem, affecting one in every 100 men and women. It tends to start between the ages of 30 and 50, and may then remain troublesome for years. It causes red, inflamed skin on the face with small broken blood vessels on the cheeks and nose; periodic hot flushes that spread over the face, making it look even redder than normal; pustules and spots on the cheeks, forehead, tip of the nose and chin; swollen, inflamed and crusty eyelids, and a red, bulbous nose.

There are several things which make rosacea worse, including alcohol, tea and coffee; hot, spicy foods; some cheeses; exposure to the sun and heat; and embarrassment. You can help yourself by identifying the things which trigger your rosacea and then avoiding them. You can also use camouflage make-up to disguise the flushing and spots. However, it is best to see a doctor to make certain of the diagnosis. An antibiotic gel such as metronidazole (Metrogel) is effective for mild to moderate rosacea, and oral antibiotics such as erythromycin or oxytetracycline are usually prescribed for more severe rosacea. A dermatologist can also prescribe the drug roaccutane which can be effective in treating severe rosacea.

Itchiness

Itchiness can ruin your sleep and disturb your concentration during the day. Certain rashes, such as eczema and lichen planus, cause itching, and skin infestations such as the scabies mite which burrows into the skin, cause intense itching which is highly distressing. On the other hand, there may be no discernible cause for the itch, in which case you will need to have blood tests to work out why it is happening.

Some causes of generalised skin itching
The following are the most common causes of generalised itching:

- iron-deficiency anaemia
- over- or under-active thyroid
- diabetes
- dry skin, especially in elderly women
- liver or kidney disease
- internal cancer, especially lymphomas.

Self-help for itching
- Treat the underlying cause, e.g. take iron tablets for iron deficiency.
- Take oral antihistamines to suppress the itch.
- Avoid alcohol, overheating, rough clothes and synthetics.
- Moisturise the skin.

Lumps and bumps on feet and hands

Most lumps and bumps that you find on your skin are harmless (see also Chapter 3). The most common small lumps that appear on the soles of the feet are verrucas, and the most common on the fingers are warts. Both are caused by a virus and will always disappear on their own eventually. They are infectious, however, so it is a good idea to use your own towel, and cover verrucas while you are showering or swimming. You can treat verrucas and warts yourself using over-the-counter preparations containing salicylic acid, glutaraldehyde or formaldehyde. Remember to protect the normal surrounding skin with Vaseline so that it does not become irritated by the treatment. Persistent warts and verrucas that are causing discomfort can be treated by a GP or dermatologist with a variety of treatments including liquid nitrogen to freeze them off.

Corns (calluses) are prominent areas on the toes which become rubbed and inflamed by contact with tight shoes. Women who have toes that stick out at an angle are more prone to corns than others. The only way to prevent corns is to be sure you do not wear shoes that squash your feet. Once corns develop, they need to be protected with raised plasters (corn plasters) available from chemists. Chiropodists (or podiatrists as they prefer to be called) can pare down the corn and may suggest treatment to correct the position of the toes.

Bunions are tender, bony lumps on the outer surface of the big toe, caused by misaligned bones in the toe. All but the widest shoes may rub against the bunion and cause painful inflammation. Wearing sufficiently wide shoes to prevent rubbing is the only way to prevent inflammation. If the bunion keeps flaring up, you may be advised to have an operation to straighten the big toe. A painful swollen big toe may also be the result of gout, which is due to a build-up of uric acid crystals in the joint. Gout is more common among men than women and is more likely to cause pain and redness at the base of the big toe than at the side where a bunion is. The difference is usually fairly obvious, but a blood test can help to determine whether a person has gout or not.

Lumps and bumps on the body

Small broken blood vessels called spider naevi are particularly common among women and can appear on the face, legs or upper chest.

The Which? Guide to Women's Health

Some women find them unsightly, and they can be treated with a small electrical current which makes them shrivel up.

Small fleshy outgrowths on the skin are often skin tags which can be tied off at their base with a piece of thick cotton, and which then fall off after a few days. Other brownish, warty-looking bumps on the skin which are very common are seborrhoeic warts. In fact they are not warts at all. They tend to crop up as you get older, and can be scraped off by your GP if they bother you.

Cysts on the scalp are usually called sebaceous cysts. They can be removed by a GP or surgeon if they catch when you comb your hair. They can grow very large but are never dangerous.

Another common sort of lump that can appear under the skin is a lipoma, or fat lump. These often occur on your arms and can be removed if you are worried about them. Again, they are totally harmless.

Any woman who becomes aware of a lump or bump on her skin wants to know if it is cancer. It is always best to err on the side of caution by consulting a GP about any suspicious or worrying skin problems, but the vast majority of lumps and bumps that crop up on the skin are harmless.

Skin cancer

Skin cancer is one of the most common cancers throughout the world. Every year more than 50 people in every 100,000 in the UK develop a skin cancer. Basal cell cancers (see below) account for more than half of these cancers; one-quarter are squamous cell cancers; and the remainder include melanomas and other rare types of the disease.

Exposure to the sun appears to be the single biggest risk factor for developing skin cancer, and short bursts of over-exposure to the sun, e.g. getting sunburnt on a foreign holiday, is more dangerous than regular, moderate exposure to the sun. People with dark skins are not usually affected by skin cancers, and the vast majority of skin cancers except melanomas occur on the head and neck, which are the parts most exposed to the sun. Fair-skinned people who live in sunny areas are most at risk. Most cases occur in people over the age of 30, and women are more susceptible to the disease than are men.

There are three main types of skin cancer: basal and squamous cell cancers and melanomas. Basal and squamous cell cancers used

170

largely to affect elderly people, although due to increasing exposure to sunburn, they are becoming more common among younger people. They are usually readily treatable with surgery and/or radiotherapy. Squamous cell cancers are more dangerous than basal cell cancers. Melanomas are less common than basal and squamous cell cancers, but they are potentially more dangerous and about half of all people who develop melanoma will die as a result. Early diagnosis and treatment can greatly reduce the death rate. Exposure to sunburn before the age of 15 can greatly increase the chance of developing melanoma in later life. Protecting children from excessive exposure to the sun is therefore vitally important.

Preventing skin cancer means avoiding excessive exposure to the sun and using effective sun-screening creams and lotions. The darker your natural skin colour, the less prone you are to skin cancer. Women with little or no colour (albino) are most at risk, and red- or blonde-haired women are at greater risk than women with dark brown hair. Black women are least at risk. Women who work outdoors, live in a sunny area or at a high altitude should take particular care.

The sun emits three main types of ultraviolet rays, divided according to their wavelength. They are UVA, UVB and UVC. UVB rays are the most damaging because they are absorbed into the skin cells and can damage the cells and predispose to cancer. UVA rays do not directly damage skin cells and are unlikely to predispose to cancer directly. However, they can cause some changes in the skin and can certainly speed up the natural ageing process. UVC rays are rapidly absorbed into the atmosphere and are unlikely to cause any damage. Modern sunbeds emit UVA – and some UVB – rays; regular use of a sunbed is likely to age your skin and may increase the risk of skin cancer.

Rodent ulcer (basal cell carcinoma)

This is the most common form of skin cancer. It is rare in people under 50 but increasingly common after that. Rodent ulcers can grow, but they never spread to other organs and never cause death. They are caused by the sun and usually crop up on the face, especially near the eyes. Initially they look like a small, raised, skin-coloured, glistening lump. Later they look like small ulcers with a rolled edge. They must be treated otherwise they gradually destroy

Tips for avoiding skin cancer

- Avoid the midday sun or the four hours during the day when the sun is hottest.
- Limit exposure to the sun, especially if you are fair-haired, fair-skinned and unused to the sun.
- Protect yourself against the sun by covering up exposed parts of the body with clothing or by using sunblocking creams and lotions of sufficient strength. Re-apply creams after swimming or as advised.

surrounding and underlying tissue. Treatment involves freezing, burning or surgically removing the lump.

Squamous cell carcinoma

These are also common cancers caused by sun damage and which do not usually spread to other organs but can cause nasty damage to surrounding skin. However, if spread does occur, it can be very damaging and difficult to treat. They usually occur on the lower lip, rims of the ears and in the mouth. They can look like a small nodule or an ulcer. They are usually cut out or treated with radiotherapy.

Malignant melanoma

Melanoma is much less common than the other two types of skin cancer but attracts more attention because it is more serious. Every ten years, the incidence of melanoma is doubling. Fair-skinned women exposed to the sun are most at risk of melanoma. Very rarely, melanoma may run in families who have numerous birthmarks. Research is continuing into the possible role of viruses in triggering melanomas.

There are seven features which may suggest that a new or existing mole is a melanoma:

- itch
- size greater than 1cm diameter
- increasing size
- irregular outline
- non-uniform colour, e.g. lighter patches in a dark mole

- inflamed
- bleeding or crusting.

Treatment involves cutting out the melanoma. No further treatment is required unless the melanoma is advanced. Younger women with early melanomas which have not invaded the skin deeply do best. Nine out of ten women whose melanoma is caught at an early stage will be alive five years later. Once the melanoma spreads to involve lymph nodes, the survival rate decreases. If it spreads to the liver or other organs, the outlook becomes very poor indeed.

Women with numerous moles can be photographed by a dermatologist annually so that any moles that are changing can be identified to pick up early melanoma. Always seek medical advice about any new moles, changes in existing moles, or any spot or sore which is present for more than three weeks.

Leg ulcers

Leg ulcers are a very common problem, especially among elderly women. They frequently occur on the lower legs, and are caused either by an injury, or by poor underlying circulation. Women with diabetes are especially prone to ulcers because their circulation tends to be poor, and diabetes delays healing. Leg ulcers may not heal easily, and they need expert medical and nursing help.

Hair

The structure of hair

Hair grows all over the body except on the palms and soles. There are two types of hair: the downy, fine hair on most of the body, and the thicker hair that grows on our scalp, eyebrows, armpits and genitals. Hair exists to help control body temperature. Hair colour and type (curly or straight) are inherited, although in an unpredictable way. The condition of hair can be affected by hormones, diet, and underlying skin and internal conditions. Hair grows in cycles of a long growing phase followed by a shorter resting phase. Because scalp hair grows rapidly (about one-third of an inch per month), it is this hair that tends to fall out after illness, certain drugs and hormone changes. Each hair on your scalp lives for about three years, then falls out.

Dandruff

Everyone gets dandruff occasionally, but severe, persistent dandruff is a major concern for the many women who suffer from it. It may not be life-threatening, but it can undermine self-confidence to an enormous degree. You can use the chart below to work out the cause of your dandruff and the steps you need to take to correct it.

Dandruff: causes and treatments

Cause	Characteristics	Treatment
Seborrhoeic dermatitis	Greasy hair and scaly scalp; red, itchy, scaly skin on face; crusts on eyebrows; patches on central chest, under arms, on breasts and in the groin	Anti-fungals, e.g. ketoconazole (Nizoral) shampoo and cream
Eczema	Diffuse, dry scaliness on scalp; temporary hair loss	Avoid any irritants. Use steroid lotions and antibiotics if the eczema is infected
Psoriasis	Discrete, scaly patches which are not usually itchy; psoriasis elsewhere on the body; temporary hair loss	Steroid lotions. Calcipotriol (Dovonex) scalp application. Tar shampoos, e.g. Polytar, once it is under control
Ringworm	Round patch of scalp scaling and hair loss	Anti-fungal drug, e.g. terbinafine (Lamisil)

Hair care

- Wash your hair only twice a week unless it tends to get particularly dirty or greasy: washing hair too frequently may wash away natural oils, leaving it dry, brittle and lifeless.
- To wash hair properly, wet hair thoroughly all over, apply a small amount of shampoo, work it gently into your scalp with your fingertips, leave for two minutes and rinse thoroughly with clean, warm water. If you are using a conditioner, make sure it is all removed when you rinse your hair. Pat your hair almost dry with a towel.
- Loosen tangles in long hair with fingers, then use a wide-toothed comb.
- Avoid hair-dryers, especially if your hair tends to be dry. Natural drying is less likely to result in damaged, brittle hair.
- Tight braiding or curlers may cause excess traction on the hair and it may start to fall out.
- Repeated bleaching, dyeing and perming may also weaken hair.
- Hair loss may be due to low iron stores or an under-active thyroid, so ask your GP for a blood test if your hair is falling out. Hair loss may also occur at about six weeks after a physical or psychological shock – including pregnancy and childbirth.

Hair loss

A normal head of hair has 100,000 hairs, which are shed at the rate of 100 hairs a day. Losing more hair than normal can be alarming, and the amount of hair in the bath or on the end of a comb can seem vast. Doctors often cannot find a reason why hair falls out, but it is worth seeing a GP who can arrange blood tests to check for iron deficiency or thyroid hormone imbalance. Severe illness, giving birth and certain drugs can make your hair fall out.

Causes of general hair loss

Cause	Characteristics	Treatment
Childbirth, severe illness, fever	Hair growth is halted because the	None. Hair usually grows back within

	body is under stress. Hair falls out two to three months later	a few months
Iron deficiency	Pregnancy, breast-feeding, heavy periods or blood loss during an operation may all cause iron deficiency. A blood test can identify the problem	Iron tablets for six weeks
Under- or over-active thyroid	Weight gain, lethargy and feeling cold (under-active); palpitations, weight loss and hot flushes (over-active)	Drugs can be used to treat both conditions
Drugs or vitamins	Excess vitamin A, the contraceptive pill and chemotherapy drugs used to treat cancer can cause hair loss	Avoid excess vitamin A. Consider taking a different contraceptive pill

Causes of patchy hair loss

Cause	Characteristics	Treatment
Alopecia areata	Small hairs are visible in a patch and look like tiny exclamation marks. There is no scaling or itching. The	Re-growth is the norm in the first attack, although it may take a few weeks. If alopecia recurs there may

	condition may run in the family	be more patches and re-growth may be slower. There is no one treatment that is effective although topical steroids may help
Traction on the hair	Hair-straightening, tight ponytails and hair rollers which pull hair too tight may make it fall out in patches	Once the traction on the hair stops, the hair usually re-grows although growth may be erratic
Male-pattern hair loss	Receding hair line and diffuse thinning. This may run in the family or it may be due to excessive male hormones (as in polycystic ovaries)	Minoxidil lotion can sometimes help re-growth but it needs to be used for life. The contraceptive pill Dianette blocks male hormones

Excess hair

There is little that can undermine a woman's self-esteem more than feeling she is growing a moustache or sprouting hairs all over her chin. Increased hair growth is more obvious if the hair is dark and the skin is relatively fair. Typically, excess hair growth (hirsutism) appears in the places where men have increased body hair, such as the chin and upper lip, chest and shoulder tips, around the nipples and in the pubic area.

Hirsutism often runs in the family, with mother, aunts and sisters having the same problem. In other cases there is a racial link – it is more common in races with dark hair and relatively fair skin – or it may be the side-effect of some medication. Excess hair that appears a few weeks after starting a new contraceptive pill may be due to progestogens. Changing to a different pill with relatively less progestogen, or to Dianette (see below), may help. Steroids taken long term for conditions such as inflammatory bowel disease, severe asthma or arthritis may also cause hirsutism. The antiepilepsy drug phenytoin is another culprit. Stopping the medication, if possible, will solve the problem.

Hirsutism is sometimes due to excess male hormones (androgens). This can be caused by cysts on the ovaries (polycystic ovaries) or, more rarely, by tumours on the ovaries or other hormone-producing glands. It needs to be investigated with blood tests and an ultrasound scan of the ovaries. Women who are overweight and whose hirsutism is related to polycystic ovaries may notice an improvement if they lose weight.

In the majority of cases, excess hair appears at puberty and tends to get worse with age, especially after the menopause. In many cases no cause is found. It often seems much worse to the woman than to anyone looking at her, but if a woman feels very self-conscious there are several options for treatment.

Electrolysis A small electrical current is passed to individual hairs. After repeated treatments, hairs may disappear altogether. This is not suitable for large numbers of hairs, and it may be uncomfortable. If you have electrolysis, check that the beautician uses new, disposable, instruments to avoid infection. Ideally, the beautician should be a member of the Institute of Electrolysis.*

Waxing Strips of hot wax are placed over the hairy area and pulled off, bringing hair with them. Waxing may irritate skin, but it gives a smooth result until hairs re-grow.

Shaving This will need to be repeated daily, and hairs grow back stubbly.

Bleaching This disguises dark hairs and is a good option for the upper lip.

Dianette An oral contraceptive pill available from your GP, Dianette contains an anti-male-hormone which can combat hirsutism. The effect lasts only while the pill is being taken, however.

When to see a doctor
See your GP if excess hair:

- is related to drugs
- appears in childhood
- starts suddenly in adult life
- is associated with periods becoming irregular or stopping altogether.

General increased hair growth (hypertrichosis)

Hypertrichosis is much less common than hirsutism. It involves hair growth which increases all over the body, rather than in the male pattern areas as in hirsutism. It happens when a woman is starved, and in the UK anorexia nervosa is the likeliest cause. Specialised medical help is needed to deal with the eating disorder (see Chapter 2).

Nails

Finger and toe nails are made of dead, hard tissue called keratin. Nails protect our sensitive fingertips and toes. Fingertips need to be sensitive to allow us to touch and feel our way. A pretty set of shiny, even, strong nails is good for self-confidence. Many women find it alarming if their nails start splitting and breaking easily. If the nails become discoloured or deeply pitted and ridged, it can be a sign of a more generalised health problem. Nails can also become discoloured or disfigured as a result of accidents, fungal infections, or contact with irritating chemicals.

Nail care

- Cut toe nails straight across – digging into the side of the nail with scissors can cause infection. If you have a troublesome piece of nail sticking into the side of your toe (an ingrowing toe nail), see a chiropodist (podiatrist) or your GP.
- Cut finger nails with nail scissors or file with an emery board. Avoid metal nail files as these can split the nails.
- Keep your hands out of water as much as possible. Wear gloves for washing-up. Dry your hands thoroughly after getting them wet, and apply moisturising hand cream if possible.
- Wear gloves when you are outdoors in the winter, and for all manual work such as gardening, to avoid chapped, rough hands.
- A coat of clear lacquer on the nails every day may help to make them less brittle.
- Acrylic nail extensions can be a good solution for women with flaky nails, but they can be expensive.

When to see a doctor

See your GP if you have:

- painful lumps under a nail
- inflammation and pus around the nail bed
- discoloration under nails which is not linked to trauma
- spoon-shaped nails
- nail changes associated with fever, lethargy or skin rashes.

Guide to nail problems

Appearance	Possible cause	Treatment
Yellow nails	Jaundice	See your GP
Discoloured and crumbly nail tip; discoloration starts at edge of nail and spreads down	Fungal infection	Anti-fungal preparation – the most effective is terbinafine tablets (Lamisil)
Discoloured and ridged base of nail with swollen surrounding skin	Infection in nail bed, caused by wet hands, damage to cuticles from picking skin, thrush or diabetes	Keep hands warm and dry. Put Canesten cream (available over the counter) around the nail bed. Antibiotic tablets will help if there is pus or painful inflammation
Flaking and fragile nail tips which split easily	Repeated wetting and drying of hands. Very common among women who work in the home	Rubber gloves for washing-up; hand creams
Longitudinal splits	Manual work, e.g. heavy gardening. Occasionally linked	Gardening gloves. See your GP if there might be a

	to psoriasis or infection of a damaged heart valve (endocarditis)	link with psoriasis or a heart problem
Thickened nails	Occasionally due to psoriasis. Thickened toe nails are usually due to ill-fitting shoes	Shoes that fit
Separation of nail from nail bed	Trauma to fingers; psoriasis; fungal infections	None; new nail will grow normally
Rough nails that feel like sandpaper	Associated with lichen planus, psoriasis and patchy hair loss	See your GP for appropriate treatment
Horizontal ridges and grooves that appear at the same time on all your nails	Severe illness a few weeks before the grooves appear. Ridges may also be due to picking the skin around the cuticle	None
Spoon-shaped nails which curve in (concave)	Anaemia due to iron deficiency	See your GP for a blood test; take iron tablets
Dark region under the nail	Trauma to the nail e.g. if it was hit with a hammer. Rarely it could be skin cancer (melanoma)	See your GP if there has been no trauma to the nail or if the dark area is growing
Brown nails	Nail varnish left on too long. Could also be a side-effect of the drug chlorpromazine	Removal nail varnish each night

Skin around the nail on the big toe is red and painful	Ingrowing toe nail due to tight shoes or because nails have been cut incorrectly	Cut nail clean across and keep the area clean and dry. See your GP or chiropodist, as you may require antibiotics and a small operation to remove part of the nail

Chapter 7

Digestive system

The digestive system is one long tube which stretches from the mouth to the anus (back passage). Its role is to break down the food we eat into carbohydrates, fats, proteins, vitamins and minerals which are then absorbed into the bloodstream and carried to the parts of the body that need them, or stored for later use. Many things can go wrong with the digestive system – some minor and some potentially very serious. This chapter covers the common problems of vomiting, diarrhoea, constipation and bleeding from the back passage, and explains the common causes, possibilities for self-help, and when to seek medical advice.

Abdominal pains may, however, be caused by other organs which lie in the abdomen. This chapter explains the common causes of pains in different parts of the abdomen, as the site and type of pain provide vital clues about the likely cause. Possibilities for self-help and advice about when to seek medical advice are also included.

How the digestive system works

The first part of the digestive system is the mouth. Enzymes (chemicals) in saliva start to break down carbohydrates such as pasta and bread. The tongue mixes food with the saliva and then pushes it to the back of the throat, down the oesophagus (gullet) and into the stomach. Mouth ulcers, which are common, are painful because the enzymes irritate the sore area.

Food is churned in the stomach and mixed with more enzymes and acid which break down most food into a semi-liquid mush. If excess acid washes back up the oesophagus it causes heartburn or pain just below the breastbone. Inflammation of the stomach

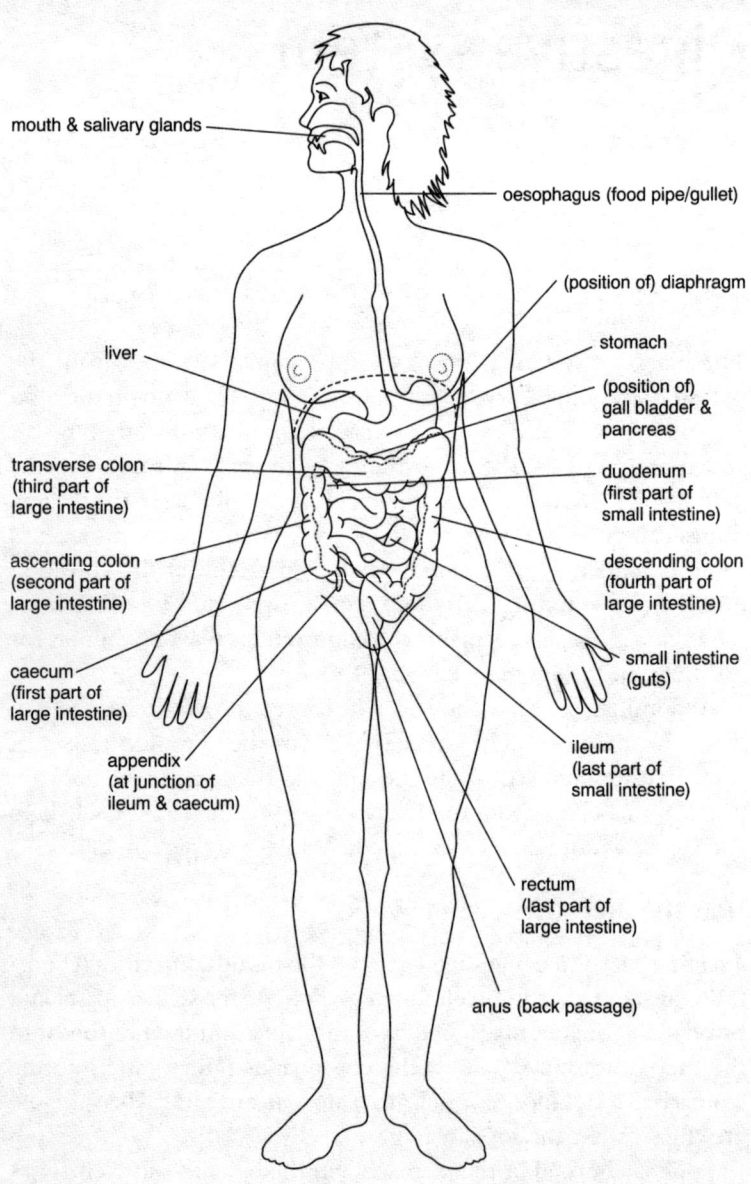

mouth & salivary glands

oesophagus (food pipe/gullet)

(position of) diaphragm

liver

stomach

(position of) gall bladder & pancreas

transverse colon (third part of large intestine)

duodenum (first part of small intestine)

ascending colon (second part of large intestine)

descending colon (fourth part of large intestine)

caecum (first part of large intestine)

small intestine (guts)

appendix (at junction of ileum & caecum)

ileum (last part of small intestine)

rectum (last part of large intestine)

anus (back passage)

Figure 6 The digestive system

because of a virus, food poisoning, excess alcohol or an allergy to a food can cause abdominal cramps and vomiting.

Semi-digested food leaves the stomach and is propelled through the small intestine and then the large intestine by waves of muscle contraction called peristalsis. Poorly co-ordinated peristalsis can result in bloating, abdominal pains and alternating constipation and diarrhoea, which are common in irritable bowel syndrome.

Soon after leaving the stomach, the semi-digested food is mixed with more enzymes and digestive chemicals which are produced in the pancreas and liver. Many foods are broken down into glucose and this is processed by insulin, produced in the pancreas. An inability to produce enough insulin is known as diabetes; this results in high levels of glucose in the blood, which is unhealthy for many parts of the body. The liver produces bile, which is a mixture of chemicals which break down fats. It also helps to break down many drugs, can store excess sugar and fats until they are needed, and to break down old blood cells when they are no longer needed. Inflammation of the liver (hepatitis) can result from viruses, drugs or alcohol and can cause loss of appetite, nausea and a yellow skin colour (jaundice) due to pigments in the bile. The gall bladder acts as a reservoir, storing concentrated bile for when it is needed after a heavy, fatty meal. The concentrated bile in the gall bladder can produce stones which may cause severe abdominal pain and nausea.

By the time food has reached the end of the small intestine, it has been broken down into small units which are absorbed from the gut into the bloodstream and other channels (lymphatics) so that they can be used to produce energy for all parts of the body. Inflammation of the small intestine in conditions like Crohn's disease and ulcerative colitis can cause abdominal pains, weight loss and dietary deficiencies because foods are not fully digested and absorbed.

The semi-solid waste that is left after the useful products have been extracted from food by digestion passes from the small intestine into the large intestine. Water is reabsorbed from liquid foods in the large intestine and the semi-solid waste moves on to the last part of the large intestine – the rectum – until it is ready to be passed out of the anus (back passage) as a bowel movement. Inflammation of the large intestine in conditions like diverticulitis, in which small pouches in the wall of the large intestine become inflamed, can cause abdominal pains and either constipation or diarrhoea.

Organs in the abdomen that are not related to digestion

Abdominal pains are often, but not always, due to a digestive problem. There are times when other abdominal organs unrelated to digestion are the root of the problem. These 'other organs' include kidneys, bladder, ovaries and the uterus.

The kidneys' role is to filter fluids, extract useful salts, minerals and water which are needed by the body, and produce urine from waste products. The urine flows out of each kidney, down a tube into the bladder (ureter) and is stored in the bladder until it is passed as urine. From the bladder, urine leaves the body down a tube called the urethra which opens into the vagina. Kidney stones and urine infections which have spread up to the kidneys from the bladder are the most common causes of kidney pain, which is felt on either side of the waist at the front or the back. An inflamed bladder (cystitis, see below) can be due to infections, friction during intercourse or bladder stones. The pain is felt just above the pubic area. An inflamed bladder causes painful and frequent urination.

The ovaries produce female sex hormones (oestrogen and progesterone) which regulate the menstrual cycle and fertility and are responsible for breast development. The ovaries contain around 400,000 eggs from the day a girl is born, and one is released every month from puberty to the menopause. Abdominal pain may be felt on either side of the belly button during release of the egg (ovulation) or during periods if a woman has endometriosis (see Chapter 11); otherwise the cause may be an ovarian cyst.

The uterus (womb) can cause abdominal pains when its muscles contract during periods (period pains) and during childbirth (labour pains).

The abdominal wall is made up of strong muscles which hold the internal organs in place. Abdominal muscles can be strained during exercise and this can also cause abdominal pains.

Common digestive problems

Vomiting

Vomiting occurs when the contents of the stomach are forced back up into the mouth as a result of the stomach muscles contracting. It is often preceded by feeling sick (nausea) and most people feel bet-

Care of the digestive system

- Stop smoking – smoking increases acid which causes indigestion; it may also delay the healing of ulcers.
- Do not drink alcohol on an empty stomach – it leads to rapid absorption.
- Keep alcohol intake moderate and avoid binge-drinking – it damages your liver, pancreas and many other organs.
- Eat a low-fat, high-carbohydrate diet, avoiding excess sugar and eating plenty of fruit and vegetables.
- Always wash hands thoroughly (with soap) after opening your bowels or having any contact with a toilet. Wash your hands again before starting to prepare food, and make sure that children do the same. Keep work surfaces and utensils clean.
- Follow manufacturers' recommendations about food storage; never use food that has passed its 'sell by' date; and keep all unused perishable food covered and refrigerated if possible.
- Follow instructions carefully when defrosting frozen foods and preparing cook-chill foods – to avoid infections such as listeria.
- Avoid raw or partly cooked eggs to avoid infection with salmonella, especially if you are elderly, pregnant or otherwise vulnerable.
- Keep pets away from areas where food is stored and prepared, and do not let cats jump on to tables or work surfaces.
- Eat small, regular meals to avoid bloating and abdominal pains.
- When you are abroad, drink reliably bottled mineral water unless you are certain that tap water is safe to drink.
- While you are visiting developing or tropical countries, avoid washed salads and fruits which cannot be peeled, as well as ice cream and ice in drinks.

For special dietary advice for pregnant women, see Chapter 13.

ter after they have vomited. The most common reason for vomiting is irritation of the stomach lining. This can be caused by excess spicy, fatty food; alcohol; or contamination of food (food poisoning) by bacteria or viruses.

There is also a vomiting centre in the brain which can cause vomiting if it is disturbed. Alcohol can affect this centre, which is why some people vomit when drunk. Some medications cause vomiting because they affect the vomiting centre or irritate the stomach. The female hormones which maintain pregnancy (HCG, progesterone and oestrogen) can affect the vomiting centre, causing nausea and vomiting, as can the contraceptive pill and hormone replacement therapy. The vomiting centre is linked to the inner ear so that vomiting is a common part of inner-ear disturbances that also cause dizziness and loss of balance. The vomiting centre in the brain can also be disturbed by a high temperature, and some women vomit readily if they have a fever, regardless of the cause. Pressure on the vomiting centre can also occur if there is swelling of the brain after a head injury or, rarely, as a result of a brain tumour.

Vomiting is usually harmless, although unpleasant. It stops on its own once the underlying problem is resolved.

Causes of vomiting

The most common causes of vomiting are food poisoning, stomach bugs (gastroenteritis), gall stones, urinary tract infections, dizziness or travel sickness, pregnancy, alcohol intoxication, drugs, migraine, appendicitis and bowel obstruction.

Self-help for vomiting

- Avoid solid food until nausea and vomiting pass.
- Drink clear fluids (e.g. water), taking small sips. Avoid milk, which may make you feel more sick.
- Avoid cigarettes, alcohol and drugs that can irritate the stomach, such as aspirin.
- Take paracetamol if you have a high temperature.
- Do a pregnancy test if you have missed a period.

Remember, vomiting makes the contraceptive pill less reliable. Continue to take it as normal, but use additional precautions for a week after vomiting stops.

When to see a doctor

It is important to see a doctor if the vomiting persists for more than 48 hours and is associated with high fever, headache and constant or worsening abdominal pains.

Diarrhoea

Doctors define diarrhoea as the passage of more than 300ml (about half a pint) of liquid stool in 24 hours. But, really, diarrhoea means having more frequent and runnier stools than normal. Some women open their bowels three times a day, others only once every three days, and most women range somewhere between these two extremes. Most attacks of diarrhoea in the UK are a result of a viral infection which is transmitted from person to person in the air or by close contact. The infection may cause some nausea and vomiting at first, then diarrhoea as the virus travels down the gut. Abdominal cramps are common, and are often relieved by a bout of diarrhoea. The diarrhoea usually clears up within 48 hours and, apart from leaving you feeling washed out, rarely has any lasting ill effects.

Causes of diarrhoea
The most common causes of diarrhoea are stomach bugs, food poisoning, irritable bowel syndrome, anxiety, drugs, bowel inflammation (Crohn's disease and ulcerative colitis), over-active thyroid, underlying constipation, gluten allergy (Coeliac disease) and other food allergies, and bowel cancer.

Self-help for diarrhoea
- Drink plenty of water to replace the fluids being lost.
- Avoid anti-diarrhoea drugs if possible as they can cause stomach cramps, and may confuse the diagnosis.
- Sachets such as Dioralyte, which replace salt and glucose, are not usually necessary for fit adults who have short-term diarrhoea and/or vomiting.
- Avoid milk products since they may exacerbate diarrhoea. Eat small amounts of bland and easily digestible foods: starving does not speed up recovery.
- If you are breast-feeding and you have diarrhoea, drink more water, but continue breast-feeding if possible as this is the best protection for your baby against stomach bugs.
- The oral contraceptive pill is less reliable if you have diarrhoea for more than 24 hours. Continue taking the pill as usual, but use additional precautions, e.g. condoms, for seven days after the diarrhoea stops.

When to see a doctor
It is important to see your GP if the diarrhoea does not settle within four days, if it contains blood, or if it is causing you a lot of pain. You should also see your GP if you are very frail and elderly.

Diarrhoea: symptoms, causes and treatment

Symptoms	Cause	Treatment
Diarrhoea, stomach cramps, fever	Gastroenteritis from a bug (virus, travel or food poisoning)	Drink clear fluids. Eat if you want to. Codein phosphate will stop the diarrhoea
Diarrhoea comes and goes; alternates with constipation; bloating	Irritable bowel syndrome	Take care with your diet. Drugs, e.g. Colofac, can be used to help with spasms
Diarrhoea which started after you took some new medication	Drugs, such as antacids, cimetidine, digoxin, antibiotics, bendrofluazide, and alcohol could all cause diarrhoea	Cut out alcohol. See your GP about medication
Diarrhoea is intermittent and contains mucus (slime) and blood. You feel feverish and unwell. There is abdominal pain and weight loss	Chronic inflammation of the bowel – ulcerative colitis or Crohn's disease	Drugs and suppositories will control symptoms. Artificial feeding and surgery are sometimes necessary
Tendency to severe constipation. Diarrhoea is hard to control. Abdomen feels hard and bloated	Overflow diarrhoea due to constipation. Stool leaks around the hard faeces that won't pass	Treat constipation with laxatives, suppositories or enemas

Diarrhoea comes on only before a performance or event	Anxiety	Relaxation techniques. Anti-diarrhoea drugs could be used if necessary
Diarrhoea with weight loss, tremor and hot flushes	Over-active thyroid	Radioactive iodine, drugs or surgery
Diarrhoea is intermittent. Stools are pale, bulky, smelly and float so they will not flush away easily. Weight loss and weakness	Malabsorption – you are unable to absorb a normal part of the diet. The most common cause is Coeliac disease – an inability to absorb fats, minerals and vitamins because of an allergy to gluten in wheat, barley and rye	Gluten-free diet
Diarrhoea with blood; weight loss and anaemia; change in bowel habit over a few months	Bowel cancer	Surgery; chemotherapy or radiotherapy, depending on the type of cancer

Constipation

Constipation is another term, like diarrhoea, which means different things to different people. Most women use the word to mean that they are opening their bowels less frequently than usual, that the stool is hard or like small pellets, and that opening the bowels causes discomfort and excessive straining. The most common cause by far is lack of fibre in the diet. Lack of exercise and inadequate fluid intake are the other common contributing factors. Pregnancy may also make you constipated because of the pregnancy hormones and the pressure of the developing baby on the intestines. Or it may be caused by something like piles or a crack in the anus from previous straining. Very rarely constipation can be the sign of an underactive thyroid which slows down the gut, or of bowel cancer.

Self-help for constipation

- Eat fresh fruit (unpeeled): at least three pieces a day.
- Cook vegetables for as little time as possible.
- Eat wholemeal bread, pasta and rice.
- Eat wholemeal oats or a higher-fibre breakfast cereal.
- Try dried fruits, e.g. dried apricots, as a snack.
- Drink extra fluid – aim for eight cups a day (about three pints).
- Exercise every day – a brisk 20-minute walk is fine.
- Avoid codeine products which may cause constipation.
- Ask your GP if any prescribed drugs may be constipating.
- Increase fibre artificially with laxatives that bulk up the stool, e.g. methylcellulose or ispaghula granules available over the counter.

When to see a doctor

It is important to see your GP if your constipation is causing you pain, or if it is not getting better even though you have been following the guidelines above. You should also get help if you are losing weight, you feel unwell, there is blood in your stool or if constipation is alternating with diarrhoea. If you are at all worried about cancer then go to your GP for reassurance.

Treatments for constipation

When constipation is due to inadequate fibre in the diet you can take laxatives which increase the bulk of the stool (e.g. methylcellulose), stimulate the gut (e.g. senna) or draw water into the gut and make the stool easier to pass (e.g. lactulose). Senna and other stimulants can make the bowel 'lazy' after years of use so that it becomes almost impossible to open the bowels without increasingly large doses. For this reason, doctors usually try not to prescribe senna and other similar laxatives except for short-term use.

If you are constipated because you are pregnant, the constipation usually gets better once the baby is born. Meanwhile, it is safe to take lactulose, but not senna and the other strong laxatives as they may start the uterus contracting.

For irritable bowel syndrome, taking anti-spasmodics and eating regularly help the symptoms, whereas if you make dramatic increases in the amount of fibre you eat you may make matters worse.

If you are constipated after giving birth you may find glycerine suppositories make it easier to open the bowels and pass a soft stool which does not cause pain. The easiest way to insert the small, bullet-shaped suppository is to moisten the end of it and put it in the back passage just after a warm bath, when the anus is relaxed.

If you are diagnosed as having an under-active thyroid, the treatment is simple: you take a tablet every day to replace the thyroid hormone. The constipation tends to improve quickly, and women usually feel much more energetic once their thyroid levels are restored to normal.

Wind and bloating

Many women have a time when they feel bloated and find they cannot do up waistbands of fitted trousers or skirts. In some cases, this is because of slow but steady weight gain which has resulted in your waist getting thicker. Women who live in lycra leggings and skirts may not notice that they are gaining weight until they try on a more fitted piece of clothing. But for other women, the tight waistbands are due to a temporary bloating caused by excess wind (gases) in the intestines. Wind does not weigh anything, so standing on the scales should enable you to tell whether you are bloated, or have put on weight. Excess wind is normally obvious because it causes gurgling noises in the abdomen, and an urge to pass wind by burping, or from the back passage. It is usually due to a change in diet, and women who switch from a low-fibre diet to a high-fibre one usually suffer from wind for a few weeks until their digestive systems adapt. Some foods, such as cabbage and pulses, produce a lot of gas as they are digested. Women who eat very fast, or bolt their food while standing up, are also more likely to swallow excess air while eating, which may cause wind. Women who do not manage to do any exercise are also more prone to wind as the food stays in the digestive system for longer and has more time to ferment and give off gases.

Excess wind is uncomfortable, embarrassing and worrying. But it is never serious unless it is accompanied by other symptoms which may suggest an underlying digestive problem, such as abdominal pains, weight loss or pale, abnormal-looking stools. Diarrhoea, hiatus hernia and irritable bowel syndrome can all cause wind.

Self-help for wind
Most self-help measures for wind and bloating are related to the food you eat and the way you eat it. Start by avoiding gas-forming foods and, if you are introducing a higher-fibre diet, do so gradually and drink plenty of non-fizzy fluids with your food. Eat your meals sitting down and in an unhurried way. Eat little and often.

When to see a doctor
It is important to see your GP if you have any of the following symptoms at the same time as wind:

- constipation which is not improving with increased fibre
- diarrhoea
- abdominal pains
- weight loss
- pale stools
- blood in the stool.

Diabetes

Diabetes is also known as diabetes mellitus or 'sugar diabetes'. It is due to a failure of the pancreas to produce sufficient insulin, the hormone responsible for breaking down carbohydrates (sugars and starches) into glucose, a simple sugar. Insulin also allows glucose to be absorbed by the bloodstream from the intestines, so the sugar can be used by muscles and tissues for energy or is stored in the liver until it is needed. Without insulin, glucose cannot be absorbed into the liver, muscles or tissues, and so remains in the bloodstream. High glucose levels in the blood can be damaging to the blood vessels and to various organs such as the heart, kidneys and eyes. Some of the excess glucose is passed in the urine and can be detected by a simple test which involves dipping a stick into the urine. This is done at health checks and antenatal check-ups to screen women for diabetes. Blood tests which check blood glucose levels are a more accurate way of detecting diabetes than are urine tests. If there is still any doubt about whether someone has diabetes, she will be given an oral dose of glucose and her blood will be tested periodically to check whether the blood glucose levels rise above normal. This is called a glucose tolerance test.

Some women do not know that they have diabetes until it is detected during a routine check-up. Others may find that they are unusually thirsty or need to urinate a great deal: this occurs because the high blood glucose levels in the urine draw out more water and produce more urine than usual. It is common to feel tired and lethargic with untreated diabetes, but tiredness is a very common problem, due more to stress than to an underlying condition such as diabetes. Rarer symptoms of diabetes are blurring of the vision, recurrent infections, e.g. boils, because diabetes lowers your immunity, and weight loss, especially among younger women.

Treatment of diabetes

Mild diabetes (i.e. where the body still produces insulin, although not enough) can be controlled by a low-sugar diet. Sugar-free jams and biscuits are available in most supermarkets, and the sufferer will have to get used to forgoing sugary products and replacing them with low-fat, high-fibre foods such as pasta and bread.

Those whose diabetes cannot be controlled by a low-sugar diet alone need other forms of treatment. Drugs to stimulate the pancreas to produce more insulin include chloropropamide (Diabinese), glibenclamide (Daonil) and gliclazide (Diamicron). They are usually taken as a single dose with breakfast. Another commonly used drug, Metformin, works in a different way, decreasing the amount of glucose that is produced in the body, and may be given in addition to one of the other drugs. Guar gum can also lower blood sugar, but tends to cause bloating and wind and is therefore not commonly prescribed.

About 25 per cent of all diabetics in the UK require regular doses of insulin; because it becomes inactivated if swallowed, insulin needs to be injected under the skin using a syringe and needle or newer devices that look like pens.

Risk factors for diabetes

Diabetes is on the increase in the UK and affects 1–2 per cent of the population. Diabetes among young people is relatively uncommon but tends to be more serious and often means that insulin injections are necessary. Most women who develop diabetes do so in middle age or later. It is more common among women who are very over-weight and among Asian and Afro-Caribbean women. There may be a family tendency to diabetes although it is not inherited in a pre-dictable way. Diabetes may be triggered by medication such as steroids, which are given for a variety of inflammatory conditions including rheumatoid arthritis, asthma and some skin conditions. The best way of preventing diabetes is to avoid obesity and to eat a diet which is low in sugar.

Diabetes and pregnancy

Women who are diabetic need advice about which contraception to use if they want to avoid pregnancy. The oral contraceptive pill is not recommended because of an increased risk of blood clots among diabetic women. The progestogen-only pill can be taken safely and the diaphragm (cap) or condoms are ideal. The coil is not recommended as diabetic women are at increased risk of infections, which can cause fertility problems with a coil if a sexually transmit-ted infection develops. Diabetic women should be able to have rel-atively trouble-free pregnancies but need specialist advice before conceiving, to minimise risks. Women who are taking oral tablets to control diabetes will need to switch to insulin while pregnant as the oral treatment may be harmful to the baby.

Women who develop diabetes for the first time while pregnant (gestational diabetes) often find that they recover after the baby is born, although they are likely to have the same problem in subsequent pregnancies. This is because pregnancy affects insulin production and requirements. There is no increased risk of abnor-malities among babies born to women who develop pregnancy-related diabetes, but they are more likely to be large, which can make delivery difficult. Controlling the diabetes during pregnancy with a strict sugar-free diet, and insulin if necessary, can minimise the dangers to mother and baby.

Jaundice

Jaundice is a yellow colouring of the skin and whites of the eyes. It is caused by a build-up of bile products in the bloodstream, which follows inflammation of the liver – where bile is made – due to a viral infection (viral hepatitis), liver damage caused by excess alcohol or (prescription or illegal) drugs, or gall stones. Jaundice is often accompanied by itching because the excess bile products in the bloodstream cause it. Jaundice may occur during pregnancy, or while you are on the contraceptive pill. It is always important to seek medical advice if you think you might be jaundiced. A blood test will confirm the presence of jaundice and help to find the cause. Other investigations may be necessary too. Very rarely, jaundice is the result of liver damage (cirrhosis) or pancreatic cancer.

Treatment for jaundice

Treatment for this condition depends on the underlying problem. Alcohol should be avoided if there is any disturbance of liver function, which will show up in a blood test. Most cases of viral hepatitis are due to a virus called hepatitis A, which you can contract when you eat food (such as some shellfish) that is contaminated by faeces. Viral hepatitis is usually a fairly mild illness which passes within six weeks.

Hepatitis B and hepatitis C are caused by viruses transmitted through blood, semen or saliva. These two forms of hepatitis may be caught through sharing contaminated needles during drug abuse, having transfusions of infected blood, having unprotected sexual intercourse with an infected person or being bitten by someone who has the infection. Further viruses that can cause hepatitis (D, E, etc.) are being discovered, but they are still relatively rare.

Vaccination against hepatitis A is available for travellers to parts of the world where food hygiene may be poor, and against hepatitis B for health workers and others who may be at risk. There is no specific treatment for any form of hepatitis, but research into antiviral drugs, e.g. interferon, is continuing.

Bleeding from the back passage

Finding bright red blood on the toilet paper when wiping your back passage after a bowel movement is extremely common and rarely serious. The cause is almost always piles (haemorrhoids), which affect around 40 per cent of the adult population in the UK. Piles are engorged veins in the back passage (anus) which may bleed, itch or hurt. They may slip out of the back passage and appear as a lump, but are usually readily pushed back in with a finger. Finding blood mixed in with the stool is less common and is usually due to bleeding higher up the digestive system. The underlying cause is usually readily treatable, such as an ulcer or irritation of the lining of the stomach or small intestine. Although bleeding from the back passage is more often than not due to piles, which can often be left untreated, it is always best to seek medical advice to be certain that there is no other underlying problem that may require treatment.

Dark blood mixed in the stool

Your stools may look black if you are taking iron tablets, stout or beetroot – in which case there is unlikely to be a problem, although it is best to take a sample of the stools to your GP, who can test it for the presence of blood – or if there is bleeding in the digestive tract. Black, tarry stools may contain blood which has become mixed in with the stool high up in the intestine. This is known as 'melaena' and warrants immediate medical attention. The first priority in hospital is to rest the digestive tract by taking no food or drink. A drip into a vein supplies all necessary fluids. Further treatment will depend on the nature of the problem. There are several possible reasons for melaena including peptic ulcers; inflammation of the stomach lining caused by alcohol, anti-inflammatory drugs such as ibuprofen, steroids and blood-thinning drugs (anticoagulants); and tears in the oesophagus caused by repeated vomiting. This may be a problem for women with bulimia. Melaena can also be caused by swallowing blood in a nose bleed, or by varicose veins in the gut as a result of cirrhosis of the liver, although this is much more common in men than women. Very rarely, blood vessel disorders or cancer are to blame. The main symptoms of cancer of the oesophagus or stomach are difficulty in swallowing, vomiting and weight loss.

Red blood in the stool

When there is bright red blood mixed in with the stool, it suggests bleeding from lower down in the digestive tract. Piles are the most common cause and are totally harmless. But see your GP if the bleeding occurs on more than a couple of occasions, to ensure that there is no serious problem. Other possible causes of bright red blood in the stool include diverticulitis, straining, ulcerative colitis, Crohn's disease and bowel cancer.

Bleeding from the back passage: symptoms, causes and treatment

Symptoms	Cause	Treatment
Bright red blood coats the stool and drips into the toilet pan or stains the toilet paper. Itching. May be a slimy discharge from the anus	Piles (haemorrhoids) – areas in the lining of the rectum which have a very rich blood supply. The blood vessels can become very engorged. They may stay in place, or slip out of the anus. Constipation is the main cause of piles. Pregnancy makes them worse	High-fibre diet. Xyloproct suppositories. Surgical options include injections, tying them with rubber bands or freezing
Sudden painless rectal bleeding. Colicky, left-sided abdominal pain which improves after you open your bowels. Nausea and flatulence. Fever and increased abdominal tenderness during flare-ups	Diverticulitis – little outpouchings in the gut wall. Most appear in the last part of the colon so symptoms occur on the left-hand side of the abdomen. The problems occur when debris stuck in the pouches gets inflamed. One in three adults in the	High-fibre diet, anti-spasm drugs, e.g. mebeverine, and antibiotics. Hospital admission may be needed during severe flare-ups or rectal bleeding

West has
diverticula by the
age of 60

Bright red bleeding, especially after you open your bowels. Pain on opening bowels	Trauma or tears of the anal canal. These can occur during childbirth, when you strain hard during constipation, as part of Crohn's disease, or as a result or anal intercourse	Glycerine suppositories and laxatives will soften the stool. Keep the anus clean. Lignocaine gel will relieve the pain
Blood and mucus (slime) in the stool which may be solid or like diarrhoea. Fever, mouth ulcers, abdominal pain, weight loss, constipation, inflamed joints and eyes	Ulcerative colitis – recurrent bouts of inflammation in the large bowel. In the West, this is the most common cause of bloody diarrhoea lasting more than a week. The cause is unknown	Treatment depends on the severity of the symptoms. Steroid foams and anti-inflammatory suppositories. Newer tablets called 5ASA drugs are often given. Drugs to suppress the immune system, e.g. azathioprine, may be needed for severe cases. Surgery can cure the condition
Rectal bleeding, fever, diarrhoea, abdominal pains and weight loss. Skin tags and abscesses around the anus	Crohn's disease – long-term inflammation which can affect any part of the gut. The cause is unknown. It is possible that the	Elemental diet in which just a few basic foods are allowed. Other foods are reintroduced to the diet one at a time. Not favoured by all

	gut over-reacts to triggers which may include exposure to measles	specialists, but can work wonders. Drug treatment is similar to that for ulcerative colitis (see above), but tends to work less well. Surgery can help but does not cure
Rectal bleeding, constipation and/or diarrhoea. Spasms in the rectum, or weight loss, pain and anaemia	Colorectal (bowel) cancer – small growths (polyps) in the bowel can become cancerous over the years	Surgery, chemotherapy and/or radiotherapy. Success depends on early diagnosis, but the outlook can be very good

Colorectal (bowel) cancer

Colorectal or bowel cancer is the second most common cause of cancer deaths in the UK. Most cases of rectal bleeding are not due to cancer, however. A family history of bowel cancer, long-standing ulcerative colitis and, to a lesser extent, Crohn's disease can all increase the risk of cancer, as can low-fibre diets.

Bowel cancer needs to be identified at an early stage to ensure that effective treatment can be given. The earliest stages of colorectal cancer can be cured by a relatively simple operation to remove the affected part of the bowel. Five years later, over 90 per cent of those treated will still be alive. But once the cancer has spread to the lymph nodes around the bowel, the percentage of people who will be alive five years later falls to 30. This is the rationale for screening – to pick up the cancer while it is still in its early, and eminently treatable, phase, or preferably at an even earlier, pre-cancerous, stage.

Who should be screened

Women who fall into either of these categories should be screened:

- members of families who inherit a tendency to bowel polyps (familial adenomatous polyposis)
- people with long-standing ulcerative colitis or Crohn's disease.

Screening should be considered for anyone with a first-degree relative who has or had bowel cancer, or members of families in which bowel, uterine and ovarian cancers are common.

What screening involves

There are several different approaches to bowel cancer screening. In the USA, for example, doctors recommend screening for everyone over the age of 40. Each year these people have a digital rectal examination – the doctor inserts a finger into the back passage to feel for lumps. After the age of 50 everyone has two tests every five years: one test examines the faeces for blood (faecal occult blood), the other is an examination of the rectum with a telescope (sigmoidoscopy). This reduces the death rate from bowel cancer but results in huge numbers of well people being unnecessarily investigated.

One suggestion in the UK is for a one-off sigmoidoscopy examination for everyone at the age of 55, with more regular screening for those at increased risk (see above). At the moment, people at increased risk usually have regular colonoscopies – examinations of the whole colon with a flexible telescope. Pilot schemes to test the feasibility of people testing their stools at home for blood as an early warning sign of bowel cancer are already under way and may become widespread if they are found to be reliable and acceptable to patients.

Abdominal pain

Everyone gets a stomach ache from time to time, and in most cases it is due to over-eating, or eating foods that do not agree with you. Most stomach aches pass on their own within a few hours. But occasionally there is a more serious underlying cause of abdominal pain which may require medical attention. The site and type of the pain, and the accompanying symptoms, provide the clues as to the likely cause. You should always get medical help if pains are severe, last for more than a few hours, or are accompanied by repeated vomiting.

Upper-central abdominal pain

The most common cause of pain in the upper-central region of the abdomen is indigestion. Other conditions which could lead to pain in the area include gastroenteritis, hiatus hernia, peptic ulcers, bacterial infections and, rarely, stomach cancer.

Indigestion

Pain in the abdomen just below the breastbone is often due to overeating, eating too much rich or spicy food, or drinking too much alcohol. Women who get repeated attacks of indigestion may be producing too much acid (which helps to break down food) in their stomachs. If this is happening, the acid can spill back or reflux into the oesophagus. This reflux is what causes the pain behind the breastbone (heartburn). It is particularly common in pregnancy. Acid production is increased by acid foods such as pickles, and by anxiety and stress. Women who have a hiatus hernia also suffer from acid reflux (see below). Being overweight and wearing clothes that are tight round the waist may also force the stomach and its acid contents up through the diaphragm, causing heartburn (see Chapter 8).

Symptoms of acid reflux are heartburn (pain behind the breastbone) which worsens on stooping or lying down; burping excessively; pain in shoulder tips and back, and beneath shoulder blades; acid taste in the mouth, especially after lying down; shortness of breath; and feeling sick or retching in the morning.

Self-help for indigestion

- Lose weight if you are overweight (see Chapter 1), as acid reflux and hiatus hernia may be exacerbated by fat around the abdomen.
- Cut down on alcohol.
- Stop smoking.
- Eat little and often.
- Avoid anti-inflammatory drugs: use paracetamol instead of aspirin.
- Avoid stooping, especially after meals.
- Loosen clothes around your waist.
- Prop up the head of your bed on books or use an extra pillow.

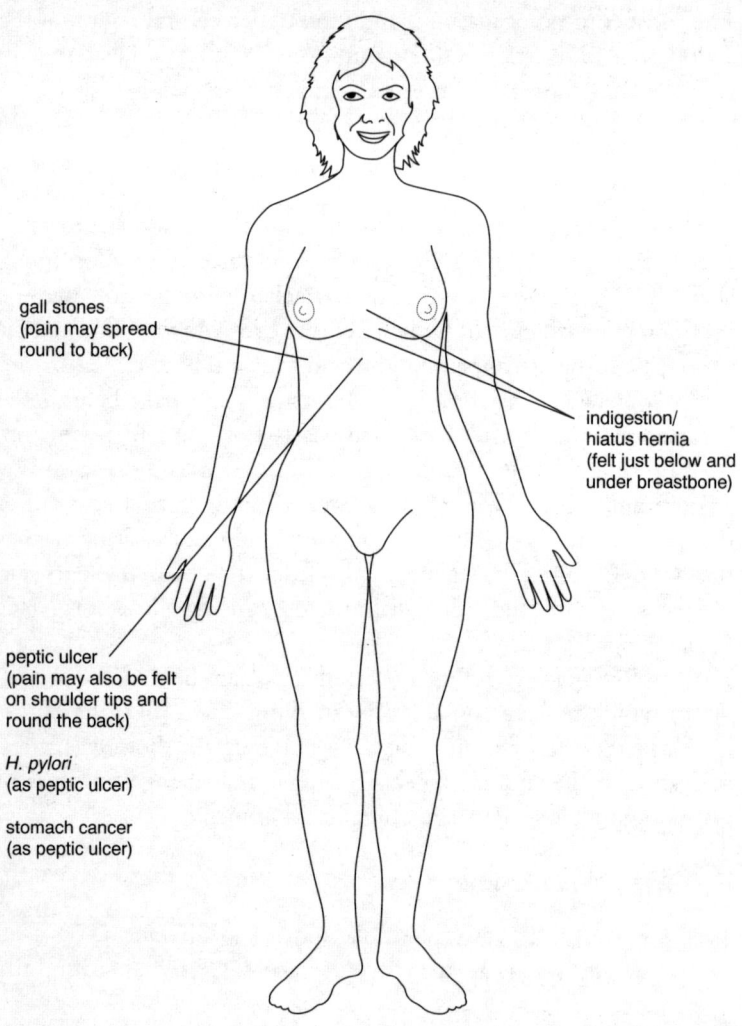

gall stones
(pain may spread
round to back)

indigestion/
hiatus hernia
(felt just below and
under breastbone)

peptic ulcer
(pain may also be felt
on shoulder tips and
round the back)

H. pylori
(as peptic ulcer)

stomach cancer
(as peptic ulcer)

Figure 7 Causes of upper-central and right-sided abdominal pain

Note: diagram shows approximate sites of pain

- Avoid spicy or acid foods, or any foods that seem to cause your symptoms.
- Take an over-the-counter antacid, which combats the acid which causes indigestion. There are numerous brands on the market including Gaviscon, Maalox, Aludrox, Rennies and Settlers.
- Try an over-the-counter drug that blocks the response to acid in the stomach, e.g. cimetidine (Tagamet) and ranitidine (Zantac).

When to see a doctor

It is important to seek medical advice if indigestion is accompanied by:

- weight loss
- difficulty in swallowing
- nausea and vomiting for more than 24 hours
- blood in the stool or in vomit.

Women who start to develop recurrent indigestion after the age of 45, having never suffered from it before, should also see a GP. The GP may recommend you see a specialist (a gastroenterologist) to rule out any underlying problem. The gastroenterologist is most likely to recommend endoscopy (viewing the oesophagus, stomach and upper intestine through a thin telescope passed down the back of the throat). The point of endoscopy is to see whether there is acid reflux damage, a hiatus hernia or an ulcer; to test for the presence of the bacterium *H. pylori,* and to rule out stomach cancer. Barium studies, in which a white mixture is swallowed which outlines the oesophagus and stomach on X-rays, are sometimes used instead of endoscopy.

Stomach bugs (gastroenteritis)

Stomach bugs are usually caused by viruses, and occasionally by bacteria. They produce inflammation of the digestive tract which results in gripy stomach pains, vomiting and then diarrhoea and often fever and lethargy at the same time. Most people recover within a few days from stomach bugs and do not require special treatment. Some persistent bugs and stomach bugs contracted abroad, especially in developing countries, may require special investigation and treatment.

Hiatus hernia

The symptoms of a hiatus hernia are the same as those of acid reflux (see above). The stomach is supposed to sit just below the diaphragm, which divides the chest from the abdomen. In a hiatus hernia, however, the stomach can roll up alongside the diaphragm or even slide up through it. The acid contents of the stomach then reflux up the oesophagus just as they do when the stomach stays in the right place but its acid spills upwards. Being overweight makes hiatus hernia more likely, but it is unclear otherwise why some women are more likely to suffer from it than others. Stooping, lying down and wearing clothes that are tight round the middle may make symptoms worse. Treatment is the same as for acid reflux. Surgery is available for very severe cases of hiatus hernia, but is rarely advised because it is a very extensive operation, and less drastic measures (see above) are usually effective.

Peptic ulcers

Peptic ulcer is the collective term used to describe a raw shallow area in the lining of the stomach (gastric ulcer) or the intestine (duodenal ulcer). Peptic ulcers cause pain which is triggered by specific foods, comes and goes, and is worse at night. The pain often goes quite quickly if you take Rennies or other antacids. There is sometimes a family history of peptic ulcers. All anti-inflammatory drugs, including aspirin, ibuprofen (Brufen) and naproxen (Naprosyn), can cause gastric ulcers as well as indigestion due to inflammation of the part of the intestines that the stomach empties into (the duodenum).

Peptic ulcers normally cause the same sort of pain as a hiatus hernia or reflux oesophagitis (see above). But they may bleed, causing blood-stained vomiting which looks like wet instant-coffee granules. Alternatively the blood may get mixed with the stool which then looks black and tarry. Ulcers can, rarely, become so deep that the crater actually makes a hole in the stomach or bowel wall. If this happens it causes severe and constant abdominal pain and profound weakness or even loss of consciousness. This is called 'perforation' and is a dangerous situation because stomach or bowel contents leak into the cavity of the abdomen causing potentially fatal damage. The vast majority of ulcers will never perforate, but the risk means that detection and treatment of ulcers are essential.

Peptic ulcers are treated in the same way as acid reflux, but it is important to get medical advice. Drugs such as ranitidine or omeprazole are commonly prescribed to heal ulcers. *H. pylori* (see below) needs to be eradicated if it is present, to prevent recurrences. Hospital care is required for bleeding or perforated ulcers.

Bacterial infection (Helicobacter pylori)

The symptoms of this bacterial infection are the same as those of peptic ulcer. *Helicobacter pylori* or *H. pylori* has been found in many people's stomachs and is almost always present in people with peptic ulcers. The bacteria produce a substance to help them survive in the acid stomach. They can increase acid production and infect the resulting damaged areas of the stomach and duodenum, causing ulcers in some people. Eradicating the bacteria not only heals the ulcers but also helps to prevent recurrences more effectively than any other treatment. Identifying the presence of the bacteria is usually done by a specialist during endoscopy. Tests for *H. pylori* will probably become widely available to GPs within the next few years.

Treatment regimes vary but consist of one or two antibiotics together with an ulcer-healing drug for 1–2 weeks. It is important to complete the course to avoid the symptoms coming back.

Stomach cancer

Stomach cancer is extremely rare. It is less common in women than in men and is rare in both sexes under the age of 45. Symptoms are initially the same as for acid reflux and hiatus hernia – indigestion and pain just below the breastbone – but go on to include weight loss, continuous vomiting, intractable or constant pain and difficulty in swallowing when the cancer is advanced. If stomach cancer is diagnosed and treated at an early stage, the outlook is good, with 90 per cent of people alive five years after diagnosis. But most cases are not picked up until they are far advanced. This means that for all people diagnosed with stomach cancer, only 10 per cent will be alive five years later. Early detection is therefore vital; it can be achieved at present only by prompt medical attention if the symptoms described above occur. Stomach cancer is often treated by removing part of the stomach. Cancer-killing drugs (chemotherapy) may also be needed.

Upper-right-side abdominal pain

Pain in the upper right-hand side of the abdomen is usually caused by gall stones or may be due to indigestion (see above). Occasionally, it may be accompanied by jaundice, in which case it could be due either to a gall stone or to inflammation of the liver (hepatitis) caused by a virus, alcohol or drugs. Pneumonia or other problems in the right lung may also cause pain in the upper right abdomen.

Gall stones

One-third of all women in the UK have gall stones at some stage in their lives. More than two-thirds of these women will never have any trouble from them and find out they have gall stones only if they have an ultrasound scan for some other reason. Women who have abdominal pain, have a scan and discover they have gall stones cannot be absolutely sure that their pain is due to the gall stones.

Bile acids are produced in the liver and stored in a concentrated form in the gall bladder nearby. When a fatty meal needs digesting, bile acids pour out of the gall bladder, down the common bile duct and into the intestine. There they get to work on the fatty food. If the bile acids are too concentrated, they can sludge up in the gall bladder and form stones. These stones cause pain as they are evicted from the gall bladder to deal with fatty food, so the pain can often be avoided if you avoid fatty food. But larger stones can get stuck in the common bile duct, and since this is also the exit from the liver, this is more serious. If stagnant bile acids cannot pass into the intestine an infection will develop. If the liver is unable to get rid of bile salts into the intestine they enter the bloodstream instead and make people look yellow. This condition is jaundice.

Gall stones cause severe pain in the upper right-hand side of the abdomen. The pain usually lasts at least half an hour and can become persistent and severe, with fever, nausea and vomiting if the gall bladder becomes infected. Other conditions which produce similar symptoms include pancreatitis (a blood test can distinguish the two) and colic, the result of passing a kidney stone.

Self-help for gall stones

- Avoid fatty foods.
- Take simple painkillers such as paracetamol and aspirin to help the pain.

- Lose excess weight, as obesity predisposes you to gall stones. If an operation is necessary, it is safer if you are not obese.

When to see a doctor
It is important to see your GP if:

- the pain is severe and lasts over half an hour
- you are vomiting or you have fever alongside the pain
- you are jaundiced
- you have recurrent attacks of pain.

Treatments for gall stones
An operation is the quickest way to deal with gall stones once and for all. However, if you wish to avoid surgery, you could opt for one of the other treatments listed below.

Antibiotics and painkillers These work after a week, but the symptoms are likely to come back at some point.

Bile acids to dissolve the stones This is slow and there is a one-in-two chance that the stones will come back within five years.

Bile acids with lithotripsy (shock waves which shatter the stones) This is most effective for small stones and again it is quite slow. To prevent the stones coming back, you need to continue the treatment long term.

Gall bladder removal The gall bladder can be removed in an operation called a cholecystectomy. This is safe, especially if you are young and fit. However, in the traditional operation you are left with a large, uncomfortable wound and you will need 7–10 days in hospital followed by two to three months at home to make a full recovery. Infections are likely in 10 per cent of cases. An alternative cholecystectomy involves a smaller incision which heals quicker: its only drawback is that surgeons might have to enlarge the incision if they have technical problems.

Keyhole surgery Four or five small incisions are made and the surgeons remove the gall bladder using a telescope instrument. The recovery time is relatively short – two days in hospital and two weeks at home. Far fewer complications and less pain are likely than after a cholecystectomy, but 4 per cent of people who opt for key-hole surgery have to have a cholecystectomy after all because of technical problems during the operation. There is a possibility of injury to the common bile duct, which is rare but serious. Try to ensure that your surgeon is well trained and experienced in keyhole surgery.

Central abdominal pain

Pains in the centre of the abdomen are very common. They are usually gripy and come in waves of tight pain that make you want to lie down with your knees curled up. A bowel movement or passing wind often improves the pain. The most common cause of a single episode of central abdominal pain of this type is a stomach bug or food poisoning, in which case it will be accompanied by diarrhoea. The most common cause of recurrent bouts of central abdominal pain is irritable bowel syndrome (see below). Constipation can also cause central abdominal discomfort (see above).

Irritable bowel syndrome

Irritable bowel syndrome (IBS) is very common indeed. It is a specific diagnosis which should be made by a GP or specialist. Women with IBS should not be dismissed as neurotic or beyond help. Because the underlying problem is still not fully understood, the treatment has to involve alleviating symptoms, rather than producing an overall cure.

It now seems that the whole of the gut is affected in IBS. When the upper part of the gut is affected it causes indigestion, burping and discomfort. The lower part of the gut is responsible for the lower abdominal pain and diarrhoea or constipation. The muscle of the gut goes into spasm, and women with IBS probably also have an increased sensitivity to pain from the gut.

The symptoms are abdominal pain and a bloated abdomen; diarrhoea and/or constipation; passing clear 'slime' from the back passage; feeling as though you need to pass a motion urgently even though nothing comes; relief of pain on passing a motion; and a feeling of incomplete emptying of the bowel. The symptoms come and go, and may be aggravated by stress, stomach upsets and specific foods. They are often worse during menstruation.

It is important to realise that IBS is a specific condition that will tend to come and go. It is not related to cancer in any way. However bad the symptoms are, they are never dangerous.

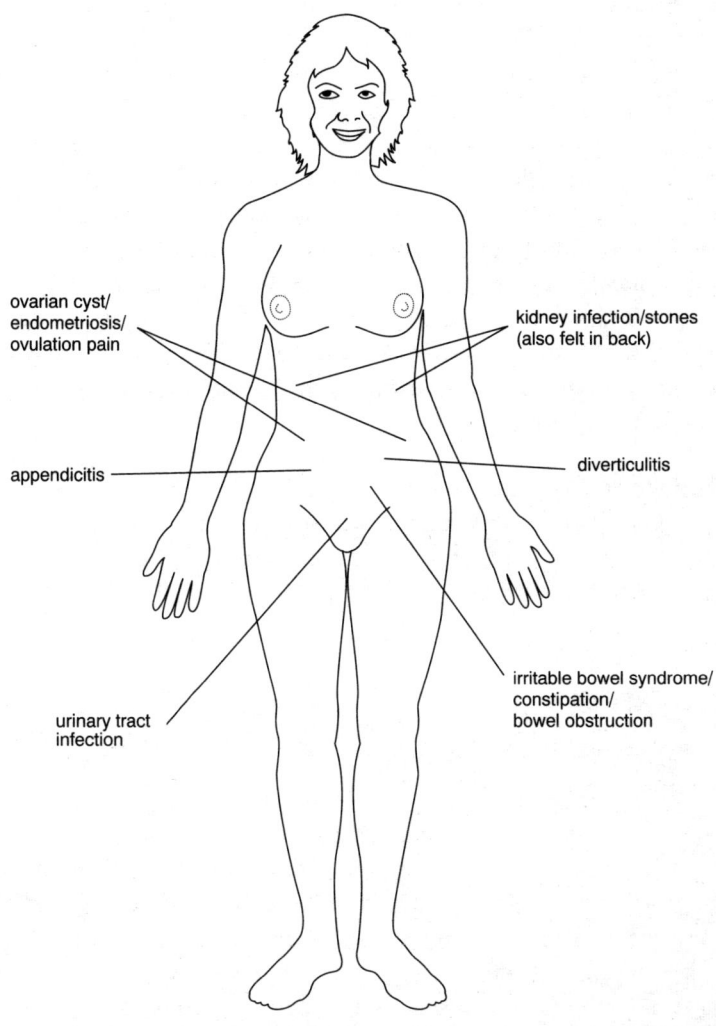

ovarian cyst/
endometriosis/
ovulation pain

kidney infection/stones
(also felt in back)

appendicitis

diverticulitis

irritable bowel syndrome/
constipation/
bowel obstruction

urinary tract
infection

Figure 8 Causes of central and lower abdominal pain
Note: diagram shows approximate sites of pain

Self-help for IBS

- Treat constipation with increased dietary fibre, e.g. dried apricots, plenty of fluids, and lactulose. Unfortunately, some women's IBS is made worse by increasing fibre, and especially by wheat bran. Most laxatives may make bloating worse. Exercise can help to relieve constipation.
- Treat pain with an antispasmodic drug – most are available over the counter. If one type does not work, try another: they are all very safe. Examples are peppermint oil capsules (Colpermin, Mintec), mebeverine (Colofac) and alverine (Spasmonal).
- Treat diarrhoea with loperamide (Imodium, Arret, Diocalm Ultra) or co-phenotrope (Lomotil) available over the counter.
- Try to maintain a positive approach, managing symptoms as and when they occur.

When to see a doctor

It is important to see your GP if you have a family history of bowel cancer, if you are unsure whether you have IBS, or if you are experiencing:

- blood in your stools
- weight loss
- persistent or worsening symptoms
- depression.

A GP will be able to confirm the diagnosis of IBS from the symptoms you describe. Examining the abdomen does not really help, and further tests are unnecessary, although blood tests are often taken to check the liver, and to test for anaemia which may be a sign of bowel cancer. If there is any doubt about the diagnosis, your GP will refer you to a specialist for a sigmoidoscopy – an examination of the lower end of the bowel with a telescope put into the back passage. Women who are over 45 when the symptoms start, and who have a family history of bowel cancer, may be referred to a physician for an examination of all of the lower bowel (colonoscopy).

Treatment for IBS

Most of the available treatments can be purchased over the counter, and can be entirely managed by the IBS sufferer without the help of a doctor. Other treatments or therapies available from a GP or a trained therapist include the following.

Exclusion diets Specially tailored diets which exclude many foods and introduce them back one by one may help diarrhoea. Exclusion diets should be supervised by a dietician. Some GP surgeries have a dietician on site.

Hypnotherapy There is a special 'gut-directed therapy' that allows the IBS sufferer to focus on her gut and learn to control symptoms. It is not generally available, but it is worth asking your GP if local specialists (gastroenterologists) offer it. General hypnotherapy is not usually as effective because it is less geared to the specific problem.

Psychotherapy This is used to explore the subconscious (to look at the underlying sources of stress and conflict that may exacerbate the symptoms) and can be helpful. Unfortunately, availability on the NHS is extremely limited.

Other causes of symptoms that are similar to those of IBS

- Crohn's disease causes bouts of colicky abdominal pain, diarrhoea and blood in the stools due to patchy inflammation along the entire length of the gut, from mouth to anus.
- Ulcerative colitis causes similar symptoms to Crohn's, although only the large intestine is inflamed.
- Constipation may cause bloating and abdominal discomfort.
- Kidney infection from a urinary tract infection causes fever, and a dull ache in the small of the back, just above the waist. This may travel round to one side of the abdomen. Urination is frequent and painful.
- Kidney stones cause severe colicky pain on one side of the abdomen. The stones usually pass on their own, but hospital admission may be needed to confirm the diagnosis and control the pain.
- Pain which occurs in the region of the ovaries, on either side of the middle of the abdomen, may be due to a twisted cyst. If the pain occurs at the same time as menstruation it may be due to bits of uterine lining which are stuck on to the ovaries (endometriosis). If the pain is in mid-cycle, it may be ovulation pain caused by the ovary releasing an egg. Ovulation pain is harmless; the other conditions require medical attention.

- An obstruction of part of the bowel can occur if there is a blockage due to a growth or the adhesions which occur after surgery. Bowel obstruction causes vomiting, constipation and a distended abdomen.

Lower abdominal pain

Lower abdominal pain is caused by a disturbance in the guts (wind, constipation, food poisoning or inflammation), bladder (urinary tract infection, cystitis) or uterus (period pains, miscarriage, labour or infection).

Urinary tract infection and cystitis

Urinary tract infections are a very common problem. They affect women far more often than men. The reason for this is that the tube leading from the bladder to the outside world (the urethra) is much shorter and more exposed in women as it leads only to an opening in the vagina, whereas the urethra in men travels down inside the penis to its tip. Cystitis (inflammation of the bladder) is often due to a urinary tract infection caused by bacteria in the bladder. Intercourse can also cause cystitis, because of friction and the presence of sperm which can enter the bladder from the urethra. Another common cause of cystitis in women after the menopause is that the vagina and the area around the urethral opening become dry and inflamed as a result of the relative lack of oestrogen – the hormone which keeps the vagina moist.

The symptoms of a urinary tract infection are pain on passing urine; getting up several times at night to urinate; urinating frequently during the day; and seeing blood in your urine from time to time.

Self-help for cystitis

Women who often get cystitis after intercourse should try to drink water before sex, and empty the bladder immediately afterwards. Using a condom also helps. Drinking barley water or using a proprietary drink or tablet to reduce the acidity of the urine, e.g. sodium citrate (Cystemme), is also useful.

When to see a doctor

It is important to see your GP if you have:

- blood in your urine
- fever
- persistent or recurrent cystitis.

Treatment for cystitis

The doctor will need to send a urine sample to the lab. This should ideally be mid-stream, which means starting to urinate, then catching a urine sample in a small pot. Laboratory examination takes at least 48 hours, identifies any bacteria in the urine and finds a suitable antibiotic. The most common treatment is trimethoprim. If a urinary tract infection recurs, further investigation is usually advised to check whether there is an underlying problem, such as a malformation of the kidneys, although this is rare in adults.

Appendicitis

Appendicitis is more common among women under 20 than in older women, but it can occur at any age. It is due to inflammation of the small 'tail' attached to the part of the bowel where the small bowel joins with the large. The appendix can be blocked, usually by a small piece of faecal material.

Appendicitis causes a sharp pain which shifts from the lower abdomen to the lower right-hand side, is aggravated by movement and gets progressively worse over a few hours. Occasionally the pain comes and goes. Other symptoms include facial flushing, nausea, vomiting, loss of appetite, constipation (or rarely diarrhoea) and mild fever.

You should seek help immediately if appendicitis is a possibility. Surgery to remove the inflamed appendix is likely. The operation may be performed through a telescope inserted into the abdomen under general anaesthetic (laparoscopy) or by making a small incision in the lower right-hand side of the abdomen. People normally recover quickly after the appendix is removed.

Chapter 8

Heart and lungs

The chest contains the heart and its blood vessels, the lungs, the oesophagus (or gullet, that takes food from the mouth to the stomach), and the trachea (windpipe) that takes air from the mouth to the lungs. These vital organs are encased by the ribs, which are joined to the breastbone at the front and the spine at the back. Chest pain, shortness of breath and cough are all extremely common problems, and many women fear that they have a serious heart or lung disease if they experience these symptoms. However, the most common causes of chest pain, shortness of breath and coughing are relatively harmless, and often easily treated. This chapter explores these problems, with details of common causes, self-help measures, when to seek medical advice and treatment options. Further details about chest pain due to indigestion can be found in Chapter 7.

The structure of the heart

The heart is a large muscle which pumps blood around the body. Veins carry blood from the body to the heart. Small veins join up, and blood enters the heart via two large veins, the superior and inferior vena cava, which bring blood into the right upper chamber of the heart (the right atrium). This blood does not have much oxygen in it as the oxygen has been taken up by the cells of the body. The blood passes from the right atrium, down past the tricuspid valve and into the lower right chamber, the right ventricle. The blood leaves the heart by passing through the pulmonary valve and enters the lungs in the pulmonary arteries to collect more oxygen. The purpose of the valves is to keep blood flowing in the right direction. From the lungs, the blood re-enters the left side of the heart in the

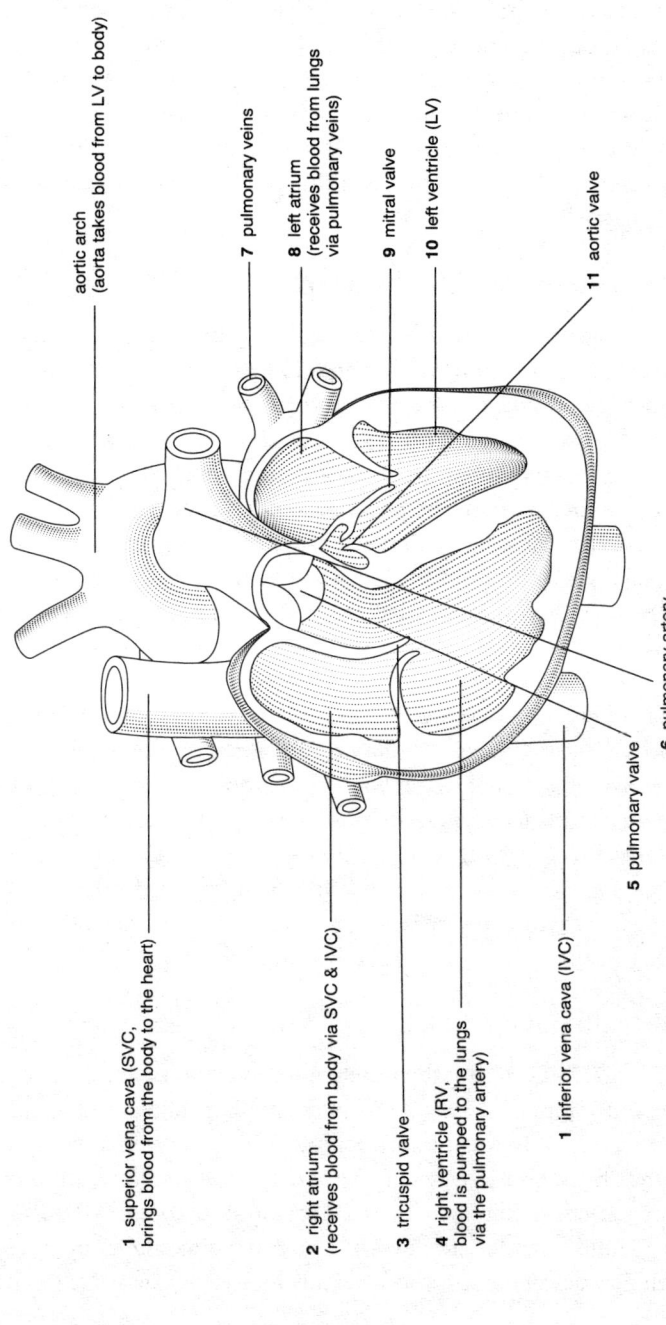

1 **superior vena cava (SVC,** brings blood from the body to the heart)

2 **right atrium** (receives blood from body via SVC & IVC)

3 **tricuspid valve**

4 **right ventricle (RV,** blood is pumped to the lungs via the pulmonary artery)

1 **inferior vena cava (IVC)**

5 **pulmonary valve**

6 **pulmonary artery**

aortic arch (aorta takes blood from LV to body)

7 **pulmonary veins**

8 **left atrium** (receives blood from lungs via pulmonary veins)

9 **mitral valve**

10 **left ventricle (LV)**

11 **aortic valve**

Figure 9 Structure of the heart: 1–11 shows passage of blood through the heart & lungs

pulmonary veins. It flows first into the upper left chamber, the left atrium, past the mitral valve and into the lower left chamber, the left ventricle. From the left ventricle, the blood passes through the aortic valve and is pumped out to the rest of the body and brain. The blood leaving the heart is full of oxygen which it will deliver to the cells of the body. The heart itself has a network of blood vessels which surround it and keep it working well. These are called the coronary arteries.

What can go wrong with the heart

Fatty deposits can build up in the arteries as a result of excess fat in the diet. These deposits can narrow the blood vessels and restrict circulation. High blood pressure means that blood flows at raised pressures through the arteries, which can also cause damage. Narrowing of the coronary arteries that supply the heart itself may result in the chest pain known as angina. If a coronary artery becomes completely blocked, the section of heart muscle which depends on that coronary artery dies: this is called a heart attack or myocardial infarction (MI). If a blood vessel in the brain becomes blocked, the part of the brain dependent on that blood vessel is severely damaged. This, known as a stroke, results in a loss of function in the part of the body which is controlled by that part of the brain (see Chapter 9). Smoking is a major cause of damage to blood vessels in the heart, brain or general circulation. High blood pressure is another major factor. High blood cholesterol, which may be an inherited tendency, can also increase the risk of damage to or blockage in blood vessels. Stopping smoking, controlling high blood pressure, keeping to a low-fat diet, treating high cholesterol levels and taking regular exercise are the best ways to prevent heart attacks, strokes and other forms of damage to the heart and circulation.

The structure of the lungs

Air is breathed in through the nose and mouth and passes down the trachea (windpipe) into a system of branching tubes in the lungs (the bronchi and the smaller bronchioles). The air is warmed up in its passage through the nose, and tiny hairs that line the nose filter out dirt particles. The air is sucked into the lungs as the ribcage moves up and out allowing the lungs to expand to take in more air. Oxygen in the air is absorbed by the lungs and passes into the bloodstream to be circulated to cells around the body. Carbon dioxide, which is a waste product in the blood, passes into the lungs and is breathed out as the ribcage sinks and the lungs are squeezed. The lungs are lined by a covering called the pleura.

What can go wrong with the lungs

Tobacco smoke, pollutants in the air and infections can all cause inflammation of the lining of the passages in the lung (bronchitis). Spasm of the airways, which may be set off by smoke, infections, exercise, dust or other triggers in susceptible people, is called asthma, and results in cough, wheeze and shortness of breath. Inflammation may also affect the lining of the lung (the pleura), resulting in pleurisy which causes pain on breathing in. Lung cancer is a growing problem for women, and has become the most common cancer among women in Scotland. It is linked to smoking and is rare among non-smokers.

Chest pain

Women can now expect to live to the age of 79. This is an average of six years more than men. The greatest causes of death by far, for both women and men, are heart disease and strokes. The death rates from heart disease in the UK have been falling since the late 1970s, but there is little room for complacency as the UK rates remain among the highest in the world. And although a baby girl born in the 1990s can expect to live four years longer than one born in the 1970s, the improvement in life expectancy in the UK is not rising as fast as it is in countries like Japan, where heart disease is less prevalent than it is in the UK. A Japanese baby girl born in the 1990s should live to the age of 83, which is four years longer than a British baby girl born at the same time.

It is true that heart disease is common, especially in old age. But most episodes of chest pain are not due to heart disease at all, but are caused by other, relatively harmless conditions such as indigestion, muscle strain, pleurisy and hyperventilation.

Chest pain and indigestion

Heartburn (see Chapters 7 and 13) has nothing to do with the heart. It is the term used to describe the pain caused when acid refluxes up from the stomach and irritates the oesophagus. The symptoms are pain behind the breastbone which gets worse when you bend down or have hot drinks; pain which spreads round to the back, below the shoulder blades; pain which may be worse after fatty, acid or large meals and after alcohol; coughing at night, which may be due to acid causing spasm in the lungs; and a lump in the throat or a choking sensation which may be due to some narrowing of the oesophagus as a result of acid reflux.

Self-help for heartburn

- Avoid wearing clothes which are tight around the waist.
- Eat little and often, avoiding foods that trigger pain, e.g. citrus fruits.
- Stop smoking (nicotine relaxes the valve between the oesophagus and the stomach and allows acid to reflux more easily).
- Lose excess weight if possible.
- Sleep with an extra pillow or raise the head of your bed on phone books or wooden blocks if night-time pain is a problem.
- Neutralise acid with antacids, e.g. Gaviscon, or block acid with cimetidine (Tagamet) or ranitidine (Zantac), both of which are available over the counter.
- Try to practise stress management, although this is easier said than done. Useful strategies may include counselling, yoga, an exercise class, a plan to delegate more, decisions about managing your time more effectively and accepting that you cannot be all things to all people.
- Avoid aspirin, non-steroidal anti-inflammatory drugs (e.g. ibuprofen) and steroids if possible. These can all cause stomach ulcers and irritation of the oesophagus. Damage can be minimised by always taking them after food, and taking them only when necessary. They can be combined with drugs that protect the stomach and oesophagus such as cimetidine, ranitidine or misoprostol. Alternative painkillers such as paracetamol or stronger preparations with codeine can be used instead, but they do not have the same anti-inflammatory properties. Specially coated preparations of aspirin and steroids are available on prescription, and these aim to minimise damage to the stomach and oesophagus by dispersing into the bloodstream without causing inflammation of the stomach lining.

When to see a doctor

What you think is indigestion could have a more serious cause. It is important to see your GP if you experience any of the following:

- weight loss, difficulty swallowing and persistent or severe pain
- vomiting blood or passing black, tarry stools which may contain blood
- recurrent episodes of chest pain which does not respond to the self-help measures above
- pain that comes on with exercise and is predominantly left-sided, spreading down the inside of the left arm
- difficulty in breathing
- severe chest pain and right-sided pain just below the ribcage.

Investigations

Blood in vomit or stools is usually due to a bleeding ulcer. Persistent pain and weight loss is also usually due to an ulcer, but doctors will want to ensure that there is no underlying cancer. Recurrent attacks of pain which does not settle with self-help are usually due to severe reflux, with or without a hiatus hernia (in which the stomach slides up into the chest, taking its acid with it). A GP is likely to suggest referral to a gastroenterologist (gut specialist) for an endosocopy (whereby a telescope is passed down the back of the throat and into the oesophagus under light sedation, to allow a direct view of the oesophagus and stomach) or barium studies (swallowing a mixture followed by a series of X-rays to outline the oesophagus and stomach). It is possible to measure the acidity in the oesophagus over 24 hours to see whether reflux is occurring.

Left-sided chest pain that comes on with exercise may be due to the heart (see below).

Treating heartburn

The most common treatment is a course of acid-blocking drugs, e.g. cimetidine (Tagamet) or ranitidine (Zantac). These are available over the counter but are cheaper on prescription if prolonged treatment is needed. An eight-week course will cure most reflux (and peptic ulcers), but relapse is common (80 per cent) after treatment. In the long term, low-dose treatment may be advised. The drug omeprazole (Losec), and related drugs known as proton pump inhibitors because they switch off the pump in the stomach that is responsible for acid production, are very effective at reducing the symptoms of heartburn.

Chest pain and inflammation

Inflammation of the ribs or the muscles between the ribs can cause chest pain. Inflammation of the lining of the heart (pericarditis) is uncommon but can cause similar symptoms. This type of pain is worse if there is any movement of the inflamed surfaces, so it will hurt more when you take a deep breath in, turn over in bed, cough or sneeze. There are several different causes of inflammation in the chest area.

Costochondritis (Tieze's syndrome)

This is inflammation of part of the rib. The upper ribs feel tender, often on one side only, in the part of the ribs near the breastbone. The inflammation is in the part of the rib that is made of cartilage rather than bone. The cause is unknown. Costochondritis gets better on its own, and no treatment other than painkillers is necessary.

Muscle strain

Your chest muscles may become tender after unaccustomed and over-enthusiastic visits to the gym. If there are no other symptoms, the link with the gym visits should be apparent. Alternative exercise and painkillers may be necessary until the pain resolves, followed by a more gradual training regime, supervised by a trained coach. Muscle strain is often caused by repeated coughing; it improves as soon as the cough does.

Viral inflammation of muscles between the ribs (Bornholm's disease)

This causes sudden and severe pain on one side of the chest. It usually occurs in young adults. A runny nose is usually present, but no other aches or pains. It is caused by coxsackie B virus, and gets better on its own in around two weeks. Painkillers are the only treatment. Other viruses such as those that cause 'flu may also cause muscle pains, fever and lethargy, but the aches are normally not restricted to the muscles in the chest (see Chapter 10).

Pleurisy

This is inflammation of the lining around the lungs and is fairly common after a severe chest infection. It causes pain when you take a deep breath in or when you cough. A chest X-ray is usually advised to make sure there is no persistent underlying lung problem. A course of antibiotics to clear the infection, and anti-inflammatory drugs such as indomethacin (Indocid) to help the pain, are usually all that is required. It is normal to recover within two weeks.

Pericarditis

This is uncommon. It is due to inflammation of the lining of the heart and causes a tightness in the middle of the chest and left shoulder which gets worse when you move around and take a deep breath in. It can be part of the widespread inflammation in rheumatoid arthritis and lupus (see Chapter 3). It occurs most often in the week after a heart attack, and treatment depends on the underlying cause.

When to see a doctor

Visit your GP if you do not know what is causing your chest pain, especially if you have had a recent heart attack or chest infection, or if you experience:

- shortness of breath
- severe pain on breathing or moving around – pain that is not helped by simple painkillers
- fever, cough, green sputum.

Chest pain and shortness of breath

Shortness of breath which is associated with chest pain requires urgent medical attention because it may be due to a serious problem such as a pulmonary embolus (see below). It can also be caused by hyperventilation, asthma or lung infections. In most cases, though, shortness of breath is uncomfortable but not immediately dangerous. The major causes, such as being overweight, acid reflux, asthma or fluid retention due to an inefficient heart ('heart failure'), are not associated with severe chest pains, and are covered later in this chapter. Shortness of breath and tightness in the chest are not usually signs of lung cancer although it is always worth seeking medical advice if these occur.

Pulmonary embolus

A pulmonary embolus is a clot on the lung. Blood clots can form in the veins of the leg (deep-vein thrombosis) after any operation, including a caesarean section, after prolonged periods in bed, and in women who are pregnant or taking the oral contraceptive pill or hormone replacement therapy (HRT). These blood clots usually stay put in the veins of the legs, where they do not cause much harm. But the danger is that the clots may become dislodged and travel in the bloodstream up to the lungs, where they become stuck in the small blood vessels. This is called a pulmonary embolus.

The symptoms are fainting, shortness of breath, chest pain, mild fever, coughing up blood, or severe shortness of breath and collapse if the embolus is very large. Investigations include a chest X-ray, an electrocardiogram (ECG) and samples of blood, which may reveal abnormalities of oxygen and carbon dioxide in the blood (blood gases). More sophisticated and accurate tests involve a type of scan that shows whether blood is reaching all parts of the lung, or a pulmonary angiogram which shows the blood vessels within the lungs.

Treatment involves thinning the blood to disperse the clot. The drugs used are heparin and warfarin. The period of treatment varies, but does not need to be longer than three months if the pulmonary embolus was caused by an operation, with no other recurring cause.

Hyperventilation

Anxiety is a common cause of shortness of breath, a pounding and rapid heartbeat (palpitations) and tightness in the chest. Women may experience panic attacks in which they start to feel sweaty, nervous and apprehensive. Overbreathing (hyperventilation) can be part of a panic attack, in which so much carbon dioxide is breathed out through rapid and shallow breathing that the acidity of the blood alters. This causes cramps and tight clenching of the hands, which only makes one more anxious. Tightness in the chest often occurs at this stage.

The trick is to breathe in and out of a paper bag several times, to breathe back the carbon dioxide, until your hands unclench. No

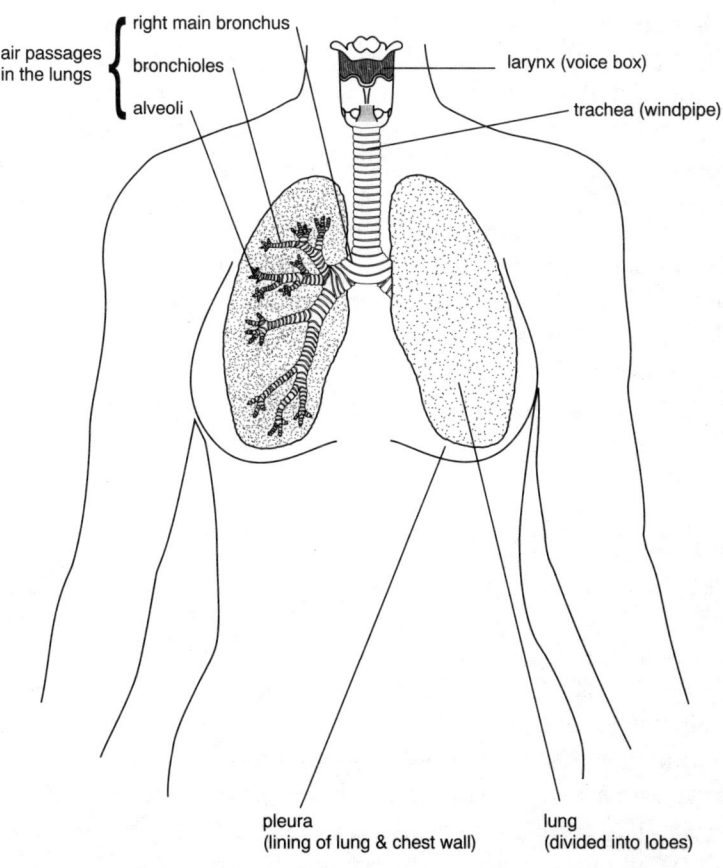

air passages
in the lungs
{ right main bronchus
  bronchioles
  alveoli

larynx (voice box)

trachea (windpipe)

pleura
(lining of lung & chest wall)

lung
(divided into lobes)

Figure 10 The respiratory system

one should dismiss chest pain as being due to anxiety, as heart disease and anxiety can and do co-exist. However, tightness in the chest that only ever occurs as part of a panic attack is unlikely to be due to heart disease. Treatment involves finding the cause of the panic attacks, avoiding the cause if possible, and having specific drug or psychological therapy.

When to see a doctor
Chest pain with shortness of breath always requires urgent medical attention. Pulmonary embolus is rare but is more common during the ten days after any operation, especially one on the pelvis or legs; after prolonged bed rest; in obese women; in pregnant women and women taking hormones such as the contraceptive pill or HRT. Higher doses of oestrogen (which are rarely used nowadays) and the newer progestogens used in contraceptive pills such as Marvelon and Femodene are associated with higher rates of blood clots. Smokers are also at increased risk of blood clots. After a heart attack, blood clots can form in the right side of the heart and travel up to the lungs, although this is less common than clots arising in the leg veins. The clots can also form in the heart if you have an irregular heart rhythm (atrial fibrillation).

Chest pain and heart disease

Chest pain caused by heart disease is a form of muscle cramp. The heart is a powerful muscle which pumps blood around the whole body. Like all muscles, it is supplied with blood by arteries. These arteries are called the coronary arteries and they can become narrowed due to build-up of debris (atheroma, or atherosclerosis). During exercise, the heart needs to increase its blood flow. If the arteries are narrowed, it cannot get the extra blood it needs, and pain results. This is called angina pectoris, or angina for short. If, as mentioned above, a coronary artery becomes totally blocked by atheroma, the part of the heart that is dependent on that artery is starved of blood and dies or 'infarcts'. This is called myocardial infarction (a heart attack).

Coronary heart disease is the single greatest cause of death in women, both above and below the age of 65. Angina is as common in women as in men, and because women tend to live longer they may spend more years suffering from angina.

There is far more scope for preventing heart disease than for either breast or cervical cancer. Yet there is no systematic national screening programme to identify risk factors for heart disease to compare with the screening programmes that exist for breast and cervical cancers. In fact, women with heart disease are less likely than men to have all the investigations necessary to make the diagnosis, and are less likely to receive interventionist treatment such as angioplasty and a coronary artery bypass graft, although this is beginning to change now.

Risk factors for heart disease

There are several established risks for heart disease.

High blood pressure (hypertension) The risk of heart disease rises steadily with rising blood pressure. High blood pressure affects 25 per cent of women in the UK, and nearly half of these are not being treated for it, increasing the risk of heart disease and strokes. After the age of 45, women have higher average blood pressures than men. Blood pressure should be checked every five years, and every six months to a year if you are taking the contraceptive pill or HRT, which can cause high blood pressure.

Diabetes This increases the risk of heart disease by contributing to furring up of the arteries (atheroma). Controlling the blood-sugar levels with diet, pills and insulin, if necessary, can reduce this risk.

Smoking Some 11 per cent of deaths from heart disease in women in the UK are attributed to smoking. About 28 per cent of women still smoke, despite all the publicity about the risks to health. Teenage girls are now more likely to smoke than teenage boys. Fewer women stop smoking than men once they start.

Cholesterol The average blood cholesterol for women in the UK is 5.9mmol per litre. The level increases with age so that by the age of 55, three out of four women have cholesterol levels over 6.5mmol per litre. There is doubt about the importance of cholesterol levels as a risk factor for women. If there are no other risk factors for heart disease, there may be little point in having cholesterol levels measured.

Lack of exercise Exercise protects the heart in a variety of ways. It increases the healthy component of cholesterol, called HDL, which counteracts the less healthy component, LDL. Only 3 per cent of

UK women take the recommended level of exercise, which is the equivalent of three 20-minute bouts of aerobic exercise each week.

Obesity People who are obese are more likely to suffer from high blood pressure, high cholesterol levels and diabetes, and are less likely to exercise, all of which increase the risk of heart disease.

Age The incidence of heart disease rises with age. Before the menopause, women are less susceptible to heart disease than men. This is because the hormones which are dominant in men, androgens, cause furring up of the arteries which can block coronary arteries and cause heart disease. After the menopause, the female hormone oestrogen no longer counteracts the androgens which also occur in women, so the risk of heart disease starts to rise. HRT can protect against this by keeping oestrogen levels nearer to premenopausal heights.

Family history A father or brother who developed or died of heart disease under the age of 55, or a mother or sister who developed heart disease before 60, constitutes a 'positive' family history. Raised cholesterol can run in the family and be a recurring cause of heart disease. But if a father smoked heavily and had other risk factors for heart disease which his daughter does not share, she may not be at any increased risk.

Minimising the risks of heart disease

The following are the three most important ways of reducing your own risk of heart disease to a minimum: stop smoking, eat healthily and avoid obesity. See Chapter 1 for more details.

Stop smoking

- Admit to yourself how many cigarettes you smoke a day and why. Is it for relaxation or stress relief? Is it to keep your weight down?
- Inform yourself about the risks of continuing to smoke and the benefits of stopping. Light smokers who stop will reduce the risk of heart disease rapidly. Heavy smokers will benefit more gradually. Stopping smoking after a heart attack halves the risk of a recurrence. It is never too late to stop.
- Set a date to stop, tell your family, remove temptation and reminders in advance of your stop date, and plan a reward for yourself if you do not smoke for a week. See your GP for support.

- Arm yourself with a self-help leaflet from ASH* or Quitline.*
- Consider nicotine replacement (chewing gum, skin patches, nasal spray) available from pharmacies. If you smoke fewer than 20 cigarettes a day, try 4mg nicotine gum or the spray. If you smoke more than that, the patches are probably best. These double the success rate for heavy smokers trying to stop smoking.
- Arrange to see your GP or nurse at regular intervals as an incentive to stay away from cigarettes.
- Hypnosis and acupuncture may help you if you are really serious about quitting.
- After one year, 5 per cent of smokers who see their GP for advice about quitting smoking manage to remain non-smokers; 10 per cent manage it if they use nicotine replacement. Nicotine is highly addictive, so anyone who does manage to quit should be very pleased with themselves.

Reduce cholesterol and eat healthily

- Reduce full-fat products and choose low-fat options. Aim to reduce the total number of calories you get from fat to 35 per cent (the current national average is 40 per cent). Boiling, grilling and baking use less fat than frying or roasting.
- Reduce saturated fats, which are found in dairy and meat products.
- Corn oil is better than animal fats like lard because it is polyunsaturated and reduces the harmful part of cholesterol, LDL. Olive oil is even better because it is mono-unsaturated and reduces LDL while raising HDL – the part of cholesterol which protects the heart. As the aim is to reduce fats overall, it is best to use olive and corn oil in moderation rather than increasing their use.
- Eat salmon, mackerel or sardines twice a week if possible. The fatty acids found in these oily fish have beneficial effects on cholesterol, thin the blood and have an anti-inflammatory effect that can help rheumatoid arthritis sufferers.
- Cakes, biscuits and pastries should be eaten only in moderation as they contain trans-fatty acids which may have an adverse effect on cholesterol and other fats in the blood.
- Fruit and vegetables which contain vitamins C, E and beta-carotene have a protective effect on the heart. Smokers require

more of these vitamins. Five or six portions of fruit and vegetables a day, in addition to potatoes, is the suggested ideal amount. This is almost double the current national average.

- Increase starchy foods such as bread, pasta, cereals and potatoes while reducing fats.
- A glass of red wine every day may help to reduce heart disease. It has a favourable effect on cholesterol and helps to prevent furring of the arteries. All forms of alcohol are harmful in excess. Excess is currently defined as more than 21 units a week for women, which is equivalent to three glasses of wine a day, 1.5 pints of beer a day, or a couple of daily shorts.
- Reduce your salt intake to lower high blood pressure. If salt has been used during cooking, do not add more at the table.

Lose weight

Obesity is defined as a body mass index (BMI) of more than 30. To work out your BMI, divide your weight in kilograms by your height in metres squared (see Chapter 1). Excess weight carried around the stomach is more harmful than that around the thighs and hips, which is a great comfort to pear-shaped women. Seventeen per cent of British women are obese, and the percentage is rising. Plumpness does not increase the risk of heart disease, however, and yo-yo dieting is more likely to be harmful than being slightly overweight.

- Set a realistic target, based on your ideal weight.
- Try to avoid 'going on a diet' which is an invitation to 'break the diet' and can lead to binge-eating. Aim to adopt a long-term plan for healthy eating which allows you to be in control of what you eat while enjoying your food.
- Keep an honest diary of what you eat and drink over a typical week, calculate your average daily calorie intake from your diary, and work out how to reduce this by 500 calories a day. Alternatively, reduce your consumption of fatty foods, snacks and alcoholic drinks.
- Continue your food diary until you have adapted to your new regime. Do not ever 'borrow' calories from the next day. Try not to overeat at all, and never tell yourself that you will not eat the following day. Try to spread your food fairly evenly throughout the day. Three regular meals, or smaller, more fre-

quent, meals are fine, depending on what suits you. Do not graze or nibble while standing at the fridge, or finish the children's food. Acknowledge what you are about to eat, put it on a plate, sit at a table and enjoy it with a clear conscience.

- If you eat 500 calories a day less than you need to maintain your weight, you will lose 1lb a week. This may not sound dramatic, but it means that over three months you will lose nearly a stone. This gradual weight loss will mean that you do not feel hungry, faint or lethargic and that the weight is more likely to stay off.
- Some women find it easier to lose weight if they are supervised by a GP, a nurse or as part of Weight Watchers★ or a similar group.
- Avoid drugs, 'miracle' weight-loss aids and expensive remedies that promise instant results. Eating less is the only way to lose weight. Regular, enjoyable exercise helps morale, self-image and muscle tone, and burns up some extra calories.

The symptoms of heart disease

With angina, the pain is felt in the centre of the chest, in the jaw, neck, and down either both arms or just the left arm. It feels as if your chest is being crushed. Shortness of breath and dizziness may occur too. Angina is usually brought on by exercise, cold weather, heavy meals and anxiety. Resting usually relieves it. 'Unstable angina' is the name given to worsening angina which comes on with little or no effort.

In a heart attack (myocardial infarction or MI), the chest pain is very severe, lasts more than 30 minutes, causes nausea and often vomiting, sweating, clamminess and great anxiety and distress. In elderly people, the chest pain may not be as severe; the main signs of a heart attack may be unexplained and sudden confusion, weakness, shortness of breath and vomiting.

When to see a doctor

Always get help immediately, by calling your GP or an ambulance, for any unexplained episodes of chest pain that may be due to heart disease. Angina sufferers quickly learn to avoid triggers to their angina, to rest when the pain occurs and to take some medication, usually a tablet or spray under the tongue which opens the blood vessels around the heart.

Investigations

Exercise ECGs are the best tests for angina. A recording of the electrical activity of the heart is made while you exercise on a treadmill. ECG changes (measuring electical activity in the heart) show lack of blood to the heart (ischaemia) in angina sufferers. Exercise radio-nuclide scanning and exercise echocardiogram are two less widely available ways of looking for disease of the coronary arteries, which supply blood to the heart muscle. A fourth test – angiography – uses dye injected directly into the coronary arteries through a catheter passed via the femoral artery (in the groin) – to show up the coronary arteries around the heart. ECGs and blood tests are performed on several occasions during hospitalisation to show that a heart attack has occurred. The blood tests measure substances released from injured heart muscle during a heart attack. A chest X-ray is also part of the investigations.

Treating angina and heart attack

Women suffering from heart disease or who have had a heart attack will be advised to lose weight, exercise more, stop smoking and reduce cholesterol levels if they are raised (see above). Angina patients may be given drug treatment to lower high blood pressure and special anti-angina drugs which work by opening up coronary arteries or reducing the work done by the heart during exercise.

There are two key techniques for resolving the problems caused by angina and heart attacks. In angioplasty, a small tube is passed into the coronary arteries until it reaches the narrowed part which has been identified during angiography (see above). A balloon is then inflated at the site of the narrowing to open it up. Recovery after angioplasty is more rapid than after more major surgery (see below) but nearly a third of patients will require more extensive surgery eventually. A coronary artery bypass graft (CABG) is offered if angina persists despite all the measures above. The idea is to bypass the narrowed coronary arteries by attaching an alternative, healthy vessel. There are two options: a long artery that runs inside the chest and has no specific function, or the long vein that runs down the leg (saphenous vein). Recurrence of angina is less likely after CABG than after angioplasty. There is no difference in the number of heart attacks or deaths from heart disease after the two procedures.

If someone suffers a heart attack, the greatest risk is in the first hour, so call an ambulance and your GP without delay. Try to be reassuring and calm. Help the victim to take her angina treatment and an aspirin, if possible, while you wait for help to arrive. Immediate treatment by the GP or ambulance crew will include oxygen, pain relief, drugs to open the coronary arteries, an aspirin, and drugs to disperse the blockage causing the heart attack (thrombolytic drugs). These need to be given as soon as possible, but if the nearest hospital is not too far away, thrombolytic treatment may be given there.

Hospital treatment is usually needed to correct any abnormalities of the heart rhythm, for pain control and to treat any complications that may occur after a heart attack, such as blood clots in the legs or high blood pressure. However, some women who have a heart attack can remain at home if their condition is stable and they have a competent and willing carer at home who can call for help if necessary. After hospital admission for a heart attack, most women will be able to go home within ten days, return to work and normal activities within three months, and start driving again after a month. There is no reason to refrain from sex and there is every reason to resume a full and active life.

It is a good idea to reduce risk factors after a heart attack (see above). An exercise programme, a daily aspirin and a daily beta blocker (a drug which reduces the work done by the heart) can all improve the outlook after a heart attack. Heart failure (see below), which can occur after a heart attack, means that the heart does not pump efficiently and fluid accumulates in the lungs causing shortness of breath. Heart failure is treated with drugs such as captopril which reduce the pressure on the heart.

Shortness of breath

Every woman has experienced shortness of breath at some stage. It may have been only momentary, while running for a bus, or pushing a baby out into the world. Or it may be a constant problem which is so disabling that it prevents all but the most limited activity. Shortness of breath is frightening and can induce panic, which in itself makes it even harder to breathe.

Lung conditions such as asthma, bronchitis and heart failure are long-term problems but they may flare up suddenly. Other causes of sudden shortness of breath are relatively rare and are usually one-off events such as a pulmonary embolus.

Sudden shortness of breath

Sudden and severe shortness of breath is much rarer than the recurrent type, but may be dangerous or even fatal. If someone cannot breathe, it is essential to call for help and practise life-support skills. The underlying cause is not immediately relevant if an individual cannot breathe: the important thing is to maintain an airway and give artificial respiration if necessary.

The possible causes of sudden shortness of breath include a pulmonary embolus (see above); severe asthma; heart failure; severe allergic reactions causing constriction of the throat and breathing; inhalation of food, e.g. a peanut which becomes lodged in the airway, and a puncture in the lining of the lung (pneumothorax).

Asthma

Asthma is an increased sensitivity of the airways. Everyone's airways are sensitive and will go into spasm if sufficiently provoked – for instance, in a very smoky pub, or while jogging on a cold day. Women who have a tendency to asthma have airways that go into spasm more readily than non-asthmatic women. The in-built tendency may be inherited from one or both parents and may be triggered by a variety of lung irritants such as pollen, viral infections which cause colds, cat fur, dust and house dust mites that live in mattresses and soft furnishings.

The symptoms of asthma are shortness of breath, wheezing, and a persistent dry cough, especially at night or when exposed to cold air or trying to exercise. Treatment involves identifying and avoiding triggers if possible. Some women can control their asthma by stopping the cat from entering their bedroom. Drugs to open up the airways which are in spasm include salbutamol (Ventolin) and terbutaline (Bricanyl) among others. Drugs that make the airways less sensitive can be used to prevent asthma attacks and include beclomethasone (Becotide) and budesonide (Pulmicort).

Treatment is usually in the form of inhalers allowing the drugs to enter the lungs directly (tablets have to be swallowed and absorbed into the bloodstream before the drug can be taken to the lungs). This minimises the chances of side-effects. Homeopathy can be useful for asthmatics but should be used in addition to conventional treatment, as stopping the inhaled drugs altogether may be dangerous.

Heart failure

Heart failure is very common among elderly people. It occurs when the heart starts to pump less efficiently than it did in its younger days. This means that the circulation of blood around the body is impaired. Conditions that put extra strain on the circulation, such as high blood pressure or anaemia, can exacerbate the problem. Fluid builds up first around the ankles: the force of gravity draws fluid to the lowest part of the body. Later, fluid can also collect in the lungs which causes shortness of breath.

Women with mild heart failure can take some of the strain off their hearts by stopping smoking, eating well, avoiding obesity, and limiting both salt and alcohol. Drug treatment is aimed at taking pressure off the heart and may involve diuretics (water pills), e.g. frusemide, or ACE inhibitors, e.g. captopril, which are also used to treat high blood pressure.

Pneumothorax

Pneumothorax is fairly common among young men but rarer among women. It describes a hole in the lining of the lung which allows air to enter between the lining of the chest wall and the lung itself. This air pushes the normal lung to one side, making breathing difficult and causing a sudden pain on that side. Pneumothorax may occur spontaneously with no obvious cause, or as a result of a broken rib puncturing the lung lining. Bruised ribs after a fall, fight or accident can also cause pain on breathing and some shortness of breath even if there is no pneumothorax. A chest X-ray is necessary to make a firm diagnosis.

Treatment is not always necessary, apart from painkillers, but a large pneumothorax may require a chest drain, which is a tube inserted to release the trapped air and allow the lung to re-expand.

Recurrent or long-term shortness of breath

Most women who suffer from shortness of breath do not have a serious underlying medical condition like the ones described above. Women who are overweight and/or smoke, often find that they are sort of breath, especially on exertion. The other common causes of recurrent shortness of breath are acid reflux (see Chapter 7), asthma (see above), chest infections caused by bacterial or viral infections (see above), panic attacks (see Chapter 2), mild heart failure (see above), anaemia or an over-active thyroid.

Thyroid disorders

The thyroid gland is the same shape and size, and sits in the same position, as a man's bow tie. It is controlled by a hormone produced by the brain called TSH (thyroid-stimulating hormone) which 'instructs' the thyroid gland to produce thyroid hormones. The thyroid hormones (thyroxine) circulate in the bloodstream and are responsible for driving many of the body's functions. Women are more prone to having too much or too little thyroid hormone than men for reasons which are not well understood but are linked to the presence of the female sex hormones.

Having an under-active thyroid is a little like having your car engine tuned too low; your whole body operates below par. This may result in weight gain, lethargy, shortness of breath, puffy ankles, feeling cold the whole time, thin hair, and heavy periods. A blood test confirms the diagnosis and treatment is by taking daily tablets to replace the thyroxine. Treatment needs to continue for life. Women normally feel very much better once their thyroid hormone levels return to normal.

Having an over-active thyroid is like having your car engine too highly tuned: your whole body is in overdrive. This may result in weight loss, shaking hands, sweatiness, palpitations, irritability and infrequent periods. In some forms of this condition, the eyes can look very bulging and staring. A blood test confirms the problem and further tests may be needed to see why the thyroid is over-active.

Treatment initially involves drugs to lower the thyroid hormones (carbimazole) and drugs to control the symptoms (such as propranolol for palpitations). Younger women may be offered an operation to remove part of the thyroid gland. This leaves a thin scar around the neck which can usually be easily covered by a necklace. Older women may be offered treatment with injections of radioactive iodine, which is absorbed by the thyroid gland and destroys some of the thyroid. Radioactive iodine may affect the foetus, so if women want to have children the advice is to go in for surgery. Both forms of treatment may be so effective that a woman ends up with too little thyroid hormone and needs to take supplements to get the level right.

Possible causes of recurrent shortness of breath

Symptoms	Possible cause	Treatment
Shortness of breath when you lie flat or stoop. Heartburn, burping and an acid taste in the mouth	Acid reflux	Avoid acid foods or other triggers. Drugs can neutralise acid (e.g. Gaviscon), block acid's effects (e.g. Zantac) or stop acid production (e.g. Losec)
Shortness of breath when you lie flat. Waking at night with shortness of breath. Swollen ankles. A recent heart attack	Heart failure – usually among the elderly	Drugs to take the pressure off your heart – ACE inhibitors and diuretics (water pills)
Shortness of breath and a wheeze which gets worse on contact with cats or other triggers, e.g. dust, exercise or cold air. Worse when you have a cold. Waking in the early morning with shortness of breath. May have hay fever and other allergies, and may have had eczema as a child	Asthma	Avoid triggers. You can take drugs to open the airways, e.g. salbutamol (Ventolin), or drugs to prevent asthma, e.g. beclomethasone (Becotide)

Shortness of breath and pain on breathing in. Recent fever and green, thick phlegm	Pleurisy – inflammation of the lining of the lung	Anti-inflammatory drugs for the pain and antibiotics for the infection
Shortness of breath, pounding and rapid heartbeat (palpitations). Feeling sweaty and nervous	Panic attack	Identify the cause. Use counselling or relaxation techniques. Beta-blocker drugs block the physical effects of anxiety
Shortness of breath, especially on exertion. Feeling weak, lethargic, faint. May have had recent heavy blood loss during a period, an operation or in childbirth	Anaemia	Identify the cause and treat it if possible. Take iron supplements if they are recommended by a doctor
Shortness of breath, pounding and rapid heartbeat, weight loss, bulging eyes, shaking hands	Over-active thyroid	Drugs, an operation to remove part of the thyroid gland, or radioactive iodine to destroy the gland
Shortness of breath on exertion. Very overweight	Obesity	Lose weight (see above)
Shortness of breath, cough, phlegm and a permanent wheeze with flare-ups caused by chest	Chronic bronchitis and emphysema	Stop smoking. Antibiotics for infection. Physiotherapy to shift the phlegm. Inhalers to open

| infections in a smoker | | the airways. Oxygen overnight |
| Shortness of breath, cough, coughing up blood, mild chest pain, wheeze, weight loss, recurrent chest infections | Lung cancer or infections such as tuberculosis (TB) – both of which are less common among women. Smokers are most at risk of lung cancer. Debilitated women, e.g. those with HIV, the homeless and drug addicts, are most at risk of TB | Depends on the cause. Lung cancer may be treated with drugs, radiotherapy and surgery |

Coughing

The sensation of needing to cough is due to irritation anywhere along the path by which air enters the lungs. The most common reason for a cough is a viral infection which causes a cold. The cough is due to inflammation caused by the virus in the nose, throat and upper airways. Viral coughs and colds require no special treatment and pass on their own within a few days. A more persistent cough with a fever and yellowy green phlegm may indicate an infection deeper in the lungs which may be caused by a virus or bacterium. An antibiotic will help if bacterial infection is present. A recurrent dry cough may be due to asthma (see above), and a cough which comes on only at night may be due to acid reflux (see Chapter 7). Some drugs such as ACE inhibitors used to treat high blood pressure and heart failure may cause a dry cough which improves with an inhaler or after stopping the drug. Many of the conditions that cause shortness of breath (see above) may also cause a cough.

Common causes of coughing

Type of cough	Cause	Treatment
Cough is dry, hacking, frequent and irritating. You may feel unwell and have a sore throat as well	Inflammation of the back of the throat (pharyngitis). It is caused by viruses such as those responsible for the common cold	Warm drinks. Try not to cough. Gargle with soluble paracetamol or aspirin before swallowing them
Dry, persistent cough which starts after taking new medication for high blood pressure	ACE inhibitors such as captopril which are widely prescribed for high blood pressure and heart failure	Discuss changing to alternative medication with your GP. An inhaler of atrovent usually helps
Cough produces thick green phlegm. There may be a fever as well	Infection – may be a simple chest infection (bronchitis) or infection deeper in the lungs (pneumonia)	Antibiotics
Dry, persistent cough that gets worse during exercise or in cold weather	Asthma	Inhalers (see above)

Chapter 9

Head and nervous system

The nervous system is made up of the brain – the control centre of the body – and the network of nerves that take messages to and from the brain. Together they control both conscious activities like stretching out a hand to pick up a cup of tea, and unconscious activities like breathing and heartbeat. We receive messages about our environment via our nerves, which register pain and temperature, and bring messages to the brain from our eyes, ears, nose, taste buds and skin so we can see, hear, smell, taste and touch the world around us.

The brain is protected by its hard, bony shell – the skull. The brain is such a complex organ that it is not yet fully understood. It consists of millions of nerves which form networks and pathways, enabling humans not only to live, walk and reproduce, but also to think, dream and create. Different parts of the brain control different functions, but the parts controlling emotions, personality and sexuality have not been properly identified yet. Nerves leave and enter the brain either directly through holes inside the bones of the skull, or via the spinal cord. The brain and spinal cord are called the central nervous system (CNS). Messages are sent out from here and received by a huge network of nerves – the peripheral nervous system (PNS) – which extend to the furthest parts of the body. Peripheral nerves can be 'motor', which means they make muscles move, or 'sensory', which means they carry messages to the brain about sensations. Messages are passed along nerves as an electric current, brought about by an electrical charge moving in and out of cells. When an electrical message gets to the end of the nerve, it has to be converted by a neuro-transmitter into chemical energy, which is released from the end of the nerve, travels across the gap between the nerves, and is picked up by receptors at the beginning of the next nerve.

What can go wrong

The brain and nerves require a good blood supply, like all organs and systems in the body. When the blood supply to part of the brain is cut off you suffer a stroke, and that part of the brain is unable to function. Injury or bleeding within the brain may also jeopardise the blood supply. Brain tissue cannot regenerate, and degeneration can occur as part of the ageing process, or as the result of infection or disease. Degeneration of the nerves in the brain that mostly rely on the neurotransmitter dopamine is the cause of Parkinson's disease, which leads to an inability fully to control movement. Patchy degeneration of the myelin sheath protecting the CNS nerves causes the very variable problems associated with multiple sclerosis. Disorders of the electrical activity in the brain may result in epilepsy. Subtle disorders or disturbances of the neurotransmitters may play a part in some psychological problems such as eating disorders and depression.

Although the brain is protected by the skull, it is also confined by it. Any growth, whether benign or malignant, that takes up a sizeable amount of space may compress normal brain tissue, causing neurological problems such as headache and visual disturbance.

The main problems that result from disorders of the nervous system are headaches, dizziness, blackouts or loss of consciousness (including faints), tremor and weakness or paralysis. Psychological problems such as depression, confusion and loss of touch with reality are covered in Chapter 2.

Headaches

Headaches are sometimes unpleasant and can be alarming if they come on suddenly or last for days or weeks. Many women go to see their GPs wanting reassurance that they do not have meningitis or a brain tumour. It may be human nature to fear the worst, but it is reassuring to remember that headaches are very rarely due to any dangerous underlying disease. In fact, the most common cause of headache is stress. For many women, stress-related headaches are a

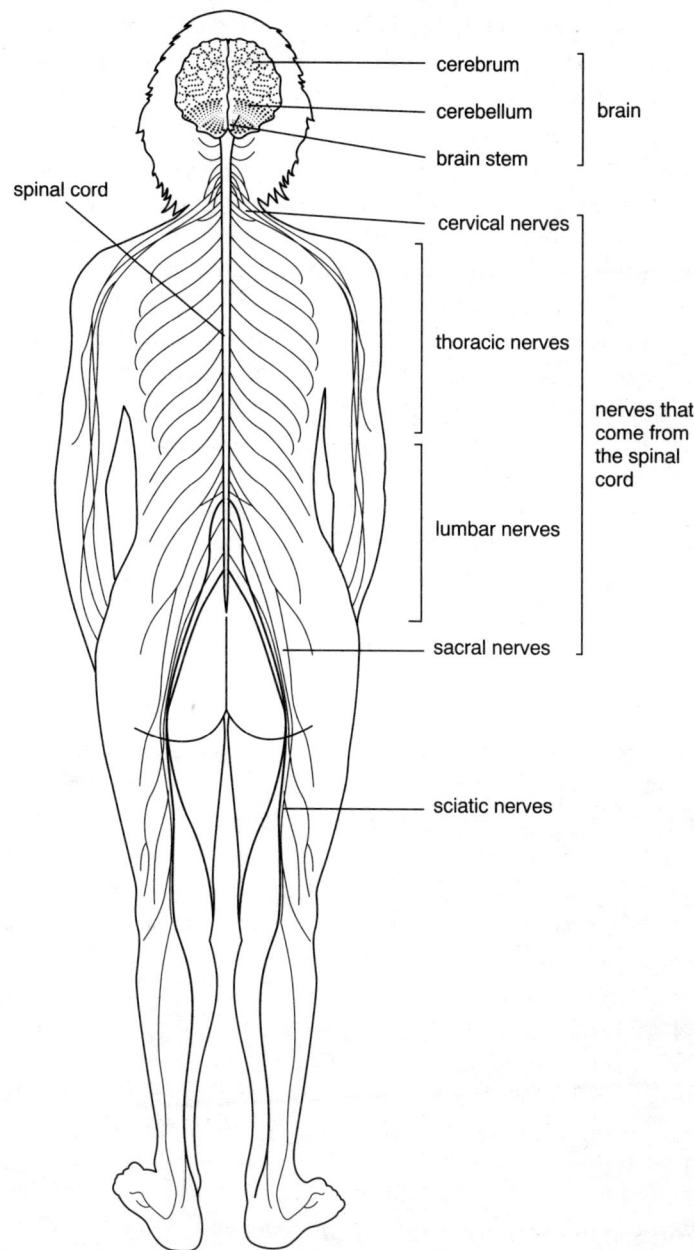

Figure 11 The central nervous system

regular occurrence and may be brought on by tension at work or home. Some women find headaches are the result of trying to juggle a number of different roles and responsibilities; feeling torn by the conflicts of being a mother, partner, housekeeper and employee, with not enough hours in the day to fulfil all the roles to their own satisfaction. Many women find that headaches get worse in the week or two before a period, and hormone-induced headaches can also occur when you are on the contraceptive pill, while you are pregnant, or if you are taking hormone replacement therapy (HRT).

Other common causes of headaches are wear and tear (osteoarthritis) in the neck, which results in trapped nerves to the head, and migraine, which can cause episodes of severe headaches, with unpleasant associated features like nausea. A car accident may result in headaches and neck stiffness as a result of a whiplash injury which jolts the head forward or back. One cause of recurrent headaches is over-use of painkillers, often taken in the first place to counter headaches. Stopping the painkillers may solve the problem.

The features and treatments of the different causes of headaches are summarised below.

Stress

The headache is present all day, in both temples or like a tight band around your head. It may feel as if your head is about to burst open. Your neck muscles may tense up too, giving similar symptoms to those of cervical spondylosis (see below). Many doctors do not like to use the term 'stress headache' as the cause of the pain is due to tense neck muscles, rather than directly due to stress. Stress headaches tend to occur every day while you are stressed, last all day, and get worse in the late afternoon. You may have other signs of stress or depression, such as disturbed sleep, tearfulness, anxiety, palpitations and an inability to concentrate. Tackling the causes of stress and using relaxation techniques are likely to be more effective than repeated painkillers, which often do not help this type of headache and may cause headaches themselves if they are used for long periods of time.

Arthritis in the neck (cervical spondylosis)

The headache is felt at the back of the head and across the scalp, which may feel tender when you brush your hair. Neck movements are often stiff and painful, especially towards the end of the day or after a bad night's sleep. Cervical spondylosis is very common in elderly people and relatively rare in young people. An X-ray will show some arthritis in the neck in everybody as they age, and it may or may not cause symptoms, so there is not much useful information to be gleaned from an X-ray in most cases. Supporting the neck with a collar is not advisable for more than 48 hours at a time as it makes the neck stiffer than ever. Careful manipulation by a physiotherapist, osteopath or chiropractor is useful for flare-ups, but the problem is likely to recur unless it is the result of a whiplash injury (see below). Staying flexible with yoga exercises or water aerobics is a good long-term strategy. Painkillers (e.g. paracetamol) and anti-inflammatory drugs help in the short term, but may be habit-forming and cause headaches themselves.

Eye strain

Doctors often say that eye strain does not cause headaches. But leaning forward awkwardly to peer at a book can certainly trigger a headache, possibly because it strains the neck muscles. You need to visit an optician for a thorough eye test if you have any difficulty in focusing clearly on either near or distant objects.

Whiplash injury

Car accidents often make the driver or passenger jolt forward and then fall back into the seat. This abnormal jerking makes the neck muscles go into spasm, trapping the small nerves that leave the spinal cord in the neck to travel to the shoulders or up across the scalp. The result can be a throbbing headache, very like that experienced by people with arthritis in the neck (see above). Painkillers or anti-inflammatory drugs, a collar to support the neck and rest for a couple of days is the usual initial treatment. After that, physiotherapy and exercises to make the neck flexible again are advised. A migraine type of headache that comes and goes can follow a whiplash injury and last for weeks. Most people, however, recover fully and rapidly after a whiplash injury.

Sinusitis

The sinuses are spaces in the skull which are normally filled with air. The sinuses interconnect and drain into the nostrils. The common cold and other viruses can clog up the nose and allow infection to enter the sinuses. The sinuses then fill up with thick, infected mucus. This causes a throbbing, constant pain in the face, often on one side, or a boring pain in the middle of the forehead. The pain is worse if you bend over. Your face may feel tender to touch, and there may be a fever. Inhaling steam and taking painkillers will ease the pressure a little. Several antibiotics may be effective for sinusitis.

Over-use of painkillers (analgesic headache) and other drug-related headaches

Regular use of anti-inflammatory drugs can cause headaches. Anyone suffering from regular headaches would do well to stop all drugs which are not strictly necessary. Stopping the offending drug may make the headaches worse, temporarily, but they quickly subside if the drug is the cause. Other drugs that may cause headaches include the combined oral contraceptive pill, the progestogen-only mini pill and nifedipine (Adalat, used in the treatment of high blood pressure). Alcohol is probably the most common drug that causes headaches – especially the morning after the night before.

High blood pressure (hypertension)

Mildly raised blood pressure does not usually cause headaches, but high blood pressure which is not controlled with treatment can cause a headache similar to that due to raised pressure in the brain (see below). Treatment to reduce the blood pressure in a controlled way may need to be given in hospital. Changing your lifestyle by stopping smoking and reducing your salt intake may be helpful in the long term, alongside drug treatment to keep the blood pressure at safe levels.

Temporal arteritis

Inflammation of the artery which runs through the temple causes a headache on one temple, which is tender to the touch. The scalp may feel tender, and pain may develop on one side of the face when you are chewing. The headache is worse when you lie flat or bend over, and it gets better if you sit upright. Temporal arteritis is a rare condition which affects elderly people and is potentially dangerous as sight can be affected if the inflammation progresses. Prompt treatment with steroids reduces the inflammation and saves eyesight. The dose is tailed off gradually over a few months but the drugs need to be restarted if the symptoms recur.

Trigeminal neuralgia

This is inflammation of the nerve which comes out of the skull to bring sensation to part of the face. The neuralgia rarely affects anyone under the age of 50, is more common among women and tends to get worse with increasing age. There is occasionally a more serious underlying neurological condition, such as multiple sclerosis, especially if trigeminal neuralgia occurs in people under 50. It is a sharp, stabbing pain on the cheek or jaw on one side which makes you screw up your face. It is triggered by cold wind on the face touching a point on the face, by eating or by talking. It is treated with drugs usually used for epilepsy – carbamazepine or phenytoin. An operation to destroy the nerve may be necessary.

Shingles (herpes zoster)

This causes pain on one side of the face – across one eye or just a part of one side of the face or scalp. The pain can precede an eruption of spots that is due to shingles, a reactivation of a long-dormant case of chickenpox. The spots of shingles crust over and heal, but the pain can persist for some time afterwards. Shingles affecting the tip of the nose can lead to damage of the cornea and requires urgent medical attention.

Pressure in the brain (benign intracranial hypertension)

Pressure in the brain may become raised for no apparent reason and causes a severe headache which is present on waking up, and which may get better during the day. Coughing and bending forward make it worse. It may be associated with vomiting and blurred vision. Young, overweight women are most often affected. Raised pressure may follow a head injury or it may occur during pregnancy. Investigations by a specialist (neurologist) are carried out to make sure there is no brain tumour. If no specific cause is found for the raised pressure, it is called benign intracranial hypertension. In 10 per cent of cases it gets better on its own. It can be treated with a drug called acetazolamide or by drawing off fluid from around the brain by putting a needle into the back (lumbar puncture).

Brain tumour

Brain tumours cause increased pressure in the brain and a similar headache to that described above. Brain tumours are the hidden fear among most people suffering from severe or persistent headaches, but it should be reassuring to know that brain tumours are rare. Nevertheless, it makes sense to seek medical help if the symptoms listed in the box persist for longer than six weeks as they may, occasionally, be signs of an underlying tumour.

Brain tumours can be non-cancerous (benign), e.g. a meningioma which grows on the lining of the brain and causes symptoms by taking up space in the brain and pressing on nerves. Meningiomas can be removed as long as they are accessible without damaging the brain. Once they have been successfully removed, there should be no further problems. Cancerous (malignant) tumours can be relatively slow-growing and amenable to treatment with surgery or radiotherapy. But they may be already far advanced

---

Warning signs of a brain tumour

Note that these symptoms may occur in stress-related headaches too and are not necessarily a sign of a brain tumour:

- persistent headaches lasting more than six weeks
- early-morning headaches as opposed to headaches that build up during the day
- headaches which wake you up in the middle of the night
- headaches which get worse when you cough, sneeze or strain to pass a motion
- vomiting when you don't feel sick; vomiting which does not relieve the pain
- seeing double
- losing sensation or power in one part of your body
- mood changes, fits or faints, increasing clumsiness, and stumbling
- headaches that do not seem characteristic of migraine, arthritis of the neck or stress
- headaches which are a dull, deep, steady ache, not pulsating like migraine.

---

by the time they are discovered and would be less likely to respond to treatment. Some cancerous growths in the brain are due to the spread of cancer from elsewhere in the body such as the lung or breast. The treatment and the outlook will depend on the nature of the original cancer.

Migraine

About 18 per cent of women and 6 per cent of men suffer from migraine. Migraine usually starts in late teens; it is most prevalent among women in their thirties, and then starts to improve. Migraine, unlike stress-related headache, is just as common among affluent middle-class women as among poorer and more deprived women. It is a major health problem costing the UK economy around £1 billion a year in lost productivity among women who work outside the home, as well as enormous misery and inconvenience to unwaged women. There are two types of migraine. The most common by far is 'migraine without aura'. The other is called 'migraine with aura'. The treatment for both types is the same.

Migraine without aura

The warning signs of an impending migraine may include behavioural changes, yawning, food craving or loss of appetite, for up to 24 hours before the attack. When the migraine comes on it is a throbbing, intense headache on one side of the head or over one eye. The headache can be severe enough to limit normal daily activities. It may be worse during a period or if you are on HRT. The migraine lasts anything from 4 to 72 hours. You may experience nausea and/or vomiting, and will probably find that bright lights and loud noise make your headache worse. You may feel too hot or too cold and look pale during an attack. Going to sleep or lying down in a quiet, darkened, peaceful room should help. Recovery after an attack may take a whole day.

Migraine with aura

This type of migraine produces all the symptoms listed above. In addition an 'aura' comes on after or with the warning signs, and between 10 and 60 minutes before the headache. 'Aura' is the term used to describe visual disturbances such as shimmering lights and blind spots. You may also feel numb down one side and be unable to find words to say what you want to say.

Causes of migraine

Although many different things can trigger a migraine, the underlying cause is probably due to inflammation around blood vessels to the brain. The chemical 5-HT, which carries messages across the gaps between nerves (a neurotransmitter), is almost certainly involved too. The drop in oestrogen levels may account for migraine associated with periods. Migraine runs in families: if both parents are affected, there is a 70 per cent chance that the children will also have migraine.

Self-help for migraine

First and foremost, you need to identify and avoid the things or situations that trigger your migraines, if possible. Keep healthy, take regular meals and exercise sensibly. Try to minimise stress in your life. You can use migraine as a barometer to assess whether you are emotionally or physically overloaded. If your migraines are increasing in frequency, you need to take action to deal with any underlying problems. Relaxation therapy, yoga and meditation can all help. Resting in a dark and quiet room, eating small snacks and gently massaging your head can help during an attack. Homeopathic and herbal remedies – especially extracts of the plant feverfew – may be useful, although convincing evidence is lacking. You could also try acupuncture, hypnosis and biofeedback. Biofeedback trains you to alter your body's physical reactions such as pulse rate. If you need to take tablets, try soluble aspirin or paracetamol, combined with an anti-nausea drug such as metoclopramide, e.g. Migravess, which is available over the counter.

Pregnancy helps 70 per cent of migraine sufferers, although it can hardly be recommended as a long-term solution.

When to see a doctor

If the self-help measures described above do not help, or if your attacks are frequent and disabling, your GP can prescribe drugs, including beta blockers which prevent attacks, painkillers, anti-nausea medication or the highly effective sumatriptan (Imigran), which mimics some of the actions of 5-HT levels in the brain.

Possible triggers for migraine attacks

Several triggers may interact to precipitate a migraine. These include:

- foods, e.g. chocolate, citrus fruits and cheese
- alcohol
- coffee (caffeine) withdrawal
- lack of food or irregular meals
- flickering lights including fluorescent lights, VDUs and watching too much TV
- stress, excitement or shock
- periods
- the contraceptive pill
- menopause
- over-exertion and physical or mental exhaustion
- lifting weights, stooping and straining (e.g. when you are gardening)
- changing your routine, e.g. going on to shiftwork
- change of climate/weather
- very hot baths
- intense smells.

Sudden headaches

A very severe and sudden headache may be caused by one of two potentially serious conditions. One is an infection which inflames the lining of the brain (meningitis) or the brain itself (encephalitis). The other is a bleed into the space around the brain and spinal cord (subarachnoid haemorrhage).

Meningitis

Meningitis is inflammation of the lining of the brain and spinal cord, the meninges, by bacteria or viral infection, and may be potentially fatal. Anyone who fears they may have it should contact their doctor or attend a hospital casualty department. The cause is either bacterial or viral infection. Immunisation has contributed to a fall in meningitis which can be caused by the polio and mumps viruses. Tuberculosis is an occasional cause, which is more common among homeless alcoholics or immigrants from developing countries. Two bacteria account for most cases of meningitis in adults – the pneumococcal and meningococcal bacteria. Pneumococcal infection causes pneumonia and ear or sinus infections which can very occasionally develop into meningitis. The very young, very old and anyone whose immunity is impaired are most at risk, although all women and men can contract it. A vaccine is available for certain vulnerable groups (e.g. people with sickle cell disease). Meningococcal bacteria live in the noses of healthy individuals but can cause epidemics of meningitis in overcrowded areas, including schools and institutions. The treatment for both types of bacterial meningitis is penicillin injections. There is a vaccine against meningococcal meningitis but it covers only two strains (A and C) which are not usually the ones which cause trouble in the UK. Anyone who is in close contact with meningococcal meningitis should be given antibiotics (usually rifampicin) to protect them from infection.

Encephalitis

Encephalitis is very similar to meningitis but is more likely to cause damage to specific areas of the brain causing lack of co-ordination, staggering about, twitching, or jerking eye movements. Encephalitis

---

Warning signs of meningitis or encephalitis

Note that these symptoms can occur with stress-related and other, less serious, causes of headaches and are not necessarily a sign of meningitis or encephalitis:

- headache which gets worse if you are jolted
- fever
- stiff neck – putting your chin on your chest causes pain (see also Chapter 3)
- vomiting
- feeling abnormally irritable, drowsy or confused
- fits
- pain in joints
- rash
- unexplained loss of consciousness.

---

may occur up to two weeks after infection with measles, chickenpox, mumps, rubella and 'flu, or as a result of infection with the same herpes virus that can cause cold sores.

Subarachnoid haemorrhage (SAH)

A subarachnoid haemorrhage is a bleed in the circle of blood vessels that help to feed the brain. There is usually an underlying weakness in the blood vessels, known as a berry aneurysm. An SAH may be preceded by a small warning bleed which causes a sudden headache with neck or back pain. A tendency to SAH may run in the family. The diagnosis is made by a lumbar puncture (needle in the back to withdraw some fluid), CT scan (multiple X-rays interpreted by computer) and an angiogram (injection of dye to show the blood vessels of the brain). An operation to clip the bleeding blood vessel can save lives and prevent damage, although the operation can be risky. Drugs to lower the blood pressure and keep the blood vessels from going into spasm are also part of the treatment.

Warning signs of a subarachnoid haemorrhage

Note that these symptoms may also occur with other, less serious, causes of headache and are not necessarily a sign of subarachnoid haemorrhage:

- sudden, severe headache at the back of the head, like a blow to the head
- faintness
- vomiting
- neck stiffness
- drowsiness
- paralysis down one side
- unexplained loss of consciousness.

Dizziness

Feeling dizzy is a sensation that most women will have experienced. It is very useful to try to pinpoint exactly what the dizziness feels like, as this will provide clues about the cause. Dizziness can be due to:

- vertigo – when the world seems to be spinning round, like being seasick
- lack of balance which results in being unable to walk in a straight line
- faintness – the feeling that you are about to pass out.

Vertigo

Vertigo is a sensation which often makes the sufferer feel sick. It is usually due to inflammation of the inner ear (labyrinthitis) and is thought to be due to a virus. Labyrinthitis comes on suddenly, makes you feel very ill, and may leave you unable to get out of bed for a few days. Hearing is not affected. The problem improves on its own over three to four weeks. Rest and not turning your head quickly will help. Drugs to calm the inner ear may also give some relief. Certain drugs can also cause vertigo, and if its onset coincides with starting a new drug, it is worth asking the doctor if the two could be related.

Recurrent attacks of vertigo may follow labyrinthitis, a head injury or a stroke, or come on for no apparent reason. The vertigo is felt with particular movements of the head, like turning over in bed. It usually gets better slowly, and physiotherapists can teach exercises to improve it.

Recurrent attacks of vertigo with nausea, deafness and ringing in the ears (tinnitus) is called Ménière's disease. This is caused by increased pressure in the inner ear. The condition comes and goes, although the deafness and tinnitus tend to get progressively worse with each attack. Many sufferers find conventional medicine cannot offer much help and turn to acupuncture, homeopathy and other complementary therapies for help. There is no evidence that any one of these therapies is particularly effective, although individuals may find relief. A low-salt diet and anti-nausea drugs such as prochloperazine (Stemetil) may help.

Lack of balance

This is a much rarer cause of dizziness than vertigo. The inability to walk straight may be due to loss of sensation in the feet, which happens to diabetics and elderly people, or to a disorder of the part of the brain that controls co-ordination (the cerebellum). If a woman finds she cannot walk in a straight line, and is finding it hard to co-ordinate movements, she must seek medical advice to find the underlying problem.

Blackouts and loss of consciousness

A 'blackout' means losing consciousness and falling to the ground. The most common occurrence is fainting, which is the body's way of rapidly shutting down when blood flow to the brain is threatened. When you fall to the ground, blood drains away from the skin and is diverted to the brain. Apart from fainting, blackouts and loss of consciousness can be caused by epilepsy, age-related insufficiency of blood to the brain (vertebrobasilar insufficiency), mini strokes, irregular heartbeat and sudden falls in blood pressure.

Faints

A wide variety of conditions can make you faint, or feel faint. Being very overtired, drinking too much alcohol, excessive dieting or fasting and severe pain from any cause may all make a person faint. Everyone has their own threshold for fainting; some people faint much more readily than others. Before fainting people often feel sick, as blood is diverted away from the gut. Blood draining away from the skin makes you look very pale. The best way to respond to feeling faint is to sit down and put your head between your knees, to allow the blood to drain back to the brain. Women who are anaemic may feel faint, breathless and tired. It is always worth having a blood test if this is a possibility as it is so easily remedied by taking iron tablets. A rare cause of fainting is low blood pressure, which is normal for healthy young women, but may cause fainting if blood pressure drops even further in a hot bath or sauna, for example. Fainting is not uncommon in early pregnancy.

Epilepsy

Epilepsy is a condition in which abnormal bursts of electrical activity in the brain trigger fits or other neurological disturbances. This may be an inherent problem, with no obvious cause, or the result of an injury to the brain such as a head injury after a road accident. Some people have warning signs of an attack, others do not. The attacks may come out of the blue, or be precipitated by flashing lights or flickering screens. During a fit, epileptics may bite their tongues, jerk, have blue lips and pass urine. There is no particular action to take if you witness a fit – intervening may cause more damage, but you can move sharp obstacles out of the way in case the person falls or jerks into them. An epileptic fit can occur during sleep or while lying down. It is usual to feel very tired for more than half an hour after an attack and it is quite common to have no memory of the attack at all. Some women with epilepsy can identify triggers which set off a fit. Avoiding these triggers may be enough to solve the problem. But most women with epilepsy will need to take long-term medication to control the fits.

If you have epilepsy it makes sense to seek specialised medical help before getting pregnant, to discuss whether you should change your medication before conceiving. Women with epilepsy do have a slightly increased risk of having a baby with some abnormality. Most of the drugs used to control epilepsy can cause some damage too. But the risk of having repeated fits usually outweighs any risk to the baby from the drugs. You may be able to stop taking medication if you have not had any recent fits. The drug phenytoin seems to cause fewer abnormalities than other drugs such as valproate or carbamazepine. Folic acid, which is recommended for all pregnant women to prevent problems with the development of the baby's

Advice for women with epilepsy

- Don't let it restrict your life more than necessary.
- Avoid swimming or bathing babies when you are on your own.
- Don't climb high ladders to change light bulbs, etc.
- You must inform the Driver and Vehicle Licensing Agency (DVLA) if you are a driving-licence holder. Drivers who have had no fits while on the same medication for two years may be allowed to drive. If for the past three years fits have occurred only while you were asleep, and never while you were awake, driving is normally allowed. Any change to your medication or the pattern of your fits must be reported to the DVLA, which will consider your case. You must not drive until a decision is made.

spinal cord, is particularly important for women with epilepsy. This is because epilepsy drugs can affect the way folic acid is absorbed from the diet. Most women with epilepsy do not have more fits during pregnancy.

Vertebrobasilar insufficiency

Older women who black out when turning their heads may have a problem with the major arteries to the brain, a problem known as 'vertebrobasilar insufficiency'. The most common cause of this is that the blood vessels become kinked as they travel up the neck over bony protrusions caused by the arthritis that affects almost everybody over the age of 60. The only solution is to avoid turning your head, hold on to the banister while you come downstairs and look straight ahead rather than down.

Mini strokes

A sudden blackout may be due to a mini stroke: a small blood clot which dislodges from another part of the body, usually the heart, lodges in a blood vessel in the brain. This usually causes loss of power down one side of the body, but may cause a sudden blackout. These attacks are known as 'transient ischaemic attacks' or TIAs and always improve within 24 hours. Anyone experiencing a TIA should contact their doctor. Finding and treating the underlying causes, and taking an aspirin a day may prevent recurrences. The risk of a heart attack or full-blown stroke is increased after a TIA.

Irregular heartbeat

An irregular heartbeat can cause palpitations and attacks in which the sufferer becomes very pale, has a very slow pulse and then falls suddenly to the ground. There is no jerking or fitting. The sudden falls, which can occur with little or no warning, can be dangerous if the fall results in injury. An electrical recording of the heart (ECG) may help to make the diagnosis. Fitting a pacemaker to drive the heartbeat artificially may be the solution, or drug treatment may be offered.

Sudden falls in blood pressure

Blackouts that occur when a person stands up suddenly may be due to an unusual and dramatic fall in blood pressure. This could be a complication of diabetes or anaemia, but may also occur as women get older. If no cause is found, the solution is to move slowly, especially when getting out of bed in the morning.

Anyone who has blackouts must inform the DVLA and will normally not be allowed to drive until there have been no blackouts for a year, and then only subject to medical advice.

Shaking or tremor

Everyone gets trembly from time to time. Trying to hand a cup of tea to someone if you are very nervous or anxious can be nigh on impossible. The hand shakes, the tea spills, the anxiety mounts . . . But, for some women, tremor is not just a sign of anxiety, but part of an underlying condition which persists and may get worse.

Tremor may run in families; may be a sign of thyroid, lung or liver disease; or may be a side-effect of medicines.

Family trait (benign essential tremor)

This type of tremor runs in the family and involves the hands and arms. It improves after drinking a small amount of alcohol but does not usually get any worse or better overall. It can be treated with the drug propranolol. It also helps if you avoid cigarettes, coffee (caffeine) and anxiety-provoking situations. Ironically, people with this condition seem to live longer than average.

Excess thyroid hormone

If you have excess thyroid hormone (see Chapter 8) the tremor will affect both hands. You may lose weight, feel hot and sweaty and have irregular periods. This condition can be treated with drugs to lower the thyroid hormone (e.g. carbimazole) and block the effects of excess thyroid (beta blockers, e.g. propranolol). Sometimes an operation to remove part of the thyroid gland is required, or radioactive iodine is injected to destroy the gland.

Lung disease

This tremor is the result of excess carbon dioxide in the blood stream. It may occur in patients with chronic bronchitis, and is

8888888

associated with shortness of breath and blue lips. It is more common in smokers. The best treatment is to stop smoking – it's never too late. Bronchitis may need treatment with antibiotics and inhalers. Oxygen may be necessary in controlled amounts.

Liver damage

The most obvious sign accompanying the tremor is jaundice, but the tremor may occur with severe liver damage from any cause and is often associated with confusion. Hospital treatment is usually necessary, but the precise treatment depends on the underlying problem (see Chapter 7). Alcohol and certain drugs such as painkillers and sleeping tablets will make the condition worse.

Parkinson's disease

The tremor is accompanied by slow, rigid movements and unsteadiness when walking; handwriting gets smaller and facial expression is lost. Symptoms of Parkinson's disease (see also Chapter 2) may be caused by certain drugs. The disease is more common among elderly men and there is no specific cure. The main drug treatment is levodopa. Transplants using brain tissue from foetuses have been performed but it is not a treatment that is widely available or wholly successful.

Multiple sclerosis (MS)

MS is caused by damage to the protective coating round the nerves in the brain and/or spinal cord. It can occur in sudden episodes with recovery between attacks, or it can cause ongoing deterioration. Relapses may be triggered by infections. MS may cause numbness in a limb or half of the body; weakness in the legs; pain in one eye with temporarily dim vision; vertigo; double vision; incontinence; difficulty in speaking clearly; mood changes and memory loss, as well as tremor. It is made worse by exertion and heat. The diagnosis may be difficult and is based on at least two typical episodes, eliminating other causes, and an MRI scan. As yet there is no cure for MS. Treatments include supplementing your diet with polyunsaturated fats, using steroids for eye problems and interferon – a drug that acts on the body's immune system and seems to prevent recurrences. Many MS sufferers have had successful pregnancies and have been able to bring up children normally. The outlook is very variable for people with MS. Some have only one attack, while others deteriorate progressively.

Weakness or paralysis

Strokes are the most common problem affecting the nervous system, causing paralysis. Other causes of paralysis include nerve damage in accidents or as a result of disease such as multiple sclerosis. They become increasingly common with age and are only slightly more prevalent among men than women. The cause is either a blockage in a blood vessel in the brain, or a haemorrhage in the brain. The part of the body controlled by the affected part of the brain cannot function. Over a few hours, one side of the body feels like a dead weight, hangs limply and then becomes rigid and numb. Vision may be impaired and speech may be difficult to understand. Severe strokes may cause total paralysis, the sufferer being aware but unable to respond by moving or talking. Underlying medical problems that may be contributing to the stroke, such as an irregular heartbeat, can be treated. But the stroke itself cannot be treated. Rehabilitation to encourage mobility can help a great deal. Measures to prevent strokes include stopping smoking, detecting and treating high blood pressure, avoiding the contraceptive pill if you are at risk of blood clots (e.g. if you are a heavy smoker or have had a previous thrombosis in the legs), controlling diabetes and high cholesterol and avoiding excess alcohol or obesity.

Part 3

Being a woman

Chapter 10

Breasts

Women worry about their breasts a great deal. Most women will admit to being preoccupied with the shape, size or general appearance of their breasts at some time in their lives. This is not just because of the understandable fear of developing breast cancer: fashion is also an important influence. Most of us put up with what nature intended, and that admits of a wide range of breast shapes and sizes.

Structure, purpose and normal development of the breast

Breasts usually start to develop when a girl is ten years old, although the process can start as early as the age of eight. Breast development is the first stage of puberty, and periods normally start one to two years later. Any breast lumps in a 9–10-year-old girl are certain to be caused by the development of breasts, which is often asymmetrical at first.

Breasts have no useful biological function other than providing sustenance for babies. The developed breast in a woman is made up of a series of lobules, small units that can produce milk when stimulated by the female hormones during pregnancy. The lobules drain into channels, or ducts, which all eventually open into the nipple. Milk is produced in the lobules and flows down the ducts into the nipple. A mesh of fibrous tissue called the stroma supports the lobules and ducts. Breast cancers and most harmless lumps develop in the lobules.

During pregnancy, the breast doubles in weight. After pregnancy, the breast often becomes softer and more droopy as breast tissue is replaced by fat. At this stage, the breasts are more prone to produce cysts.

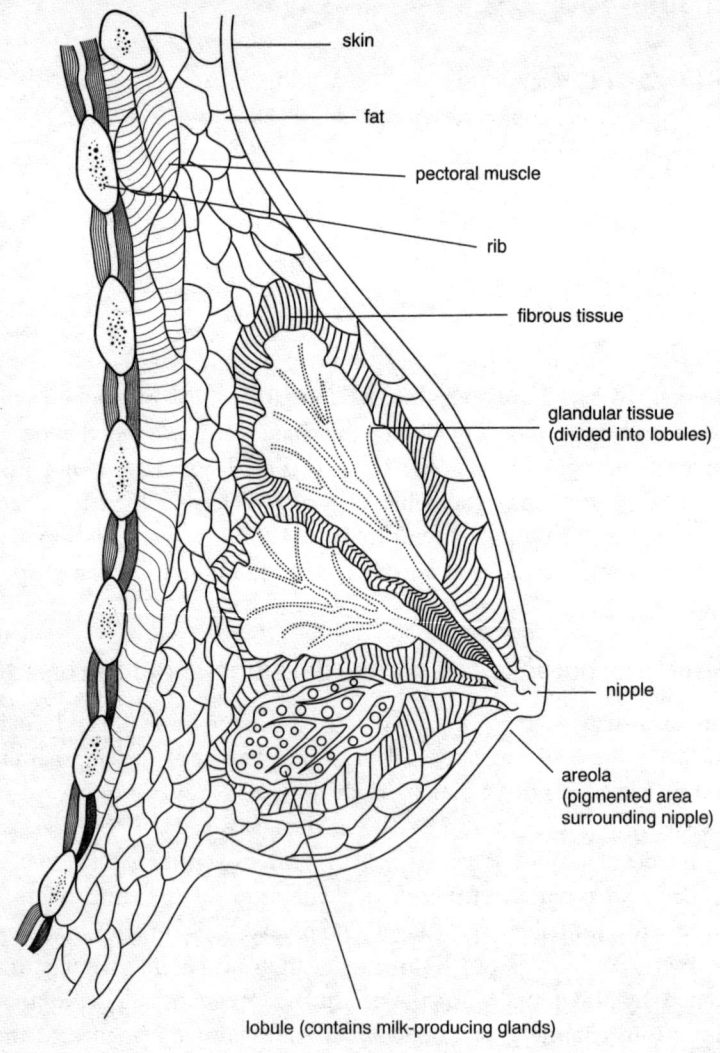

skin

fat

pectoral muscle

rib

fibrous tissue

glandular tissue
(divided into lobules)

nipple

areola
(pigmented area
surrounding nipple)

lobule (contains milk-producing glands)

Figure 12 Structure of the breast

Breast care

- Wear a professionally fitted bra. Ill-fitting bras can contribute to backache, breast tenderness, nipple soreness and rashes under the breasts.
- Support breasts adequately when exercising. A professionally fitted sports bra is best.
- A rash which develops on the shoulders or back may be caused by allergy to nickel in bra clasps. Covering the metal with a piece of cotton will help.
- Breasts start to sag after the age of 30 as breast tissue is replaced by fat. This process is natural, normal and inevitable.
- Adopting a low-fat diet and avoiding obesity are two lifestyle measures that may help to prevent breast cancer.
- Be aware of what is normal for your breasts (see *Plan for breast awareness,* below).
- Have a mammogram at least once every three years over the age of 50.
- Always seek medical help if you find a breast lump. Remember that nine out of ten breast lumps in women under 30 are not due to cancer, although cancer does become more common as you get older. See your GP first, and insist on referral to a specialist if the lump persists after your next period.
- Seek referral to a specialist centre if your mother, sister, or grandmother has had pre-menopausal breast cancer.

If women do not become pregnant, the breast tissue starts to be replaced by fat at the age of 30. The process continues gradually, and speeds up after the menopause. By the age of 70, the milk ducts shrink, so that the nipple, which the ducts open on to, may get pulled inwards, making it look like a small slit.

Breast-feeding

Breast-feeding is widely acknowledged to be the best way of feeding babies in the first weeks of life. However, although it is estimated that in the UK 64 per cent of women give breast-feeding a go, only 38 per cent of babies are still breast-fed at the age of six weeks.

Many mothers are disappointed to find that breast-feeding is not the natural and satisfying experience they had believed it to be. It can be painful for the mother and frustrating for the baby. Like other techniques, breast-feeding has to be learnt, and requires patience. But women who are already exhausted from childbirth may feel they do not have the stamina to put up with cracked nipples and a screaming baby, and resort to bottle-feeding. Once the baby tries a bottle, getting it to go back on the breast could be difficult, largely because it has to suck much harder to get milk from the breast than from a teat on a bottle.

Women need a great deal of support, encouragement and practical advice at this stage. It usually takes no more than a few days for the process to become established and for the baby to start feeding efficiently and contentedly.

Advantages of breast-feeding

It protects baby against infections A baby suffers from 10–15 per cent fewer episodes of diarrhoea and chest infections in his or her first year if breast-fed for at least three months; is less likely to be admitted to hospital with gastroenteritis; and has 50 per cent fewer ear infections in his or her first year if breast-fed for at least four months.

It protects against allergies A baby has 20 per cent less chance of wheezing up to the age of seven if breast-fed for any length of time, after allowing for other causes such as passive smoking, overcrowding and parental poverty among children from non-allergic families; gluten allergy (Coeliac disease) in later life is less common if babies are breast-fed.

It confers long-term health advantages There is less diabetes in children from families which are prone to the disease if they have been breast-fed for 9–12 months; it is reported that premature babies fed breast milk by tube compared with premature babies fed formula milk by tube have a higher IQ.

It reduces mortality from gut infection Breast-fed babies have negligible mortality rates from gut infection (necrotising enterocolitis), while over 500 formula-fed babies suffer from it a year, of whom 100 die.

It is advantageous to the mother No preparation or sterilisation of equipment is needed; the milk is a nutritionally complete food for baby and is cheap and portable; breast-feeding uses up about 500 calories a day, which helps weight loss if desired.

Tips for successful breast-feeding

- Wait until the baby's mouth is gaping.
- Move the baby's head quickly so that its mouth is still open when it reaches the breast. The baby's gaping lower jaw and tongue should come into contact with the breast first, as far from the nipple as possible so that the correct amount of breast is pulled into the baby's mouth, rather than the baby just chewing on the nipple.
- Feed enough of the nipple and surrounding areola (the darker area that surrounds the nipple) into the baby's mouth so it is sucking on a teat that is two-thirds breast and one-third nipple.
- Offer the breast whenever and for however long the baby wants, within limits, to allow complete emptying of the breast.

Tips for avoiding problems when breast-feeding

- Ask hospital staff not to give your baby a bottle while you are in hospital unless this is essential.
- Seek experienced help early. Do not wait until you are desperate.
- Speak to friends who have breast-fed.
- Do not stop breast-feeding abruptly: tail off gradually.
- For painful breasts, take an anti-inflammatory medicine such as ibuprofen, which is safe when breast-feeding, to relieve the pain while persevering with feeding if possible.
- Request an antibiotic from your GP if you have a high temperature or feel 'fluey' as a result of mastitis (see below).
- See your GP if you think a breast abscess is developing. This is a hard, red lump which is very painful. It causes a high fever and does not empty out despite correct breast-feeding technique. It will be filled with pus and needs to be surgically drained in hospital. Abscesses are rare.

What can go wrong with breasts

The main problems and concerns that women have about their breasts are cosmetic problems, nipple discharge, breast pain, breast-feeding problems, breast lumps and breast cancer.

Cosmetic problems

These are all appearance-related, and although some of them are very much a matter of the woman's self-perception, they may need treatment. See Chapter 15 for information on cosmetic surgery.

Extra breasts or nipples

As many as five in every hundred men and women have an extra nipple, or occasionally even an extra little breast. These are usually just below the normal breasts or in the armpit. The extra nipples and breasts rarely cause any trouble although they can get the same diseases as normal nipples and breasts. They can be removed by a surgeon if they are unsightly or rub on clothing.

Different-sized breasts

Like our faces, our breasts are slightly asymmetrical in that one is sometimes a little larger than the other. Occasionally, there can be a dramatic difference between the sizes of the two breasts and in its most extreme form a woman might have one well-developed breast and one which is totally flat. In such a case, the muscle underlying the breast may be poorly developed or even absent. Many women with this sort of asymmetry will want surgery to even up the two breasts. This can mean enlarging the under-developed breast (breast augmentation) or making the larger breast smaller (breast reduction) or a combination of the two.

Excessively large breasts

Breasts develop during puberty and growth normally slows down in adolescence. Sometimes the breasts keep growing throughout adolescence and end up much larger than average (bra size 36B in the UK). If very large breasts make a young woman very self-conscious, stop her doing sports and activities she would otherwise enjoy, or give her backache and breast discomfort, she should consider seeing a specialist with a view to having breast reduction (see Chapter 15). It may be hard to get the operation on the NHS, although it is worth seeking referral from a GP and consulting the surgeon about the pros and cons of the operation.

Excessively small breasts

As mentioned above, there is a wide range of breast shapes and sizes among women. There is no relation between breast size and the ability to breast-feed a baby successfully. Some women feel that their breast size reflects their femininity and cannot come to terms with having small breasts.

Breast augmentation using a prosthesis filled with silicone gel or saline (salt water) can be done by a plastic surgeon. It is extremely rare to be able to have this operation on the NHS; the exceptions are if the breast is being reconstructed after a mastectomy for breast cancer (see below) or if one breast is very under-developed compared to the other one (see above). There have been concerns about the safety of some implants, so if you are considering having breast reconstruction or cosmetic surgery, you should get advice from experts (see Chapter 15).

Nipple discharge

An amazingly high percentage of women can produce fluid from their nipples even when they are not breast-feeding. Two-thirds of women who still have periods will find that their nipples ooze fluid if someone sucks them. This can be very alarming, especially because the colour of this fluid may be anything from the whitish yellow colour one might expect to inky blue-black, but it is usually harmless. It is much less common to find fluid oozing from nipples if there has been no stimulation such as sucking. If your nipples ooze spontaneously, an examination to check for lumps and a mammogram (see below) are advisable, particularly if the fluid is blood-stained.

If both examination and mammogram are normal, there is nothing to worry about. If the fluid is oozing from just one spot on the nipple and if it is bloodstained or persistent, your doctor may suggest an operation to make sure there is no cancer lurking in the duct.

Milk oozing from nipples is, of course, normal in women who are pregnant or breast-feeding. Milk production at times other than pregnancy or breast-feeding is called galactorrhoea and can occur in men as well. Drugs such as cimetidine, taken for heartburn or ulcers, or spironolactone taken for water retention, are a common cause. Excess production of the hormone prolactin is another possibility as this is the hormone that primes the breasts to produce milk during pregnancy and after delivery. A relatively harmless brain tumour known as prolactinoma can cause this excess production.

Breast pain

Two-thirds of women experience recurrent breast pain, and many others suffer from it occasionally. It is usually uncomfortable and can be alarming, but breast pain is very rarely a sign of serious underlying disease, and hardly ever a sign of cancer. Women who have frequent breast pain are no more likely to develop breast cancer than women who never have such pain.

There are three types of breast pain: one is related to periods (cyclical), a second is constant (non-cyclical) and the third occurs during breast-feeding.

How to determine whether the pain is cyclical

Two-thirds of women who seek help for breast pain have cyclical pain, which means it is linked to periods. Keeping a careful record every day of the occurrence (or non-occurrence) of pain for at least three months is the best way of distinguishing cyclical from non-cyclical pain. This is important, because the causes of and treatments for the two kinds are different.

Keeping and interpreting a breast-pain record

In the example below, the woman had mild pain on 1–3 March, severe pain on 4–8 March and a period from 9 March. After the period, she had no pain until the next cycle.

Month	1	2	3	4	5	6	7	8	9	10	11	12	13	14	15	16	17	...	28	29	30	31
Mar	o	o	o	●	●	●	●	●	p	p	p	p	p	p	p	p	–	–	...	–	o	o	o
Apr	●	●	●	●	●	p	p	p	p	p	p	p	p	–	–	–	–	–	...	o	●	●	●

Key: ● severe pain
    p period
    o mild pain
    – no pain

Her pain is clearly cyclical, in that she experiences increasing severity of pain in the two weeks leading up to her period (after ovulation) and then has relief from the pain for at least a week after the period.

If the pain were non-cyclical there would be moderate pain throughout the month, no build-up of severity leading up to the period and no relief after a period.

Cyclical pain

For some ill-understood reason, cyclical breast pain is worse in women in their early to mid-thirties. Women who suffer from it say that their breasts feel heavy and tender to touch. They often find that the pain gets worse after heavy exercise, and that lifting clothes or groceries on to or from high shelves is very uncomfortable. Moreover, the breasts feel heavier and lumpier for a few days before the period.

Women with cyclical breast pain welcome their periods because, as mentioned above, for the duration of the period and for at least a week afterwards they have no pain. Then the whole process starts again. Given that the pain is so closely related to menstruation, to many it may seem that the menopause is the best cure for cyclical breast pain. Some women improve while they are pregnant or taking the contraceptive pill, but others do not.

Causes of cyclical breast pain

Why some women get cyclical breast pain and a minority does not is a mystery. It may seem that either hormones or water retention – both related to the period – must be the cause. But studies have not been able to show any clear difference in terms of hormones between sufferers and non-sufferers, and women with swollen breasts do not in fact have more water in their bodies than women who do not suffer from breast pain – they just feel that way. That is why water pills (diuretics) are of no help.

It is possible that part of the answer lies with fats in the blood. Women who suffer from cyclical breast pain may have lower essential fatty acids and higher amounts of saturated fatty acids than women who do not suffer from such pain. The essential fatty acids which are found in oily fish, some margarines and evening primrose oil may be relatively low in women with cyclical breast pain. The theory is that excess saturated fatty acids, which are found in red meat and dairy products, for instance, make the breast tissue more sensitive to the naturally circulating oestrogens.

Self-help for cyclical breast pain

Most women live with their discomfort. After all, it is not a sign of cancer, it does go away each month, and it becomes so familiar that you can almost ignore it.

Simple measures that can help while you have pain are:

- wear a soft bra at night
- avoid metal under-wired and tight bras
- avoid heavy exercise (e.g. high-impact aerobics) and repeated lifting
- if you are taking hormones, think about stopping them. Stopping the contraceptive pill, mini pill or hormone replacement therapy (HRT) helps some women, especially if the cyclical breast pain has worsened since taking them
- reduce fats in the diet, especially saturated fats, but increase carbohydrates and eat oily fish, e.g. salmon and mackerel, which are rich in unsaturated fatty acids, at least twice a week
- try taking evening primrose oil – see below

Using evening primrose oil

Evening primrose oil (EPO) is extracted from the seeds of the evening primrose plant. The active ingredient is gamolenic acid, which is an essential unsaturated ('healthy') fatty acid that the body needs to fight inflammation. As mentioned above, oily fish contain unsaturated fatty acids too, but for many EPO is a more convenient way of taking in relatively large amounts of gamolenic acid.

Women with cyclical breast pain may have low levels of unsaturated fatty acids which make the breast cells over-sensitive to the effects of female hormones. Taking EPO can make the breasts less sensitive and painful. EPO can also be useful for other conditions in which inflammation causes pain or irritation, such as eczema or rheumatoid arthritis.

Preparations of EPO like Epogam and Efamast are available on prescription or over the counter. Studies have found that an estimated 45 per cent of women who take it find it helpful. EPO is to be taken daily (the dose is 6–8 500mg capsules a day) for at least four months. It may cause mild nausea but has no other side-effects. Bear in mind that it could take as long as three months for any improvement to become apparent. It is therefore best to take it for six months and then stop. More than half of the women who find EPO helpful will experience a recurrence of the pain, but it may well be less intense. A further six-month course may help if severe pain recurs.

- techniques which are claimed to be effective include firm massaging of the side of the leg (kinesiology) or the scalp (cranial osteopathy).

Treatments for breast pain that do not work
None of the following has been found to help this problem: vitamin B6; water pills (diuretics); progestogens (hormone creams or tablets); or antibiotics.

Prescribable treatments for cyclical breast pain
Reassurance that breast cancer is not the cause of their breast pain will make it easier for the 85 per cent of women who seek medical help to put up with their discomfort without wanting further medical attention. But going to see the GP, and perhaps being referred to a hospital clinic, could have a therapeutic effect in itself. One study found that some 19 per cent of women who are given placebo treatment (an inactive tablet) reported feeling better.

Drugs used in treatment of cyclical breast pain
Four main drugs are used to treat women with cyclical breast pain. Each of them works differently.

Drug	How it works	Side-effects
Bromocriptine	Blocks the hormone prolactin which stimulates breast tissue	Nausea, constipation, headache, dizziness on standing up in 33 per cent of women
Danazol	Possibly blocks actions of the female hormone progesterone and male hormones on the breast. Usually more effective than bromocriptine	Irregular periods, weight gain, headache, nausea in 20 per cent of women

Tamoxifen	Counteracts oestrogen. Not officially licensed to use for breast pain although effective. Used in treatment of breast cancer	Must not be used during pregnancy, so contraception is vital. Hot flushes and irregular periods may occur
Goserelin	Fools the body into thinking there is enough oestrogen and progesterone in the system, so the ovaries do not produce more hormones. Induces temporary menopause	Hot flushes, dry vagina, mood changes, loss of bone density on prolonged use, i.e. symptoms of early menopause

A step-by-step guide to treatment of cyclical breast pain
In consultation with your GP:

1. Start with EPO and take it for at least four months. It has the fewest side-effects of all the prescribable treatments, but is as effective as bromocriptine and danazol.
2. If EPO has not been effective after four months' use, choose between danazol and bromocriptine. Danazol works more rapidly and may cause fewer side-effects.
3. If danazol/bromocriptine have not proved effective after six months, ask for referral to a breast clinic.

When to see a doctor
You should consult your GP if:

- breast pain is constant, not cyclical
- you feel a breast lump which is still there after a period
- breast pain is interfering with your life
- you want to try prescribable medication
- you have other symptoms such as discharge from nipple.

Constant or non-cyclical breast pain

Of the millions of women who suffer from breast pain, two-thirds have problems related to their menstrual cycle, which means the pains get worse in the two weeks before a period, and then improve. But the remaining third cannot find any pattern to their breast pain. The unluckiest have continuous pain, but most women say that it comes and goes in a totally random way.

Unlike the heavy, lumpy feeling that characterises cyclical pain, non-cyclical breast pain feels more like a burning sensation. It can seem like a draw-string around the breast being pulled tightly together. Whereas cyclical pain typically affects women in their early to mid-thirties, non-cyclical pain usually affects women a decade older.

It is worth knowing that breast cancer is very rarely a cause of this type of pain. However, examination by a doctor is a good idea to ensure that there are no breast lumps, and to determine the reason for the pain. The pain could be coming from the actual breast or from the ribs or other organs, such as the lungs, that underlie the breasts.

Possible causes of non-cyclical breast pain

Non-cyclical breast pain could be caused by an abscess or infection in the breast (most commonly caused by breast-feeding), although occasionally what seems to be breast pain may actually be caused by an ailment in a part of the body nearby.

Ribs Tenderness at the junction of bone and cartilage just to the side of where the rib joins the breastbone (costochondritis or Tieze's syndrome) or an inflammation of the muscles between the ribs (Bornholm's disease) could be experienced as breast pain.

Back Neck and upper-spine pains may be felt in the upper part of the breasts.

Lung Inflammation or infection of the lung underlying either breast could lead to pain in the breast.

Gall stones Pain may be felt in the right breast.

Treatment of non-cyclical breast pain
The treatment will depend on the underlying cause.

Cause	Treatment
Costochondritis	Resolves on its own, but anti-inflammatory drugs (e.g. ibuprofen) can be used to ease the discomfort
Bornholm's disease	Anti-inflammatory drugs (e.g. ibuprofen) are used
Diffuse breast pain	Wear a bra 24 hours a day; ibuprofen or evening primrose oil may help
Breast abscess/infection	Antibiotics can be given and the abscess(es) drained
Back pain	Osteopathy, chiropractic or physiotherapy could relieve pain. Alexander Technique helps correct posture. Wearing surgical collars is not advisable except for short-term relief of neck pain
Lung	Antibiotics are given for infections, and anti-inflammatory drugs for pleuritis (i.e. inflammation of the lining covering the lung), which may cause pain in the breast. Lung cancer is a very rare cause of pain. Not smoking is the best way to prevent lung disease
Gall stones	An operation to remove the gall bladder is the best treatment for recurrent pain and inflammation caused by gall stones

Pain while breast-feeding

The advantages of breast-feeding are very widely publicised, but the disadvantages for mothers tend to be played down. Many women suffer from pain while breast-feeding, and this could be due to one of two main causes: cracked and sore nipples, or mastitis.

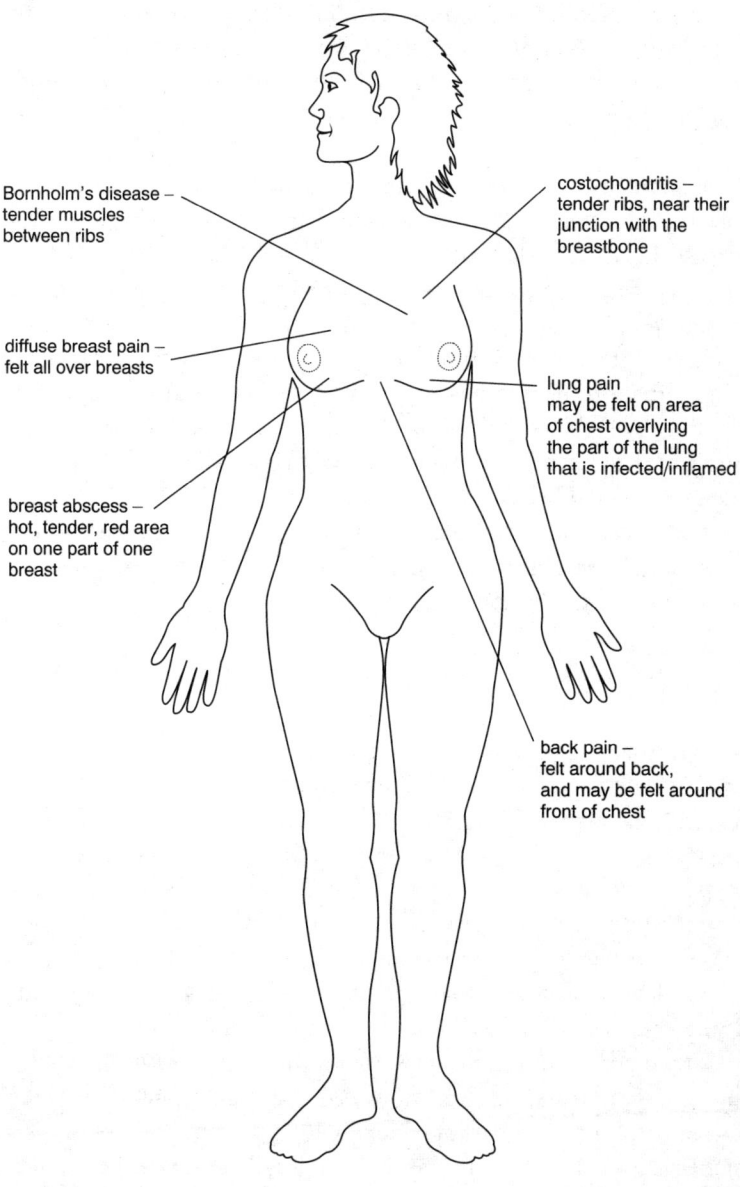

Bornholm's disease –
tender muscles
between ribs

costochondritis –
tender ribs, near their
junction with the
breastbone

diffuse breast pain –
felt all over breasts

breast abscess –
hot, tender, red area
on one part of one
breast

lung pain
may be felt on area
of chest overlying
the part of the lung
that is infected/inflamed

back pain –
felt around back,
and may be felt around
front of chest

Figure 13 Possible causes of non-cylical breast pain
Note: diagram shows approximate sites of pain

Small cracks in the nipple can heal if the baby continues to feed. The breast milk itself has healing properties, and smearing some of the milk on the nipple after a feed can help. Cold, lightly steamed cabbage leaves put inside the bra also help because they contain natural healing chemicals.

Even worse than cracked nipples is mastitis. This is the term used to describe a red, swollen, painful area that may develop in the breast during breast-feeding. Not only does the breast itself hurt, but it is often accompanied by a fluey feeling with aches, shivers and a high temperature. In its early stages, mastitis is not caused by a bacterial infection and antibiotics are neither necessary nor helpful. The initial problem is that the breast does not get fully emptied of milk at each feed. The most important way to solve mastitis and prevent it recurring is to focus on the way that the baby feeds (see *Tips for successful breast-feeding,* above).

Help with the techniques of breast-feeding is essential and can be sought from a health visitor, midwife or from trained counsellors at the National Childbirth Trust* or La Leche League.*

Lumps in the breast

It is normal to have lumpy breasts before a period. Every month the hormones progesterone and oestrogen prepare the body for possible pregnancy after ovulation, which occurs two weeks before a period is due. This makes the breasts lumpier, heavier and more sensitive. If pregnancy does not occur, the hormone levels drop again, the breasts become less sensitive and lumpy, and a period starts. Pregnancy, the contraceptive pill and HRT all keep the hormone levels relatively high so that breasts may feel constantly lumpy and sensitive.

Any woman who thinks she has a lump in her breast should see her GP. It is reassuring to know that the vast majority of lumps either turn out to be part of generally lumpy breasts and of no particular significance, or are found to be totally harmless lumps that will never become cancer.

The following are causes of a breast lump:

Localised benign lumpiness This is an area of lumpiness in the breast that contains only normal breast tissue but which, instead of lying smoothly under the skin, has become knotted and lumpy for no apparent reason. No specific treatment is necessary. This is common at all ages, but especially among women aged 25–40.

Breast cancer A cancerous lump is distinct, hard and not painful to touch. It is rare in women under 35, but becomes progressively more common after the age of 50 (see box below).

Cyst A cyst is a fluid-filled lump which occurs when a lobule gets blocked. Some women are prone to cyst formation and may develop several different breast lumps over the course of their lifetime. A cyst can be drained by inserting a needle into it and draining the fluid into a syringe. Cysts are common at all ages, but especially in women aged 35–55.

Fibroadenoma These lumps are very common, harmless and caused by an overgrowth of a breast lobule. They tend to get bigger just before a period, and may disappear after a period. They are most common in young women, accounting for 60 per cent of all breast lumps in women under 20. They can safely be left alone in women under 40, but are usually removed by surgery in women over 40 to ensure that there are no cancer cells in the lump.

Mastitis and breast abscess Infection can cause a swelling which is hot, red and painful to touch. Infections are most common during breast-feeding. Treatment is with antibiotics, and surgical drainage is occasionally necessary.

Duct ectasia The ducts that are designed to take milk from the lobules to the nipple shorten and widen as women get older. As mentioned above, by the age of 70, 40 per cent of women have very shrunken ducts. This change can pull in the nipple so that it looks like a slit, cause a cheese-like discharge from the nipple owing to a build-up of natural secretions and lead to a hard, doughy lump under the nipple if the secretions accumulate. This is a harmless condition but can be differentiated from breast cancer only by tests done in a breast clinic, e.g. mammography (see below). This is found mainly in women over 55.

Fatty lump (lipoma) This common type of benign lumps in the breast can arise at any age.

How to detect lumps

There are three main ways of detecting lumps: by finding a lump in your own breasts; through examination by a health professional, or by a partner finding a lump; and through mammography.

Breast cancer in the UK: the facts at a glance

- Breast cancer affects one in 12 women.

- It is the main cause of deaths among women from cancer.

- The UK has the highest death rate from breast cancer in the world.

- It is relatively rare among men: in 1992 there were 90 deaths from it among men compared with 15,220 deaths among women.

- Most cases of breast cancer occur in women over 50. The rate continues to rise as women get older, and breast cancer is very rare in women under 35.

- The earlier breast cancer is detected, the greater the chance of survival.

- Some 62 per cent of women in England and Wales who were diagnosed as having breast cancer in 1981 were still alive five years later (65 per cent in Scotland). This rate is starting to improve. It must be remembered that most of those affected were elderly by the time of diagnosis.

- Women with a mother, sister or daughter with breast cancer are twice as likely as the general population of women to develop breast cancer themselves. But 80–95 per cent of breast cancer arises in women who do not have an affected relative.

- Two genes (BRCA1 and BRCA2) that predispose women to breast cancer have been identified so far.

- The NHS Breast Screening Programme introduced in 1988 offers a three-yearly mammogram to all women aged 50 or over and aims to reduce the death rate in the screened population by 25 per cent by the year 2000. Women aged between 50 and 64 are routinely invited; those aged above 64 are encouraged to make their own appointments.

- Breast awareness (see below), whereby women consciously discover what is normal for their own breasts, is the best way of detecting a lump apart from mammography.

Checking breasts for lumps

The point of checking breasts is to detect breast cancer at an early stage, while the lump is still small and before the cancer has a chance to spread. Fear of finding a lump prevents many women from examining their own breasts regularly. This is a great pity as there is no one better able to detect a change in the appearance or feel of a breast than the woman herself.

Plan for breast awareness

The NHS Breast Screening Programme and Cancer Research Campaign have produced a five-point plan to help women check for normality and report any changes without delay:

1. Know what is normal *for you*
2. Look and feel
3. Know what changes to look for
4. Report any changes *without* delay
5. Attend for breast screening if you are aged 50 or over.

The changes they advise women to look out for are:

- appearance – any change in the outline or shape of the breast, especially those caused by arm movements, or by lifting the breasts; any puckering or dimpling of the skin
- feelings – discomfort or pain in one breast that is different from normal, particularly if new and persistent
- lumps – any lumps, thickening or bumpy areas in one breast or armpit which seem to be different from the same part of the other breast and armpit: this is very important if new
- nipple change – nipple discharge that is new and not milky; bleeding or moist reddish areas which do not heal easily; any change in nipple position (pulled in or pointing differently); a rash on or around the nipple.

An awareness of what your own breasts look and feel like (see above) is more important than a rigid way of examining them. But some women like to do it in a systematic way. The following is one method:

1. Check your breasts in the week after a period, because this is when they are least lumpy, or at a regular day of the month if you no longer have periods.
2. Stand in front of a mirror in good light, stripped to the waist. Look at your breasts with your arms by your sides, raised above your head and with your hands on your hips. Look out for dimpling of the skin or a change in outline of the breast which might mean an underlying lump.
3. Lie down with your right arm behind your head. Feel your right breast with the flat of your left hand, then *vice versa*. Reach into the armpit, as the breast tissue reaches into the armpit. Feel the entire breast including the nipple, with your hand held flat. If you knead the breast like dough, you will feel lumps that are not true lumps, and will frighten yourself unnecessarily. Lumps are fairly easy to feel as they have a distinct border, like feeling an egg buried in soft dough.
4. If you feel a lump, do not panic. Make an appointment to see your GP. If your breasts are generally lumpy on both sides, with no specific lump, your GP will be able to reassure you. If there is a specific lump, or the lumpiness is one-sided, your GP will refer you to a hospital breast clinic, where you will be seen by a surgeon.

Examination by a health professional

It is quite reasonable to ask a GP or practice nurse to do a breast check whenever you attend the surgery for family planning, HRT or general health checks. Sporadic examinations by health professionals are, however, no substitute for self-awareness and mammography screening.

Mammography, its advantages and disadvantages

Mammography, which is an X-ray of the breasts, is the best way of screening women to detect early breast cancer.

Early detection Cancers which are detected by mammography tend to be smaller and less advanced than cancers which show themselves as a lump. This makes treatment more effective and less traumatic.

Fewer deaths from breast cancer In Sweden, which has a very well-organised national breast cancer screening programme, there has been a decline (of 29 per cent in women over 50, and 13 per cent in women under 50) in the number of women who were screened for 12 years or more dying of breast cancer.

British screening programme In the UK, the national screening programme began in 1988. All women aged 50–64 are invited for a mammogram every three years. The reason why women under 50 are not offered routine screening mammograms in the UK is that their breast tissue is denser and therefore mammograms are not accurate at detecting cancer in its early stages. There is, as yet, no reliable way of screening women under 50. They may be offered mammography if they are at increased risk of breast cancer (see below) or if a lump is found. A trial is under way to discover what benefit, if any, may be gained by screening women from the age of 40. Women over 64 can request their own appointments for screening but do not receive automatic invitations. Recent studies (1998) suggest that mammography offered from ages 50 to 69, every two years, would be beneficial.

Psychological effects of mammography Women who are called to have a mammogram do not seem to get particularly anxious about the test. This might be because breast cancer is such a worry to women anyway that being called for screening is more reassuring than frightening. Women who are called back for further tests obviously do feel worried, but as soon as they are reassured that all is well, they feel better.

However, there are some disadvantages of mammography.

Risks of mammography Radiation can itself induce cancers. But the radiation from a mammogram is very small and the increased risk of developing cancer from the mammogram is negligible compared to the chances of getting breast cancer naturally.

Unnecessary investigations and stress A mammogram sometimes suggests an abnormality which cannot be felt. About two-thirds of these abnormalities are shown by a second mammogram or an ultrasound scan to be harmless. If the second mammogram or ultrasound scan is not reassuring, the surgeon can guide a needle into the abnormal area by viewing it on an X-ray screen, retrieve a tiny sample of the abnormal area and send it for microscopic examination to see if cancer cells are present. This is called fine needle aspiration (see below).

Discomfort of the mammogram Each breast in turn has to be squashed fairly flat between two plates to get a good view and to reduce radiation. This is very uncomfortable for some women, especially those with tender breasts. It is, however, only temporary discomfort and will not damage the breast in any way.

What happens when a lump is found or suspected

The important things to remember are not to panic – most lumps are not cancer – and to see your GP within a week. You will probably be referred to a breast clinic for proper diagnosis.

What happens at a breast clinic

If you have been referred to a breast clinic you will almost certainly be apprehensive, but knowing what to expect at the clinic can help. Clinics are based in hospitals and are run by surgeons who specialise in breast problems.

The first stage of the consultation will be a series of questions. In some clinics, these may be in the form of a questionnaire which you can fill in while waiting to be seen. Relevant questions include details of any previous breast lumps, and the outcome; age of first menstruation; number and dates of pregnancies if any; years of use of oral contraceptive pill and/or HRT; other medication; and whether there is any history of breast cancer in the family.

During the interview with the doctor, other questions will be asked such as when the lump first appeared and how quickly it has grown. Harmless breast cysts, for example, may appear overnight, whereas breast cancers usually grow more slowly.

The doctor will examine your breasts in a method similar to the one described above for self-examination. He or she will also measure any lump with a pair of callipers and will feel armpits and the area above the collarbones for lymph glands which may be enlarged if the lump is cancerous. However, enlarged glands do not necessarily mean bad news – in the armpits this could just as easily be the result of a minor infection from shaving under the arms.

The lump may well have disappeared by the time you are seen in the clinic or you may discover that it is just part of a generalised lumpiness and that there is nothing to worry about. Reassurance is very often the outcome of that much-dreaded trip to the breast clinic.

If, following the clinical examination, a breast lump is confirmed at the clinic, the doctor will suggest an ultrasound scan (if you are under 35) or a mammogram (if you are over 35), and cytology.

Ultrasound scan This is a painless method which uses high-frequency sound waves. A clear gel is smeared on to your breasts and a hand-held instrument glides over them. High-frequency sound waves are emitted by the instrument which 'bounce' off the inner structures of the breast. The operator can tell from the picture which appears on the screen whether there are no lumps, fluid-filled cysts or solid lumps.

Mammogram As described above, mammography can be uncomfortable, but it is a better way of detecting abnormalities in women over 35, whose breasts are less dense than those of younger women.

Cytology or fine needle aspiration This is the study of cells in a small sample of the lump. The sample is removed with a needle and syringe: the needle is put in to the lump, cells are sucked into the syringe and then spread on to a glass slide. The cells are examined under a microscope to establish whether they are cancerous. Theoretically, a report can be available within 30 minutes.

The combination of these three steps – the clinical examination, the scan or mammogram, and cytology – gives an accurate idea of whether a lump is cancerous or not. A survey done in 1996 of 1,511 women in the UK with breast cancer showed that the use of these three steps led to 99.8 per cent of the lumps being diagnosed correctly. The three steps together are rarely wrong but no test is ever wholly infallible. Two in every 1,000 women who are told their lump is cancerous will be unnecessarily alarmed. Cells in a lump can sometimes look abnormal under the microscope but turn out, when it is removed during an operation, to be a harmless fibroadenoma.

Removal of a breast lump

The breast lump does not have to be removed if examination, mammogram or ultrasound scan, and cytology are all normal. However, some breast clinics advise all women over 40 who have a painful lump to have it removed as it is unlikely to disappear. If the cytology suggests that there are cancerous cells in the lump, but examination and mammogram or ultrasound scan seem normal, removal of the lump is advised in order to achieve a clear diagnosis. The same happens if the cytology is normal but the mammogram looks suspicious. The removal of a lump is usually carried out under general anaesthetic in a short operation, often as a day-case.

Breast surgeons will often agree to remove a lump if the woman is desperate to have it done. However, as long as the investigations all suggest that the lump is harmless, it can be left alone.

Hope for the future

A test has recently been developed to check whether benign-feeling breast lumps are cancerous. In the new technique sensors are placed over the breast lump and the electrical changes at the skin's surface on normal skin and over the lump are measured. This technique may save the need for half the biopsies performed on breast lumps.

Women at increased risk of breast cancer

Known risk factors account for only about 40 per cent of cases of breast cancer. The majority of cases arise in women who are not known to have been at extra risk.

Women who are at increased risk of breast cancer (see below) should ask their GPs to refer them to a breast clinic which can offer specialised screening and counselling. They should also ask for regular screening. Mammograms should be offered to women with a family history of breast cancer, starting from when they are 5–10 years younger than when their relative developed the disease. As mentioned earlier, mammograms are not routinely offered until the age of 50, so women would need to persuade their GPs to refer them.

There is no proven way of preventing breast cancer in high-risk women. Trials involving different variables are under way but results will not be available until at least 2006. A very few women opt to have both breasts and ovaries removed while they are younger than their family members who got breast cancer were when they developed the disease. This is obviously an extreme option.

Risk factor	Chance of developing breast cancer
No increased risk	One in 12 women in the UK
Previous benign lumps whose cells show a pre-cancerous abnormality called atypical hyperplasia	One in ten women within 20 years

| Atypical hyperplasia and mother, daughter or sister with breast cancer | One in five to one in three will get breast cancer within 20 years |
| Carries the cancer gene which causes multiple cases of breast and other cancers in one family | Eight in ten will get breast cancer during lifetime |

Factors that marginally increase the risk of breast cancer

The contraceptive pill causes a small increase in breast cancer risk in women who are taking it. The risk decreases gradually once a woman stops taking it; ten years after stopping it there is no increased risk compared with non-pill-users. The number of years of pill use does not appear to affect the risk – what matters is the age at which a woman last takes the pill. Women who stop taking it at the age of 20 have a much lower risk than those who take it up to the age of 45. HRT appears to cause no increased risk of breast cancer if used for less than five years. After five years, the risk of breast cancer rises by 50 per cent, with older women being at even greater risk. This needs to be balanced against the lower death rate from heart disease among women on HRT. Not having children or having a first child after the age of 35, not breast-feeding, and eating a high-fat, low-fibre diet are all said to raise the risk of breast cancer, but not to a significant degree. Smoking for 30 years or longer may increase the risk of breast cancer.

Cancerous lumps in the breast

The news that a lump is cancerous is shocking, frightening and panic-inducing. However, it has been found that nearly 80 per cent of breast cancer patients want to take an active role in decisions about treatment. Younger, better-educated women are the most willing to be involved and the least likely to be passive about treatment options. Participating in the decisions requires up-to-date, easy-to-assimilate information and a good and trusting relationship with the doctor. It is every woman's prerogative to be fully informed about the options facing her.

Further tests to determine whether the breast cancer is at an early or advanced stage will be carried out before the treatment options can be discussed. The size of the lump, involvement of lymph glands and spread to other organs determine the severity of the cancer. Blood tests to check the liver and a chest X-ray to check the lungs will be done to ensure that the cancer has not spread to other organs. Spread is rare if the lump is small, but bone and liver scans are often requested if the lump is large, because spread is then more likely.

Treatment of breast cancer

When a woman develops breast cancer, the treatment for it has two main objectives. One is to remove the lump by lumpectomy or mastectomy (see below), and the other is to control any spread of the disease.

Lumpectomy vs mastectomy

Contrary to what many women think, in a high proportion of patients with breast cancer the breast does not have to be removed. An operation to remove just the lump (lumpectomy) or the quarter of the breast which the lump is in, followed by a course of radiotherapy to the whole breast, may give as good a result as removing the whole breast (mastectomy).

	Lumpectomy	**Mastectomy**
Time in hospital	1–2 days	4–5 days
Time taken for wound to heal	1 week	Slightly longer than 1 week
Main advantages	Smaller scar	Less worry because there is no remaining breast tissue
Main disadvantages	More anxiety that lump may recur; course of radiotherapy more likely than after mastectomy	Fear of loss of femininity; more major operation

As has been pointed out, mastectomy is hardly ever the only option. However, it may be advised if the lump is more than 4 cm across, especially if the breast is fairly small and removing a large lump will look worse than mastectomy, which allows use of a prosthesis or implant (see below). Younger women are more prone to cancer which spreads into the ducts within the breast tissue. This type of cancer is more likely to recur, and removing the whole breast may improve the outlook. If either examination or the mammogram shows more than one area of cancer within the breast, mastectomy will be advised.

Some women prefer the idea of having the whole breast removed once cancer has been detected. They feel more confident that it will not recur after mastectomy, even though studies have shown that there is no real difference between mastectomy and lumpectomy followed by radiotherapy.

The operation

The date of the operation for either a lumpectomy or a mastectomy may be fixed so that it falls in the second half of the menstrual cycle, i.e. in the two weeks before the next period if a woman still has periods. The long-term outlook seems to be better if this is done.

The operation will usually include the surgeon taking samples of the lymph nodes in the armpit (axillary nodes). If cancer is found in these nodes, the chances are that further treatment to mop up cancerous cells will be offered, in the form of cancer-killing drugs (chemotherapy, see below).

Recovering from the operation

Removing a lump or even an entire breast is a relatively straightforward operation and physical recovery is usually rapid and free of complications.

A lumpectomy is a simpler and quicker operation, but the psychological consequences are just as serious as after mastectomy. In fact, more women report feeling depressed and anxious after lumpectomy than after mastectomy. After mastectomy, the patient's main preoccupations are, understandably, to do with how losing the breast will affect her femininity and how her partner and friends and family will react. But after lumpectomy, women worry about whether the cancer will recur, and some check their breasts constantly to ensure that they do not miss any new lump.

It is unrealistic to expect to be able to shrug off the enormous shock that the diagnosis of having breast cancer will cause. After the upheaval caused by the diagnosis, operation and immediate post-operative recovery, the woman has to deal with all her fears and uncertainties herself, even if she has a very supportive family.

Information about the future is vital. It is very hard to assimilate all the details that the surgeon imparts at your bedside when you are still fuddled after the operation. Moreover, the follow-up out-patient appointment may be hurried and not conducive to asking the necessary questions.

To get the most out of consultations with hospital surgeons:

- make a list of questions to ask at the outpatient appointment
- ask to see the consultant dealing with you, rather than a more junior member of staff
- take a close friend or partner with you. Do not be afraid of tak-ing notes if you want to refer back in the comfort of your own home to things said at the hospital
- ask to see a breast counsellor if there is one, who may have more time to talk
- see your GP, who may be able to clarify what the hospital doc-tors have said
- contact the Breast Care and Mastectomy Association* or BACUP,* which are excellent self-help groups with good, up-to-date information.

Treatment after the operation

The main forms of post-operative treatment are radiotherapy and chemotherapy.

Radiotherapy uses X-rays to destroy abnormal cells. After the removal of a breast cancer lump, a course of radiotherapy to the whole breast and armpit helps to prevent recurrence of lumps in that breast. It does not affect long-term survival, which is depen-dent on the type and size of the cancer, and whether the disease has spread to other organs, rather than on the treatment. Radiotherapy is not necessary after mastectomy if the glands in the armpit have been removed. It used to cause irritation to the skin and damage to the underlying lung in some women, but side-effects are much rarer with modern, low-dose radiation.

Chemotherapy The other treatment, chemotherapy, is often not necessary if the outlook is thought to be very good. Lumpectomy and radiotherapy are sufficient treatment if the surgeons think that the risk of the cancer recurring is very low. But drugs to kill cancerous cells are worthwhile if there is a higher chance of recurrence: for instance, if there has been cancer in the nodes in the armpit.

Women who have not reached the menopause are likely to live longer if treated with a combination of chemotherapy drugs or by switching off female hormone production by destroying the ovaries. The latter can be done by treatment with drugs, radiotherapy or an operation to remove the ovaries.

Women who have passed the menopause fare best when given the drug tamoxifen, sometimes with other chemotherapy drugs as well. Women over 70 are usually offered tamoxifen on its own. Tamoxifen has few side-effects although it can cause hot flushes, vaginal bleeding and nausea.

Results of the largest-ever collection of data on a cancer drug, done in May 1998, suggest that tamoxifen should now be given to any woman with breast cancer – regardless of age – who has had surgery for a hormone-dependent cancer. Overall, tamoxifen is said to do 30 times more good than harm. Although some deaths result from the side-effects of the drug (chiefly from pulmonary embolus and womb cancer), they are outweighed by the reduction in death rates and recurrences of breast cancer. However, other studies have shown that tamoxifen may not be beneficial in preventing cancer in women who are at increased risk because of their family history but who have never had breast cancer themselves.

Breast reconstruction

Losing a breast is always difficult to come to terms with. But if the breast is reconstructed at the same time as or soon after the mastectomy, the psychological impact can be minimised. An implant can be put under the muscles of the chest wall. There have been some scares about the safety of silicone-filled implants, although silicone remains the best material currently available. Before the final implant is inserted, the tissue and muscles are often stretched by gradual inflation of a tissue expander. Plastic surgery may be required to fashion a larger breast. Sometimes, the normal breast has to be made smaller to match the reconstructed breast. Your surgeon will discuss with you the relative pros and cons of this breast reconstruction in your particular case. See Chapter 15 for more details.

Breast cancer – the outlook

One in 12 women in the UK will get breast cancer. Many of these women will die of some totally unconnected cause, such as a heart attack or stroke, but some will die prematurely because of their cancer. The outlook for women with breast cancer has started to improve at last, especially among younger women. This is very encouraging news after many years of little improvement in the statistics.

Women who have the odds in their favour (i.e. older women or those with smaller cancers which have not spread to other organs) will not die of their breast cancer. After initial treatment they can expect not to be troubled by breast cancer again. Those who have the odds stacked against them (i.e. younger women or those with bigger and more virulent tumours) stand only a 13 per cent chance of being alive 15 years after the diagnosis is made. Overall, 62 per cent of women diagnosed with breast cancer in England in 1981 were alive five years later. Given that many of the women were elderly anyway, this is not as bleak a picture as one might expect.

The more advanced the cancer is when detected, the worse the outlook will be. Tumours which are big, have spread to lymph nodes in the armpits and whose cells no longer resemble normal cells at all are the worst type. Although breast cancer is rare in women under 35, if they do get it they tend to fare badly. If the cancer has spread to other organs such as bones and liver, it is far more difficult to control. The search for other ways of predicting which women with breast cancer are likely to fare well and which have a more aggressive type of the disease is still continuing.

Research is focusing a great deal on the role of abnormal genes which lead to breast cancer running in some families. However, it must be remembered that a genetic tendency probably accounts for fewer than 20 per cent of all cases of breast cancer.

Breast cancer can recur. Having had breast cancer once, a woman has a fivefold chance of developing it again. Despite the fact that screening and treatment are improving all the time, there is no room for complacency about breast cancer – the UK has the highest death rate from the disease in the world. But developments in identifying the genes that predispose women to breast cancer and improvements in early detection and treatment mean that we should see dramatic improvements in the next ten or so years.

Chapter 11

Gynaecology

Women have two ovaries, one on either side of the abdomen around the level of the hip bones. A tube called the fallopian tube runs into the upper part of the uterus (womb) and collects eggs from the ovaries. The bottom end of the uterus opens into the cervix (the neck of the womb), which is connected to the vagina. The urethra, which drains urine from the bladder, also opens into the vulva so that urine can be passed out of the body.

Every month from puberty to the menopause, one of the ovaries releases an egg from its vast store, held from the day a girl is born. The egg travels along the fallopian tube. If it is fertilised by a sperm in the tube, the fertilised egg embeds in the wall of the uterus and a pregnancy starts to develop. If the egg is not fertilised by a sperm, the lining of the womb which has been plumped up by hormones is shed, and a period results two weeks after the egg was released by the ovary. The menstrual cycle is controlled by hormones (FSH and LH) which are released by the brain and which stimulate the ovaries to produce the female sex hormones, oestrogen and progesterone. The levels of these hormones in the bloodstream determine when the ovary releases an egg, and prepare the lining of the uterus for possible pregnancy each month. The fall in the hormone progesterone which occurs if the egg is not fertilised causes a period. The contraceptive pill works by giving a small regular dose of the two hormones oestrogen and progestogen (a synthetic progesterone), so that the body does not produce its own hormones. Without the natural rises and falls in hormones, the ovaries do not release an egg, and pregnancy cannot occur. At the menopause, women's ovaries stop working and no longer produce oestrogen or release a monthly egg, pregnancy cannot occur naturally, and periods stop. The loss of oestrogen affects some women more than others, and may cause a variety of symptoms (see Chapter 14). Hormone replacement therapy (HRT) replaces the naturally occurring oestrogen.

A woman's external genitals (the parts you can see) consist of the hair-covered pubis, the vagina which is the opening or 'front passage', and the clitoris which lies just above the urethra and is the woman's equivalent of a penis. The clitoris becomes erect when a woman is sexually aroused and is very erotically sensitive. Clitoral stimulation contributes to most women's orgasms. On either side of the vagina are two sets of 'lips' called the labia. The labia and clitoris are known as the vulva. The skin between the vagina and the anus is called the perineum, and it is this area that may tear or be cut during childbirth, to allow the baby to come out.

Problems relating to the reproductive system

Many women suffer repeated problems with their reproductive system. A lucky minority sail through periods, pregnancy, childbirth and the menopause with very few problems. There is no consistent reason why some women seem to suffer more than others. Any gynaecological problem can cause distress and anxiety, affect relationships and undermine a woman's self-image and femininity.

This chapter covers the most common gynaecological problems: period problems, vaginal bleeding, gynaecological cancers, pelvic pain, painful intercourse, vaginal discharge, lumps, bumps and spots in and around the vagina, and itchy vulva and vagina.

Periods

The average age for starting periods is 13, and this is getting younger as girls are heavier at a younger age. The average age for stopping periods (the menopause) is around 50. Periods are the bane of many women's lives and a comforting thought for those who have troublesome periods is that women nowadays can expect to live for more years without periods than with them, whereas at the turn of the century most women died before they even got to the menopause.

Every month, or thereabouts, the ovaries produce an egg. Hormones prepare the womb by plumping up its lining and

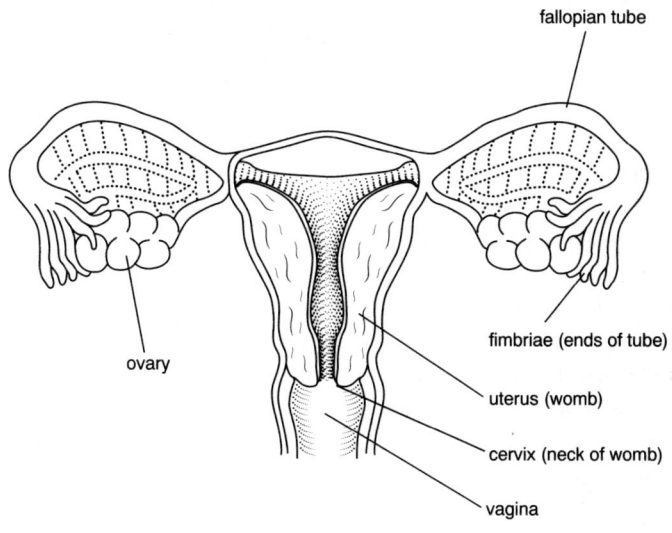

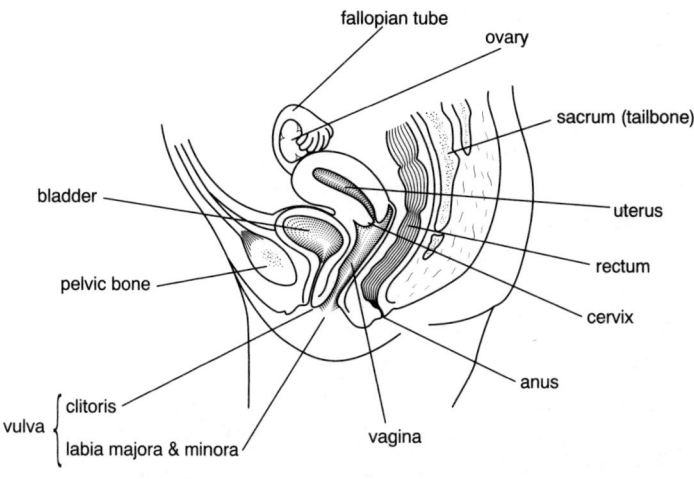

Figure 14 Female reproductive system

increasing its blood supply, in case the egg is fertilised by sperm and pregnancy occurs. If pregnancy does not occur, the egg, lining of the womb and excess blood are all shed, and come out of the vagina as a period. The hormonal fluctuations which occur during the menstrual cycle are responsible for the mood changes, bloating and breast tenderness which affect many women before a period.

Painful periods (dysmenorrhoea)

Period pains usually start just as the period is starting, and feel like an ache in the lower abdomen, back and legs. Pelvic congestion, due to a build-up of blood in the veins of the pelvis, is probably to blame for this aching, which could pass in a few hours or last a couple of days. Cramp-like pains which come in spasms may last for a couple of hours and be associated with nausea and even vomiting. These are probably due to the effect of chemicals called prostaglandins which make the blood vessels in the womb squeeze shut. Period pains are usually worst for girls in the two years after they start having periods. Most women find that their periods tend to improve, especially after the birth of their first child, although during the menopause they may become painful again.

Endometriosis is a condition in which cells from the lining of the womb (the endometrium) are deposited on other organs, such as the ovaries. The endometrium outside the womb becomes plumped up and full of blood, just like the endometrium in the womb. This causes inflammation and cysts, and bands of tissue get stuck together (adhesions) which can cause fertility problems. Period pains may become much more severe. The only way to diagnose the condition with any certainty is by laparoscopy. This involves a gynaecologist inserting a telescope (a laparoscope) into the abdomen, usually under general anaesthetic, to have a look at the ovaries and other organs.

Self-help for painful periods

- Try doing aerobic exercise, e.g. swimming, cycling, walking fast and jogging, to reduce the pain.
- Have a warm bath or use a hot-water bottle while the cramps are bad.

- Take mefenamic acid (Ponstan), aspirin or ibuprofen preparations – all of which are available over the counter and can block the prostaglandins which are partly responsible for the cramp-like pains.

When to see a doctor
It is important to see your doctor if you have painful periods which seem to be getting worse – there is a possibility that you may have endometriosis. You should also get help from your GP if you have heavy, painful periods which are interfering with your lifestyle – your job or exams, for example. If you feel particularly tired and you are pale and short of breath, you could be anaemic as a result of heavy periods.

Treatment for painful periods
Acupuncture and cranial osteopathy (manipulation of the skull by an osteopath) may help period pains. Various relaxation therapies may also make the pains more bearable. Doctors may suggest stronger painkillers or hormones, including the contraceptive pill. If endometriosis is the problem, drugs which cause a temporary menopause and 'switch off' the ovaries may be given (e.g. buserelin) or hormone treatment (e.g. danazol) may be advised. By stopping the body's natural hormone cycles for a while, the inflamed tissues can recover. Endometriosis may recur after treatment, but often does not. Surgery to release adhesions and remove cysts caused by endometriosis is occasionally necessary, especially if they are interfering with fertility. Hospital investigation may be necessary for tests in suspected cases of endometriosis.

Premenstrual syndrome

Premenstrual syndrome (PMS, one element of which is premenstrual tension, PMT) is a common problem which may severely affect a woman's life. It is important to be certain that tension is related to periods, rather than a result of depression that may be affecting the woman throughout the month. Keeping a symptom diary is the best way of clarifying this. There are several ways of relieving PMS, which are discussed in Chapter 2.

Heavy periods (menorrhagia)

Heavy periods are those which make a woman anaemic, and which involve losing clots or flooding despite tampons and pads. It is worth seeing a doctor if these things happen, or if your periods seem to be getting heavier. There may not always be a specific cause, but some of the possible causes are:

- hormone imbalance. This can be corrected with the contraceptive pill or progestogens
- a coil (intrauterine contraceptive device or IUCD). This causes heavier and more painful periods. A new coil which releases a small amount of progestogen (Mirena) may be preferable as it produces lighter and less painful periods (see Chapter 12)
- under-active thyroid which causes weight gain, lethargy and dry skin as well as heavy periods (see Chapter 8). This can be treated with thyroid supplements
- the onset of the menopause (see Chapter 14)
- fibroids. These are non-cancerous lumps which develop in the muscle layer of the womb. If the lumps stick out of the womb they can cause pain during intercourse and a swollen abdomen. If the lumps project into the cavity of the womb, they can cause heavy and painful periods. Fibroids tend to shrink after the menopause. If they are causing excessive problems, small ones can be easily removed using a cutting instrument on the end of a 'telescope' (a resectoscope) inserted through the vagina. Larger fibroids can be cut out (a procedure called a myomectomy). Occasionally women are advised to have the entire womb removed (a hysterectomy)
- endometriosis (see above)
- pelvic infections. These cause fever, pain during intercourse, discharge and heavy periods (see below).

Treatment for heavy periods

If the blood loss is so heavy that you are anaemic, you will need iron supplements. Medical treatments, such as hormones, or drugs which affect the 'efficiency' of the endometrium in stopping bleeding, such as tranexamic acid, can be effective especially in younger women. If this is not successful, surgery is an option and you may be offered a trans-cervical resection of the endometrium (TCRE). This is an alternative to hysterectomy. Hormone treatment is given first to thin out the womb lining prior to the operation. A telescope (hysteroscope) is inserted into the womb via the vagina, under a general anaesthetic. The lining of the womb (the endometrium) is then destroyed using a heated cutting instrument or laser. The advantages over hysterectomy are less post-operative pain, a shorter hospital stay, quicker recovery, and no scar. The disadvantages are that, in unskilled hands, hysteroscopy may cause complications whereas gynaecologists have ample experience of carrying out hysterectomies. Your periods may not stop and as pregnancy can be dangerous after this procedure, it must be prevented – usually by sterilisation. It is also possible that the original problem of heavy periods may recur. Up to a quarter of women who have TCRE need to have it done again, and one-sixth end up opting for a hysterectomy. Many women are pleased with the results of the TCRE initially, but long-term satisfaction is not as high as with a hysterectomy. Nevertheless, women may prefer to try a procedure which is far less drastic than a hysterectomy, knowing they can always have the hysterectomy at a later date if the TCRE fails.

A hysterectomy – the complete removal of the womb – is the only operation that will guarantee complete absence of periods and certain contraception. It is the only possible operation if there is cancer of the womb (endometrial cancer). It is also the best option for severe prolapse (see below). It can be combined with removal of the ovaries if they are diseased, as in severe endometriosis (see above), or if there is a family history of ovarian cancer. There are various ways of doing a hysterectomy. In most cases, the cervix is removed along with the womb, so that there is no chance of developing cancer of the cervix in the future. The cervix may be left if a woman feels that its removal may interfere with her sex life, although most women who have it removed do not notice a great change in their enjoyment of sex. When a hysterectomy is performed because of cancer, the top part of the vagina, the tissue alongside the womb and some lymph glands are removed at the same time in a more extensive operation. The operation can be done by making an incision across the lower part of the abdomen which leaves a scar just below the bikini line, through the vagina, or through a laparoscope (a telescope inserted into the abdomen). This latter method, also known as keyhole surgery, can be technically tricky for the gynaecologist and should be performed only if he or she has extensive experience of this relatively new technique. Always ask the gynaecologist about his or her experience before agreeing to this, or any other, operation. Recovery time after a hysterectomy is variable, depending on your general level of fitness, the skill of the gynaecologist, the extent of the operation, the method used (recovery is quickest after keyhole surgery and slowest after abdominal surgery), and whether any complications such as infection set in. Most women find that it takes around six weeks for them to feel that they are back to normal. A gradual return to normal activity is best, such as taking a daily walk for a few days after the operation and building up from an initial five minutes to a brisk half-hour after three weeks or so. After the wound has healed, swimming is an excellent way to regain strength and fitness.

Absent periods (amenorrhoea)

Periods are normally irregular and infrequent for the first couple of years after they start and then, later, towards the menopause. Periods stop during pregnancy and may not restart for three to six months, or longer if you are breast-feeding. In between times, however, many things can make you skip a period or several in a row. These include stress, travel and change of job; weight gain, weight loss, excessive dieting or excessive exercise; certain contraceptives, e.g. depo-provera, the three-monthly progestogen injection; polycystic ovaries (see below); medical conditions such as diabetes, over-active thyroid or colitis (inflammation of the bowel); and hormone imbalance, e.g. over-production of the hormone prolactin, which can also make your breasts produce milk even if you have not had a baby.

If you have never had a period at all, that is a different matter. Girls normally start menstruating by the age of 16. Breast development, which is the first sign of puberty in girls, starts a year or two earlier. Girls who have not started to develop breasts by the age of 14, or whose periods have not started within two years of breast growth, should see their GP. The most common reason for this is that the girl is going into puberty rather late, just as some girls start their periods rather early. Girls who weigh below 47kg (103lb) may not start their periods until their weight increases, as puberty is weight-dependent. Other, less likely, causes include hormonal problems, a chromosome disorder which means the ovaries are not fully developed or are absent, or – very rarely – tumours of the ovaries.

When to see a doctor

If your periods have stopped – or never started – and you have had sexual intercourse, it is wise to do a pregnancy test, as pregnancy is by far the most common reason for missing periods. There is no urgent need to seek medical help unless you are trying to get pregnant, or you are unwell and may have an underlying illness. However, it is a good idea to see a doctor if your periods are very irregular or stop altogether for more than six months.

You should also see your GP if you have noticed a recent increase in facial hair, or if your breasts are producing milk. Girls older than 16 who have not started their periods should see a GP, as should girls who have not started their periods despite having developed breasts more than two years earlier.

Tests and treatment for absent periods

Your GP will perform a general examination and a vaginal examination, and arrange for an ultrasound scan and blood tests. Alternatively he or she might arrange for you to see a gynaecologist. Treatment obviously depends on the underlying cause. Often no treatment is necessary, and the periods restart on their own. The drug clomiphene may be prescribed to 'kick-start' the ovaries back into ovulating. HRT or the contraceptive pill can correct hormone imbalance in a woman who does not want to get pregnant.

Frequent periods

Most women have a period around once every 28 days, from puberty until the menopause. Some women have a naturally shorter or longer cycle. Towards the menopause, the cycle may change, and for a few years women may have a period every three weeks instead of every four. If there is any possibility that the bleeding may be abnormal, it is best to see a doctor. Erratic vaginal bleeding, bleeding after intercourse and irregular periods should always be taken seriously. Do not automatically assume they are part of the menopause or due to the contraceptive pill. In most cases, there will not be any particular underlying problem. A few simple tests can ensure that the bleeding is not due to cancer of the cervix or womb (see below).

Bleeding between periods

Vaginal bleeding between periods, after intercourse or after the menopause is very common, and usually harmless. But it is very important to get medical advice because occasionally the bleeding can be a sign of a potentially dangerous but treatable condition like cancer of the cervix or endometrium (womb lining).

Breakthrough bleeding This is bleeding that occurs while you are on the contraceptive pill or HRT. It is completely harmless. Changing to a different formulation may help, but it is important that other possible causes of bleeding are excluded.

Hormone imbalance The most common cause of abnormal vaginal bleeding is a hormonal imbalance. But it is important to see a doctor and have any necessary investigations to rule out the more serious conditions below before assuming that hormonal imbalance is to blame. Hormones in the form of the contraceptive pill, HRT or progestogens can usually correct any imbalance.

Polyps These are small fleshy outgrowths from the cervix or endometrium, and they may cause bleeding after intercourse. They can be easily removed by a gynaecologist.

Cervical erosion This is not really erosion at all, but the name given to a natural process whereby the surface of the cervix changes. The cervix has tough cells which line the surface in contact with the vagina, and delicate cells which line its inner surface. The hormones of pregnancy and the contraceptive pill may lead to a harmless overgrowth of these delicate cells. This is called an erosion and it bleeds easily if it is irritated by a smear test, intercourse or tampons. An erosion usually clears up on its own once the pregnancy ends or the pill is stopped. If troublesome, it can be easily and painlessly treated with cautery or 'cold coagulation' treament.

Pelvic inflammatory disease (PID) PID comprises sexually transmitted infections such as chlamydia, which can cause fever, pain on intercourse, lower abdominal pain, vaginal discharge and vaginal bleeding. It is important to get medical advice quickly if you have these symptoms, to get an accurate diagnosis and correct antibiotic treatment. PID can cause infertility if it is left untreated as it can spread to the fallopian tubes and cause damage.

Miscarriage or ectopic pregnancy Unexpected vaginal bleeding and lower abdominal pain may be due to a pregnancy in a fallopian tube (an ectopic pregnancy) or a miscarriage. In both cases, the previous period will have been missed. If you are in any doubt, do a pregnancy test and seek medical help (see below and in Chapter 13).

Cervical cancer Abnormal vaginal bleeding may be a sign of cancer of the cervix. It is thought to be more common among women who have the wart virus (although not necessarily warts), those who start to have sex at an early age, and those who smoke. Having regular (minimum three-yearly) smear tests from the age of 20 helps to identify early changes that may eventually lead to cancer unless they are treated. Having a smear, waiting for the result and then being told that the result is abnormal can be very stressful, but the overall aim is to prevent cancer, so the stress is worth putting up with. Smears may be reported as 'inadequate', which means that the person taking the smear did not manage to get enough cells on the slide to allow a proper report. If that happens, you will be invited to have another smear. Having a smear when you are in mid-cycle helps to ensure that the smear is adequate. Smears may be reported as showing 'inflammation or severe inflammatory changes' which may mean an infection is present. Smears may show 'dyskaryosis', which can be mild, moderate or severe. These changes may never develop into cancer if they are left untreated, but there is a small chance that they will progress to localised cancer (carcinoma in situ) or to more extensive cancer. Because of this, treatment – usually laser treatment of the abnormal area – is advised if the abnormality is confirmed after further examination with a colposcope. A colposcope is a piece of equipment that allows the gynaecologist to look at a magnified view of the cervix.

In recent years there have been several high-profile cases of hospitals needing to recall women for repeat smears after errors in the interpretation of smears have come to light. Tragically, in a few cases, this has meant that women have developed cervical cancer soon after a smear had been reported as being normal. This has led to widespread loss of confidence in the whole screening programme. However, there are three important points to remember when one of these scares hits our headlines. First, most women who develop cervical cancer have never had a smear in their lives. Second, the vast majority of smears are correctly interpreted, leading to the identification of pre-cancerous changes which, once treated with laser, do not go on to develop into cancer. Third, as a result of these scares, standards throughout the country are being improved so that smears are more likely to be reliable now than ever before.

Cervical cancer is diagnosed in 4,000 women each year in the UK. The majority of these women, as mentioned above, have never had a smear. This is a great tragedy since cancer is preceded by these early, pre-cancerous changes which can be detected and treated. If they are treated in the early stages, cancer will not develop. But women who do not have regular smears will not know that something is amiss until they have developed full-blown cancer, which is what causes the abnormal vaginal bleeding. By this stage, treatment is still possible with surgery and/or radiotherapy, but is less likely to be effective. It is a real tragedy that this largely preventable cancer still claims around 1,600 lives a year in the UK.

Endometrial cancer Abnormal vaginal bleeding, especially after the menopause, can also be a sign of cancer of the endometrium (womb lining). This is rare in women under 50, and is less common in women who have taken the contraceptive pill. It is more common in women who are childless, older than 50, obese or who have had a late menopause. Oestrogen without progestogen can cause endometrial cancer, which is why women who have not had a hysterectomy need to take progestogen with their oestrogen in HRT.

Endometrial cancer is diagnosed by taking a small sample of the endometrium in a simple procedure called an endometrial biopsy. This does not require a general anaesthetic. Alternatively, the sample can be taken in a 'D&C' (dilatation and curettage, also called a 'scrape') which requires a general anaesthetic. Treatment of endometrial cancer can be very effective as it is often detected early if women who have abnormal vaginal bleeding seek medical help promptly. It involves a complete hysterectomy in which the womb, ovaries and tubes are removed, and possibly radiotherapy.

Ovarian cancer Ovarian cancer does not usually cause abnormal vaginal bleeding. This type of cancer is difficult to detect because it does not cause many specific symptoms until it is well advanced and difficult to treat. Once it starts to spread to other organs it can cause abdominal pains, bloating, nausea, vomiting, pain on intercourse, erratic vaginal bleeding and bowel disturbances including diarrhoea, constipation or blockage of the bowel. It affects 5,000 women a year in the UK, and causes 4,000 deaths a year. It is more common among women who have a sister, mother or daughter who has had ovarian cancer or breast cancer which developed at a young age. The gene BRCA2 is responsible for some cases that run in families. Ovarian cancer is also more common among women who have never had children. It is less common among women who have been on the oral contraceptive pill and rare in women under 50; it becomes more common as women get older. The diagnosis is often made by chance if a woman has a vaginal examination or an ultrasound scan. Most ovarian cysts are not due to cancer but are totally benign and harmless. They may need to be removed in an operation to be certain that they are not cancerous. There is no specific screening test for ovarian cancer which is reliable, but women who have a family history of the disease should see a specialist who can advise about blood tests and regular ultrasound scans, which may help to pick it up at an early stage.

The treatment of ovarian cancer involves surgery to remove the growth, and further surgery to remove the womb, ovaries and tubes if the growth is cancerous. Chemotherapy, using powerful cancer-killing drugs, is also given.

Vulval cancer Cancer of the vulva is rare and usually, but not always, affects elderly women. It does not usually cause abnormal vaginal bleeding. It may start as a white, thick area or a red, thin, shiny patch on the vulva which is usually itchy. These pre-cancerous changes can be treated with a simple operation or a cream containing the anticancer drug 5-fluorouracil. If left untreated, these changes have a 20 per cent chance of becoming cancerous within ten years. If that occurs, a more extensive operation to remove the vulva is required.

Investigations
It is important to see a doctor for any abnormal vaginal bleeding. The doctor may be able to diagnose the problem after listening to your description of the symptoms and performing an internal examination. Tests are necessary if there is any doubt. These may include the following.

Blood tests A full blood count is needed to check for anaemia due to excessive bleeding, and thyroid function tests check that an under- or over-active thyroid is not the cause of the bleeding. Measuring the hormone FSH may determine whether you are going through the menopause.

Vaginal examination A doctor or nurse inserts a lubricated, gloved finger into your vagina while you lie on your back with your knees bent and spread apart. They use the other hand to feel your abdomen. In this way they can examine the size and position of the womb, and tell whether there is any tenderness or any growths or enlargement in the ovaries.

Cervical smear While you lie on your back as for a vaginal examination, the doctor or nurse inserts a metal instrument (a speculum) into your vagina and gently opens it to allow a good view of the cervix. You can ask the nurse or doctor to warm the speculum and allow you to put it in yourself if you like. Once the speculum is in place and open, a wooden or plastic spatula is scraped round your cervix to obtain cells which are then smeared on to a glass slide, sprayed with a fixative and sent to the lab for examination under a microscope. The result normally takes 4–6 weeks (see above).

Ultrasound scan This is the best way of detecting fibroids (see above) or cysts on the ovaries. Vaginal ultrasound scans, in which the probe is put in the vagina, are the most accurate way of detecting problems in the womb.

Endometrial sampling For this simple technique, which is replacing the old 'scrape' or D&C, a narrow tube is inserted up the vagina and into the womb to sample cells from the womb lining. It is an easy way of checking whether abnormal bleeding is harmless or due to cancer of the womb lining (endometrial cancer). No anaesthetic is necessary and it is only slightly more uncomfortable than a smear. It is done in an outpatient clinic.

Hysteroscopy A telescope is used to look into the womb under local or general anaesthetic. The womb is filled with fluid or gas and the hysteroscope is used to get a good view inside. Samples (biopsies) can be taken if there are any abnormal-looking areas.

Toxic shock syndrome

This is an extremely rare but potentially serious condition requiring urgent medical attention. About ten cases a year occur in the UK, and roughly half of all cases occur in women who use tampons. The infection is more likely if you forget to change a tampon and leave it in your vagina for many hours. Toxic shock syndrome is caused by a poison produced by a bacterium which normally lives on the skin (*Staph. aureus*). The signs occur during a period and include high fever (over 39°C), a rash in which skin peels off, vomiting and diarrhoea, and dizziness and fainting.

Pelvic pain

Some gynaecological problems may cause a constant pain in the lower abdomen and pelvis, the area between the two hipbones at the front and the tailbone (sacrum) at the back. Sometimes the pain may be mainly in the back, and may feel like a constant backache. At other times, the pain may come and go and be felt mainly at the front. Some gynaecological problems cause pain during intercourse, such as some ovarian cysts. Other conditions such as endometriosis cause pelvic pain during periods (see above). The main causes of pelvic pain are described below.

Pelvic inflammatory disease (PID)

Pelvic inflammatory disease is the name given to infection in the uterus and tubes. The symptoms are vaginal discharge (although this may not always occur), pain during intercourse, fever and lower abdominal pain. You should always see a doctor immediately if PID is a possibility. Prompt treatment with antibiotics is necessary to prevent any damage to the tubes, which need to be open for future fertility.

Ectopic pregnancy

A fertilised egg can sometimes start to develop in one of the fallopian tubes that lead from the ovary to the uterus. Part of the tube containing the ectopic pregnancy (see also Chapter 13) usually becomes sealed off, damaging the tube and causing severe pain but no fever. There is no vaginal discharge. There may be some vaginal bleeding after the pain starts (unlike a miscarriage, in which the bleeding starts before the pain). You might suspect you are pregnant because the symptoms will usually start about two weeks after a missed period. Pregnancy tests will be positive. Occasionally, the part of the tube containing the ectopic pregnancy ruptures, causing tremendous abdominal pain on one side, rendering you pale, sweaty, clammy and even unconscious. Any suspected ectopic pregnancy needs to be taken very seriously.

Hospital treatment will include immediate resuscitation if necessary, a pregnancy test and an ultrasound scan to confirm the diagnosis. Laparoscopy (viewing the abdominal contents through a 'telescope') allows the gynaecologist to treat the ectopic by opening the tube and removing the pregnancy. Sometimes part or the whole tube has to be removed. More major surgery is occasionally needed for more serious cases.

When to see a doctor

See your GP immediately if you have a combination of the following symptoms:

- a missed period and/or a positive pregnancy test
- one-sided lower or central abdominal pain
- vaginal bleeding that starts after the pain
- a coil in place, you are taking the progestogen-only pill, or you have had previous pelvic inflammatory disease or ectopic pregnancy – all of which make an ectopic more likely.

Miscarriage

One in five confirmed pregnancies ends in a miscarriage (see also Chapter 13). The vast majority of these occur within the first 12 weeks of pregnancy. Usually the foetus miscarries (or 'aborts') because it cannot develop further. There is very rarely a recurrent problem. It does not mean that miscarriage is more likely in any subsequent pregnancies. There is nothing one can do to prevent a miscarriage. Abstaining from intercourse and resting make no difference to the outcome. Miscarriages start as vaginal bleeding followed by crampy abdominal pains, like period pains. Warm baths and painkillers should help you to cope with the cramps. An injection is necessary if a woman's blood group is rhesus-negative, to mop up any of the foetal cells that may enter her bloodstream from the foetus. The foetal cells may be rhesus-positive, which will be 'foreign' to the woman's body and can trigger production of antibodies to fight the 'foreign' cells. These antibodies can cause damage to any subsequent rhesus-positive pregnancies (see also Chapter 13).

Further intervention by gynaecologists is often not necessary. The pains and bleeding of a miscarriage settle down on their own in most cases. A 'scrape' to clear the womb is necessary only if the bleeding and pains persist for more than a few days or if a woman is more than 8 weeks pregnant. After a miscarriage there is no real need to avoid pregnancy, unless you and your partner wish to. Pregnancy will not occur until the body is ready. Any woman who has had three or more miscarriages in the first 12 weeks of pregnancy, or who miscarries later in pregnancy, should be offered tests by a gynaecologist to look for an underlying problem.

Labour pains

Small contractions of the uterus frequently occur in the last third of the pregnancy (see also Chapter 13). These are called Braxton Hicks. But the rhythmic, painful contractions that characterise the start of labour (see Chapter 13) are quite different. Signs of labour include a 'show' – a thick, blood-stained or clear plug of mucus from the vagina; persistent low back pain; waters breaking – a sudden loss of clear fluid from the vagina; and regular cramping abdominal pains, which become more frequent, last longer and usually get more painful over a few hours. Antenatal or parentcraft classes will help you to know what to expect. A TENS machine and a warm bath as well as massage by a partner or friend can be helpful in the early stages of labour. It is important to phone the labour ward or the attending midwife, for guidance.

Ovarian cysts

Cysts are harmless, fluid-filled growths that occur frequently on the ovaries. Cysts and other harmless growths are often detected if you have an ultrasound scan for some reason. Most cysts do not cause any symptoms, remain small and disappear of their own accord. Some grow big enough to cause abdominal discomfort, bloating and pain during intercourse. To avoid further discomfort, these larger cysts are usually removed in a short operation. Cysts are sometimes caused by endometriosis (see above). Growths may also be removed even if they are not causing symptoms: they are examined under a microscope to check whether they are cancerous. An operation to remove a cyst (a cystectomy) should not interfere with future fertility at all. Ovarian cysts and benign growths are extremely common, whereas ovarian cancer is relatively rare (see above).

Retroverted uterus

The womb normally tilts forwards, but many women have a womb that tends to tilt backwards. This does not normally cause any problems, except that a doctor fitting a coil may find it more tricky than usual. Getting pregnant and having a baby should not pose any particular problem. A retroverted uterus is occasionally responsible for any pain or discomfort, and some positions during intercourse may be uncomfortable. If you are told that your womb tilts backwards, do not worry about it. No treatment is necessary.

Painful intercourse

When intercourse is painful, it is not pleasurable. Fear of the pain can put a woman off sex for a long time, even when the actual pain has gone. There may be an underlying physical reason why sex is painful, or it may be entirely psychological. Either way, it is worth seeking help either from a GP or from a family planning clinic or gynaecologist. Physical causes of painful intercourse include:

- childbirth – the vagina normally remains swollen and tender for six weeks after delivery. Pain after that time may be due to poorly healed vaginal tears, a badly repaired episiotomy (surgical cut), scars, or an infection
- infections – thrush, trichomonas, herpes and other infections may make the vagina sore (see below)
- a dry vagina – the vagina often becomes dry after the menopause. HRT helps. The vagina may also be too dry if a woman is not adequately stimulated by her partner. Being frank with your partner, and using K-Y jelly for extra lubrication, may be helpful
- a sore vagina – the vagina may feel sore after vigorous sex. In this case the pain will settle on its own. Tampons can also cause soreness – in which case using sanitary towels will solve the problem

- endometriosis – inflammation of the patches of womb lining which lie outside the womb, usually around the ovaries, can cause a deep-seated pain during intercourse (see above)
- pelvic inflammatory disease – infection which spreads up into the womb and fallopian tubes can also cause deep-seated pain during intercourse. Usually it causes a fever and vaginal discharge as well (see below).

Psychological causes of painful intercourse include:

- a previous physical cause of pain, e.g. childbirth. Many women find it hard to relax sufficiently to enjoy sex again if they have had a particularly painful or traumatic delivery. Reassurance by a doctor that there is no longer a physical problem, use of K-Y jelly for lubrication, and an understanding and attentive approach by the woman's partner all help
- previous bad experiences of sex. Women who have been raped or abused may find sex painful, as memories are rekindled during intercourse. Expert counselling is better than suppressing the memory of the experience
- vaginismus – sex is painful for women whose vagina tightens during intercourse. There is usually an underlying psychological problem. If fear of pregnancy is the cause, then getting reliable contraception sorted out may solve the problem. Otherwise, it is best to seek help.

Vaginal problems

Discharge

The vagina normally produces fluid to keep it moist, and it has a natural acidity produced by special bacteria that live there. This acidity keeps infections at bay. If the bacteria are destroyed, by antibiotics or vaginal deodorants, or douching for example, or if the acidity is disturbed by pregnancy, the contraceptive pill or after the menopause, then vaginal infections become more likely.

Vaginal discharge may be normal (see below) or it may be due to an infection. Medical help is available from your GP or from clinics (known as genito-urinary medicine clinics) that specialise in sexually transmitted diseases. GUM clinics are usually found in local hospitals and most offer a walk-in service, without the need for a letter from your GP. Staff will not communicate with your GP without your permission. Most will perform an HIV test if you wish. Another source of specialised help for sexually transmitted infections is family planning clinics.

Normal discharge

Many women notice an increase in their normal discharge when they are pregnant, on the pill, at ovulation (two weeks before a period) or after intercourse. This is normal, and does not require any special treatment. Excessive washing may cause infections because it may destroy the normal bacteria and predispose you to thrush. Normal discharge does not smell, itch or cause any irritation to the vagina.

When to see a doctor

Abnormal discharge would include any discharge which is blood-stained or foul-smelling. You need to see a doctor if discharge is accompanied by fever, abdominal pain and pain on intercourse. You should also see a doctor if discharge is itchy or causing irritation and soreness in your vagina. If you cannot find an explanation for the discharge – such as your cycle, a recent pregnancy or the contraceptive pill – and it is increasing, it is worth discussing it with a doctor. If a male partner has discharge from his penis he should see a doctor.

Thrush

There are a number of things you can do to prevent thrush. After a bowel motion, always wipe from front to back to avoid introducing bacteria that normally live in the bowel into the vagina. Do not wear synthetic tights and leggings, and keep the vagina as cool and dry as possible by wearing loose skirts or trousers and cotton knickers. Avoid destroying normal vaginal bacteria that keep thrush at bay: take antibiotics only if necessary and avoid vaginal deodorants and excessive washing. Consider alternative contraception if being on the pill gives you thrush. Eat yoghurt containing lactobacillus (it does not have to be 'live') to restore the natural bacteria to the vagina. Tampons soaked in yoghurt are soothing but not as effective as eating the yoghurt.

Thrush can be treated with an anti-fungal pessary (clotrimoxazole or Canesten), available over the counter or on prescription. Antifungal creams may help soreness but they are not as effective as the pessary which is inserted into the vagina. An oral tablet called fluconazole (Diflucan) can be swallowed to rid the bowel of thrush and prevent recurrent vaginal infections. Partners do not usually need any treatment unless they also have symptoms (e.g. rash/itch).

Vaginal discharge: causes and treatments

Cause	Type of discharge	Smell	Other symptoms
Thrush (candida)	Creamy white	None	Itchy, sore vagina
Bacterial vaginosis	Grey-white and watery	Fishy – especially after sex	Vagina not sore
Trichomonas	Frothy and green	Foul-smelling	Sore vagina
Chlamydia	May not be any; may be thick and bloody	No smell usually	Fever, pain during intercourse, partner may have pain passing water
Gonorrhoea	May not be any; may be thick and bloody	Smelly	As chlamydia

Bacterial vaginosis
Bacterial vaginosis (BV) is more likely if the naturally occurring vaginal bacteria are destroyed (see *Thrush*) or if you have been fitted with a coil. It can be treated with a course of an antibiotic called metronidazole (Flagyl) or with a vaginal cream (Dalacin). There is

nothing you can do to prevent the condition; it is not sexually transmitted, although it is rare among women who never have intercourse, and partners do not require any treatment. A recent report found a link between bacterial vaginosis and premature labour or miscarriages late in pregnancy, in view of which pregnant women may be screened for BV in the future.

Trichomonas

Since this is a sexually transmitted infection you can prevent it by using barrier methods of contraception (male/female condom). Like BV, it is treated with metronidazole. Although it is sexually transmitted, male partners rarely have any symptoms and it does not necessarily mean that one partner has had intercourse with someone else. To get rid of the infection, both partners should take a course of antibiotics.

Chlamydia

Since chlamydia is sexually transmitted, you can prevent it by using barrier methods of contraception (cap or condom). Having a coil fitted can cause a severe attack if chlamydia is present on the neck of the womb. It is therefore important for the doctor to check for chlamydia and treat it before inserting a coil. Chlamydia can make a woman very unwell. It causes inflammation of the vagina, womb and fallopian tubes, resulting in severe lower abdominal and pelvic pain. The inflammation may also cause fertility problems later on if it damages the fallopian tubes. Prompt treatment is necessary to ease the pain and fever and minimise fertility problems. The treatment involves antibiotics, e.g. tetracycline, for the woman and her partner. Hospital admission is occasionally necessary for severe attacks.

Researchers in the USA have recommended that sexually active teenage girls should be screened for chlamydial infection every six months because the infection could cause pelvic inflammatory disease, infertility and ectopic pregnancy.

Gonorrhoea

As for chlamydia and trichomonas, barrier methods of contraception will help prevent the spread of gonorrhoea. The treatment is antibiotics (penicillin) for the woman and her partner.

Vaginal and vulval lumps, bumps and spots

The vagina is the passage from the outside up to the cervix (the neck of the womb). The vulva is the skin which makes up the 'lips' on either side of the vaginal opening. The skin between the back passage and the vagina is called the perineum. Most conditions that affect the vagina also affect the vulva and perineum as they are all very close.

Ulcers and genital herpes

Herpes is one of the most common sexually transmitted infections in the UK, and the most common cause of ulcers on the vulva or vagina. It is caused by a virus (herpes simplex virus, HSV type 2, sometimes just called 'herpes') of the type that causes cold sores (HSV type 1). It is usually, but not invariably, caught by intercourse with a man who has herpes blisters on his penis. Four to five days after contact, the vulva starts burning. Within a day or two, a cluster of tiny blisters appears on the vulva. They burst, leaving small, painful ulcers which take between ten days and six weeks to heal. The first attack is often the worst, causing fever, headache, swollen glands in the groin and difficulty passing water. Occasionally, even more widespread and serious infection can occur, causing inflammation of the liver and brain. Further attacks can crop up for years to come, often precipitated by being very run-down.

Herpes can be prevented if men with herpes abstain from sex or use condoms until the blisters are fully healed. Oral sex should be avoided if either partner has herpes or cold sores. Pregnant women who have herpes just before they are due to deliver are sometimes advised to have a caesarean section to ensure the baby does not catch the virus. The treatment for genital herpes involves painkillers to damp down the pain, and antibiotics only if the blisters become infected with bacteria. Antiviral drugs (e.g. acyclovir or famciclovir) help to speed up healing and reduce the pain. They are effective only if they are started as soon as the attack starts. Oral tablets or a cream to put on the blisters are both available. Continuous use of oral acyclovir can prevent frequent recurrences. Support groups and counselling are helpful for those women who suffer repeated attacks. Acupuncture may alleviate painful attacks, and homeopathic remedies are available to help prevent recurrences and relieve pain. Relaxation techniques may be useful for pain control.

Warts

Warts on the genitals are common and are sexually transmitted. They appear between one and six months after intercourse with a man who has warts on his penis. They can cause itching, irritation and sometimes bleeding in the vulva and perineum, and can spread up into the vagina and reach the cervix. They look like the small warts that many people get on their hands. Occasionally they become large, with little tendrils that protrude. They are caused by a virus called HPV and can cause changes to the cells of the cervix which can, in time, become cancerous.

A cervical smear is always advisable if genital warts appear. Women with warts often have other sexually transmitted infections, particularly trichomonas (see above). Men with warts should abstain from intercourse or use condoms until the warts have been treated. The treatment involves preparations which can be painted on to the warts (podophyllum and podophyllotoxin). These are available only on prescription. They irritate normal skin, so they must be used with care, and surrounding skin must be protected with Vaseline. Male partners must be treated, too. Large, numerous or inaccessible warts are treated with a laser or liquid nitrogen. Warts on the cervix are usually treated with lasers. Other infections are treated at the same time if they are present; trichomonas, for example, is treated with a course of antibiotics.

Bartholin's abscess

Tender, hard lumps on either side of the vagina are usually due to infection of the small glands that lubricate the vagina, called Bartholin's glands. A course of an oral antibiotic cures the infection. Occasionally, large abscesses may need to be drained in hospital, although this is rare.

Prolapse

Women sometimes have a feeling that something is coming down the vagina. Backache, leaking urine after coughing, sneezing or straining (stress incontinence) may occur at the same time. All these symptoms will be worse after standing for a long time, and will usually improve after lying down. The cause is a prolapse, which means that the walls of the vagina and/or the womb itself are not held firmly in place but are sagging downwards. If the front wall of the vagina which separates it from the bladder is sagging (a cystocele), it may be difficult to pass water properly. If the back wall of the vagina which separates it from the rectum (bowel) is sagging (a rectocele), it may be hard to pass a motion easily.

Repeated and difficult childbirth is a major cause of prolapse. Stopping getting pregnant and doing pelvic floor exercises after childbirth can help to prevent prolapse later on. The menopause weakens the supports that hold the womb in place and keep the vaginal walls strong. HRT may help to prevent this weakness and so reduce the chance of a prolapse. Obesity increases pressure in the abdomen, which in turn increases the pressure downwards on the womb and predisposes to a prolapse. Coughing also increases the pressure on the womb and smokers tend to cough more than non-smokers. Constipation and straining to open the bowels also increase the pressure on the womb and back wall of the vagina.

Treatment of a prolapse involves losing weight, stopping smoking, preventing constipation and possibly taking HRT. Such action may help to ensure that the problem does not get worse. A ring pessary is a rubber ring which can be fitted in the vagina to hold up the womb. It is changed every 3–12 months by a GP or gynaecologist. An operation to 'darn' the front or back walls of the vagina to strengthen them can be done for a cystocele or rectocele. It is also possible to have an operation called a colposuspension to 'hitch up' the womb. It takes less time to recover from this than from a hysterectomy, and the woman still can have children. In addition, it is a less major operation than a hysterectomy so it may be advisable for older women who are not in good general health. The procedure is usually successful, although the prolapse may recur in time. Hysterectomy is the most effective treatment available if the womb is prolapsed (see above). The womb is removed via the vagina, and the front and back walls of the vagina can be repaired at the same time. Getting back to normal after a hysterectomy takes about six weeks.

Itchy vulva or vagina

An itchy vulva and vagina can drive a woman to distraction. Many of the common causes can be treated at home, but you should see a doctor if you have any persistent itching or skin changes. The causes include:

- vaginal discharge – thrush is a very common cause of itching (see above)
- warts and herpes (see above)
- incontinence – women who leak urine may often walk around with damp pads or underwear, which can cause irritation and itching
- allergy – bubble baths, vaginal deodorants, powders, soaps and underwear washed in a new soap powder can all cause irritation of the vulva and vagina and make them itch. Make sure you wash with water only, dry yourself carefully using a soft towel or hair-dryer, and avoid contact with all chemicals. An antihistamine at night (e.g. Piriton, which is available over the counter) combined with a steroid cream (e.g. hydrocortisone, also available over the counter) often relieves the itch. It is important not to use a steroid cream for longer than a week without seeking medical help to exclude other causes of itch, e.g. thrush
- skin conditions – conditions that affect all the skin, e.g. eczema and psoriasis, can also affect the vulva and vagina. See a doctor for advice
- infestations – threadworm is a common problem among women who are in contact with young children who have the problem. Small thread-like worms crawl out of the back passage at night, causing intense itching of the back passage round to the vagina. Pubic lice or scabies can live in the pubic hair and also cause very intense itching. See a doctor for advice
- abnormal skin changes – the skin of the vulva may become red and shiny, with white patches, as a result of long-term inflammation of the skin. Alternatively, the skin may become thickened and tight-looking with white patches. These skin changes cause intense itching. It is important to see a doctor. Referral to a gynaecologist for a biopsy, removal of a small sample of the abnormal skin, is normally recommended. This is because the skin changes may eventually become cancerous. Treating pre-cancerous skin changes with a cream (5-fluorouracil), or a simple operation to remove the abnormal areas, prevents cancer of the vulva developing

- diabetes – the symptoms include abnormal thirst, passing a great deal of urine, tiredness and sometimes weight loss and blurred vision. Excess glucose is passed in the urine and this can cause itching. It is very rare, however, for the only sign of diabetes to be an itchy vulva. See your doctor if diabetes is a possibility.

Urinary problems

The structure of the urinary system

The kidneys filter blood and extract useful minerals and water which are reabsorbed into the bloodstream to be used by the body. The remaining liquid, which contains waste products, including drugs and medicines which have been broken down by the body, excess salts, acids and water, is called urine. Kidney disorders may affect the ability of the kidneys to filter the blood and lead to an imbalance of chemicals (urea and electrolytes) in the blood.

The urine drains into the central part of the kidneys, trickles down tubes called ureters and is stored in the bladder. When the bladder is nearly full, a signal is sent from the bladder to the brain and another signal comes back to tell you to release the urine from the bladder, through a tube called the urethra and out through an opening in the vagina, when you reach a toilet. This control of the bladder is a conscious skill that has to be learned in childhood. Some disorders that affect the nervous system, such as strokes, multiple sclerosis, dementia, brain tumours and diabetes, may affect bladder control. The bladder is supported by muscles, and damage during childbirth may lead to loss of support of the bladder exit and an inability to hold on to urine during coughing, sneezing and running.

As explained above, in women, the urine flows down a short tube called the urethra and out through an opening in the vagina. Men have a longer urethra which travels down the inside of the penis. Because of their shorter urethra, women are much more prone to urine infections than men. Inflammation around the urethra after intercourse or as a result of dryness during the menopause may cause burning when passing urine. Urination can also be painful if there is any inflammation in the bladder (cystitis) or vagina (vaginitis).

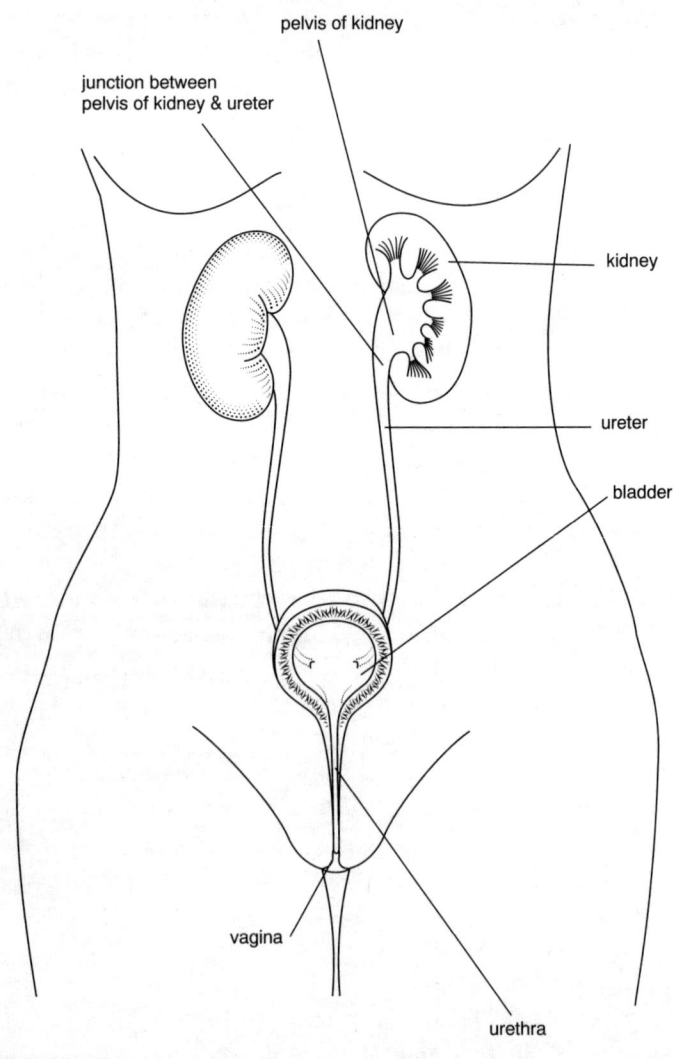

pelvis of kidney

junction between
pelvis of kidney & ureter

kidney

ureter

bladder

vagina

urethra

Figure 15 The urinary system

Painful urination: symptoms, causes and treatment

Symptoms	Cause	Action
Burning sensation when urinating; strong and frequent urge to urinate; urge and burning may be brought on by cold, stress, intercourse and tight synthetic underwear	Cystitis	Wear cotton underwear. Empty your bladder after intercourse. Drink extra fluids. Take potassium or sodium citrate mixtures, e.g. Cystemme. See your GP if the problem persists or recurs
As above, plus fever, vomiting, backache and blood in the urine	Urinary tract infection	See your GP for antibiotics and a urine sample test
Vaginal discharge and stinging sensation when urinating	Vaginal infection or inflammation	See *cystitis,* above
Urge to pass something that will not pass; blood in urine	Stone which has formed in the kidneys or bladder and is stuck in the ureter	See your GP. Stones often pass on their own, but hospital tests and treatment may be necessary

Frequent urination

Women differ in the number of times they urinate. Some women regularly get up at night to urinate, others never do. There is a wide range of what is 'normal', and it is partly dependent on habit and the amount you drink, the quantity of alcohol, tea and coffee – all of which encourage urine production. If your normal pattern changes, or there are additional symptoms like blood in the urine, pain or fever, it is important to get medical help. The most common cause of needing to urinate more often than normal is a urinary tract infection. Many women experience a gradual increase in frequency of urination as they get older, together with a strong urge to go. This may result in incontinence if you cannot get to the toilet in time. This common and distressing problem can be treated effectively and it is well worth seeking help (see below). Excessive thirst, tiredness and frequent urination may be a sign of diabetes. A simple urine or blood test is necessary to make the diagnosis.

Blood in the urine

Red urine is not always due to blood. The drug rifampicin, for example, given for protection after contact with meningitis, turns the urine red. Beetroot and some food colourings can have a similar effect. But blood in the urine always needs to be taken seriously. It is usually due to a urine infection, which is readily treated with antibiotics. Passing a stone which can originate in the kidney or bladder may also cause intense pain and blood in the urine. Kidney diseases of various kinds may cause blood in the urine. This may be visible or invisible, but detectable in a urine test which may be done as part of a routine medical check-up. Blood can appear in the urine when you have a period, or you may pass a blood-stained discharge after childbirth, miscarriage or a termination of pregnancy. Any inflammation or infection in the vagina can also cause bleeding which appears in the urine. Blood from the back passage, due to piles for instance, may appear in the toilet and seem to be mixed in with the urine. Women who bleed particularly easily because of a problem with clotting or because they are on drugs to 'thin the blood', e.g. warfarin or heparin, may notice blood in the urine, which is not necessarily harmful in itself. Blood in the urine which is causing no other symptoms may be an early sign of bladder cancer, which is eminently treatable if caught then. This is one of the reasons why it is so important to see a doctor as soon as any blood is noticed in the urine.

Leaking urine: incontinence

Incontinence is the involuntary loss of urine which is bad enough to be a problem. It is amazingly common, affecting 30 per cent of women aged 25 to 55, and an even higher percentage of older women. Up to 10 per cent of all women over 25 wear some type of pad or protection at all times, and many more use protection when doing sports. Incontinence often affects a woman's self-esteem. It can put a woman off sex, sports and work, and can make going out at all a daunting experience. The shame of it is that most types of incontinence are treatable, if only women would admit their problem and seek help from experienced health professionals.

Urge incontinence

The symptoms of urge incontinence are an intense urge to urinate; losing urine before getting to the toilet; frequent urination day and night, and passing large amounts of urine at a time. In urge incontinence, the bladder becomes very sensitive and fires off messages to the brain even when it is not full. It often comes on gradually and may start after a gynaecological operation. It is more common as you get older, and may be combined with a dry, sore vagina after the menopause. Other causes of these symptoms may be water pills (diuretics) taken for high blood pressure or water retention; a urine infection; a kidney stone; or neurological problems such as multiple sclerosis.

Stress incontinence

Stress incontinence occurs when the bladder supports become weakened or overstretched. Urine leaks out when the pressure in the bladder increases – when you cough, sneeze, laugh or exercise, for example. There is no urge to urinate. Very small amounts may be passed at a time. Stress incontinence can affect women of all ages, although it is more common among young women. It usually starts suddenly – after childbirth, for example.

Mixed urge and stress incontinence

Some women are unfortunate to suffer a mixture of both stress and urge incontinence: they have a strong urge to go, and they leak when they cough. This is more common among older women.

Overflow incontinence

If leaking occurs at any time without any kind of trigger – like coughing – then it is likely you are suffering from overflow incontinence. In such a case urine is flowing out of the bladder round a blockage such as constipation. The leak is likely to be a slow, constant dribble rather than suddenly wetting yourself.

Dementia, some types of stroke, and epileptic fits may leave a woman completely unaware of her need to go to the toilet.

Self-help for incontinence
Stress incontinence

- Empty your bladder before taking exercise.
- Restrict your fluid intake to 1.5 litres per day (though not less than this).
- Put a large tampon in your vagina before exercising.
- Learn pelvic floor exercises or use vaginal cones (see box below).

Urge incontinence

- Restrict your fluid intake to 1–1.5 litres per day.
- Learn the bladder drill (see box opposite).

Pelvic floor exercises

These exercises are known as Kegel's pelvic floor exercises after the physician who devised them. The exercises should be taught by a trained physiotherapist or continence nurse. The exercises involve learning to squeeze the pelvic floor muscles for increasing lengths of time to tone up the muscles and improve bladder control. It is similar to stopping yourself in the middle of passing urine and holding the stream before letting go again. You need to have a vaginal examination first to check that you can contract your pelvic floor muscles – put your own finger in your vagina and squeeze it to check if you can identify the muscles. Improvement takes three to six months, and you should continue to do the exercises indefinitely. You may wish to try biofeedback, which uses electrical gadgets to encourage you to do the exercises even better.

Vaginal cones can also be used to treat stress incontinence. They are like weight training for the pelvic floor. Cones of increasing weight are put in the vagina and held there by contracting the muscles for 15 minutes twice a day while doing normal activities. They can be bought from chemists or on mail order. If there is no improvement after six weeks you need to seek help. Around 85 per cent of women say it improves their symptoms; 21 per cent become completely dry as a result of using cones.

Bladder drill

The aim of the bladder drill is to retrain the bladder to stop it being so sensitive. You first need an examination from a doctor to ensure there is no underlying disease. The drill should be explained by a trained physiotherapist or continence nurse. You are encouraged gradually to reduce the frequency of trips to the toilet to urinate, so that the bladder gets used to holding more urine before sending a message to the brain that you need to go. At first, you are told to urinate every one and a half hours by the clock, even if you do not need to go, but you mustn't go in between. Once you can last for an hour and a half without wetting yourself, the interval is increased by half an hour at a time, making sure you can stay dry and comfortable at each stage. You are asked not to drink more than 1.5 litres per day and you are asked to keep an accurate chart of the time and volume of all drinks, and the time and volume of all urine passed (which means urinating into a measuring jug). It is a hassle but, with an 80 per cent cure rate, many women feel it is worthwhile.

When to see a doctor

No one should have to put up with being incontinent. It is important to seek effective help. The GP, who has access to specially trained nurses, continence clinics and specialists, is the first port of call. The Continence Foundation* provides excellent advice and support. Tests include a vaginal examination to check for a dry vagina and prolapse; a urine test (the sample is sent to the laboratory to check for infection); and a urine and/or blood test to check for kidney disease or diabetes, both of which can cause excess urination. You may also be referred for specialist tests of your bladder function (urodynamics). Stress incontinence which has not improved with pelvic floor exercises (see above) may be cured with an operation. Surgeons offer various operations. These involve hitching up or supporting the bladder and the bladder neck. Urge incontinence which has not improved despite bladder drill (see above) may respond to drug treatment (e.g. oxybutynin).

Chapter 12

Fertility

Contraception is, arguably, the single greatest contribution to equality of the sexes. This chapter looks at the different methods of contraception available today and discusses their advantages and disadvantages. It also examines the emotive topic of infertility and outlines the options for assisted conception.

Contraception

Women are potentially fertile from the time they start periods until a year after periods have stopped. Today, women expect to be able to control their fertility rather than be controlled by it. But even the best methods of contraception have drawbacks. The choice of contraceptive method depends on the needs of the individual.

Natural family planning
Natural family planning involves avoiding intercourse in the most fertile time of the menstrual cycle – that is, 12–16 days before a period starts. There are various methods, including:

- taking your temperature every day to detect the rise that occurs in the fertile period
- observing changes in the vaginal mucus (the Billings method)
- a combination of temperature and mucus methods to give a double check
- using a calendar to work out the most fertile period (five days either side of ovulation).

The advantages of natural family planning are that it does not involve any hormones so it does not interfere with your body at all. It is acceptable to all religions – some of which may not allow more artificial methods. There are no complications or side-effects. The disadvantages are that it is more fallible than other methods (see below), it limits the times when you can have sex, and it can be a hassle.

Breast-feeding after childbirth is an effective natural contraceptive if no supplement feeds are given, periods have not restarted and the baby is less than six months old. However, you cannot really rely on breast-feeding to act as a contraceptive, and most women prefer to use more reliable methods rather than risk getting pregnant soon after having given birth.

Persona

This product, first marketed in 1996, consists of a series of disposable test sticks and a hand-held computerised monitor to help you know when you are fertile. You dip a stick into a sample of your urine every morning and then put the stick into the monitor. A red light shows on the monitor when hormone levels in your urine indicate that your are 'unsafe' to have sex (i.e. you are in the fertile period when you ovulate). A green light means you are no longer in the fertile period and thus it is *relatively* safe to have sex without getting pregnant. Some women also find Persona useful when they are trying to get pregnant as it indicates the fertile period.

Combined oral contraceptive (the pill, COC)

The combined oral contraceptive is a tablet containing two hormones which are similar to the two naturally occurring hormones produced by the ovaries, oestrogen and progesterone. These two hormones override the normal hormonal cycle and so prevent ovulation. The pill is taken every day for 21 days and then there is a 7-day pill-free break. The advantages are that it is very effective so long as it is taken regularly. Periods tend to be lighter, and the pill gives protection against ovarian cancer, endometrial cancer and pelvic inflammatory disease. The disadvantages are a slightly increased risk of thrombosis (blood clots in the legs and lungs) more so with the newer pills containing desogestrel and gestodene. This is greatly increased among smokers. There is also concern about a slightly increased risk of breast cancer (see Chapter 10). Intermittent vaginal bleeding, acne, headache and weight gain are common side-effects. The pill is not recommended for breast feeding women as it tends to reduce the milk supply.

Progestogen-only pill (the mini pill)

The mini pill is a tablet containing progestogen only, taken every day without a break. It must be taken at the same time every day, and is unreliable if you take it more than three hours late. It works by making the mucus in the cervix (the neck of the womb) thicker so that the sperm cannot get through, and altering the lining of the womb so that implantation cannot occur. The advantages are that there is no increased risk of thrombosis, unlike with the COC, which makes it safer for older women, smokers and diabetics. It does not affect the flow of breast milk, unlike the COC, which makes it suitable for breast-feeding mothers. The disadvantages are that it is less reliable than the COC, many women find it hard to take it at the same time every day, it may cause erratic or absent periods, and pregnancies that do occur are more likely to be ectopic (in the fallopian tube).

Injectable contraceptive (depo-provera)

Depo-provera involves an injection of a hormone similar to progesterone every 12 weeks. The advantages are that it is very effective; there are no oestrogens so there is no increased risk of thrombosis or concern about breast cancer; and it may help premenstrual tension. It is a very good option for women who cannot remember to take a pill every day. The disadvantages are that periods may stop altogether, which some women find worrying (although it is not harmful); frequent irregular vaginal bleeding may occur; return to normal fertility may be delayed by up to one year when you stop having the injections; occasionally your weight and blood pressure may rise; and the protective type of cholesterol may decrease which may in turn leave people at risk of heart disease, so it is not ideal for older women.

Implants (Norplant)

Norplant is a set of six rods containing a hormone similar to progesterone inserted under the skin in the upper arm. The advantages are that it is very effective and hassle-free for five years. The disadvantages are that, as for depo-provera, insertion requires a trained doctor and may cause bruising, and removal can be tricky. Norplant usually causes irregular bleeding for the first six months, which can be helped by other hormone treatments. It can sometimes cause bloating, headaches and skin problems in the first few months.

Diaphragm (cap)

A diaphragm is a rubber dome, individually fitted and inserted before each act of intercourse. It is smeared with spermicide (sperm-killing gel or cream), left in place for a minimum of six hours after sex and then removed. It can be re-used for one year, then needs replacing. A woman may need to get a different-sized one if she loses or gains more than half a stone, or after childbirth. The advantages are that it is good for women who do not want to take hormones or who have intercourse only occasionally. You use it only when you need it. It is effective if it is used properly and with spermicide. It also acts as a barrier against sexually transmitted infections including HIV although less so than the male condom. The disadvantages are that it can be messy; you have to remember to use it each time; it can interfere with the spontaneity of sex; and it is not as effective as hormonal methods or the coil. Some women or men can be allergic to the rubber or spermicide, and some women find they cannot keep a diaphragm in their vagina. Recent evidence has shown that it is not an effective enough method for a woman who really wants to avoid pregnancy. A male condom is more effective.

Male condom (sheath)

A condom is a rubber sheath with a teat on the end. It is rolled on to the erect penis and removed after intercourse. The advantages are that it is widely available; it does not require special fitting; it does not involve hormones; and it gives protection against sexually transmitted infections including HIV. The disadvantages are that condoms can be fiddly; you have to remember to use one each time; they may split; they can interfere with the spontaneity and enjoyment of sex; they may cause allergies in men or women; they are available free only from family planning clinics, otherwise they have to be paid for, unlike most other methods; and they are not as reliable as hormonal methods or the coil.

Female condom

The female condom is a soft sheath available at chemists or free from family planning clinics. It is put inside the vagina just before intercourse, and removed afterwards. The advantages are that it does not require special fitting, and it protects against sexually transmitted infections including HIV. It may be preferable if a man finds it hard to maintain an erection and keep a male condom on his penis throughout sex. The disadvantages are that it can be fiddly; some women cannot retain one in their vagina; the penis can slip between the sheath and vaginal wall; and it may cause allergies.

Intra-uterine contraceptive device (IUCD – coil)

An IUCD is a small copper and plastic device which is inserted into the womb by a trained doctor. It prevents a fertilised egg from implanting in the womb. The advantages are that it is very effective; it can remain in place for five years or, in some cases, more; it is usually hassle-free once it has been fitted; and it can be fitted up to five days after unprotected intercourse to prevent pregnancy. The disadvantages are that it tends to cause heavier and more painful periods; it does not protect against sexually transmitted infections, and any infections that do occur are more likely to spread up the coil and into the womb and tubes which can impair fertility. For that reason the IUCD is not usually recommended for women who have not yet started a family. If pregnancy does occur it is more likely to develop in the tube (an ectopic pregnancy) than in women using hormonal contraception. The IUCD may need to be removed or changed if a smear shows an infection called acinomyces.

Levonorgestrel-containing IUD (Mirena)

This is an intra-uterine device (IUD) that slowly releases a hormone, such as progesterone (levonorgestrel), into the womb. It lasts for a minimum of five years, has all the advantages of the IUCDs (listed above) and is extremely effective. The hormone reduces heavy periods and is even being used for women with heavy periods (see Chapter 11) who do not need contraception. It also reduces period pains. The disadvantages are that insertion may be painful and may require a local anaesthetic as it is wider than a normal IUCD. It needs to be fitted by a trained doctor. Intermittent vaginal bleeding (spotting) is very common in the first three months and then usually settles down. The hormone may cause acne, headache and bloating, like the mini pill, but all the side-effects are unlikely.

Female sterilisation

Sterilisation involves an operation under general or local anaesthetic using a telescope (a laparoscope) introduced into the abdomen via two small incisions in the abdominal wall. The fallopian tubes leading from the ovaries to the womb are tied, cut or clipped to stop any eggs released from the ovaries being fertilised. The advantages of sterilisation are that it is extremely effective; is hassle-free after the operation; does not involve hormones, and does not interfere with periods. The disadvantages are that it is irreversible (although an operation to try to restore fertility can be attempted); it requires an anaesthetic, and there is some discomfort after the operation.

Male sterilisation (vasectomy)

A vasectomy is an operation under local anaesthetic in which a cut is made in the scrotum, and the tube that takes sperm from the testicles is cut or burnt. Three semen samples which are free of sperm are required after the operation before a man is assured that he is sterile. The advantages of vasectomy are that it is extremely effective; is hassle-free after the operation; and that it allows the man to take responsibility for contraception. The disadvantages are that it is irreversible (although an operation to try to restore fertility may be attempted); there may be some discomfort and bruising of the scrotum after the operation.

Post-coital contraception (the 'morning-after' pill)

The so-called morning-after pill is contraception taken after unprotected sex to avoid pregnancy. Four tablets containing a mixture of high-dose oestrogen and progestogen can be taken within 72 hours (two tablets at first, then two more taken 12 hours later). Alternatively, a coil (IUCD) may be fitted within five days of unprotected intercourse. The advantages are that you can prevent pregnancy after contraceptive failure, or after rape. Both pill and IUCD methods are highly effective. The disadvantages are that the contraception depends on access to a doctor (although the post-coital pills may soon become available over the counter); and the pills often cause nausea. For the disadvantages of the contraceptive pill and IUCD, see above.

A task force set up by the World Health Organisation (WHO) recommended in 1998 that a progestogen-alone pill is a more effective post-coital contraception than the currently prescribed 'morning-after pill'. Two doses of 750 micrograms of levonorgestrel taken 12 hours apart produced a more reliable effect than the usual 'morning-after pill', which contains oestrogen and a progestogen. It may be some time before GPs take this new information on board.

Reliability of different methods of contraception

There is considerable overlap between the effectiveness of the different methods. A careful diaphragm-user may have better protection than a haphazard pill-taker, for example. The list below groups together contraceptive methods that offer similar levels of protection if they are properly used, starting with the most effective.

Method	Numer of pregnancies per 100 women[1]
Male sterilisation	0–0.2
Norplant	0–0.2
Mirena	0–0.2
Female sterilisation	0–0.5
Depo-provera	0–1
IUD (coil)	1–2
Combined pill	0.2–3
Mini pill	0.3–4
Male condom (sheath)	2–15
Female condom	2–15
Diaphragm (cap)	4–18
Spermicides alone	4–25
Persona	5

Natural family planning or fertility awareness	6–25
No contraception: women aged 50	0–5
No contraception: women aged 45	10–20
No contraception: women aged 40	40–50
No contraception: women under 40	80–90

[1]Among women using this method of contraception in the first year of use.

Hopes for the future

The following methods are likely to be available within the next ten years. None of these methods is due for release in the near future.

Vaginal ring This is a rubber ring, inserted into the vagina, which releases synthetic progesterone (a progestogen), and is changed every three months. There is also a combination oestrogen and progestogen ring which is kept in the vagina for 21 days, with a 7-day break, like the combined pill.

Contraceptive patch A patch which is stuck on the skin of the buttock and which releases oestrogen and progestogen will also be an option. It is changed weekly for three weeks, then there is a 7-day break.

Injections Regular injections of the male hormone, testosterone, with or without a progestogen, could be given to men every three to four months.

Fertility

Preparing to have a baby

Women who are planning to have a baby are usually keen to provide the ideal conditions for it. The major organs and parts of the baby develop in the first three months in the womb and the first few weeks of pregnancy are crucial for the baby's well-being. By the time a woman has missed her period, she will be at least two weeks pregnant. And women with irregular cycles may be even further into their pregnancies by the time they realise. So it makes sense to sort out any health problems or medication, and adopt a healthy lifestyle, as soon as you decide to try for a baby (see also Chapter 13). The following is a checklist for women trying to get pregnant:

- stop smoking
- restrict alcohol to 1–2 glasses of wine a week and avoid binge-drinking altogether. Researchers in Denmark found (in 1998) that women drinking five or fewer units of alcohol a week were twice as likely to conceive within six months as women drinking double that amount
- avoid handling raw meat, eating under-cooked meat or handling cat-litter trays to avoid toxoplasma infection
- avoid unpasteurised cheeses or cook-chill foods which may not have been properly cooked, to avoid listeria infection
- avoid raw or under-cooked eggs to avoid salmonella infection
- avoid eating liver: it may contain excess vitamin A
- have a blood test to check your immunity to rubella (German measles) and a blood test for anaemia if your heavy periods make anaemia likely
- ask your GP to refer you to a specialist to stabilise any pre-existing conditions such as diabetes, epilepsy or thyroid disorders. Your medication may need to be changed
- ask your GP for a referral to a genetic counselling centre if there is a family history of an inherited condition, or if you are part of a high-risk group for a particular condition, e.g. Afro-Caribbeans are at risk of sickle cell anaemia, and Ashkenazi Jews are at risk of Tay Sachs disease
- ask your GP to investigate any vaginal discharge or possible sexually transmitted conditions that you or your partner may have
- have a cervical smear test to check there are no pre-cancerous changes in your cervix
- take 400 micrograms of folic acid each day to prevent spinal cord disorders such as spina bifida in the baby. Folic acid tablets are available from chemists or health food shops, or on prescription
- try to adopt a regular, controlled eating pattern and exercise routine. Lose weight if you are significantly overweight, but do not start yo-yo dieting.

Fertility problems

One in six couples has difficulty conceiving a baby. The average time that it takes a couple to conceive is four months; 80 per cent of couples conceive within one year. So for every friend one hears of who gets pregnant as soon as she even thinks about it, there will be another couple who wait over a year. There are several ways you can improve your chances of getting pregnant. To start with, make love every other day at least, especially around the most fertile time of the month, which is three days either side of ovulation. Ovulation (release of the egg from the ovary) usually occurs 14 days before your next period is due. Temperature charts, fertility thermometers and ovulation-testing kits can help show when ovulation occurs. Some women get signs of ovulation – some vague pains or a change in their normal vaginal mucus, which becomes more slippery and clear.

You could also try cutting down or even stopping smoking, and encourage your partner to do the same. Smoking may affect fertility and increase the miscarriage rate. Excess alcohol, being very overweight, and certain prescribed drugs can affect a man's sperm count. However, age is one of the biggest factors in infertility. A woman's fertility decreases from the age of 35, although with men it is a more gradual process. So the later you leave it to have a baby, the harder it gets.

There is no one position for making love that enhances the chances of getting pregnant. It does not matter, for example, if fluid runs out of the vagina after intercourse – the sperm move very fast to get through the cervix; nor does the woman have to have an orgasm to get pregnant.

When to see a doctor
You should see your GP if:

- you have been trying for a baby for more than a year and you are both under 30, or for six months if you are over 30
- you are not having periods regularly, or you are having heavy and painful periods
- there are sexual problems which make intercourse infrequent or unsuccessful
- there is pain after intercourse, abnormal vaginal discharge, vaginal or penile warts or other sexually transmitted infections that need treating
- if your partner has an undescended testicle, swollen scrotum with large veins, sexually transmitted infections like gonorrhoea, or problems with intercourse.

Causes of infertility

In about four out of ten infertile couples the woman has a specific problem. In another four out of ten couples, the man has a specific problem. In the remaining two out of ten couples, there are problems with both the man and woman, or no cause can be found. One common reason for infertility is that the woman does not produce an egg (ovulate) regularly or at all. Many women find that their periods stop for a while if they lose or gain a lot of weight suddenly, travel, change job or are otherwise stressed. Stopping the contraceptive pill is said not to cause periods to stop, but some women find that their cycles take a while to get back to a normal pattern when they stop taking the pill. Periods normally restart on their own once normal weight is regained or the stress subsides. The drug clomiphene is sometimes prescribed to stimulate ovulation.

A condition that causes irregular periods, facial hair, spottiness and sometimes infertility is polycystic ovaries (PCO). PCO is more common in overweight women and describes the appearance of the ovaries which are filled with cysts. PCO may not cause any problems or it may cause a hormone imbalance with excess male hormones (androgens) which are responsible for the infertility. Losing excess weight, drug treatment with drugs that stimulate ovulation (e.g. clomiphene), or an operation to modify the internal structure of the ovaries to stimulate them to work, can all be successful.

Another cause of irregular or absent periods and therefore infertility is a premature menopause. Some women experience the menopause before the age of 40. This means that the ovaries stop working and will not produce eggs. The only hope for pregnancy in these cases is using donor eggs (see below). There are also various hormone disorders that can prevent ovulation and conception. The GP or gynaecologist can take a blood sample to test for various hormone levels. Treatment obviously depends on finding a specific cause.

Blockage of the fallopian tubes, which lead from the ovaries to the womb, is another important cause of infertility. The tubes can be blocked because of previous infections or operations. An ectopic pregnancy (pregnancy in the tube), appendicitis, infections which have spread up from the vagina and womb (pelvic inflammatory disease) or inflammation from endometriosis (see Chapter 11) can all make the tubes stick together or be plastered down by adhesions (which are bands of tissue that form when there is inflammation or infection). The tubes need to be able to float freely and be totally unblocked. An operation to achieve this may be attempted but IVF (see below) may offer more hope.

An obstruction in the womb is a rare cause of infertility. A gynaecologist can look into the womb with a telescope (hysteroscope) to ensure there is no problem in the womb, as part of the investigation for infertility.

Male problems are to do with sperm. In many cases, the man's sperm may not be healthy enough to fertilise an egg. As part of the investigations for infertility, men are asked to produce a semen sample by masturbating. The sample is then analysed in a laboratory. Men with low sperm counts used to be told there was nothing that could be done, and treatment still presents a great challenge, but the semen can be treated in the laboratory to improve the chances of pregnancy. Techniques like ICSI (see below) are offering hope. An operation to retrieve sperm from the exit to the testicle where they are produced can now be done without a general anaesthetic. This is useful if there is a blockage in the tube from the testicle. It has been established that male fertility is declining, possibly owing to modern environmental hazards. The effect that drugs, smoking, infections and stress have on fertility, both male and female, is still unclear.

Assisted conception – the options

IVF

In vitro fertilisation (IVF) is the procedure used to fertilise eggs with sperm outside the body (in a test tube). The fertilised eggs are then placed in the womb. Drugs are given to the woman to stimulate her ovaries to produce several eggs, instead of the usual one. The eggs are then taken from the ovaries using a vaginal scanner which is passed up the vagina. A sedative and painkiller are given, but a general anaesthetic is not necessary. The egg is mixed with the sperm sample supplied by the man. If sperm fertilise the eggs, the fertilised eggs (embryos) are put in the woman's womb a couple of days later, in a procedure similar to having a smear test. A maximum of three embryos are usually replaced. Hormone pessaries put in the vagina keep the lining of the womb primed to accept the embryo.

Possible problems with IVF include a one-in-four chance of having twins and a one-in-20 chance of triplets, if pregnancy occurs. Minor problems such as sickness, headaches and feeling irritable may be due to the drugs. The ovaries may be too sensitive to the hormones and produce numerous eggs. This can cause vomiting, lower abdominal pain and bloating and occasionally leads to hospital admission. There is also an increased chance of a pregnancy in the tube (ectopic pregnancy) but the ultrasound scan, which is done if a pregnancy test is positive, should pick this up.

IVF is particularly useful for women with blocked or damaged fallopian tubes. It is also offered to women who have unexplained infertility, or are having difficulty getting pregnant for a variety of reasons such as lack of ovulation, endometriosis, or a partner with a slightly low sperm count.

Gamete intra-fallopian transfer (GIFT)

GIFT is an alternative to IVF. Drugs to stimulate the ovaries are given as for IVF. The difference is that the woman has a general anaesthetic, the eggs are collected, and eggs and sperm put into the fallopian tube, which leads from the ovaries to the womb. The eggs and sperm are left to fertilise themselves in the tube. Obviously, only women with normal tubes can have GIFT.

Pro-nuclear stage embryo transfer (PROST)

PROST is just like IVF, but the fertilised eggs are put into the fallopian tubes using a laparoscope, rather than into the womb through the vagina.

Intra-cytoplasmic sperm injection (ICSI)

ICSI is offering hope for men with very few active sperm who cannot fertilise an egg with IVF. A single sperm is injected directly into an egg which has been retrieved from the woman as it is with IVF.

Zygote intra-fallopian transfer (ZIFT)

ZIFT is a combination of IVF and GIFT. In this technique the woman's ovaries are stimulated and eggs retrieved as for IVF. The eggs are mixed with sperm in a test tube, but as soon as fertilisation has occurred the zygote (the fused egg and sperm) is placed in the fallopian tube. ZIFT is used when fertilisation of egg and sperm has been problematic (so GIFT is unlikely to work), and when the fallopian tubes are fully functioning (which renders IVF unnecessary).

Artificial insemination

Artificial insemination can be done using the partner's sperm, or sperm from a donor. In artificial insemination by husband (AIH) the man produces a semen sample by masturbation. The semen is syringed into the woman's cervix (the neck of the womb) at the time in the month when she is producing an egg (ovulating). This is usually exactly 14 days before the next period is due. If the sperm are few, slow moving or have many abnormalities, the semen can be processed to select the most active sperm, which can then be syringed into the cervix.

In donor insemination (DI) the sperm comes from donors, usually students, and has been screened for sexually transmitted diseases including HIV and genetically inherited diseases. The sperm donor has no legal rights or obligations. The sperm is introduced into the neck of the womb at the time of month when the woman is ovulating, as for AIH.

Intra-uterine insemination (IUI) introduces the sperm straight into the womb, through the vagina and neck of the womb. The sperm are specially treated, and the woman may be given drugs to help her produce more than one egg to increase the chances of pregnancy.

Egg donation

This is the only option for women who are not producing eggs. The eggs can be fertilised by the woman's partner's sperm, and the embryo can be replaced in the womb while hormones keep the pregnancy going.

Which technique for which problem?

Problem	Techniques which may be suitable
Sperm – too few or too slow	ICSI or DI or IVF
Woman's body 'hostile' to sperm, e.g. she makes antibodies to sperm or the cervix produces a barrier to sperm	AIH or IUI or IVF
Problems with intercourse, e.g. spasm in the vagina (vaginismus) or male impotence	AIH or IUI or DI
Unexplained infertility	AIH or IUI or IVF
Poor-quality eggs and lack of response to IVF	ICSI
Sperm cannot get to eggs, e.g. blocked fallopian tubes due to previous sterilisation, endometriosis or previous ectopic pregnancy	IVF
Irregular ovulation	IVF

GIFT, ZIFT or PROST techniques may be offered in place of IVF, so long as the fallopian tubes are normal. Donor or preserved sperm may be used if the man has chemotherapy for cancer and sperm has been stored from before his treatment. DI can also be used for lesbian women who do not wish to have intercourse with a man but who would like to have a baby.

Adoption

Adoption remains an alternative to assisted conception. Couples who do not conceive using assisted conception, and who cannot or do not want to adopt, have to face childlessness. This can be a period of bereavement for all the lost experiences they had looked forward to. Counselling and help from support groups can be enormously useful (see address list).

Chapter 13

Pregnancy

Most women know they are pregnant because they miss a period. Some women have an intuitive 'feeling' that they are pregnant. Feeling sick and tingling of the breasts can start soon after the sperm fertilises the egg (conception) and may be noticeable even before the next period is due. Modern pregnancy-testing kits can be bought in supermarkets or chemists, and are easy to use and very accurate. They can detect pregnancy just ten days after conception, which may be four days before a woman will notice a missed period. The kits all test for the presence of a pregnancy-related hormone called HCG in the urine. To get an instant result you can either do a test at home or take a urine sample to a chemist, who will carry out the test. Some GPs test on the premises, others will offer to send a sample to the hospital laboratory. A charge may be made and the results are likely to take a week if the sample is sent off. All the tests are equally accurate. A negative result may mean the test was performed too early, so it may be worth repeating it a week or two later. A positive result means pregnancy in the vast majority of cases.

Forty weeks and three stages

The pregnancy is counted from the first day of the last menstrual period and lasts 40 weeks, give or take two weeks either side of that date. Eighty-five out of a hundred women deliver their babies within a week of the expected date of delivery. The pregnancy is divided into three stages called trimesters. The first trimester, from conception until the end of the 12th week, is the time when most of the baby's organs develop. The middle trimester, until the end of the 28th week, is when the pregnancy starts to show. You begin to

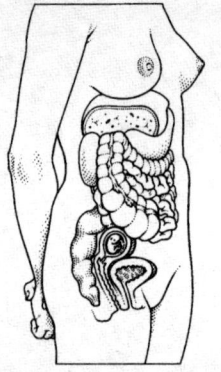

First and second months

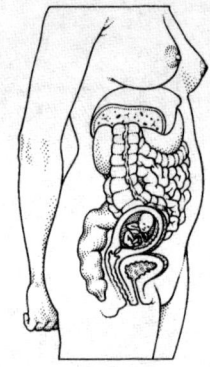

Third and fourth months

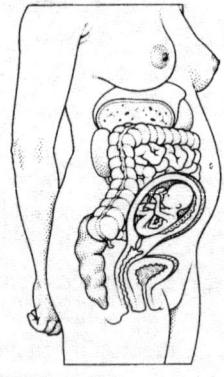

Fifth month

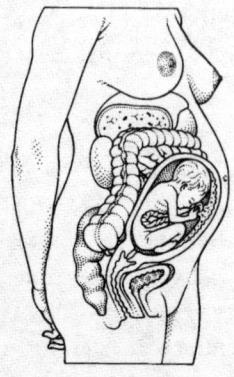

Sixth and seventh months

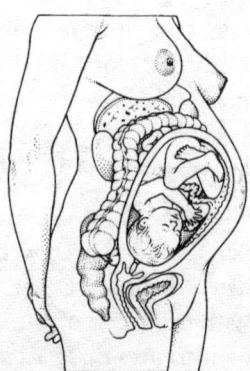

Eighth month

Figure 16 The developing foetus

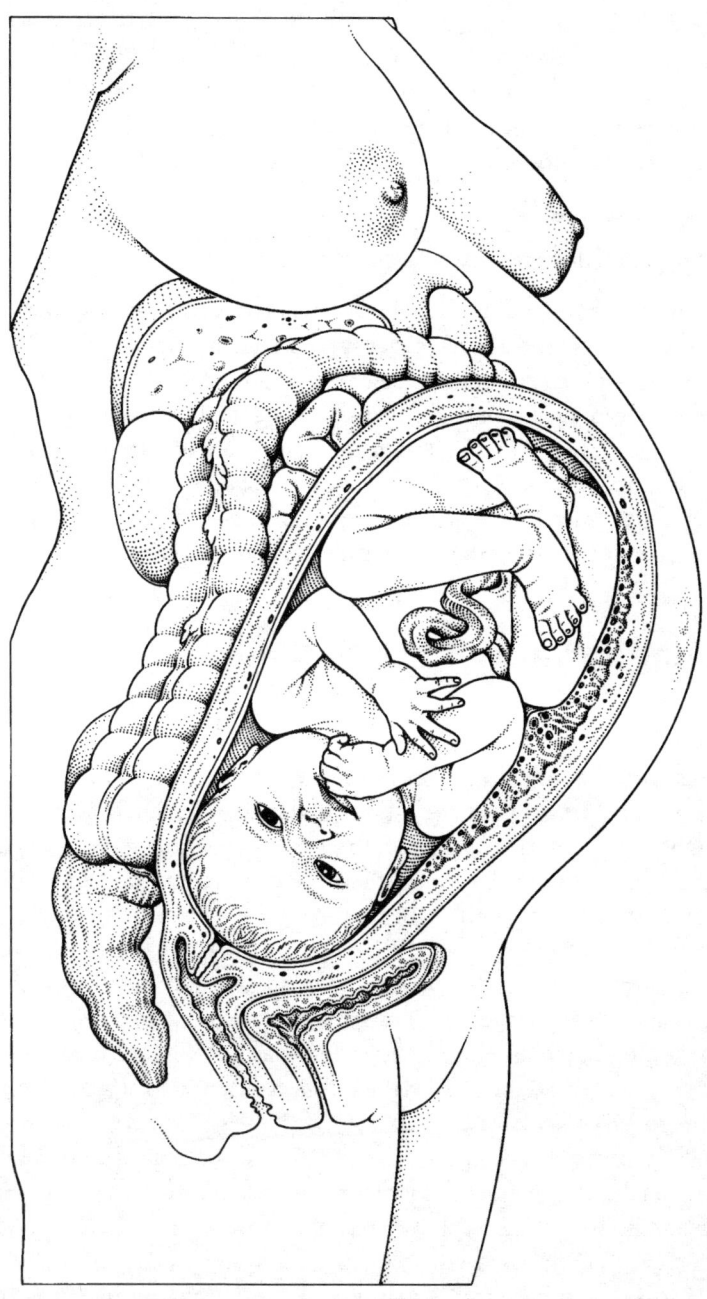

Baby at 40 weeks, ready to be born

feel the baby's movements around 18–20 weeks. The baby's organs continue to develop and the baby grows from now until the end of pregnancy. By the end of the second trimester, most babies can survive if they are born prematurely. In the last trimester, the baby's lungs become more mature and it continues to grow.

Pregnancy and pre-existing medical conditions

Women who have a pre-existing medical condition, such as high blood pressure, diabetes, epilepsy or a thyroid disorder, should ideally seek medical advice before getting pregnant. The aim of pre-conceptional care is to stabilise any pre-existing medical conditions, and to alter drug treatment if necessary to minimise any risk to the baby without jeopardising the mother's health. Women who are taking any medication for any condition should ask the GP or specialist whether they need to avoid getting pregnant.

Caring for yourself and the baby

Diet

Pregnant women often get very worried about what to eat and what not to eat during pregnancy, how much to eat, and how much weight they should be gaining. Apart from avoiding certain foods which may put the baby at risk, there are no hard and fast rules. Eat a balanced diet with regular meals and do not consciously eat more or less than normal.

With one exception, vitamin and mineral supplements are not necessary unless your diet is unusual or you are prone to certain deficiencies. Folic acid is the exception to this as it is vital for the development of the baby's spinal cord and nervous system. Folic acid is found in Marmite, Bovril, green leafy vegetables, citrus fruits, pulses, breads and cereals and dairy products. It is also recommended that women take a supplement of 400 micrograms a day prior to conception and in the first 12 weeks of pregnancy. Iron supplements are not necessary unless a blood test shows iron-deficiency anaemia.

During the first ten weeks of pregnancy there is no need to eat any more than usual. Women often do have an urge to eat more, because the pregnancy hormones can induce hunger. If you are worried about gaining extra fat during the pregnancy, just try to eat as normally as possible. As the pregnancy continues it does use up extra energy, but this amounts to only about 500 extra calories – the equivalent of a medium-sized bar of chocolate or a small packet of peanuts – a day, and therefore does not really warrant 'eating for two'. A lot of women who have hang-ups about food find they enjoy their food and worry about it less when they are pregnant. Bulimic women tend to get better while they are pregnant. Obsessive preoccupation with weight gain in pregnancy is not helpful or justified on medical grounds. In a normal pregnancy the weight gain tends to be between 6kg and 19kg (1–3 stones), with the average being around 12kg.

Alcohol

Most women who drink alcohol during pregnancy do so in moderation. The evidence suggests that moderate intake does not put the baby at any risk. Drinking in moderation means having one or two glasses of wine or a pint of beer up to twice a week (see Chapter 1). Women who are pregnant, or are trying to get pregnant, are best advised either to give up alcohol or to restrict their intake to this level. Women who drink heavily – more than 40cl or around half a bottle of wine a day over a period of months – put their developing babies at increased risk. The babies are more likely to be underweight when they are born, have difficulties feeding and sleeping, and be more irritable than normal. In extreme cases, the babies may be born with a variety of abnormalities which result in low IQ, an odd-looking face, cleft palate and so on. This is the so-called fetal alcohol syndrome. Women who find it hard to control the amount of alcohol they drink should really try to abstain altogether during pregnancy. If this applies to you, seek expert help before you get pregnant, to correct any vitamin deficiencies or other alcohol-related health problems that you may have as a result of drinking too heavily.

Smoking

Smoking during pregnancy may result in the baby being underweight. Babies normally grow a great deal in the last 24 weeks of the pregnancy, but smokers' babies tend to fall short of the expected growth rate. By giving up smoking in the first 16 weeks of pregnancy, you can ensure that your baby has a normal chance of growing to its expected weight by the time of delivery.

There are other very good reasons for giving up smoking before pregnancy. For example, non-smokers may find it easier to get fit before getting pregnant. Premature labour is more common among smokers. And there is growing evidence about the risks of passive smoking once the baby is born. These risks include an increase in allergies, respiratory infections and asthma. Children of smokers are also far more likely to smoke themselves than children of non-smokers, with all the health risks that smokers incur. In short, it is not much of a birthright for a baby to inherit. Pregnant women often find that pregnancy is a strong and persuasive incentive to quit. The challenge is not to restart once the baby is born.

Recreational drugs

Drugs which are smoked with tobacco, such as marijuana, pose the same hazards to the developing baby as smoking cigarettes. Whether specific drugs such as Ecstasy have an adverse effect on the baby is hard to say because women who regularly use illicit drugs during pregnancy often expose themselves to other harmful drugs too, like alcohol and cigarettes. Addictive drugs such as heroin pass through the placenta to the baby and the baby may be born dependent on these drugs too. Newborn babies of heroin addicts experience withdrawal signs of shaking and agitation, and often have to be cared for in special units until they are stable. Coming off all addictive drugs before pregnancy is obviously the ideal.

Exercise

In principle, pregnancy should not stop you continuing your normal level and type of exercise. If you are used to playing badminton twice a week, for example, and swimming from time to time, there is no reason whatsoever to change your normal routine. It obviously does not make sense to go from being a couch potato while not pregnant to doing two hours a day of high-impact aerobics as soon as the pregnancy test turns positive. It is a good idea to increase your fitness while you are pregnant, but it should be a gradual process.

Low-impact activities that increase general fitness are ideal, such as using the stairs rather than lifts, brisk walking and swimming. During very strenuous exercise blood is diverted away from all organs other than the muscles, heart and lungs. This includes the uterus, so sustained bouts of very intensive exercise may be harmful in theory. In practice, few women exercise to that extent.

Work

Three-quarters of women in paid employment continue to work until the 34th week of pregnancy. Women with more than 26 weeks' service are entitled to 18 weeks' pay – 6 at 90 per cent of full pay and 12 at statutory maternity rate. The earliest time that maternity leave can start is 11 weeks before the expected date of delivery (EDD). A Mat B1 form has to be signed by a doctor or midwife to confirm the EDD. Many women prefer to work as long as they can, leaving as much maternity leave as possible once the baby is born. In some cases, an employer can leave a woman's job open for up to a year. Average maternity pay in the UK works out as the equivalent of 8 weeks' full pay. This does not compare very favourably with other European countries: women in Denmark, for example, get the equivalent of 22 weeks' full pay, and those in Germany get the equivalent of 14 weeks' full pay. Some employers require women to stop working after a particular number of weeks of pregnancy. But so long as the workplace is safe from toxic chemicals and hazards, and you are enjoying a normal pregnancy, there is no medical reason not to go on working for as long as you want to.

Specific hazards at work and at home

Breathing in tobacco fumes is probably the greatest hazard for pregnant women, but there are many things they should avoid or be careful about. For example, you should avoid X-rays in early pregnancy or if there is any chance that you are pregnant. Serial X-rays of the kidneys and intestines are particularly hazardous to a developing baby. However, ultrasound scans have been performed on over 50 million women during pregnancy without any pattern of problems to the developing babies having emerged. Likewise, visual display units (VDUs) have not been shown to cause any consistent pattern of problems.

You should discuss any specific concerns you have about chemicals in the workplace with the Health and Safety Executive★ or your local union official. Employers are bound by a code of practice, and must offer alternative, non-hazardous work to pregnant or breastfeeding women. Normal exposure to chemicals in the home such as cleaning fluids should not pose a hazard, although it is always wise to ventilate all rooms in which chemicals are sprayed or used. You should take care when you are gardening: stand well back when pesticides are being used, and wear gloves when applying chemicals such as weedkillers. Handling pets or animals can occasionally expose you to infections that may damage your baby. Pregnant women are advised to avoid handling ewes at lambing, because of the risk of catching chlamydia. If you have to handle cat-litter trays, wear gloves, to avoid infection with toxoplasma. Silage and silage-like products should also be avoided because of the risk of catching listeria.

Childhood infections such as rubella (German measles) and chickenpox may occasionally infect a pregnant woman with risks to the developing baby. Immunity to rubella should ideally be checked prior to pregnancy, and is checked routinely in the antenatal clinic. But if you come into contact with a child who has an infectious disease, or if you develop an infection yourself while you are pregnant, you need to get specific advice because the outcome depends on the type of infection and the stage of pregnancy.

High levels of stress may not be good for the mother or the baby. Stress may contribute to high blood pressure, which can be harmful in itself, although it is hard to find conclusive proof of a link between stress and complications in mother or child. Extreme agitation can divert blood away from the uterus. Pregnant women in full-time employment do not have lighter babies on average than women who are not in paid work, and working outside the home is not dangerous to the health of the mother or developing baby. However, travelling to work, especially in large, crowded, dirty cities, may increase the likelihood of premature labour. It makes sense to try to arrange more flexible working hours to avoid travelling during rush hours, if possible.

Day-to-day health problems in pregnancy

Heartburn

Heartburn is due to acid refluxing up the oesophagus from the stomach. It can happen all the way through pregnancy, but is often worse towards the end. One of the hormones that keeps the pregnancy going, progesterone, also has the effect of allowing the acid to rise out of the stomach more easily. In later pregnancy, the pressure of the developing baby pushes acid up out of the stomach too. This causes belching and pain behind the breastbone which can spread round the back and up to the shoulder tips, especially when you lie down. Ways of dealing with this are to prop yourself up on an extra pillow in bed, avoid stooping, avoid acid foods, eat little and often and neutralise the acid by drinking milk or taking an antacid such as Gaviscon.

Piles

Piles or haemorrhoids are due to pressure on the veins in the back passage (anus). They are common in pregnancy because the hormone progesterone relaxes the vein walls and lets them become more engorged. Progesterone also slows the gut down, making constipation – and therefore straining – more likely. The developing baby can also cause pressure on the veins. Piles can bleed, itch and hang down out of the anus, especially after you have passed a motion. Avoiding constipation by eating a high-fibre diet with plenty of fluids is the best way to minimise problems from piles. Suppositories such as Xyloproct can be used, but it is best to seek medical advice first. The piles usually improve after pregnancy, but occasionally remain troublesome and require treatment such as an injection to shrivel them up.

Varicose veins

Varicose veins are the same as piles, except that they occur in the legs, not the anus. Standing for long periods of time exacerbates the aching and throbbing that varicose veins can cause. Hairdressers and other workers who have to stand for long periods should try to sit on a stool while working whenever possible, and try to put their feet up during breaks and after work. Support stockings are available on prescription, although they have to be paid for. Engorged veins can also cause problems in the vulva, the area surrounding the vagina. A heavy throbbing, which is worse at the end of the day, is felt around the outside of the vagina. Engorged veins may be visible. There is no specific treatment except lying down. They almost always get better soon after the baby is born.

Nausea

Nausea is very common in the first 12 weeks of pregnancy. It is due to the rising hormone levels which are necessary to keep the pregnancy going and usually passes after the first 12 weeks, but it can be very debilitating for some women. Eating little and often, trying not to get too tired, and avoiding foods and drinks that exacerbate the nausea, may be helpful. If vomiting becomes so severe that you are becoming weak, losing weight or are worried, then drug treatment may be advised. This could be antihistamines which are usually used for allergic reactions, or a drug called promethazine which is used for travel sickness.

Tiredness

Tiredness is very common especially during the first 12 weeks of pregnancy, probably because of the rising hormone levels, and again at the end of pregnancy when the baby is much bigger and heavier. The middle third of the pregnancy is normally the stage when women feel particularly well and relatively full of energy. Anaemia can make a woman more tired than usual, and the blood test carried out as part of routine antenatal checks will detect anaemia so that iron supplements can be given if necessary.

Check-ups and tests

The pattern of regular check-ups during pregnancy (antenatal care) that exists in the UK today started in the 1920s. Many tests have been added as scientific technology has moved on. The result is a rather bewildering array of measurements, blood tests and scans, and a ritual of antenatal appointments that is the same for high- and low-risk pregnancies alike. The whole point of antenatal care is to identify those women who are at increased risk of problems during pregnancy or childbirth. A lot of the 'sacred cows' of antenatal care, such as routinely weighing pregnant women, checking a urine sample on each visit to the antenatal clinic, and insisting on a set number of antenatal appointments irrespective of whether the pregnancy is high or low risk, are being questioned at the moment. The ideal is to devise a personalised package of antenatal care and options for childbirth for each individual woman. The better-informed a woman is about what is being offered and why, the more she can formulate a plan of care with her midwife, GP or obstetrician (hospital doctor).

The aim of antenatal care is to:

- deal with the problems women experience during pregnancy, e.g. heartburn, varicose veins and high blood pressure
- deal with signs that the baby is not thriving in the womb, e.g. by delivering the baby early if problems are detected, or correcting abnormalities while the baby is still in the womb
- prevent problems for the baby, e.g. offering termination of pregnancy if the baby is found to have Down's syndrome
- prepare the mother and partner for childbirth
- prepare the mother and partner for parenting.

Screening for Down's syndrome has previously been reserved for women aged 35 or over, on the basis that Down's syndrome becomes more common among older mothers. Although this is true, it is also the case that since most women who have babies are younger than 35, at least half of all Down's syndrome babies are born to younger mothers who were not offered screening. More tests (e.g. nuchal translucency and blood tests, see below) are therefore being offered to women irrespective of their age.

Women in the UK have an average of 15 checks per pregnancy. This is about the same as in the Netherlands, and about three times as many as in Switzerland. Yet there is very little difference in the outcomes of pregnancies in the three countries. The most important times for checks and their rationale are summarised below.

Week 12 A doctor or midwife will record details of previous medical problems, previous deliveries, the date of your last smear test and the date of the first day of your last menstrual period (LMP), in order to calculate your EDD. You will probably have a physical examination to check for undetected problems such as a heart murmur. But a vaginal (internal) examination is not necessary, and it is quite reasonable to delay having a smear test until after the pregnancy.

Blood tests are done to find out the blood group, rhesus factor (see box) and antibodies to detect anaemia, syphilis and hepatitis B. They are also used to check to see if the woman has antibodies to rubella. Other blood tests may be offered to those at particular risk, e.g. Afro-Caribbeans may be tested for sickle cell, and women from Asian and Mediterranean countries may be tested for thalassaemia. Screening for HIV may be done anonymously on all women booking at the clinic, or it may be offered to those women at increased risk, e.g. intravenous drug users. Urine is checked for glucose (a sign of diabetes), protein (a sign of pre-eclampsia – see below) and sometimes for bacteria (a sign of urinary tract infection which is more common in pregnancy). You will probably be given general advice about diet, smoking, alcohol and drugs in pregnancy.

Many pregnant women have an ultrasound scan early in pregnancy. In most parts of the UK this is done around 12 weeks, though it is increasingly offered even earlier than that. The purpose of this first scan is to confirm the date the baby is due and to ensure

---

Rhesus factor

'Rhesus' refers to a group of chemicals carried on cells of the body. Factor D is the most common of these chemicals. If your cells carry factor D, you are classified as rhesus positive; if they do not, you are rhesus negative.

If blood containing factor D enters the bloodstream of a rhesus-negative woman (say, during blood transfusions or pregnancy, even if the latter results in a miscarriage), her body will produce antibodies against the factor because it does not recognise it and treats it as a foreign body. These antibodies stay in the woman's system and may 'attack' future pregnancies, which may cause anaemia in the baby and prevent its normal development.

Giving an injection of anti-factor D to a rhesus-negative woman immediately after a miscarriage or during a pregnancy mops up any stray factor D that may be in her bloodstream and prevents her from producing potentially harmful antibodies.

that the baby's growth is appropriate for the stage of pregnancy. Owing to the constant improvements in technology and knowledge of the baby's developing anatomy, this scan also allows for the early detection of abnormalities. The nuchal translucency test (see below) is one measurement that can be taken during this scan.

Now is a good time to discuss the pattern of antenatal care that would suit you and your options for giving birth. Your GP will ask you to sign two forms – a book which allows the GP to be paid for offering care during pregnancy, and a form which is returned to your local Family Health Services Authority which then sends you a certificate entitling you to free prescriptions and NHS dental care for all the time you are pregnant and for a year after the baby is born.

Week 18–20 You will now be offered another (or in some cases the first) ultrasound scan. This is used to measure the size of the baby, firm up the expected delivery date, and check for abnormalities (see below). A blood test for alpha fetoprotein (AFP) is sometimes offered around this time (see *AFP and other blood tests*, below). This test can indicate an increased risk of Down's syndrome or spina bifida (an abnormality of the spinal cord). However, a normal result is no guarantee of a normal baby. Some women prefer not to have the AFP test on the basis that they would not terminate the pregnancy even if there were signs of an increased risk of Down's syndrome. Amniocentesis (see below) is offered if blood tests suggest a problem.

Week 22 The midwife or doctor takes your blood pressure and feels your abdomen to check the size of the baby. Your weight gain is not a very useful measure of the baby's growth. You could ask to hear the baby's heartbeat. From week 24 you can ask the midwife or GP to sign a Mat B1 form, which will entitle you to maternity benefit.

Week 30 A repeat of the checks done in week 22. An additional ultrasound scan can be arranged if there is any concern that the baby is not growing well. This is the time when blood pressure can start to rise, so particular attention is paid to checking that.

Week 36 A repeat of the same checks. This is the time to find out which way the baby is lying. If it is breech (bottom first), or transverse (lying across), the GP or midwife will ask you to see an obstetrician in the hospital, to discuss your options – you may want them to try and turn the baby, for example.

Week 40 A repeat of the same checks. Once a pregnancy goes more than two weeks beyond the normal 40 weeks or if there are signs that the baby is distressed at any stage once it is fully developed, inducing labour with a hormone pessary in the vagina may be advised. If the former is the case, the worry is that the placenta, which is the unit in the womb which is sustaining the baby, will run out of steam and that the baby may be deprived of vital nourishment.

Women having their first baby need additional blood pressure checks because they are at greater risk of pre-eclampsia (see below). Check-ups at 26, 34, 38 and 41 weeks are advisable in addition to those above.

Ultrasound

Ultrasound bounces sound waves off internal surfaces and uses the echoes that come back to form a picture on a screen. There is no radiation involved, and the overall scientific view is that there is no evidence of harm for either mothers or unborn babies. Before an ultrasound scan, you are asked to drink three or four glasses of water to fill your bladder. This allows loops of bowel to float out of the way and helps the person doing the scan to get a clear view of the uterus. A clear gel is smeared on to the abdomen and the technician guides a smooth instrument over the abdomen while the images appear on the screen. Vaginal scanning, in which a probe is put into the vagina, is being used increasingly, as it gives clearer and more accurate results. Many technicians give some feedback while they are doing the scan, pointing out where the baby is, and later showing its organs. A full and final report may not be available until a week or so after the scan. The report is added to the pregnant woman's medical notes in the hospital, but neither she nor her GP is informed of the result unless there is a specific problem.

Are ultrasound scans useful?

In the UK, ultrasound scans may be carried out at 12 weeks to confirm when the baby is due in order to allow accurate timing of other tests such as AFP. If the dates are fairly certain, most pregnant women in the UK have a scan at 18–20 weeks. This is to firm up the expected date of delivery, and measure the size of the baby. This baseline measurement could be useful if there is any worry about the baby's growth later in pregnancy. A scan at 20–24 weeks shows the most detail when looking for abnormalities, and some hospitals offer this.

Ultrasound can also be used to confirm pregnancy: the embryo (developing baby) can be seen by 7–8 weeks, and a heartbeat may be visible. This is useful if there is any doubt as to whether the embryo is in the fallopian tube (an ectopic pregnancy) or in the womb. Ultrasound can also confirm that there is just one baby. It is important to know if a woman is carrying twins or even more babies, to ensure adequate care during pregnancy and childbirth. But this can be detected in other ways. The level of AFP in the mother's blood is raised if there is more than one baby in the womb.

Not only can the scan locate the baby or babies, it also locates the position of the placenta. The placenta occasionally grows over the exit of the womb into the vagina (placenta praevia). Often, as the womb grows, the placenta moves so that it no longer covers the exit, but if this does not happen, it means that the baby will have to be delivered by caesarean section. The scan will also pick up if there are any obstructions in the womb which may hinder the baby's growth or delivery. Large fibroids, for example, are harmless swellings of the muscle layer of the womb, but if you have them you may need a series of scans during pregnancy to keep an eye on them and the baby.

Probably the major reason women want to have a scan is to check for abnormalities. At 18 weeks, the major abnormalities that can be detected are spina bifida, in which the spinal column does not fuse properly, causing variable degrees of neurological damage, and kidney problems. Major heart problems can be picked up, but less obvious heart problems may not be apparent until 22–24 weeks. Major growth problems may not become apparent until 26–28 weeks.

Later in pregnancy scans can be used to measure the baby's growth if there is any cause for concern. A series of measurements of the baby's girth around the abdomen gives a good assessment of whether it is growing well.

Nuchal translucency test

This new test, which is offered by the NHS in only a few areas of the UK, is used to detect Down's syndrome. An ultrasound scan is done at 10–14 weeks and the technician measures the pad of fat at the back of the baby's neck. A high thickness could indicate Down's syndrome. This test can pick up 80 per cent of babies with the abnormality. However, the false positive rate (when the test suggests that the baby has Down's but is wrong) is 8 per cent. Therefore, if the test indicates that a baby could have the condition, women should have chorionic villus sampling (CVS) or amniocentesis (see below) – which are the only foolproof tests – to confirm the diagnosis.

AFP and other blood tests

A blood test to detect Down's syndrome is sometimes offered to women at 18–20 weeks. It measures the level of AFP and up to three other hormones (HCG, oestriol and inhibin) in the blood. If the levels of all four chemicals are looked at, as many as 75 per cent of babies with Down's can be detected. However, most hospitals measure only two or three of the chemicals. Measuring three – the so-called triple or Bart's test – picks up only 60 per cent of Down's syndrome babies.

Chorionic villus sampling (CVS) and amniocentesis

CVS or amniocentesis can be used to screen babies who may have a major problem with the chromosomes which carry genetic material. An increasing number of inherited (genetic) disorders are being identified and may be detectable using these techniques. Chromosomal abnormalities can impair mental and physical development, and parents may wish to terminate the pregnancy if an abnormality is found. Those at risk of chromosomal abnormalities are women:

- over the age of 35. The risk of having a baby with Down's syndrome is greater the older a woman is. Blood tests to measure AFP and three other hormones of pregnancy can identify possible cases so that CVS or amniocentesis can be considered
- whose previous babies have had a chromosomal abnormality
- who have an inherited disorder or a faulty gene. If a parent carries a gene which if inherited causes a major disease, or if both parents carry a gene which, if combined, put the baby at risk, then CVS or amniocentesis may be offered. This would apply, for example, if both parents were known to carry the gene for cystic fibrosis.

In CVS, an ultrasound scan is used to identify the baby so that the needle used to draw off some cells from the placenta does not damage the baby. The probe can be introduced through the mother's abdominal wall or up the vagina and through the neck of the womb. In amniocentesis, the doctor takes a sample of the fluid surrounding the baby (amniotic fluid), after identifying the baby and placenta using ultrasound scanning.

A new technique is now being developed which may offer an alternative to these two methods. Known as coelocentesis, it involves taking fluid from the space outside the sac in which the baby lies. It can be performed between six and ten weeks but it is still in the experimental stages.

Comparing the two techniques

CVS	Amniocentesis
Can be done at 9–11 weeks	Cannot be done until 12 weeks at the earliest
Results are available within a couple of days	Final result takes three weeks
Causes miscarriage in 1–3 per cent of cases, but fewer if the operator is experienced	Causes miscarriage in only 0.3–1 per cent of cases, but it is done later in pregnancy, by which time the risk of miscarriage has fallen naturally
Damage to babies' faces was reported, but has fallen now that the probe is introduced through the vagina rather than the abdomen	Does not cause abnormalities

Monitoring

Babies who are not growing well or are at greater risk of problems need extra monitoring. If they are not thriving in the womb, they may need to be delivered to be 'fattened up' in the outside world. Monitoring is usually done in the hospital, often in a day ward so that the mother can be monitored during the day and go home at night. Monitoring may involve:

- recordings of the heart rate and any contractions of the womb (cardiotocographs, CTGs)
- ultrasound scans to measure growth and assess whether the baby is thriving. Measurements of the baby's estimated weight, its movements, the amount of amniotic fluid surrounding it and even the pattern of blood flow in the blood vessels between mother and baby (Doppler studies) are all used to build up a picture of how the baby is faring
- cordocentesis, a technique to sample the baby's blood from the umbilical cord, which is rarely used because it carries a 1–2 per cent risk of killing the baby. It is done only if the pregnancy is putting the mother at great risk, and it is vital to know whether the baby is normal before subjecting her to further treatment and risk.

Medical conditions affecting the mother

Pregnancy and childbirth are safe for both mother and baby in the vast majority of cases. The death rate for babies in late pregnancy and just after delivery is at an all-time low and has continued to fall steadily since the Second World War. Babies who die in the womb in the last third of pregnancy, are stillborn or who die in the first week of life make up the perinatal mortality rate. In 1990, this rate was 8.3 for every 1,000 births. In the 1930s, it was nearly eight times as many. The huge improvements in perinatal mortality rates are largely due to the better standard of living enjoyed by most women in the UK today.

Despite these huge advances, some pregnancies still end with a less than perfect outcome. Of every 1,000 births in England and Wales in 1990, about eight babies were stillborn or died within the first week of life, 20 had some kind of abnormality and 60 weighed under 2.5kg (5.6lb), which made them more vulnerable than heavier babies. The pregnancies at greatest risk are those where the mother is under 20, or poor, or was born in Pakistan. The main dangers for the mothers are high blood pressure and blood clots on the lungs (pulmonary embolism). Infection and haemorrhage used to be the main dangers, but are much more readily treatable nowadays.

Being pregnant and giving birth used to be far more hazardous for women than it is today. In Victorian times, 6–7 women died per

1,000 pregnancies. The rate now is less than one-hundredth of that. Taking into account deaths of women during pregnancy, childbirth and six weeks after childbirth, and including death after miscarriages and ectopic pregnancies, the rate was 7.6 per 100,000 deliveries (1985–7). Every pregnancy-related death of a mother is investigated individually, and a report is compiled every three years by the Department of Health.

The main dangers for the babies are low birthweight, lack of oxygen, and severe abnormalities (congenital malformations) such as the non-development of the brain or other vital organs. The whole point of antenatal care is to help to identify potentially treatable problems early enough to prevent damage to either mother or baby.

Potential problems for the mother

The four main kinds of problems expectant mothers are likely to face are:

- vaginal bleeding in early pregnancy, including miscarriage, ectopic pregnancy and hydatidiform mole (see below)
- vaginal bleeding in late pregnancy, including placental abruption and placenta praevia
- high blood pressure and pre-eclampsia
- abdominal pain, including miscarriage, fibroids, ectopic pregnancy, twisted ovary or ovarian cysts, stretched ligaments, urine infection, appendicitis, placental abruption and uterine contractions.

Vaginal bleeding in early pregnancy

Bleeding in pregnancy is always worrying for a woman because of the fear that this is the start of a miscarriage. It is true that at least one in five confirmed pregnancies does miscarry in the first three months (12 weeks) of pregnancy. Modern medicine does not have an explanation for the majority of these miscarriages except that the egg and sperm have made an embryo that is not viable. There is rarely a specific underlying problem, and having one miscarriage does not mean you are at greatly increased risk of having another. Women who have two miscarriages at around 12 weeks may have a clotting disorder and need specialist investigation. Miscarriages that occur later than 12 weeks also need to be investigated. Sometimes the cervix opens in the middle or last thirds of the pregnancy for no obvious reason. A stitch can be sewn around the cervix at 14 weeks and removed at the end of the pregnancy to prevent this problem.

Miscarriages start with vaginal bleeding and often period-like abdominal cramps. If the bleeding and abdominal pains settle on their own, the pregnancy can continue normally with no increased risk to the baby. This is called a 'threatened' miscarriage. A miscarriage becomes inevitable if the bleeding and pains continue, the neck of the womb is seen by a doctor to have opened, and you have passed small amounts of tissue which are the contents of your womb. A blood test to check whether you need an injection if you are rhesus negative (see *Rhesus factor* box above) is always necessary, so it is important to seek medical advice. Hospital admission to 'scrape' the womb to prevent further bleeding and infection is often advised but it is not always necessary.

Mild bleeding may be due to a cervical erosion, which is a harmless raw area on the neck of the womb (cervix) which occurs because of the pregnancy hormones. Other causes of vaginal bleeding can include vaginal irritation from thrush, which also causes a creamy white discharge and polyps (small pouches) from the cervix which may cause bleeding after intercourse.

Ectopic pregnancy

An ectopic pregnancy (see also Chapter 11) is a potentially dangerous condition in which the pregnancy develops in the fallopian tube, instead of in the womb. Ectopic pregnancy is more likely if the tubes are damaged either by a previous ectopic, an operation on the tube, or infection. An ectopic pregnancy can burst, causing sudden pain and collapse. It may even be life-threatening. More commonly, the ectopic pregnancy and the damaged part of the tube seal themselves off and do not burst dramatically but cause severe abdominal pains on one side and later a small amount of vaginal bleeding. This typically happens around the sixth week of pregnancy. Urgent medical attention is essential for any woman with a suspected ectopic. She will be admitted to hospital for laparoscopy (a telescope is used to look into the abdominal cavity) and possibly an operation to remove the damaged part of the tube and resew the tube. After an ectopic pregnancy, women are at increased risk of another, but many go on to have perfectly normal pregnancies and deliveries.

Hydatidiform mole

Another very rare cause of vaginal bleeding in pregnancy is a hydatidiform mole. This occurs in just six out of 10,000 pregnancies. It causes excessive vomiting and vaginal bleeding at eight weeks of pregnancy, and makes a woman feel unwell. Occasionally grape-like globules are passed vaginally. The cause is an abnormality of the fertilised egg which causes an overgrowth of the vessels that normally go on to form the placenta. The diagnosis is made on an ultrasound scan. Treatment is a 'scrape' of the womb which sucks out the contents, so the pregnancy cannot continue. Follow-up is co-ordinated by a specialist centre and involves regular measurements of the pregnancy hormone (HCG) which is particularly high in this condition. If the HCG levels remain high, drug therapy is given to prevent further problems. It is not safe to embark on another pregnancy until the condition has been fully treated.

Vaginal bleeding later in pregnancy

Bleeding in late pregnancy may not have any obvious cause in many cases. Small blood vessels from the placenta or membranes which surround the baby may bleed, and this rarely places the mother or baby at any increased risk. Bleeding of unknown cause is usually dealt with by advising the mother to go into hospital for ten days so that the baby can be monitored. If the bleeding stops, the baby is growing well in the womb, and no underlying problem is found, the mother is normally sent home to wait for labour to start spontaneously.

But there are two potentially very serious causes of vaginal bleeding after 24 weeks of pregnancy.

Placental abruption

Placental abruption means that the placenta starts to separate from the womb. It causes sudden abdominal pain, dark red vaginal bleeding and clots. It is potentially very dangerous for both mother and baby. The cause is unknown. It is more common if there is an underlying abnormality of the womb, or if you have had a previous placental abruption. Placental abruption requires emergency hospital treatment. Stabilising the mother's condition is essential before rapidly delivering the baby.

Placenta praevia

Placenta praevia means the placenta has developed in the lower part of the womb, partially or completely blocking the exit from the womb through which the baby needs to pass to be delivered. It can cause painless, bright red vaginal bleeding which does not cause the same degree of weakness or collapse as a placental abruption. Placenta praevia is usually diagnosed on an ultrasound scan before it causes any bleeding. A placenta which lies low in the middle of pregnancy may well move higher to a normal position by the end of the pregnancy, when the womb has grown. But if it is still encroaching on the exit of the womb by 32 weeks, a caesarean section will be planned before labour is likely to start, at 36–38 weeks.

High blood pressure and pre-eclampsia

Mothers may have high blood pressure prior to pregnancy. The ideal situation is to reduce blood pressure to normal levels before pregnancy by losing excess weight, cutting down on salt in the diet, and taking medication if necessary. If blood pressure is well controlled, and has caused no kidney damage (i.e. there is no protein in the urine), the pregnancy should be uneventful for both mother and baby. Some women who do not normally have a problem with their blood pressure develop high blood pressure for the first time while they are pregnant. Normally blood pressure tends to fall in the second half of pregnancy to accommodate the extra volume of blood that pumps from the mother to the baby. If this process fails, blood pressure rises. High blood pressure can trigger a series of events that can damage the kidneys, causing protein to leak into the urine – a situation called pre-eclampsia. That is why a urine sample is checked at every antenatal clinic, especially if blood pressure is high. If there is no protein in the urine, the treatment for high blood pressure may be bed rest at home. If this does not work, and the blood pressure remains high, or if protein is found in the urine, hospital admission is needed to enforce bed rest, monitor the baby and mother and give drug treatment to lower the mother's blood pressure. There was a great deal of optimism that low-dose aspirin would help to reduce the incidence of pre-eclampsia, but trials have proved disappointing. Hope is now focusing on a drug used to treat heart disease (angina): glyceryl trinitrate, skin patches of which have shown good results in treating women with pre-eclampsia and babies who are not growing well in the womb.

Delivering the baby usually solves the problem of high blood pressure, but the baby needs to be at least 28 weeks old to have the best chances of survival. Pregnancy-induced high blood pressure normally returns to normal within ten days of delivering the baby. The baby may be smaller than average, but should otherwise be unharmed by its mother's high blood pressure. The danger of not controlling pre-eclampsia is that it can progress to a more serious condition called eclampsia, which is rare nowadays. It involves convulsions like epileptic fits. Signs of imminent eclampsia are headaches, flashing lights, an itchy face and stomach pains. Treatment of eclampsia involves drugs to control the fits (principally magnesium now) and delivering the baby as speedily as possible.

Abdominal pains

Abdominal pains are always worrying in pregnancy because women are understandably worried that they may be about to have a miscarriage. In fact, abdominal pains are common during pregnancy and may be due to relatively minor problems like a urine infection. It is always best to ring a GP, a midwife or the labour ward if you have abdominal pains. Abdominal pains that come and go after 28 weeks may be Braxton Hicks contractions (see below).

Fibroids
Fibroids are harmless growths of the muscle layer of the womb. They are most common in 30- to 40-year-olds, and among Afro-Caribbean women. During pregnancy the fibroids can break down, causing pain over the abdomen, mild fever and vomiting. They are usually diagnosed in an ultrasound scan, although it may be necessary to look inside the abdomen with a telescope (laparoscopy). Treatment is bed rest and painkillers, and the symptoms usually settle down without further intervention.

Twisted ovary
This is rare, occurs in younger women in early pregnancy and can cause pain and tenderness on one side of the abdomen. A laparoscopy is needed to make the diagnosis.

Ovarian cysts
Cysts on the ovary can burst and cause pain. Ultrasound is used to confirm the diagnosis. An operation to remove the cyst may be necessary.

Stretched ligaments
The growing womb can pull on the ligaments that hold it in place. Less commonly, small blood clots in these ligaments may cause abdominal pains at the side and down into the area behind the pubic hair. Rest, painkillers and a hot-water bottle held on the sore spots will help.

Urine infection
A urine infection spreading up to the kidneys is quite common in pregnancy. It causes fever, a burning sensation when you pass urine, a frequent urge to pass urine, and pain in the lower abdomen. If the infection spreads from the bladder into the kidneys it causes loin pain, vomiting and a higher fever. It is important to take a urine sample to the GP, and to start an antibiotic that is safe in pregnancy, e.g. amoxycillin, stay warm and drink plenty of fluid.

Appendicitis
This can occur during pregnancy, causing sickness, loss of appetite and abdominal pain. It can be tricky to diagnose in pregnancy because it does not always cause pain in the lower right of the abdomen, as the baby can shift the position of the appendix. An operation to remove the inflamed appendix should be achieved without disrupting the baby in any way.

Medical problems affecting the unborn

Abnormalities

Some women refuse tests designed to identify babies with abnormalities, because they feel they will want to have the baby regardless of the results. Other women request all the tests available, and consider terminating the pregnancy if tests suggest a serious abnormality. But there are other reasons to have screening tests, even if you would not consider termination. A growing number of conditions which are potentially dangerous for the baby, such as kidney obstruction and some heart and gut abnormalities, can be detected while the baby is still in the womb; moreover, procedures to correct some of them, like kidney obstruction, can be performed on the foetus itself. Treatment of many other abnormalities can be carried out soon after the birth of the baby, so detection in the womb gives parents and doctors time to make arrangements with specialist centres to expedite the treatment. Some women and their partners would also like to know in advance if their baby is likely to have significant problems, so they can start to adjust psychologically and prepare their family and friends for the new baby.

Around one in ten babies is born with some kind of abnormality. Many will be minor and remediable such as an extra toe, or more major but still readily repairable such as a cleft palate or hare lip. Less commonly, babies are born with an abnormality that is likely to affect their development and is going to mean they have special needs. Parents of babies born with an abnormality often go through a kind of bereavement, mourning the loss of the 'perfect' baby they had hoped for, and later grieving about the extra challenges involved in nurturing the child. It is impossible to take in all the implications in the first instance. The responsibilities of caring for a tiny baby usually push more long-term worries to the background for the first few weeks of the baby's life. There is time after that for parents to request extra meetings with specialists, to ask detailed questions about the outlook for their baby, and to find out what help is available.

Abnormalities may be caused by the environment, including radiation, drugs and infections. Or they may be inherited (genetic). One of the best known drug-related abnormalities was caused by thalidomide, a drug prescribed for nausea in the 1960s which caused limb abnormalities. Radiation in high doses is also known to cause abnormalities, which is why unnecessary X-rays are avoided during pregnancy. Infections such as rubella can also cause abnormalities.

Genetic problems such as Down's syndrome may cause abnormalities in the baby and impair his or her physical and intellectual development in later life. Screening tests aim to identify these babies so that parents have the choice of terminating the pregnancy if they wish. Treatment of genetic diseases, e.g. cystic fibrosis and sickle cell disease, may be possible in the future.

The cause of many conditions is unknown. For instance spina bifida, in which the spine fails to fuse properly, results in variable neurological damage, and is still not fully understood, although it is now recognised that if women take adequate folic acid (400 micrograms a day) the risk of spina bifida is reduced.

Low birthweight

'Low birthweight' refers to babies who are in the bottom 3 per cent of weight for babies born at that age. There is no absolute cut-off point. Being underweight at birth puts the baby at increased risk of problems during delivery and after it is born. However, the fact remains that most underweight babies are small but perfect, and encounter no serious problems at all. The most common reason for babies being underweight is that the mother smokes. But some babies are small because the placenta is not functioning well, and this would be the case if the mother had high blood pressure. Occasionally, babies are small because they have an abnormality. The best way of detecting whether a baby is likely to have a low birthweight is by ultrasound scans. Other factors that affect the weight of the baby include the size and race of the mother. Larger women tend to produce larger babies, although there is often no predictable connection between the size of a baby and his or her mother. Contrary to common belief, the size of the father plays little part. Women living at high altitudes have smaller babies.

Preventing low birthweight

- Do not smoke while you are pregnant. Smoking by the mother is the single most common cause of low-birthweight babies, which in turn is the most common cause of death and illness among babies in the first weeks of life.
- Have regular antenatal checks to detect high blood pressure. High blood pressure in the mother can cause damage to the placenta and restrict the baby's growth. Rest, drug treatment and early delivery of the baby may be necessary if maternal blood pressure is high (see above).
- Restrict alcohol to two glasses of wine or a pint of beer about twice a week and avoid binge-drinking (getting very drunk in one heavy drinking session) while you are pregnant.

- Discuss antenatal screening tests with a midwife. Ultrasound scans and blood tests aim to identify problems in advance. Treatment of some conditions is becoming possible while the baby is still in the womb.

- Seek specific medical advice if you are concerned that you have been in contact with or infected by an illness. Rubella (German measles) can cause numerous abnormalities and restrict growth. Widespread MMR vaccination of all children aims to eradicate this virus. Pregnant women are screened to check their immunity, although ideally immunity should be checked before conception. Other infections such as toxoplasmosis and cytomegalovirus are relatively rare in the UK. To avoid toxoplasmosis, pregnant women should not touch raw meat with their bare hands or handle cat-litter trays, since these are the main sources of infection.

Prematurity

Babies who are born more than three weeks early – that is at 37 weeks or before – are considered 'premature'. Women who start to have contractions and go into labour prematurely may be given drugs (ritrodine and salbutamol) in hospital, to try to stop labour. If labour cannot be stopped by drug treatment, transfer to a hospital with specialised care for premature babies may be necessary. Although it is always alarming to go into labour a few weeks before expected, problems are rare unless you are less than 34 weeks pregnant. Two out of a hundred of all babies born in the UK are born before 32 weeks of pregnancy. They can actually survive after 24 weeks or even earlier, and the possibilities for keeping very premature babies alive are improving all the time. Babies who are under 28 weeks when born require a great deal of medical care in a special care baby unit (SCBU) to help them survive. The aim of the care is not just to keep the baby alive, but to minimise the risk of any handicap as a result of the prematurity.

The specific cause of many premature births is not known. However, premature babies are more common among young, poor mothers, and among all women who have had a previous premature birth. The cervix sometimes opens of its own accord, resulting in a premature birth. It is possible to have a stitch sewn around the cervix to stop it opening, and you may be advised to have this done at around 14 weeks if you have had this problem previously. The stitch is removed at around 36 weeks, after which labour can proceed normally.

Twins or multiple pregnancies often result in premature labour because of the extra pressure on the mother's body. Hard, physical work and repetitive, boring, noisy or unpleasant work may bring on premature labour. Women who feel that a previous premature birth may have been triggered by their work may consider giving up work earlier in subsequent pregnancies, or being signed off as sick. Abnormalities of the baby can also result in premature birth, especially abnormalities that cause excess amniotic fluid. For example, if the baby cannot swallow any of the fluid because it has an abnormality in its food pipe, the amniotic fluid builds up and puts extra pressure on the womb, triggering labour. Ultrasound scans at around 20 weeks can pick up many foetal abnormalities, and scans later in pregnancy can detect excess amniotic fluid.

Vaginal infections can enter the womb by passing up the vagina and through the cervix. Once in the womb, the infection can weaken the membranes surrounding the baby, making them rupture prematurely (i.e. the waters break). This leaves the baby susceptible to the infection. If a woman's waters break prematurely, she is usually given antibiotics to control any possible infection, and to avoid transmission of any infection to the baby.

Labour

Recognising the onset of labour

Women are often surprised how hard it can be to know for certain when labour has begun. Many women rush to the labour ward at the hospital, or contact their midwife, only to be told that they are definitely not in labour. However, it is probably best to err on the side of caution. Tales of babies born in the back of the car, or unplanned home deliveries, may make good stories, but the situation may be far from ideal for mother or baby, especially if the labour does not go smoothly.

Early labour pains may feel like crampy period pains, but they are intermittent. They may feel like a band of pain rippling across the abdomen, or a gradually worsening backache. During the wave of pain, the abdomen feels hard and tight as the womb contracts. The wave of pain reaches a climax, then dies away. The pattern is often variable in the early stages. Weak contractions may follow strong ones, and *vice versa*. There may also be a show – a blood-tinged glob-ule of mucus which may come out of the vagina looking like pink-ish slime. This is the plug of mucus which has been lodged in the neck of the womb. But many women never see a show. Your waters may break, causing a sudden gush of a variable amount of clear fluid from the vagina. This is painless: it simply means that some of the membranes surrounding the baby have ruptured. Contact the labour ward when this happens, but you do not have to dash into hospital immediately.

Minor contractions of the womb do not necessarily herald the start of labour. They are called Braxton Hicks and can occur any time towards the end of pregnancy. If the contractions are lasting progressively longer, and coming progressively more frequently, it is likely that you are in true labour, and not just experiencing Braxton Hicks. If you are in any doubt, phone the labour ward or your midwife.

Place of delivery

Some 98.4 per cent of all deliveries in the UK take place in a hospi-tal or maternity unit. Just 1.6 per cent take place at home, or in a car or ambulance on the way to hospital. But half of these happen because the labour is very fast or starts unexpectedly. A mere 0.8 per cent of all deliveries are planned to take place at home. There are moves afoot to try to increase a mother's choice concerning place of delivery, and this may result in more home deliveries. There is a great deal of variation in the services and choices offered by the NHS in different parts of the UK. Private midwives are increas-ingly available for home deliveries, but adequate cover by a nearby hospital team is essential, in case of sudden emergencies.

The key to successful home deliveries is assessing which preg-nancies are risky for the mother or baby, and which are low risk. Low-risk pregnancies can be delivered safely at home, as has been seen in the Netherlands, where there are far higher numbers of home deliveries than in the UK. Women who are having their first baby can opt for a home birth, but they are more likely to require transfer to a hospital during labour. In a study of 285 women in inner London who gave birth at home between 1979 and 1989, over 77 per cent had a normal delivery at home with a midwife, without needing specialist help.

Women who have successfully given birth at home often say it is a very satisfying experience, minimally disruptive to other children and comforting from a mother's point of view to be on home territory. The disadvantage is the delay in getting expert help in an emergency. Women who opt for hospital delivery may prefer the fact that all the expertise is 'on tap' if needed. You can be discharged from hospital within six hours from most units if there are no problems with the delivery.

An alternative approach is to have a midwife come to you at home until delivery is imminent. She then accompanies you into hospital and stays with you during the delivery. This is called the Domino scheme. Some hospitals also have a GP-run unit attached to the main maternity wing where GPs are responsible for monitoring midwives, and where women can have a relatively low-tech birth unless a complication arises. Hospital units are increasingly aware of the need for a woman to know her midwife when she is in labour as this can make the whole experience less bewildering. Some areas are now reorganising midwives into small teams: you have a chance to meet the team while you are pregnant and one of them should be available to attend you whenever you go into labour.

Vaginal delivery or caesarean sections

The numbers of caesarean sections in the UK have increased in recent years to nearly 15 per cent of all deliveries in 1997. This is still far fewer than in the USA, where nearly a quarter of all deliveries are by caesarean. Throughout Europe the rate varies between 10 and 20 per cent, and there is a lot of variation within different areas of the UK too. The disadvantages for a woman in having a caesarean are the abdominal pain after the operation, the feeling of losing out on a valuable experience in not giving birth 'in the normal way', and being separated from the baby after the birth while the operation is completed. It also takes longer to get up and about and may be harder to care for the baby in the first few days.

Obstetricians feel that caesarean sections are usually performed because it is the safer option for the baby and/or the mother. But one reason for advising a caesarean is the obstetrician's fear of being sued if something goes wrong: in some cases it might be argued in court that doing a caesarean would have improved the outcome. So even in cases where the value of doing a caesarean has not been proved, like breech (bottom-first) babies, a caesarean may be carried out for fear of litigation. The same is true for doing a caesarean just because the mother had one last time, even if there is no recurring reason to do one.

The best way to keep caesareans to a minimum, without jeopardising the care of either mothers or babies, is for low-risk women to be cared for by GPs and midwives without unnecessary monitoring or intervention. Higher-risk pregnancies which are more likely to have complications require a different pattern of antenatal care, with electronic monitoring where necessary. Keeping low-risk women away from high-tech hospital units is likely to reduce the caesarean section rate, reserving the operation for when it is really necessary. If low-risk women develop any complications, they can be transferred from the care of a midwife or GP to a hospital consultant (obstetrician).

Types of vaginal delivery

The position in which a woman delivers a baby depends on her own preference, whether there are any complications which mean that intervention is necessary, and the resources and attitude of the midwife or doctor helping her to deliver the baby. Walking around during labour, lying in a birthing pool and being able to take up any position will all help to make a woman feel more relaxed and in control. But if the labour is not progressing smoothly, or there are any signs either the mother or baby is getting exhausted, intervention may be needed. To help get the baby out, a doctor may recommend putting a suction cup on the baby's head. This is called a ventouse. Forceps, metal instruments a bit like a pair of salad servers, are put into the vagina and clamped around the baby's head to ease it out into the world. Cutting the woman's perineum – the skin between the vagina and anus – is almost always necessary before using forceps or ventouse. This is called an episiotomy. An episiotomy may also be performed if the baby is breech (bottom-first), stuck or distressed, or if the perineum looks as though it is about to tear badly, damaging the anus. The cut has to be sewn up after delivery.

Pain relief

Giving birth is a painful business. But fear of the unknown can make the pain much more intense and frightening. Attending classes while you are pregnant, having a look around the labour ward, and giving some thought to how you would ideally like the birth to be managed can all help to minimise the panic that labour pains can cause. Most women like to have their partner with them during labour, but some opt to have a calm and reassuring person whom they trust, such as a mother, sister or close friend instead. Knowing the midwife who is to deliver the baby is better than meeting her for the first time once the intense pains have already started.

Some women go into labour with very fixed ideas about pain relief. But every labour is different, and it is a good idea to have worked out a preference while still keeping an open mind.

Hypnosis, acupuncture and self-help

These may be effective at relieving pain in the early stage of labour, but it may be hard to organise an experienced therapist to be available when the pains start. In practice, many women rely on self-help techniques such as yoga, relaxation exercises, a warm bath or a comforting back massage by a partner to help them through the early stage.

TENS (transcutaneous electrical nerve stimulation)

TENS machines (see also Chapter 3) can be hired or bought during pregnancy. They work by stimulating nerve endings in the skin. This is supposed to block the brain's perception of other sources of pain, such as labour pains. TENS has no side-effects and may be effective, although many women find it disappointing once strong labour pains start.

Gas and air

Another option for pain relief is breathing in a gas through a mask when a contraction starts. The gas (nitrous oxide) is mixed with oxygen in a 50:50 mixture known as Entonox. It can cause nausea and light-headedness. It makes many women feel as though they are 'floating', which makes the pain rather unreal.

Pethidine

Pethidine is a strong painkiller which can be injected in the early stage of labour. It can be very effective at blocking the pain, but may cause nausea and make the head swim. Pethidine can also make the baby's breathing slow and shallow after delivery, although this is rarely a problem because of the low dose given, and can be reversed by giving the baby a drug called naloxone.

Epidural

Epidurals, which are injections of anaesthetic drugs into the space around the spinal cord, produce very good pain relief, blocking sensation from the waist down. But having an epidural means that a caesarean section or forceps delivery is more likely, as you lose the sensation to push. Women who have epidurals occasionally suffer long-term backache afterwards. Changes in the type and amount of drugs given mean that the pain control has been improved but that the mothers' muscles are less paralysed, so they can walk around a bit more during labour. So far, though, these improvements have not reduced the need for forceps or caesarean section, and it remains to be seen whether they will reduce the risk of long-term backache. The vast majority of women who deliver a baby with an epidural are highly satisfied with the result.

After delivery

Women tend to stay in hospital for much less time after delivery than they used to. Many women are pleased to go home as quickly as possible so they can have a private bath, and sleep without being woken by the cries of other women's babies. In fact, hospitals often harbour infections, so both the mother and the baby may be better off at home. The flip side of early discharge from hospital is that help may not be on hand when a woman wants help with breast-feeding, or has concerns about her own or the baby's health. The homecoming may be a lonely and bewildering experience for women who do not have a good support structure at home. Even if there is a supportive partner at home, the parents of a newborn baby may feel they are floundering at first.

In the UK, a midwife visits every day for the first ten days of a baby's life. She checks the baby and the mother, who will find that it a good idea to make a list of questions as they arise to ask her when she visits. A heel-prick test is carried out to check whether the baby is low on thyroid hormone or has a rare but preventable deficiency which can cause mental impairment if not picked up. A health visitor normally comes round on the tenth day.

Health visitors are good people with whom to discuss feeding problems and the very common low mood that affects most mothers around this time. You should be able to speak to your GP on the phone and he or she may visit if necessary. Many GPs pay up to five visits after the delivery as part of their package of care which started with antenatal check-ups. Other sources of specialised help are the National Childbirth Trust* and La Leche League,* which have networks of local counsellors who can give help and advice about breast-feeding and other problems. It is important to ask for help from family, friends or professionals who may be able to ease the pleasurable but very taxing burden of becoming a parent.

Feeding the baby

Breast-feeding (see also Chapter 10) is better for the baby than bottle-feeding. That does not mean that bottle-fed babies cannot fare perfectly well, as the vast majority of them obviously do, or even that women who choose to bottle-feed are not good or caring mothers, as that is obviously not the case. But the hard fact remains that breast-feeding confers many advantages on the baby, and to a lesser extent on the mother. Yet the number of babies who are still being breast-fed at six weeks is a staggeringly low 38 per cent in the UK. If there were no readily available alternative to breast-feeding, almost all mothers would be able to breast-feed. Breast-feeding may be natural, but it does not always seem to come naturally to either babies or mothers. Help and support are essential if women who experience difficulty breast-feeding are going to persevere with it.

Hospitals are often at fault in giving newborn babies 'top-up' feeds from a bottle. Midwives on the maternity ward should be available to help women get breast-feeding established, and there is a good case to be made for staying in hospital until feeding is going smoothly. Alternatively, help at home from a community midwife should be available for as long as it takes to get the breast-feeding going smoothly.

Recovery after delivery

Vaginal bleeding after delivery normally tails off over about ten days. Fresh, heavy bleeding with clots and painful cramps may mean that some membranes or bits of placenta remain in the womb. Breast-feeding releases the hormone that makes the womb contract, and this may be enough to clear out the womb. A GP can visit and give an injection to encourage the womb to contract and empty itself if necessary. Sometimes readmission to hospital for a 'scrape' is necessary. Antibiotics may be prescribed if there is a chance that infection has entered the womb and is prolonging the bleeding or causing heavy discharge.

Feeling tearful and rather deflated is normal and often hits women about four days after delivery. A study of first-time mothers in Cardiff in 1988 found that twice as many women had the 'blues' as did not: it was apparently more normal to feel low than to feel happy. A number of factors probably contribute – plummeting progesterone levels, a sense of anti-climax after the initial euphoria, tiredness and the responsibility of caring for the totally dependent newborn. Having a good cry, and confiding in a partner or trusted confidante, is enough for most women. The mood normally passes within two weeks. It is perfectly legitimate, and advisable, to seek help from the GP, midwife or health visitor if this low mood persists, is worrying, or is interfering with your ability to care for your baby. Help is available in the form of counselling, regular visits from the health visitor, antidepressant drugs and hormone patches of oestrogen which some experts believe can help postnatal depression. More serious forms of depression which prevent a woman from caring for her baby are rare, and require expert help from a psychiatrist.

Pain from a sore vagina, perineum piles and cracked nipples can be depressing and make a woman feel that she aches in every bit of her body. But these pains heal well, rarely causing any problems beyond the first few weeks. Paracetamol is safe while breast-feeding, and you can use that as well as hot-water bottles, rubber rings to sit on, and cold, lightly steamed cabbage leaves inside your bra to ease sore nipples (see Chapter 10). Problems such as leaking urine when you cough or sneeze also tend to improve with time, but may require expert help such as physiotherapy to strengthen pelvic floor muscles. These are problems to discuss with your GP at the postnatal check-up, which is usually offered six to eight weeks after delivery. Contraception is another issue to discuss at that time.

Terminating a pregnancy

A pregnancy can be unwanted because a woman feels physically, psychologically or financially unable to cope with caring for a baby and bringing up a child. Less commonly in the UK, a woman may want to terminate a pregnancy because screening tests have found that the baby has a major abnormality. Rarely, a doctor will advise a woman to terminate a pregnancy because it is putting her life in danger.

About one in three pregnancies among unmarried women, and one in 14 pregnancies in married women, are terminated (aborted). Most unwanted pregnancies could be avoided by using effective contraception (see Chapter 12), although no contraceptive method is 100 per cent effective, and accidents such as condoms splitting do happen. Post-coital contraception is available from a GP or family planning clinic: the morning-after pill involves taking two tablets and then another two tablets 12 hours later. This can prevent pregnancy in 98 per cent of cases if it is started within 72 hours of unprotected intercourse. Alternatively, a coil can be fitted up to five days after unprotected intercourse, with a similarly high success rate in preventing pregnancy.

But if pregnancy does occur, a woman may opt for a termination. Late termination of pregnancy is possible to allow time for women to get the results of screening tests. The vast majority of terminations are performed before 12 weeks, when a simple suction method is used to remove the contents of the womb under a short general anaesthetic. Most women seeking a termination for 'social' reasons, as opposed to an abnormality in the baby, see their GPs first, and should ideally discuss the pros and cons before being referred either to an NHS hospital, if termination services are available, or to a private clinic. Counselling is offered by the hospital or clinic prior to the termination. Future contraception should be discussed at the same time. Recovery from an early termination (before 12 weeks) is usually rapid and uneventful, although depression is common and prolonged bleeding and infection can occur. Occasionally the pregnancy can be left intact, necessitating a second operation. A termination does not affect future fertility or childbirth.

Terminations after 12 weeks normally involve inducing a mini-labour. After 24 weeks, termination is legal only if the mother's life is at risk if the pregnancy continues. A caesarean section to deliver the baby is usually performed in these rare circumstances.

Chapter 14

Menopause

The word 'menopause' simply means cessation of the menses, or monthly periods. The underlying reason for this happening is that the ovaries stop functioning. As the ovaries stop producing eggs, or do so only erratically, the levels of the hormones produced by the ovaries, oestrogen and progesterone, fall. It is the fall in oestrogen that causes some of the problems that women may experience after the menopause, such as hot flushes and a dry vagina. Many women sail through this period in their lives, grateful that their periods have finally stopped. A few suffer numerous physical and psychological symptoms. The hormone changes are certainly responsible for many of these problems. But for many women the menopause coincides with a period of adaptation and changing roles. Children will have moved on, partners may be retiring from work, working women may feel vulnerable at work, and some women just find the ageing process hard to accept. For others, it is a time of personal growth – a chance of an existence independent of the family's needs, to develop other interests or share more time with partner or friends. About 30 per cent of all women in the Western world have passed the menopause. Of these, about 30 per cent suffer from specific problems related to the menopause.

Hormone replacement therapy (HRT) can get rid of specific symptoms such as hot flushes in 90 per cent of cases. But in the UK fewer than one in five women who could take HRT choose to do so. For some this is a conscious decision. For others, HRT is never explained or offered. Each woman going through the menopause needs to weigh up the pros and cons of HRT for herself, and make an informed decision about whether to try it or not.

How to recognise the menopause

- **Cessation of periods.** The menopause has been reached when there has been no bleeding for 12 months. In the run-up to the menopause periods may become erratic – they could be frequent or infrequent, heavy or scanty. Some women may find that their periods do not change at all, they stop suddenly one month and never recur.

- **Hot flushes.** These are caused by blood vessels in the skin becoming more sensitive as oestrogen levels fall. A hot flush can come on out of the blue or when you are hot and flustered. It makes you feel, and look, bright red in the face and spreads to the neck, ears and hair. You may break out in a sweat and feel uncomfortable. Not all women get hot flushes, but some get more than their fair share. On average, women experiencing the menopause have hot flushes for about 18 months.

- **Night sweats.** Similar to hot flushes, night sweats come on while a woman is in bed. They may be mild or, in extreme cases, may cause your nightclothes and sheets to be drenched.

- **Breast tenderness.** Some women notice as they approach menopause that their breasts are more sensitive and tender to touch as well as more lumpy. Always see a doctor about lumps – do not assume that they are caused by the menopause.

- **Vaginal dryness.** Loss of oestrogen means that the vagina is less well lubricated. This may make sex uncomfortable and may also make you prone to urine infections.

- **Other symptoms.** Dry skin, lacklustre hair, brittle nails, mood changes, loss of concentration and tiredness are experienced by some women around the time of the menopause. It is not clear whether the conditions are directly related to loss of oestrogen, and hence whether they will be helped by HRT.

Women may be advised to stop HRT if they develop the following problems: migraine-type headaches starting for the first time; any signs of thrombosis in the legs or lungs; a rise in blood pressure; impending major surgery or a period of immobilisation, e.g. after a back injury; jaundice; or pregnancy.

Is HRT right for you?

Ask yourself the following questions to see whether you would benefit from HRT:

1. Am I suffering from the menopause? (hot flushes, breast tenderness, night sweats?)
2. Am I at risk of osteoporosis? (see box opposite)
3. Am I at risk of heart disease? (see box on page 382)
4. Am I low risk for breast cancer? (see Chapter 10)
5. Am I low risk for thrombosis? (i.e. no previous thrombosis, no strong family history of thrombosis, not obese/immobile/smoker)

If your answer to questions 1, 2 or 3 is 'yes', you may want to try HRT.

If you also answer 'yes' to both questions 4 and 5, HRT should be safe for you.

If your answer to any of these questions is 'no', the advantages of HRT may be less clear cut for you, but that does not mean you should not consider it.

The pros and cons of HRT

HRT is the most effective treatment for hot flushes, night sweats and a dry vagina. It reduces deaths from heart disease by half, and it reduces the incidence of broken hips and the other complications of osteoporosis. Without HRT, 50 per cent of women will break a bone because of osteoporosis.

One of the main disadvantages of HRT is that it causes 'minor' side-effects in around 15 per cent of users. These include breast tenderness, weight gain, nausea, headaches, itchy skin, rashes, mood swings and fluid retention. There is also a monthly bleed with most preparations, although some produce three-monthly bleeds or no bleed at all (see below). HRT can also cause abnormal vaginal bleeding, usually spotting throughout the cycle. This needs to be investigated if it persists. There is a possible increased risk of breast cancer after HRT has been taken for 5–10 years, but studies show conflicting results. Of two major recent studies, one showed

---

Risk factors for osteoporosis

The following factors could predispose a woman to osteoporosis:

- having menopause before the age of 45
- having a first-degree female relative with osteoporosis
- consuming a lot of alcohol
- smoking
- having a small build (short, small bones)
- using steroids or thyroid hormones long term
- having had prolonged anorexia
- having a high caffeine intake
- being of Asian or Caucasian origin
- having bone density scan which shows bone thinning.

---

no increase in breast cancer, the other showed a small increase starting after five years of use. The reduction in deaths from heart disease with HRT has to be balanced against uncertainty about breast cancer. Endometrial cancer (cancer of the lining of the womb) is no longer a risk since the progestogen hormone is given for at least 10 days out of 28, to balance the oestrogen in women who have not had a hysterectomy. Taking oestrogen on its own would increase the risk of endometrial cancer.

Types of HRT

There are basically four different types of HRT.

Oestrogen only This is for women who have had a hysterectomy. It can be given as a skin patch which needs changing twice a week; a skin patch that needs changing once a week; a skin gel to rub on daily; a tablet to take daily; a vaginal cream to apply as directed; a vaginal pessary to insert as directed; or as a vaginal ring to have inserted.

Oestrogen and progestogen combined This is for women who have not had a hysterectomy. Progestogen must be used for a minimum of ten days in each cycle, either combined in one product, or as two products. These preparations give a monthly bleed. The treatment can be given as a skin patch to change twice a week; a skin patch and tablets to use as directed; or as tablets only to use as directed.

Risk factors for heart disease

The following factors could predispose a woman to heart disease:

- menopause before the age of 45
- inherited high levels of cholesterol
- high blood pressure
- diabetes
- cigarette smoking
- obesity causing diabetes or an increase in high blood pressure
- first-degree relative with heart disease.

Oestrogen and progestogen combined, but giving a bleed every three months only. This comes as tablets to use as directed.

Oestrogen and progestogen combined, but producing no bleed at all. This can be used only by women over the age of 54, or after a whole year without periods. In other words, it is not suitable for women whose natural periods may not have ceased in case there is any undiagnosed vaginal bleeding. Spotting is common in the first four to six months but usually settles after that. It comes as tablets to use as directed.

Alternatives to HRT

Alternatives to HRT include:

- vitamin E for hot flushes
- counselling for depression
- homeopathy for menopausal symptoms
- a high-calcium diet, regular exercise and no smoking – to reduce the risk of osteoporosis
- a low-fat diet including fatty fish, regular exercise and no smoking – to prevent heart disease
- non-hormonal medication available for treating osteoporosis, e.g. calcium, calcitonin or biphosphonates
- non-hormonal medication for hot flushes (clonidine) and depression (antidepressants)
- vitamins A, C and E and the mineral selenium – these may offer protection against heart disease and breast cancer as they neutralise damaging chemicals (free radicals) in the body.

Chapter 15

Cosmetic surgery

Plastic (from the Greek *plastikos*, meaning 'to mould') or reconstructive surgery aims to restore to normal part(s) of the body that have been injured or physically damaged in some way. Cosmetic or aesthetic surgery aims to surpass or enhance the normal, and hence arouses strong passions. Media coverage has given it the image of being a pastime of the rich and famous: newspaper reports abound of celebrities who repeatedly subject themselves to the knife in an endless quest to achieve physical perfection and stave off the signs of ageing. However, the majority of patients are ordinary men and women who, after years of low self-esteem, are eager to correct a physical feature they are unhappy with or to achieve a more youthful look. Few of us would quibble with treatment for children who have such protuberant ears that they are made fun of in school and stared at in the street or for women who seek breast-reduction operations because they have such large breasts that they suffer constant backache and discomfort, as well as offensive comments and stares.

Hundreds of thousands of women, and a growing number of men, in the UK have had some cosmetic surgery, in the belief that it will make them feel more confident and better about themselves. It is estimated that some 65,000 people had cosmetic surgery in the UK in 1995, of whom 90 per cent were women. About 90 per cent of the procedures were to reverse signs of ageing.

If your mis-shapen nose, wrinkles, large breasts or roll of tummy fat is really the one thing that is preventing you from being happy, then it probably is worth fixing. However, some women have major surgery only to find that they then fixate on something else because the real problem is low self-esteem caused by other factors – and possibly ones that are better tackled by counselling than by surgery.

Is cosmetic surgery for you?

A decision to opt for cosmetic surgery is not to be made lightly. To help you make up your mind whether you should have it, ask yourself the following questions.

- Once I have this operation, will I be happy with the way I look?
- Am I prepared for the fact that the operation can cause damage?
- Am I being realistic about the likely result? Have I seen photos/slides/computer-generated pictures of the likely outcome?
- Am I satisfied that the surgeon is experienced in doing this particular operation and is a member of a recognised professional body (see below)?
- Do I know how much pain, swelling and bruising will result, how long I will need off work, how long healing will take and whether I will be left with any scars?
- Can I afford it?

If your answer to all these questions is 'yes', then cosmetic surgery may be for you.

The pros and cons of cosmetic surgery

Any woman contemplating cosmetic surgery must try to balance the advantages against the disadvantages before deciding if she should opt for it.

For those at a low ebb about a physical feature, improving it through cosmetic surgery can improve their self-esteem and make them less self-conscious. It can also make them less of a target for bullies. Physical discomfort, such as that experienced by women with excessively large breasts, can also be alleviated.

However, no surgery – even if it is a minor procedure – is risk-free. The anaesthetic used may cause an adverse reaction, complications (e.g. haemorrhaging and scarring) and infections may result, and the outcome may not be successful. For breast reductions and tummy tucks the body mass index (BMI, see Chapter 1) should be under 28. A higher BMI and cigarette-smoking lead to increased complications from both anaesthesia and the surgical procedure.

The risks and side-effects of specific types of cosmetic surgery are discussed under the relevant headings below.

Treatment providers

If you are contemplating surgery, consult your GP first to discuss options, including the possibility of getting help on the NHS (see below). Referral to a cosmetic surgeon should ideally be done by your GP so all your medical details can be forwarded to him or her.

As the availability of cosmetic surgery on the NHS is severely restricted, most women have to have it done privately. Moreover, because private medical insurance companies almost always exclude any type of cosmetic surgery, a woman wanting to have such surgery will have to pay for it out of her own pocket.

Cosmetic surgery on the NHS

For cost reasons cosmetic surgery is rationed on the NHS and is available only if the surgeon feels there are overriding physical or psychological reasons for doing it. Operations offered on the NHS include:

- implants for women with severe breast underdevelopment or asymmetry
- breast reductions for women with back and shoulder problems
- nose surgery for people with breathing problems
- tummy tucks for patients with abdominal wall bulges as a result of pregnancy or abdominal surgery
- eyelid reductions if the eyelids affect vision.

Waiting lists for these operations can be long, and some hospitals refuse to do any cosmetic surgery on the basis that it is not a priority for the NHS.

Cosmetic surgery and private medical practice

Cosmetic surgery has few legal safeguards. Anyone can set up a private cosmetic surgery clinic, call him- or herself a consultant, advertise for patients, and even operate, as long as he or she does not pretend to be a doctor.

A lot of cosmetic surgery is done in private hospitals and clinics by NHS surgeons trained in plastic and reconstructive surgery, but anyone wishing to have an operation must bear in mind that there are no set minimum training levels in cosmetic surgery, so surgeons from any field can, and do, use skills learned in other operations for cosmetic surgery (for example, an ENT surgeon may do cosmetic surgery on the nose). While many of the skills they need are the same, the lack of regulations means that a patient has no guarantees that her operation will not be the first of its sort for the surgeon.

If your GP cannot or will not refer you to a cosmetic surgeon or you want to look for one yourself, make sure you follow the guidelines given below.

Surgery checklist

Once you have decided that cosmetic surgery is for you, make sure that you have a clear idea of the look you want to achieve through it. Bear in mind that even fairly minor operations involve risks, and balance these against your motives for surgery. If you develop a wound infection, for example, it can seriously affect how the scars will look. There is also a chance that you might not be happy with your new appearance. Use the following checklist to make sure you get all the information you need to make a decision.

The surgeon
- What are his or her qualifications?
- Is he or she a member of BAAPS?
- How many times and how recently has he or she done the operation?
- Will the surgeon you meet do the operation?
- Does he or she have insurance?

Good surgeons will be candid about risks and should quiz you thoroughly about your motivations for surgery. They should take a full medical history, ask about your lifestyle and general health, and dissuade you if you are not fit for surgery. They should also explain clearly what results are achievable.

How to choose a clinic or surgeon

If you are contemplating cosmetic surgery, your best chance of achieving what you want is to find a good surgeon. This is not just a question of avoiding dodgy ones; it is equally important to find one you are happy with.

Some private clinics employ non-medically trained people (called 'advisers' or 'consultants') to talk first to potential patients. Many 'advisers' or 'consultants' are known to play down potential dangers and complications, thereby misleading people. Often they also pressurise patients into signing up for an operation and paying a deposit after the first meeting. Beware of clinics that ask you to

---

The surgery
- How do you need to prepare for surgery?
- How will the surgery be done?
- What are the risks? How often do complications arise?
- Where will you go for the operation?
- Will you have a local or general anaesthetic?
- How long will the results last?
- Will you be left with visible scars?

Recovery time
- How much pain, bruising or swelling should you expect?
- When will the stitches be removed?
- How long will your wounds take to recover?
- How long will you need to recover?
- What will you be able and unable to do once you get home?
- How long will you need off work?

The clinic or hospital
- What do the staff do if things go wrong? Do they have resuscitation equipment and medical help on hand 24 hours a day?
- Who can you contact if you need advice after the operation?

The cost
- Does the price include the cost of the anaesthetist, drugs, overnight stays and follow-up appointments?
- Who pays to fix complications or to re-do surgery if this is needed?

---

make a decision and to put down a payment even before you are allowed to meet a surgeon. Ideally, you should meet a surgeon at your first consultation. Insist on seeing one before you put down a payment: if you are not allowed to, do not use the clinic. He or she should explain the operation and the risks involved, examine you and advise you on your suitability for it.

If possible, see two or three surgeons and ask about their experience and qualifications (see below for an explanation of the letters after a surgeon's name). Do not be fobbed off by generalisations or jargon. Choose a surgeon you are comfortable with and avoid one who urges you to have surgery.

Surgeons' qualifications

Private clinics often proudly advertise that their surgeons are Fellows of the Royal College of Surgeons (FRCS), but on its own this guarantees only that the surgeon has a basic level of surgical training.

The British Association of Plastic Surgeons (BAPS)★ and the British Association of Aesthetic Plastic Surgeons (BAAPS)★ are the two professional bodies recognised by the Royal College of Surgeons. Members of the latter are consultant plastic surgeons who have had six years of specialist training in plastic and reconstructive surgery. However, BAPS or BAAPS membership in itself is not enough: you must check that the surgeon has experience of doing the particular operation you want.

Some surgeons are members of the British Association of Cosmetic Surgeons (BACS),★ a rival to BAAPS. Surgeons need no training in plastic surgery (just general surgery) to join BACS, although they do need to prove they have cosmetic surgery experience.

The General Medical Council (GMC) has a specialist register with the names of qualified surgeons; you can now telephone a GMC hotline★ to check whether a surgeon is on it.

Major procedures

Cosmetic surgery operations considered to be 'major' are those that generally involve the use of a general anaesthetic and usually some time in hospital. They include nose reshaping, breast surgery, face-lifts and liposuction.

Nose reshaping

Although everyone has a slightly asymmetrical nose, some people hate the look of their nose so much that they feel only surgery would alleviate their low self-esteem. Noses can be damaged from birth, in accidents, or by sniffing illicit drugs such as cocaine. Most requests for nose reshaping come from women who think their nose is too big, too long, too hooked or too bumpy. The tip of the nose tends to droop a bit as people age, and surgery to tilt the end up a little is fairly easy to do.

The upper third of the nose is a pyramid-shaped piece of bone, the lower two-thirds are softer cartilage and the tip of the nose is made of two domes of this cartilage. A septum, or wall, runs inside the nose, dividing it in two.

As the nose usually continues growing till a person is 20, surgery is not recommended for women under that age.

Before the operation
It is usual to meet the surgeon twice before the operation. At the first meeting the surgeon will take a full medical history and examine you physically. After you tell him or her what you would like done to your nose, he or she will examine it carefully, inside and out, and tell you whether it is possible. Photos will be taken and some surgeons will use computer images to show you what you might look like after surgery, although they will not be able to guarantee the final result. At the second consultation you will be told more about the operation itself. Make sure you get all the answers you need (see checklist above).

The operation
Surgery takes one to two hours under a general (or occasionally local) anaesthetic and usually requires an overnight stay in hospital. For nose reduction, the surgeon corrects any major problems with the septum which may be interfering with breathing. Then he or she may file down any humps on the nasal bones. The bones are cut at their base and moved inwards to make the bridge of the nose narrower. If the tip needs moving upwards, which it usually does, the septum is trimmed through small cuts in the nostrils and the cartilage is trimmed to reshape the tip of the nose. All the work is usu-

ally done from inside the nose, with no need for external cuts. This is called 'closed rhinoplasty'. Sometimes, a cut is made in the fleshy part between the nostrils, resulting in a small, inconspicuous scar, and this is known as 'open rhinoplasty'. To build up a squashed-looking nose, the surgeon can add cartilage from the ear or a rib, bone from the skull, or silicone implants.

After the operation

The nasal bones have to be encouraged to reset, so after the operation you will have plaster of paris or a plastic splint taped over your nose. Having ice packs over the nose and sitting up help to reduce bruising and swelling round the nose and eyes. The pain is usually quite bearable and may be quite mild. Gauze packs in the nose may be removed the morning after the operation or may need to stay in place for a few days if surgery has been extensive. Sneezing, nose blowing, hot baths and spicy foods which make the nose run are discouraged. Any stitches between the nostrils come out after 4–5 days, and the plaster or splint after 10 days. Simple camouflage make-up can be used to disguise bruising. Most people can return to work within two weeks. The swelling can take a few months to totally settle and in that time it may be hard to breathe through the nose. The stiffness will gradually disappear although numbness at the tip of the nose may take up to six months to improve.

The risks

The main risk with nose surgery is that you may not like the final result: about 5 per cent of those who have had it done have some additional surgery to try to get their nose looking even better, although this cannot be done for at least a year after the initial surgery. Side-effects are generally quite rare. Persistent swelling over the nose, nose bleeds, infection and a constant runny nose occur occasionally. Tiny broken blood vessels on the nose are fairly common. Dark patches of skin under the eyes may develop in people with fairly dark skin.

Cost and outlook

An operation on the nose can cost between £3,000 and £4,000, and the results usually last forever.

Breast enlargement

Women seek breast enlargement, or 'augmentation', after breast cancer surgery or because they dislike being flat-chested, or having shrunken breasts after pregnancy, or droopy breasts as they get older. Rarely, breasts never grow at all at puberty or grow into abnormal shapes. Augmentation is usually done on women between their late teens/early twenties and late forties.

Before the operation
The surgeon will want to meet you to discuss why you want to have the operation done and what your expectations are. He or she will take a full medical history including whether you have any history or family history of breast cancer and whether you have any pre-existing connective-tissue diseases such as rheumatoid arthritis which might otherwise be blamed on the implants. You will have a full physical examination, and your breasts will be checked for lumps. You should take a bra with you that you would like to be able to fill to show the size you would like to be. If your nipples are low, you may be advised to have surgery to re-site them. If your breasts are very unequal sizes, you may need different-sized implants to even them up. Breast surgery will not help stretch marks or other skin abnormalities.

The operation
The surgeon makes a cut in the armpit, around the lower half of the areola (the darker part of the breast surrounding the nipple), or on the underside of the breast. Keyhole surgery allows much smaller cuts to be made. An implant is inserted either just in front or just behind the muscle of the chest wall. All implants consist of a silicone bag with a filling, which could be soft silicone gel, saline (salt water), soya-bean oil or hydrogel. A fifth substance, polyethylene glycol, is being tried in implants. The operation is always done under general anaesthetic and a one-night stay in hospital is usual. A tube may be left in the breast for a day to drain blood and fluid.

After the operation
The new breasts are taped in position with plaster. The whole chest wall will feel sore and bruised. The drain is usually removed the day

after the operation. Painkillers may be necessary for 4–5 days. You will have to wear a special bra or bandaging to hold the breasts in position for a month after surgery. You will be able to drive after ten days and return to gentle exercise after 3–4 weeks. It is best not to stretch upwards (for example, to hang washing out on a line) for at least six weeks.

The risks

The most common risk of breast augmentation is a poor cosmetic result, with uneven or lopsided breasts. Blood clots, bruising, infection and pain may all occur. Numbness round the nipple or occasionally increased sensation and tenderness round the nipple are possible risks. Scar tissue will develop around the implants and the extent of the scar tissue will determine the extent of your cleavage and the final appearance of your breasts – this could take up to six months. The silicone gel implants can feel hard at first and usually soften up, but for some women they remain hard, lumpy and painful. It may be more difficult to feel cancerous lumps if you have lumpy implants, although ultrasound and mammograms will be able to distinguish between implant and cancer. Implants should not affect the ability to breast-feed.

There has been a great deal of controversy, and litigation, about the safety of silicone implants. Claims have been made that they can cause breast cancer, birth defects in offspring, ME, fatigue, memory loss and a range of auto-immune disorders in which the body attacks its own cells. Although most of the links have been refuted, concerns remain that silicone may leak out of the implants and cause auto-immune connective-tissue disorders such as rheumatoid arthritis. In the USA silicone gel implants are currently restricted to use in clinical trials only. In the UK a report in July 1998 by the Independent Review Group (IRG) set up by the government found no 'conclusive' evidence that women with silicone gel implants are any more likely to have health problems than other women. Despite this conclusion, however, the safety debate still rages. Indeed, the IRG report points out that 'there is some risk associated with the use of any implant'. On balance, the evidence would appear to support the view that silicone gel implants are relatively safe, but each woman considering having such implants should discuss this issue with her surgeon before the operation.

No perfect alternative to silicone exists. Saline implants have a tendency to wrinkle and the wrinkles may show through the skin. Some 10 per cent of saline implants rupture and then need to be removed. Soya-bean-oil implants have the advantage of letting X-rays through so mammograms are easy to perform, whereas with silicone the mammogram has to be taken from a special angle as X-rays do not pass through it. If soya-bean-oil implants rupture, they should be harmless but further trials are needed to establish this for certain.

Cost and outlook
Breast augmentation costs between £3,000 and £4,000. The life of most implants is currently accepted as being between 10 and 15 years.

Breast reduction

Women may opt for breast-reduction surgery if they have very large breasts causing them discomfort or embarrassment, or if one breast is very much larger than the other. At puberty some girls start to develop very large breasts which can keep growing throughout the teenage years until they are uncomfortably big.

Before the operation
Preparation for the operation is very similar to that described above for breast enlargement. The operation itself is a major one, under general anaesthetic, and requiring a night in hospital, but generally causes minimal pain.

The operation
Cuts are made around the nipple to reposition it, then vertically down from the nipple to the underside of the breast and round the underside of the breast. The lower part of the breast is removed to make it smaller. Fat in the armpit may also be removed by liposuction. The skin is trimmed to the new, smaller breast and stitched back in place. The scars that form correspond to the cuts – around the nipple, down the lower half of the breast and round the underside of the breast.

The risks
Risks include blood clots under the skin which usually drain away but may need to be removed, poor scar healing, damage to the nip-

ple reducing sensation and the ability to breast-feed, and changes to the nipple colour. Ending up with unsightly scars and uneven-sized and shaped breasts are fairly common risks. Small areas of fat in the breast may die as they are deprived of their blood supply and this can cause a red, hot area which may drain away or form a lump which can be removed if it is causing concern.

Improved techniques to stitch inside the breast and leave fewer scars may be offered in the future.

Cost and outlook
Breast reduction costs between £3,500 and £4,500. The result is permanent, but changes in weight and age will still affect the size of breasts.

Face-lifts

As we age, our skin gets thinner and less elastic and the underlying facial muscles sag. The fat that pads our cheeks while we are younger slips down round the jaw. The overall sagging causes deep grooves from the nose to the mouth, wobbly jowls, a 'turkey' neck, hooded eyes and bags under the eyes as eyebrows droop, and fine lines around the mouth and eyes where thin skin is tethered to underlying muscles. Whether we see the effects of ageing as resulting in a face full of character which looks lived-in, or in a ravaged face which needs fixing, depends on us.

We age at different rates. The factors that affect the ageing process are:

- **genes** Women tend to look like their mothers, especially as they age.
- **facial type** Women with wide cheekbones and little facial fat age slower because there is less fat to slip down to the jaw and neck.
- **smoking** The effects of nicotine and tar – and of screwing up one's eyes against cigarette smoke – speed ageing.
- **sun** Excessive tanning caused by the sun or sunbeds makes skin lose elasticity more rapidly.
- **loss of teeth** Poor teeth have an ageing effect.
- **lifestyle** A good diet, regular exercise, moderate alcohol and avoidance of excessive stress probably all contribute indirectly to helping a person look younger for longer.

A face-lift can improve a scraggy neck and jowls, and restore a more youthful appearance. It cannot remove the fine lines around the mouth and eyes, and may not affect the grooves between the nose and the mouth. You can get some idea of the final result by pulling up the skin in front of your ears. The operation will be most successful for women aged 40–60, because their skin is still elastic.

Before the operation

It is usual to meet your surgeon twice before the operation. At the first meeting, a full medical history will be taken and an examination will be done, especially of your face. The surgeon will have a discussion with you about the pros and cons of surgery, and may take photographs. You may want to take along photos of yourself when you were younger so the surgeon can see what effect you would like to achieve. The second consultation is to discuss the details of the surgery – which operation would be best for you and what you can expect. Use the checklist above to make sure you have the answers to all your questions.

You may have a face-lift alone or have additional surgery at the same time to, say, enhance your chin or cheekbones with silicone implants.

To optimise the results of a face-lift, it is best to lose any excess weight beforehand and then keep your weight steady rather than letting it yo-yo up and down. Stopping smoking, or at least cutting own drastically for a minimum of three weeks before surgery, will reduce the risk of blood clots during the operation and help you to heal better after it. If you are on hormone replacement therapy (HRT) or are taking the contraceptive pill you need to ask your surgeon about stopping them to minimise the risk of blood clots during the operation. You should also ask about whether you should avoid aspirin and other anti-inflammatory drugs in case they make you bleed more and bruise more easily after the surgery.

The operation

There are six main types of face-lift:

- **the mini-lift** In this type of operation the surgeon cuts a line in the skin from the temples down in front of the ears and then behind the ears and across the scalp. The skin is lifted up and pulled taut, any excess is trimmed off and the wound is stitched. The advantages of the mini-lift are that it can be done quickly, sometimes even without general anaesthetic, is suitable for older women who do not want major surgery, and gives quick results. The disadvantages are that the results may not last for long, it does not help nose–mouth grooves, it can result in blood clots under the facial skin, and when the scars heal it can pull the ears out of place. Repeated mini-lifts can give the face a tight, unnatural look.

- **the standard lift** This standard form of the face-lift pulls both skin and deeper underlying structures upwards, resulting in a more lasting effect than the mini-lift. The cuts are similar but deeper. Muscles in the lower part of the face and neck are tightened and tethered to underlying bones if possible. The advantages are that it can help correct a scraggy neck and it gives a better and more lasting result than the mini-lift. The disadvantages are that it always requires a general anaesthetic, takes three weeks to recover from, and can result in bad scars and occasionally in damage of facial nerves, which can cause facial paralysis (usually temporary).

- **the extended standard lift** This lifts deeper facial structures off the cheeks and pulls them up so the middle of the face looks better. The advantages are that it helps sagging cheeks, jowls and neck, and flattens deep nose-mouth grooves. It causes less swelling than the standard lift and the recovery time from it is shorter. The main disadvantage is a greater chance of damage to facial nerves with more risk of facial paralysis.

- **the composite lift** This extensive operation combines the extended standard lift with lifting the eyebrows and lower eyelid surgery. It is used chiefly for older women who want to reduce bags under the eyes and around the cheeks. The disadvantages are increased risk of damage to facial nerves and swelling which takes up to six months to go down.

- **the mask lift** In this type of operation the cuts are made across the top of the head and inside the mouth. The surgeon burrows deep under the structures of the face to get under the layer which covers the bones. In this way all the tissues of the face, including the deepest layers of fat, can be pulled up and tightened. The advantages are that it works well on lines around the mouth and eyes. The disadvantages are that it can give you an unnatural appearance with more slanted eyes, does not improve the lower part of the face such as jowls, can produce swelling for up to 12 weeks and may cause infection in the cheeks, hair loss round the incision in the scalp and permanent loss of sensation or prickling in the scalp.

- **'keyhole' lift** Keyhole, or endoscopic, surgery is carried out through five very small cuts in the scalp, under the lower eyelids and mouth, through which a narrow fibre-optic light and camera and cutting instruments are passed. The surgeon then burrows into the deep layers under the covering of the facial bones as in the mask lift. The advantages are much smaller scars. The disadvantages are the same as for a mask lift and include prolonged swelling, temporary restriction of facial movements and numbness.

After the operation

Stitches are usually removed five days after surgery. After two weeks, most of the bruising round the eyes and on the face will have improved and you will probably be able to return to work after three weeks. Within two months, your face will have fully healed. You will be advised to use moisturisers regularly to keep the skin soft and supple.

The numbness of the face and scalp usually improves within three months. Paralysis or weakness of facial muscles usually disappears within six weeks of the face-lift. Rare side-effects of face-lifts which may be permanent include persistent pain on cheeks or ears, asymmetrical facial expressions owing to muscle weakness, darkened skin in the areas where bruising occurred, the formation of red spider veins which stretch the skin, hair loss over scars and lumpy, thick scars.

Cost and outlook

Depending on the type of surgery a face-lift could cost between £3,000 and £10,000, and could last up to 10 years.

Liposuction

Women seek liposuction to remove unwanted fat. It is not a way to lose weight and should really be used only as a last resort after dieting and exercise have helped you to get as near as possible to your ideal weight. It is most successful if used on women in their twenties and thirties, as their skin is still stretchy, and is effective on excess fat – on the thighs, waist, lower abdomen, hips and inner part of knees – which will not shift with diet or exercise. Cellulite, which is visible sub-cutaneous fat, cannot be tackled by liposuction.

Before the operation

The surgeon will meet you to discuss the pros and cons of liposuction, check you over and advise you to lose any excess weight if at all possible. It is particularly important that you are given a realistic idea of what can be achieved, and are made aware of any potential side-effects such as blood loss, pain and bruising (see below).

The operation

Liposuction is almost always carried out under general anaesthetic but you may not need to stay in hospital overnight. The surgeon inserts a fine tube attached to a vacuum pump through your skin and into the fat layer. The tube is moved around to suck out an even layer of fat, and the same amount of fat is taken from the other side of the body for an even result. Liposuction on the hip and thighs takes about an hour. The small wound is stitched and an elasticated dressing put over the treated area.

Alternative methods use other ways of breaking up the fat, such as laser, ultrasound or electrical current, but the results and risks are similar.

After the operation

The treated area may be sore but not very painful on the whole. You may have a drain left in for 24 hours to take away blood and fluid. Stitches come out after 5–10 days. The dressing stays on for at least three weeks. You will be encouraged to walk about as much as possible and to wear tight-fitting garments over the treated areas for up to six weeks.

Risks

Bruising, clots under the skin and discomfort are common problems after the surgery. In the longer term, excess skin may look wrinkled and saggy. Persistent swelling and loss of sensation in the skin usually settle down by six months but occasionally remain a permanent problem. Anaemia from excess loss of blood during the operation may make you tired but can be corrected by taking iron tablets. A major risk is that you may be disappointed by the result.

Cost and outlook
Liposuction costs between £1,000 and £5,000. The fat may return as you gain weight or as you get older.

Tummy tuck

This operation is available for women who have a fold of skin hanging down from their lower abdomen like an apron, usually after an operation such as a caesarean section or a hysterectomy. Tummy tucks are best for fit women who do not have (or have lost) any excess weight and want merely to get rid of the fold of skin.

Before the operation
It is usual to meet the surgeon twice before the operation. He or she will check you over, weigh you and examine your tummy. You need to have enough loose skin to be able to pull your belly button right down to where your pubic hair starts, otherwise in addition to the cut from one hip bone to the other you may need a cut up to your belly button. Toning up your abdominal muscles as much as possible before the operation will help healing and help you to achieve a tauter stomach.

You will be advised not to have a tummy tuck until you have had all the children you want to.

The operation
The surgeon makes a long incision from one hip bone to the other, just above the pubic hair, and also cuts around the belly button so it is left on a stalk. Skin and fat are pulled down taut, the excess is cut off and then the incision is stitched up. The belly button is repositioned. A drain is left in to take away fluid and blood for up to two days, stitches are removed after about ten days and a pressure dressing may be left on for up to three weeks.

After the operation
After the operation you will need to stay in hospital for one or two nights. You may feel sick, be unable to eat and feel full of wind.

Swelling and bruising round the scar are common, and usually settle down after a few days. Infection is always a possibility after any surgery and can result in a fever and a tender, hot, red scar which starts to ooze pus or blood. The scar round the belly button will take a while to heal. Numbness around the belly button and lower abdominal scar is also common and may occasionally be permanent. The scar fades over the next year.

Cost and outlook

A tummy tuck costs about £3,000, and the effect lasts forever.

Minor procedures

Some cosmetic surgery procedures are considered to be minor, not in terms of cost, risks or discomfort, but because they are done under local anaesthetic. They include collagen injections, the removal of tattoos and non-surgical face-lifts.

Cosmetic dentistry

Increasing numbers of men and women of all ages are spending money on fixing their teeth. If your teeth look good, you will smile more and feel more confident. Compared with other more invasive types of cosmetic surgery, dental work is relatively safe. The main risk is that you may not be satisfied with the result, so a realistic chat with a dentist, and a second opinion, before embarking on the work, may be a good idea.

Options include:

- **braces** to straighten crooked teeth. It is increasingly hard to get orthodontic work done on the NHS, and private costs may be in excess of £2,000
- **dental contouring**, to file down crooked or pointed teeth
- **whitening** to remove coffee, tea or tobacco stains. This can be done by polishing as part of a 'scale and polish' by the dentist or hygienist. Further whitening can be achieved by bleaching, using gels containing hydrogen peroxide. The dentist makes you a plastic mould which fits over your teeth, you squeeze in a little gel and wear the mould for a variable time depending on the strength of the gel. You pay up to £200 for the moulds, and

around £15 for each tube of gel. The main risk with this procedure is gum sensitivity, especially if you have some gum recession with a lot of tooth showing where the gum should be. Another way of whitening teeth is to replace old metal fillings, which can make a tooth look dull and grey, with white fillings. The disadvantage is the expense and the possibility that white fillings may not last as long as metal ones

- **crowns and caps**, which are false covers that fit over a damaged tooth. After the tooth is filed into a cone shape to accommodate the cover, the dentist takes an impression of it and makes a mould. A crown is then made to measure, and is cemented on to the tooth stump. It usually lasts for years. Bridgework covers gaps caused by missing teeth by preparing teeth on either side of the gap and placing a crown across the prepared teeth and the gap. Costs about £500 per crown

- **implants**, which are false teeth that can be anchored into the bone to look and work like ordinary teeth to disguise missing teeth. Costs about £2,000 per tooth

- **bonding**, in which the material used in white fillings can be stuck on to the surface of chipped or damaged teeth, or used to fill gaps between teeth, and then polished up so it looks like the rest of the tooth. The bonding may stain and chip and it lasts five years at the most, so veneers (see below) are often fitted instead

- **veneers**, which are very thin sheets of porcelain stuck with resin on to the surface of damaged teeth. The veneer is made to measure, the surface of the tooth is roughened so the plastic resin will stick and the veneer is stuck in place by shining ultraviolet light on to it.

Broken capillaries ('spiders')

The broken blood vessels which look like red spiders and appear on our thighs, noses and cheeks as we get older bother some women a lot. Some women are more prone to spiders than others are. Occasionally they are an inherited tendency, but generally they are caused by too much sun or alcohol or by previous injury. Treatments include:

- **sclerotherapy**, in which a very fine needle is inserted into the centre of the spider and an irritant solution is injected so that

the spider shrivels up. It leaves a little bump which disappears after a few weeks. Further treatment may be needed six weeks later. It is not always successful. Costs around £200
- **electrolysis**, in which a small electrical current is passed through a needle inserted into the centre of the spider. It may leave a small scar or even cause more spiders to develop. Costs from £20
- **pulse-dye laser treatment** to destroy cells. This involves a few sharp pricks and causes some bruising, swelling and numbness, but it produces by far the best results. It is available from dermatologists (skin specialists) and some plastic surgery units only, unlike electrolysis which may be available at beauty clinics. Costs around £250.

Sun spots

These flat brown areas of skin develop on parts of the body exposed to the sun, such as cheeks, hands and throat. The best treatment is with laser, which causes a sensation like a quick slap across the face. After treatment, you will feel like you have been sunburned, and a scab will develop but heal after a couple of weeks, leaving the skin as normal. After treatment you will be told to use sunblock on the treated areas.

Wrinkles

Wrinkles and furrowed brows can make you look old and grumpy. Treatments include:

- **injections of botulinum toxin**, which is a chemical that causes temporary muscle paralysis. The toxin is injected into facial muscles to make furrows and frown lines on the forehead and crow's feet around the eyes relax. The effects last for about three to six months. If the wrong muscles are injected, the eyebrows may droop, although this too wears off after three to six months
- **dermabrasion**, which is a way of smoothing down skin to get rid of fine wrinkles and scars from old acne or chickenpox. Under a local or general anaesthetic, depending on the extent of the work to be done, the skin is 'sanded' down using a small

rotating brush instrument. The newly exposed skin will be delicate, red and sore and will need to be kept away from the sun and moisturised regularly. The skin may become pale, blotchy and shiny. Costs around £400

- **collagen injections**, which can get rid of furrows, pits, grooves and wrinkles. Collagen is the stuff that binds our bones, skin, muscles and ligaments, and as it decreases in our skin over the years, wrinkles appear. For the treatment, collagen is made up into a paste with salt water and injected into wrinkles. The salt water gets absorbed, leaving the collagen in place. Two or three treatments may be needed to fill out a wrinkle. Allergic reactions causing hard, red, itchy blotches may develop after the injection and take months to disappear. Injections may be painful and local anaesthetic cream may be rubbed on to the area about half an hour before injection to lessen pain. The effects last for up to six months. Costs around £300 per session
- **laser skin re-surfacing**, in which a laser is used to vaporise outer layers of the skin such that when the skin heals, surface wrinkles and small scars may be obliterated
- **chemical peels**, which involve chemically burning off superficial skin layers. The regenerated skin will be smoother, tighter and shiny. The precautions to be taken are the same as those after dermabrasion.

What to do if something goes wrong

Complaining is something that most people find difficult, but if you had cosmetic surgery done privately and genuinely feel that you have suffered as a result of it, follow these guidelines. The NHS complaints procedure is covered in the appendix.

It is important to think about what you want to achieve by complaining. Most people want someone to say they are sorry, explain exactly what happened and why, and say what will be done to stop it happening to others. If this is what you want, start by making a complaint in writing to the surgeon or clinic. Find out if the clinic has a procedure for dealing with patients' complaints which you can follow.

If your complaint is about professional misconduct you should refer the matter to the GMC. A practitioner found guilty of a breach of professional conduct may be struck off the register.

If you feel strongly that the private treatment you received was unsatisfactory you could initially withhold payment. (To prepare for such an eventuality, you could, before treatment begins, ask your insurance company – if you are in a private insurance scheme that covers the costs of your cosmetic surgery – whether it is prepared to send the payment cheque to you rather than to the hospital or doctor concerned.) Thereafter, you have the option of starting court action.

Depending on what recompense you are seeking, there are two grounds for pursuing legal action: breach of contract or medical negligence.

Breach of contract

Your rights under the Supply of Goods and Services Act 1982 (common law in Scotland) are to receive a service that has been carried out with reasonable skill and care, within a 'reasonable time' where no time limit has been fixed, and for a 'reasonable charge' where no charge has been agreed in advance. If you feel that your surgery did not meet these criteria (e.g. you were charged too much or you did not achieve the effect you wanted), you could pursue a claim for your losses through the court, where you would first have to establish that a breach of contract occurred.

If you paid for treatment with a credit card, you could try contacting your credit card company because it will be jointly liable if there has been a breach of contract.

Medical negligence

If you have suffered some sort of injury as a result of the surgery, you do not have to have been through the clinical complaints procedure first, but obtaining compensation will almost certainly mean taking legal action.

Whereas a serious complaint about the NHS could lead to your suing the hospital or the health authority/board, in the private sector you have to sue the practitioner personally because the doctor probably works independently, rather than being an employee of the private hospital or clinic where he or she works. Any action for personal injury you take must (for adults) start within three years of the incident that gave rise to the complaint. In the case of children, the three-year period does not begin until they are 18, so they have until they are 21 to bring proceedings.

You can obtain guidance on pursuing the claim from your local community health council or Action for Victims of Medical Accidents (AVMA);* the latter, as well as giving you free basic legal and medical advice, can refer you to a solicitor with the appropriate experience.

Claims for medical accident or negligence are not to be undertaken lightly, even if you qualify for legal aid. As well as being expensive, and likely to take a long time, such cases are difficult to prove. Negligence is much more than a professional misjudgement. You will need a lawyer who is experienced in medical negligence cases, and having proved the existence of negligence your lawyer will have to show that this negligence caused you harm.

Your solicitor will take a statement from you about what happened and discuss costs. You may be able to fund the case by way of a 'no win, no fee' agreement. This means that if you lose the case you will not have to pay your solicitor anything; if you win, you will have to pay his or her normal charges plus a success fee which you will have agreed to at the start. If the matter seems worth pursuing, and you have the money to proceed or are eligible for legal aid, the solicitor will obtain your medical records, identify the issues and then send them to a medical expert prior to preparing a report. This will be sent with your statement and records to a barrister for advice as to the strength of the claim and on how to proceed.

If your case is sufficiently strong, the surgeon or clinic may settle your claim out of court.

Appendix

You and the health system

To get the best out of the National Health Service (NHS), it pays to know how the system works. In addition, a good relationship with the doctors and other medical staff you come in contact with would help.

General practitioners

Your first port of call for health matters is your general practitioner (GP). He or she is the central figure in the 'primary care' team – the group of professionals from various health disciplines who work

---

What do you want from your GP?

- **services and staff** Do you want services such as counselling, health education and complementary therapies to be available? Would you value access to, for example, a well woman or family planning clinic? Would you like to be able to see a nurse about minor problems? (This is more likely to be available from a fund-holding or large group practice.)
- **location** Do you need a practice within walking distance, on a bus route or simply one that is accessible by car?
- **sex** Do you particularly want either a male or a female GP, or don't you mind?
- **age** Does the GP's age matter to you?
- **practice size** Have you any preference for a group practice or for a GP working alone? The trend in Britain is strongly towards group

---

from a surgery or health centre. This team might include a district nurse, health visitor, practice nurse, community psychiatric nurse, therapists, social worker, receptionist and medical secretary. So choosing a GP is one of the most important health decisions you ever make. The checklist will help you decide what your priorities are when you are looking for a new GP.

Hospital treatment

From time to time you may need to attend the outpatient department of your local hospital, because you have been referred by your GP to a consultation or examination, or to have hospital treatment that does not involve staying overnight, or for assessment and care in a nurse clinic. Before you attend a consultant's outpatient clinic, you will be put on a waiting list; the hospital will write to you with details of your appointment. The Patient's Charter (see below) now states that all patients should be seen in the outpatient clinic within 26 weeks of referral (and 9 out of 10 of them within 13 weeks); once you have arrived, you should be seen within 30 minutes of your appointment time.

If you are about to go into hospital as an inpatient – say, for an operation – have a proper discussion with your GP about the pro-

---

practices comprising four or more doctors. Note that although, at a group practice, you may have more choice, you may still face a long wait to see 'your' doctor.

- **opening hours** Do you want a walk-in surgery, fixed appointments or a mixture of both? Do you want an evening or weekend surgery? Do you need a mother-and-baby clinic, and is it at a convenient time? Do you want telephone access to your GP (or a nurse)?
- **approach/attitude** Do you want a GP who is sympathetic to complementary medicine, one who involves you in decisions, or one who decides what is best for you and then informs you of this?
- **special interests/expertise** Do you want a GP who has an interest in or knowledge of a specific condition, such as eczema or asthma?
- **facilities** Do you want a child-friendly practice? Do you need wheelchair access?

cedure and the possibility of alternative treatment. It is also advisable to talk to the surgeon. If you are worried or feel you have not been given enough information, remember that you are entitled to ask for a second opinion.

Under the Patient's Charter, you should be given, before or at the time of admission, a written and a verbal explanation of what will happen during your hospital stay. Before any surgical procedure takes place, you will be asked to sign a consent form. First, be sure that you know the answers to all of the following questions:

- what is the reason for the operation?
- what is going to be done and what are the risks?
- will I be treated by experts in the appropriate field of medicine or surgery?
- how long will I be in hospital?
- how long will it take me to recover?
- will I be in pain afterwards, and if so what pain relief will be available?
- are there likely to be any permanent after-effects?

The rights of patients

The Patient's Charter, launched in 1991 and extended several times since, sets out the rights and standards that you can expect throughout the NHS. Your rights under it are:

- to receive health care on the basis of clinical need, regardless of ability to pay
- to be registered with a GP
- to be able to change doctors easily and quickly
- to be offered a health check on first joining a doctor's list
- to receive emergency medical treatment at any time through a family practitioner, the emergency ambulance service and hospital accident and emergency departments
- to have appropriate drugs and medicines prescribed and to have any proposed treatment clearly explained to you, including any risks involved and any alternatives
- to be referred to a consultant acceptable to you when your GP thinks it necessary, and to be referred for a second opinion if you and the GP agree that this is desirable

- to have access to your (post-1991) health records, and to know that those working for the NHS are under a legal duty to keep their contents confidential
- to choose whether or not to take part in medical research or medical student training
- if aged between 16 and 74 and not seen by your doctor in the previous three years, to have the health check to which you are entitled under the existing health promotion arrangements; and to be offered an annual health check (at home if you wish) if 75 years old or over
- to be given detailed information about local family doctor services, including quality standards and waiting times, through your health authority/board's local directory
- to receive a copy of your doctor's practice leaflet, setting out the services he or she provides
- to receive a full and prompt reply to any complaints you make about NHS services
- to be guaranteed admission for virtually all treatments by a specific date no later than 18 months from the day when your consultant places you on a waiting list.

If you are pregnant, you have rights under the Maternity Services Charter, which is part of the Patient's Charter.

It grants the mother:

- the right to choose where her baby is born (in hospital or at home)
- access to a named midwife who will be responsible for her care
- the opportunity to see a consultant obstetrician at least once during the pregnancy
- the opportunity to see a consultant paediatrician if the obstetrician anticipates problems with the baby
- the right to see her maternity records during pregnancy and, if she chooses, to keep them with her
- the right to be given information about local maternity services and an explanation of any treatment proposed, including benefits, risks and alternatives
- specific appointment times, and to be seen within 30 minutes of these times

How to complain to the NHS

What outcome do you want?

The NHS to investigate, and to give an apology, an explanation, and assurances that it won't happen to others?

yes

STAGE 1: Make a complaint (local resolution)

Make your complaint within six months if possible. Go direct to the person involved. Talk to them about what happened and what you would like done about it. It may clear the air.

Alternatively, write to the complaints manager at the trust (or health authority if about a family practitioner such as a GP or dentist). The address will be in the phone book. If you want to take up the complaint later, ask for the complaints leaflet.

What will happen?

This depends on who you've complained to and what about. A complaint made on the spot could be sorted out immediately.

If you complain about a GP, then the staff in the surgery or the complaints manager in the health authority might investigate. They may need to look at records and meet with you to gather the facts. A lay conciliator may discuss the complaint with everyone involved to see if the problem can be resolved.

Either way, you can expect to get an acknowledgement of your complaint within two days and a full investigation and a written response within 20 working days if the health authority or trust investigates, ten days if by a family practitioner.

Are you satisfied with the response?

yes → **Complaints process ends.**

Disciplinary action against the person involved; e.g. sacked, suspended, or struck off?

yes / **no**

Contact professional body

If you think a health professional has behaved unethically or unprofessionally (e.g. drunkenness or indecency), you can complain to the professional body he or she is registered with. For example, the General Medical Council or the UK Central Council for Nursing, Midwifery and Health Visiting. They can strike members off the professional register or suspend them from practising.

A complaint to a trust or health authority might lead to a disciplinary action but this may delay the complaints procedure.

Financial compensation? This means taking legal action.

yes

Legal action

You will usually have to take legal action and prove negligence in court. In some cases, trusts or health authorities will settle outside of court and award 'ex-gratia' compensation (as a goodwill gesture rather than through legal obligation).

It's vital to get advice from a lawyer who knows the area and has experience in medical negligence. Action for Victims of Medical Accidents (a national charity) can put you in touch with a solicitor and support groups. The service is free.

STAGE 2: Request an independent review panel

You must make your request within 28 calendar days of the written reply to your complaint. The response should tell you who to contact if you want to request an independent review panel. If not, ask the complaints manager.

The person who sets up the panel – the convener – will ask you to explain in writing exactly why you are still dissatisfied.

What will happen?

The convener will decide within 20 working days (or within ten if your complaint is about a family practitioner) whether or not to set up an independent review panel.

Is a panel set up?

If agreed, the panel is set up within 20 days (within ten for family practitioners).
They will write to tell you what they'll investigate.

no →

The review

The independent review panel has access to background papers, your health records and any written statements. It won't undertake a formal hearing but you might be interviewed or asked to meet with some or all of the parties involved. The investigation should be over within three months of your first approaching the convener.

You will get a copy of the draft report to comment on. The final report is sent to you and the other people involved. The chief executive of the trust or health authority will write and inform you of any action they will be taking as a result.

Are you satisfied?

yes →

Complaints process ends.

Are you satisfied with the reason why?

yes → **Complaints process ends.**

no →

yes →

no →

Appeal to the Ombudsman

The Ombudsman (Health Service Commissioner) is independent of the NHS and the Government. You must appeal to the Ombudsman in writing within a year of the event. If the Ombudsman decides to take on your case, he will undertake a thorough and rigorous investigation (he has legal access to any NHS records), and make recommendations to the relevant NHS bodies. In 1994–95, 60 per cent of the 508 complaints the Ombudsman investigated were upheld. Investigations in 1997 took an average of 60 weeks.

or → Take **legal action** or contact the **professional bodies.**

- the choice of whether to have her partner or a friend or relative with her while she is in labour or giving birth
- the choice of having her baby with her in hospital – unless there are clinical reasons why she should not
- the right to have friends and relatives visit her in hospital at all reasonable times as long as this does not disturb others.

The Patient's Charter is to be replaced in 1999 with a new NHS Charter, which will set standards of care you can expect but also state what the NHS can expect from you: your responsibilities. Patients will have to keep – or call to cancel – appointments, think twice before calling a GP to their home and treat NHS staff with respect. The change in emphasis could undermine the whole point of a charter – to drive up standards. It is hoped that a balance will be struck between the rights and responsibilities of patients.

Complaints procedure

The new complaints procedure for the NHS, put in place in April 1997, is designed to be simpler, quicker and fairer than the old one. It should have well-publicised local-level procedures (known as 'local resolution') to sort out most complaints as they arise. Each stage should be completed within particular time limits. If complaints are not resolved satisfactorily at local level, they may be investigated by an independent review panel.

The chart on pages 410–11 summarises the complaints procedure in the NHS. For complaints about private medicine see Chapter 15.

Glossary

abdomen The part of the body from the lower ribs to the groin and pubic area

acute Short-lived, sudden onset (e.g. acute appendicitis), opposite of chronic (q.v.)

amenorrhoea Absence of periods for more than six months

anaesthetic Loss of sensation. Local anaesthetic gel or injection induces loss of sensation in one area only, general anaesthetic gases or injection induce loss of consciousness

analgesia Methods of pain relief, e.g. drugs (analgesic drugs), acupuncture, hypnosis

androgens Hormones (q.v.) present in men and women, but more so in men

anovulation Failure of the ovaries to release an egg each month at ovulation (q.v.)

antibiotics Drugs to halt or kill infections caused by bacteria (e.g. tonsillitis). Not effective against infections caused by viruses (e.g. common cold, 'flu).

antibody A substance produced by the body to fight infections or chemicals that may harm the body (antigens)

arthritis Inflammation of joints which may be due to wear and tear (osteoarthritis q.v.), infection, or auto-immune conditions (q.v.) such as rheumatoid arthritis

aspiration Removal of fluid, air or blood from a cyst or space in the body using a needle and syringe

auto-immune When the body reacts against its own cells by producing antibodies which damage its own organs

benign Non-cancerous. Benign lumps may grow but will not spread to other parts of the body or cause widespread damage

biopsy The surgical removal of a sample of tissue to make a diagnosis after examination under a microscope

blood pressure A measurement of the pressure with which blood is flowing through the blood vessels. High levels can damage blood vessels and increase the risk of CVA or CHD (q.v.)

cancer (carcinoma) An abnormal proliferation of cells which may cause a lump (tumour) and may spread to other parts of the body, interfering with normal function

carcinoma in situ A cancer which is localised to one site and has not yet spread

cardiovascular system The heart and blood vessels

cataract Opacity of the lens of the eye which makes vision increasingly hazy

cerebrovascular accident (CVA) or 'stroke' Blockage of blood vessels in the brain resulting in damage to the part of the brain which relies on that blood supply

cervical erosion Raw area on the surface of the neck of the womb (cervix) due to overgrowth of more delicate cells (columnar cells) that normally line the cervical canal

cervical smear test *see smear test*

cholesterol One of the fats in the blood which is used to produce hormones and other vital functions. Excess levels in the blood may cause cholesterol deposits which can block blood vessels and cause coronary heart disease

coronary heart disease (CHD) Narrowing of the blood vessels around the heart (angina), or blockage of a blood vessel (heart attack or myocardial infarction)

chemotherapy Treatment with powerful cancer-killing drugs. Normal cells may also be destroyed, causing side-effects such as hair loss

chromosome A tiny particle containing genetic material which determines inherited characteristics. There are 46 chromosomes in all human cells. Each chromosome has two strands of DNA. Segments of DNA make up genes which contain codes for specific characteristics.

chronic Long-term, persistent or recurring condition, e.g. chronic bronchitis

colposcope A binocular instrument to magnify the surface of the cervix and allow more detailed examination if a smear test (q.v.) shows an abnormality

combined oral contraceptive (the 'pill') Contraceptive pill containing two hormones (q.v.), namely oestrogen (q.v.) and normally a progestogen (q.v.)

cyst A fluid-filled sac found in any part of the body

cystitis Inflammation of the bladder causing painful urination

diabetes Insufficient production of the hormone (q.v.) insulin produced by the pancreas, to deal with glucose (sugar) from the diet. High blood levels of glucose result which can be damaging for many parts of the body

diaphragm ('cap') A rubber contraceptive device which a woman inserts in her vagina to cover the neck of the womb and prevent sperm from reaching the womb

dilatation and curettage (D&C) A 'scrape' performed under general anaesthetic to remove cells from the lining of the womb (endometrium q.v.) to be examined under a microscope to rule out the presence of cancer

discharge Abnormal or unusual fluid produced by a part of the body, e.g. vagina

diuretics ('water pills') Drugs to help the body to get rid of excess fluid

dysmenorrhoea Painful periods

dyspareunia Painful intercourse

endometriosis A pelvic condition in which cells of the endometrium are found outside the womb (e.g. on the ovaries) and may cause pain, adhesions and cysts (q.v.) as they swell and bleed during periods

endometrium Cells lining the womb

fallopian tubes Two small hollow tubes that lead into the cavity of the womb (uterus). They have delicate finger-like ends (fimbriae) which catch the egg released by the ovary. The egg and sperm fuse in the fallopian tube (fertilisation) to start a pregnancy

fibroadenoma A common, benign (q.v.) breast lump

fibrocystic disease A common benign breast condition with multiple small cysts (q.v.)

fibroids ('leiomyoma' or 'myoma') Benign lumps in or on the wall of the uterus

first-degree relative A close relative, e.g. mother, sister, maternal grandmother or aunt

genital herpes Painful lesions of the genitalia which may recur and are caused by the herpes simplex virus which may be sexually transmitted

genital warts Lesions of the genitalia caused by the papilloma virus which may be sexually transmitted

glaucoma Raised pressure inside the eyes resulting in impaired vision

gonadotrophic hormones Hormones such as follicle-stimulating hormone, FSH, and luteinising hormone, LH, produced by the pituitary gland at the base of the brain; direct the ovaries to produce the female sex hormones oestrogen and progesterone (q.v.)

gynaecologist Doctor specialising in the treatment of problems affecting the female reproductive system. Gynaecologists are also trained as obstetricians (specialists in pregnancy and childbirth)

hirsutism Abnormal or excessive facial or body hair which may be due to excess androgens (q.v.)

hormone A chemical produced by a gland which has an effect on other parts of the body, e.g. FSH and LH by the pituitary gland, thyroid hormone by the thyroid, adrenaline by the adrenal glands, hormones controlling calcium by the parathyroid glands, insulin by the pancreas, oestrogen and progesterone by the ovaries

hormone replacement therapy (HRT) The use of hormones to treat symptoms of the menopause caused by functional failure of the ovaries

hyper . . . Excessive or over-active, e.g. hyperthyroid is an over-active thyroid gland resulting in excess thyroid hormone in the body

hypo . . . Low or under-active, e.g. hypothyroid is an under-active thyroid gland resulting in too little thyroid hormone in the body

hysterectomy Surgical removal of the uterus and usually the cervix

immunity The body's defence system against infections and attack by foreign particles

incontinence Lack of urinary or faecal control

inflammation The reaction of tissue to infection, irritation or injury which may result in redness, heat, pain and swelling as well as adhesions

intra-uterine contraceptive device (IUCD or 'coil') A small plastic and metal device inserted into the womb by a doctor to prevent pregnancy by interfering with implantation of a fertilised egg

laparoscopy Insertion of an instrument into the abdomen under general anaesthetic to view internal organs and diagnose and treat specific problems

laxatives Drugs or substances to allow the body to pass softer, more frequent stools. Used to treat constipation or to empty the bowel prior to an examination

malignant Cancerous

mastectomy Surgical removal of a breast

menarche Age at which periods start for the first time

menopause Age at which last period occurs

menorrhagia Excessively heavy bleeding during periods

menstrual cycle Time from first day of one period to first day of the next

menstruation Monthly bleeding from the uterine cavity caused by specific hormone (q.v.) changes

mini pill Contraceptive pill containing a synthetic form of the hormone progesterone (q.v.) called a progestogen (q.v.), and no oestrogen (q.v.)

myomectomy Surgical removal of a fibroid (q.v.) without a hysterectomy (q.v.)

nodule A small lump which may be benign (q.v.) or malignant (q.v.)

oestrogen A hormone (q.v.) produced by the ovaries which is responsible for female sexual characteristics. Levels fall after the menopause (q.v.) and are replaced in hormone replacement therapy (HRT)

oöphorectomy Surgical removal of an ovary

osteoarthritis Joint damage caused by wear and tear

osteoporosis Loss of bone cells leading to brittle and weak bones which may cause pain and fractures. Loss of bone cells accelerates after the menopause (q.v.)

ovary Female reproductive organ in which the eggs are produced

ovulation Discharge of an egg from the ovary

pelvic inflammatory disease (PID) Infection and/or inflammation of the internal female genital organs

peri-menopausal Around the time of the menopause (q.v.)

platelets Blood cells required for clotting

polycystic ovaries (PCO) Multiple small cysts (q.v.) on the ovaries which may be linked with infertility, irregular periods and anovulation (q.v.)

polyp Growth, usually benign, on a stalk, e.g. laryngeal polyp on the vocal cords, cervical polyp on the cervix or endometrial polyp in the womb

premenstrual syndrome (PMS) Physical and psychological symptoms, e.g. bloating and irritability, which start up to two weeks before a period and improve after a period

progesterone Hormone (q.v.) produced by the ovaries which has a role in the menstrual cycle and pregnancy

progestogen A synthetic progesterone used for contraception or to treat menstrual irregularities, or to protect the uterus if oestrogen is given as HRT (q.v.)

prolapse The downward movement of any organ, usually the womb, due to weakening of its supporting structures such as ligaments and muscles. May be accompanied by weakness of the wall between the womb and bladder (cystocele), or the wall between the womb and rectum (rectocele)

radiotherapy Treatment with X-rays which can kill cancerous cells

salpingitis Infection or inflammation of the fallopian tubes (q.v.)

sinusitis Inflammation and/or infection of the lining of the sinuses (air-filled spaces in the skull and face)

smear test or 'cervical smear' or 'PAP smear test' The screening test for cancer of the cervix. A sample of cells from the cervix is taken by scraping a spatula round the cervix. The sample is sent to the laboratory for the cells to be examined under the microscope for pre-cancerous, treatable changes

steroids Hormones (q.v.) produced by the adrenal glands that control blood pressure (q.v.) and other vital functions. Also given as medication to treat auto-immune (q.v.) and chronic inflammatory (q.v.) conditions such as rheumatoid arthritis

systemic Involving the whole body as opposed to a localised reaction

testosterone The male sex hormone (q.v.) found in small amounts in women

trichomonas An infection which causes vaginal discharge

ultrasound A non-invasive diagnostic technique which uses sound waves to bounce off internal organs and give an image on a screen which can be interpreted

urethra The tube leading from the bladder to the outside of the body

urinalysis Testing of a urine sample for glucose, protein and blood which should not normally be present

uterus The womb

vaccine (or **'immunisation' or a 'jab'**) A substance which when introduced into the body will provide protection against a specific disease or infection

vagina The birth canal extending from the uterus to outside the body

vulva Female external genitalia

Addresses

Acne Support Group
PO Box 230
Hayes
Middlesex UB4 0UT
Write enclosing an sae

Action for ME
PO Box 1302
Wells
Somerset BA5 1YE
Tel: (01749) 670799
Fax: (01749) 672561
Web site: www.afme.org.uk

Action for Victims of Medical Accidents (AVMA)
Bank Chambers
1 London Road
London SE23 3TP
Tel: 0181-686 8333

Action on Pre-Eclampsia (APEC)
31-33 College Road
Harrow
Middlesex HA1 1EJ
Tel: (01923) 266778

Action on Smoking and Health (ASH)
16 Fitzhardinge Street
London W1H 9PL
Tel: 0171-224 0743
Fax: 0171-224 0471
Email: ash-uk@dial.pipex.com
Web site: www.ash.org.uk

African-Caribbean Mental Health Association
Suite 37
49 Ferra Road
London SW2 1BZ
Tel: 0171-737 3603

AL-ANON
61 Great Dover Street
London SE1 4YF
Tel: 0171-403 0888
Fax: 0171-378 9910
Email: alanonuk@aol.com
Web site: www.hexnet.co.uk/alanon

Alcohol Concern
Waterbridge House
32-36 Loman Street
London SE1 0EE
Tel: 0171-928 7377
Fax: 0171-928 4644
Email: alccon@popmail.dircon.co.uk
Web site: www.alcoholconcern.org.uk

Alcoholics Anonymous (AA)
General Service Office
PO Box 1, Stonebow House
Stonebow
York
North Yorkshire YO1 7NJ
Helpline: (0345) 697555 *(24 hours)*

Alzheimer's Disease Society
Gordon House
10 Greencoat Place
London SW1P 1PH
Tel: 0171-306 0606
Fax: 0171-306 0808
Email: info@alzheimers.org.uk
Web site: www.alzheimers.org.uk

Arthritis Care
18 Stephenson Way
London NW1 2HD
Tel: 0171-916 1500
Helpline: (0800) 289170
(Mon-Fri, 12 noon-5pm)
Fax: 0171-916 1505
Web site: www.vois.org.uk/arthritiscare

Association for Improvements in the Maternity Services (AIMS)
40 Kingswood Avenue
London NW6 6LS
Tel: 0181-960 5585

Birth Control Trust
16 Mortimer Street
London W1N 7RD
Tel: 0171-580 9360
Fax: 0171-637 1378
Email: bct@birthcontroltrust.org.uk
Web site: www.casynet.co.uk/bct

Breast Cancer Care/Breast Care and Mastectomy Association of Great Britain
Kiln House
210 New Kings Road
London SW6 4NZ
Tel: 0171-384 2984
Fax: 0171-384 3387
Helpline: (0500) 245345

British Acupuncture Council
Park House
206 Latimer Road
London W10 6RE
Tel: 0181-964 0222
Fax: 0181-964 0333
Email: info@acupuncture.org.uk
Web site: www.acupuncture.org.uk

British Agencies for Adoption and Fostering
Skyline House
200 Union Street
London SE1 0LX
Tel: 0171-593 2000
Fax: 0171-593 2001

British Association for Counselling (BAC)
1 Regent Place
Rugby
Warwickshire CV21 2PJ
Information line: (01788) 57832

British Association of Aesthetic Plastic Surgeons (BAAPS)
35-43 Lincoln's Inn Fields
London WC2A 3PN
Tel: 0171-405 2234
Fax: 0171-430 1840
Web site: www.baaps.org.uk

British Association of Cancer United Patients (BACUP)
3 Bath Place
Rivington Street
London EC2A 3DR
Information service: (0800) 181199
Counselling service: 0171-696 9000/
0141-553 1553
Fax: 0171-696 9002
Web site: www.cancerbacup.org.uk

British Association of Cosmetic Surgeons (BACS)
17 View Road
London N6 4DT
Tel: 0181-341 0158

British Association of Plastic Surgeons (BAPS)
35-43 Lincoln's Inn Fields
London WC2A 3PN
Email: secretariat@baps.co.uk
Web site: www.baps.rcseng.ac.uk

British Association of Psychotherapists
37 Mapesbury Road
London NW2 4HJ
Tel: 0181-452 9823
Fax: 0181-452 5182

British Chiropractic Association
Blagrove House
17 Blagrove Street
Reading RG1 1QB
Tel: (01189) 505950
Fax: (01189) 588946
Email: britchiro@aol.com
Web site: www.chiropractic-uk.co.uk

British Deaf Association
(information department)
1-3 Worship Street
London EC2A 2AB
Tel & textline: 0171-588 3520
Advocacy lines: Voice: (01270) 501600
    Textline: (01270) 501300
Fax: (01270) 501400
For advice on legal issues including benefit

British Diabetic Association
10 Queen Anne Street
London W1M 0BD
Helpline: 0171-636 6112
Fax: 0171-637 3644

British Digestive Foundation
see Digestive Disorders Foundation

British Epilepsy Association
Anstey House
40 Hanover Square
Leeds LS3 1BE
Helpline: (0800) 309030
Fax: 0113-242 8804
Email: epilepsy@bea.org.uk
Web site: www.epilepsy.org.uk

British Heart Foundation
14 Fitzhardinge Street
London W1H 4DH
Tel: 0171-935 0185
Information line: (0990) 200656
Fax: 0171-486 5820
Web site: www.bhf.org.uk

British Homeopathic Association
27a Devonshire Street
London W1N 1RJ
Send an sae for list of registered doctors

British Medical Acupuncture Society
(BMAS)
Newton House
Newton Lane
Whitley
Warrington
Cheshire WA4 4JA
Tel: (01925) 730727
Fax: (01925) 730492
Email: bmasadmin@aol.com
Web site: www.medical-acupuncture.co.uk

British Migraine Association
see Migraine Action Association

British School of Reflexology
Holistic Healing Centre
92 Shearing Road
Old Harlow
Essex CM17 0JW
Tel: (01279) 429060
Fax: (01279) 445234

British Tinnitus Association
4th Floor
White Building
Fitzalan Square
Sheffield S1 2AZ
Tel: 0114-279 6600
Fax: 0114-279 6222
Email: tinnitus@dial.pipex.com

British Wheel of Yoga
1 Hamilton Place
Boston Road
Sleaford
Lincolnshire NG34 7ES
Fax: (01529) 303233
Email: wheelyoga@aol.com
Web site:
http://members.aol.com/wheelyoga
Write enclosing an sae

Centre for Autogenic Training
(BAFATT)
c/o Royal London Homeopathic Hospital
NHS Trust
Great Ormond Street
London WC1N 3HR
Tel: (01803) 312098

The Chartered Society of Physiotherapists
14 Bedford Row
London WC1R 4ED
Tel: 0171-306 6666
Fax: 0171-306 6611
Email: pa@csphysio.org.uk

Coeliac Society
PO Box 220
High Wycombe
Buckinghamshire HP11 2HY
Tel: (01494) 437278
Fax: (01494) 474349
Email: admin@coeliac.co.uk
Web site: www.coeliac.co.uk

The Continence Foundation
307 Hatton Square
16 Baldwin's Gardens
London EC1 7RJ
Tel: 0171-404 6875
Fax: 0171-404 6876
Helpline: 0171-831 9831
(Mon-Fri, 9.30am-4.30pm)
Email:
continence.foundation@dial.pipex.com
Web site: www.vois.org.uk/cf

CRY-SIS
BM CRY-SIS
London WC1N 3XX
Tel: 0171-404 5011 *(24 hours)*
Support for families with babies who cry excessively

Depression Alliance
35 Westminster Bridge Road
London SE1 7JB
Tel: 0171-633 9929 *(answerphone)*
Fax: 0171-633 0559
Web site: www.gn.apc.org/da/

Depressives Anonymous
36 Chestnut Avenue
Beverley
East Riding of Yorkshire HU17 9QU
Tel: (01482) 860619
Fax: (01482) 887634
Web site: www.ribblewebdesign.co.uk/fda

Diabetes Foundation
177A Tennison Road
London SE25 5NF
Tel: 0181-656 5467 *(answerphone)*

Digestive Disorders Foundation
PO Box 251
Edgeware
Middlesex HA8 6HG
Tel: 0171-487 5332 *(answerphone)*
Web site: www.digestivedisorders.org.uk

Disability Wales - Anabledd Cymru Llys Ifor
Crescent Road
Caerphilly CF83 1XL
Tel: (01222) 887325
Fax: (01222) 888702
Email: info@dwac.demon.co.uk

Eating Disorders Association
1st Floor
Wensum House
103 Prince of Wales Road
Norwich NR1 1DW
Adult advice line: (01603) 621414
(9am-6.30pm)
Youth line: (01603) 765050 *(4pm-6pm)*
Fax: (01603) 664915
Email: eda@netcom.co.uk
Web site: www.gurney.org.uk/eda

The Exercise Association of England Ltd
Unit 4, Angel Gate
City Road
London EC1V 2PT
Tel: 0171-278 0811
Fax: 0171-278 0726

Eye Care Information Service
PO Box 3597
London SE1 6DY
Send an sae marked 'VDU information' for leaflets

Family Planning Association
2-12 Pentonville Road
London N1 9FP
Tel: 0171-837 5432
Helpline: 0171-837 4044
Fax: 0171-837 6785

Fibromyalgia Association UK
35 Seymour Road
Lye, Stourbridge
West Midlands DY9 8TB
Tel: (01384) 820052

GMC specialist register hotline
0171-915 3638

Health and Safety Executive
(see also Leafletline)
Public Enquiry Point
Broad Lane
Sheffield S3 7HQ
Web site:
www.open.gov.uk/hse/hsehome.htm
Letters only – no personal callers

Hearing Aid Council
Witan Court
305 Upper Fourth Street
Central Milton Keynes MK9 1EH
Tel: (01908) 235700
Fax: (01908) 235770

Heartburn Hotline
Tel: (0800) 556611

Herpes Viruses Association
41 North Road
London N7 9DP
Helpline: 0171-609 9061

Human BSE Foundation Helpline
Tel: (01380) 720033

Huntington's Disease Association
108 Battersea High Street
London SW11 3HP
Tel: 0171-223 7000
Fax: 0171-223 9489
Web site: www.hda.org.uk

Institute for Complementary Medicine
PO Box 194
London SE16 1QZ
Tel: 0171-237 5165 *(10am-3pm)*
Send an sae with 2 stamps for list of practitioners or courses

Institute of Electrolysis
138 Downs Barn Boulevard
Downs Barn
Milton Keynes MK14 7RP
Tel: (01908) 695297
Send an sae for list of members

International Glaucoma Association
c/o King's College Hospital
Denmark Hill
Camberwell Green
London SE5 9RS
Tel: 0171-737 3265
Fax: 0171-346 5929
Email: ita@kcl.ac.uk
Web site: www.ita.org.uk/iga/

ISSUE (The National Fertility Association)
114 Lichfield Street
Walsall
West Midlands WS1 1SZ
Tel: (01922) 722888
Fax: (01922) 640070
Email: webmaster@issue.co.uk
Web site: www.issue.co.uk

La Leche League of Great Britain
BM 3424
London WC1N 3XX
Tel: 0171-242 1278
Information and counselling for women wanting to breast-feed

Leafletline (Health and Safety Executive)
Health and Safety Executive Books
PO Box 1999
Sudbury
Suffolk CO10 6FS
Tel: (01787) 881165
Fax: (01787) 313995
Web site: www.hsebooks.co.uk

Lupus UK
St James House
Eastern Road
Romford
Essex RM1 3NH
Tel: (01708) 731251
Fax: (01708) 731252

Marie Stopes Clinic
108 Whitfield Street
London W1P 6BE
Tel: 0171-388 0662/2585
Fax: 0171-388 3409

Menière's Society
98 Maybury Road
Woking
Surrey GU21 5HX
Tel: (01483) 740597
Fax/Minicom: (01483) 771207
Support for sufferers of Menière's and like conditions

Migraine Action Association
178 High Road
Byfleet, West Byfleet
Surrey KT14 7ED
Tel: (01932) 352468
Fax: (01932) 351257
Email: info@migraine.org.uk
Web site: www.migraine.org.uk

Migraine Trust
45 Great Ormond Street
London WC1N 3HZ
Tel: 0171-831 4818
Fax: 0171-831 5174

MIND (National Association for Mental Health)
Granta House
15-19 Broadway
Stratford
London E15 4BQ
Tel: 0181-519 2122 ext 275
Helpline: (0345) 660163
Fax: 0181-522 1725
Email: contact@mind.org.uk
Web site: www.mind.org.uk

Miscarriage Association
c/o Clayton Hospital
Northgate
Wakefield
West Yorkshire WF1 3JS
Tel: (01924) 200799 *(answerphone)*

Multiple Sclerosis Society
25 Effie Road
London SW6 1EE
Tel: 0171-736 6267
Fax: 0171-736 7861
Email: info@mssociety.org.uk
Web site: www.mssociety.org.uk

Myalgic Encephalomyelitis (ME) Association
4 Corringham Road
Stanford-le-Hope
Essex SS17 0AH
Tel: (01375) 642466 *(10am-4pm)*
Information line: (01375) 361013 *(1.30pm-4pm)*
Fax: (01375) 360256

National AIDS Helpline
Tel: (0800) 567123 *(24 hours)*

National Association for Colitis and Crohn's Disease
4 Beaumont House
Sutton Road
St Albans
Hertfordshire AL1 5HH
Tel: (01727) 844296
Fax: (01727) 862550
Email: nacc@nacc.org.uk
Web site: www.nacc.org.uk

National Association for Premenstrual Syndrome
7 Swists Court
High Street
Seal, Sevenoaks
Kent TN5 0EQ
Tel: (01732) 760012
Send A5 sae for information

National Association for the Relief of Paget's Disease (NARPD)
1 Church Road, Eccles
Manchester M30 0DL
Tel: 0161-789 6755
Email: 106064.2032@compuserve.com
Web site: www.demon.co.uk/narpd

National Asthma Campaign
Providence House
Providence Place
London N1 0NT
Tel: 0171-226 2260
Fax: 0171-704 0740
Helpline: (0345) 010203 (9am-7pm)
Web site: www.asthma.org.uk

National Back Pain Association
16 Elmtree Road
Teddington
Middlesex TW11 8FT
Email: 101540.1065@compuserve.com
Web site: www.backpain.org/
Send £2.50 p&p for information

National Childbirth Trust
Alexandra House
Oldham Terrace
London W3 6NH
Tel: 0181-992 8637
(Mon-Fri, 9.30am-4.30pm)
Fax: 0181-992 5929

National CJD Support Network
Tel/Fax: (01630) 673973
Tel/Fax: (01630) 673993 (*administration*)

National Eczema Society
163 Eversholt Street
London NW1 1BU
Tel: 0171-388 4097
Helpline: 0171-388 4800
Fax: 0171-388 5882
Web site: www.eczema.org

National Endometriosis Society
Suite 50
Westminster Palace Gardens
1-7 Artillery Row
London SW1P 1RL
Tel: 0171-222 2781
Helpline: 0171-222 2776
Fax: 0171-222 2786

National Osteoporosis Society
PO Box 10
Radstock
Bath BA3 3YB
Tel: (01761) 471771
Helpline: (01761) 472721
Fax: (01761) 471104
Email: info@nos.org.uk
Web site: www.nos.org.uk

National Schizophrenia Fellowship
28 Castle Street
Kingston-upon-Thames
Surrey KT1 1SS
Tel: 0181-547 3937
Helpline : 0181-974 6814
(Mon-Fri, 10am-3pm)
Fax: 0181-547 3862
Email: info@nsf.org.uk
Web site: www.nsf.org.uk

Northern Ireland Association for Mental Health
80 University Street
Belfast BT7 1HE
Tel: (01232) 328474
Helpline: (01232) 237937
Fax: (01232) 200335
Email: niamhbel.aol.com

Northern Ireland Community Addiction Service
40 Elmwood Avenue
Belfast BT9 6AZ
Tel: (01232) 664434
Fax: (01232) 664090

Parkinson's Disease Society
215 Vauxhall Bridge Road
London SW1V 1EJ
Tel: 0171-931 8080
Fax: 0171-233 9908
Helpline: 0171-233 5373
Email: mailbox.edsuk.demon.co.uk

**Pelvic Inflammatory Disease Network –
Women's Health**
52 Featherstone Street
London EC1Y 8RT
Tel: 0171-251 6580
Fax: 0171-608 0928
Email: womenshealth@pop3.poptel.org.uk

Positively Women
347-349 City Road
London EC1V 1LR
Tel: 0171-713 0444
Fax: 0171-713 1020
Email: poswomen@dircon.co.uk
Support for HIV-positive women

Psoriasis Association
7 Milton Street
Northampton
Northamptonshire NN2 7JG
Tel: (01604) 711129
Fax: (01604) 792894

QUITLINE
Tel: (0800) 002200 *(9am-11pm)*
Help for those who want to quit smoking

Rape Crisis Centre
Tel: 0171-837 1600
(6pm-10pm weekdays, 10am-10pm weekends)

Raynaud's and Scleroderma Association
112 Crewe Road
Alsager
Cheshire ST7 2JA
Tel: (01270) 872776
Fax: (01270) 883556
Email: webmaster@raynauds.demon.co.uk
Web site: www.raynauds.demon.co.uk

Relate National Marriage Guidance
Herbert Gray College
Little Church Street
Rugby
Warwickshire CV21 3AP
Tel: (01788) 573241
Fax: (01788) 535007
Email: info@relate.org.uk
Web site: www.relate.org.uk

**Release (The National Drugs and Legal
Helpline)**
388 Old Street
London EC1V 9LT
Helplines: 0171-729 9904 *(10am-6pm)*
0171-603 8654 *(24 hours)*
Fax: 0171-729 2599
Email: info@release.org.uk
Web site: www.release.org.uk

Repetitive Strain Injury Association
Chapel House
152 High Street
Yiewsley, West Drayton
Middlesex UB7 7BE
Tel: (01895) 431134 *(Mon-Fri, 2pm-4pm)*
Fax: (01895) 437300

**Royal National Institute for the Blind
(RNIB)**
224 Great Portland Street
London W1N 6AA
Tel: 0171-388 1266
Helpline: (0345) 669999
(Mon-Fri, 9am-5pm)
Fax: 0171-388 2034
Email: helpline@rnib.org.uk
Web site: www.rnib.org.uk/

**Royal National Institute for Deaf People
(RNID)**
19-23 Featherstone Street
London EC1Y 8SL
Tel: (0870) 605 0123 *(9.30am-5pm)*
Textline: (0870) 603 3007 *(9.30am-5pm)*
Fax: 0171-296 8199
Email: helpline@rnid.org.uk
Web site: www.rnid.org.uk
*Write to PO Box 16464, London EC1Y
8TT for information*

The Samaritans
General Office
10 The Grove
Slough
Berkshire SL1 1QP
Tel: (01753) 216500
Helpline: (0345) 909090 *(24 hours)*
Fax: (01753) 819004
Email: admin@samaritans.org.uk
Web site: www.samaritans.org.uk

**Schizophrenia - A National Emergency
(SANE)**
1st Floor
Cityside House
40 Adler Street
Whitechapel
London E1 1EE
Tel: 0171-375 1002
Helpline: (0345) 678000 *(2pm-midnight)*
Fax: 0171-375 2162
Email: mkn.co.uk/help/charity/sane/index

Scottish Association for the Deaf
Clarewood House
96 Clermiston Road
Edinburgh EH8 8AQ
Tel: 0131-314 6075
Telephone for the deaf: 0131-558 3390
Fax: 0131-314 6077

Scottish Association for Mental Health
Cumbrae House
15 Carlton Court
Glasgow G5 9JP
Tel: 0141-568 7000
Fax: 0141-568 7001
Email: enquire@samh.org.uk

Scottish Council on Alcohol
166 Buchanan Street
Glasgow G1 2NH
Tel: 0141-333 9677
Fax: 0141-333 1606
Email: sca@clare.net

Scottish Women's Aid
Norton Park
57 Albion Road
Edinburgh EH7 5QY
Tel: 0131-475 2372
Fax: 0131-475 2384
*Information, support and refuge for abused
women and their children*

**Seasonal Affective Disorder (SAD)
Association**
PO Box 989
Steyning
West Sussex BN44 3HG
Tel: (01903) 814942
Fax: (01903) 879939

Sickle Cell Society
54 Station Road
London NW10 4UA
Tel: 0181-961 4006/7795
Fax: 0181-961 4386

Society of Chiropodists
53 Welbeck Street
London W1M 7HE
Tel: 0171-486 3381
Fax: 0171-935 6359

**Society of Teachers of the Alexander
Technique (STAT)**
20 London House
206 Fulham Road
London SW10 9EL
Tel: 0171-351 0828
Fax: 0171-352 1556
Email: office@stat.org.uk
Web site: www.stat.org.uk

**Stillbirth and Neonatal Death Society
(SANDS)**
28 Portland Place
London W1N 4DE
Tel: 0171-436 7940
Helpline: 0171-436 5881
Fax: 0171-436 3715

Stroke Association
Stroke House
123-127 Whitecross Street
London EC1Y 8JJ
Tel: 0171-566 0300
Fax: 0171-490 2686
Email: stroke@stroke.org.uk
Web site: www.stroke.org.uk

**Support Around Termination for
Abnormality (SATFA)**
73 Charlotte Street
London W1P 1LB
Tel: 0171-631 0280
Helpline: 0171-631 0285
Email: arcsatfa@aol.com
*Support at all stages for those considering
antenatal screening/testing and for those who
choose to terminate a pregnancy after diagnosis*

Tinnitus - RNID
Royal National Institute for Deaf People
105 Gower Street
London WC1E 6AH
Helpline: (0345) 090210 *(10am-3pm)*
Advice on overcoming tinnitus caused by inner-ear damage

Tisserand Aromatherapy Institute
65 Church Road
Hove
East Sussex BN3 2BD
Tel: (01273) 206640
Fax: (01273) 329811

Wales Council for the Blind
3rd Floor, Shand House
20 Newport Road
Cardiff CF2 1DB
Tel: (01222) 473954
Fax: (01222) 455710

Wales Council for the Deaf
Glenview House
Court High Street
Pontypridd CF5 7JY
Tel: (01443) 485687
Fax: (01443) 408555
Minicom: (01443) 485686

Wales Council for the Disabled
see Disability Wales

Weight Watchers UK
Kidwells Park House
Kidwells Park Road
Maidenhead
Berkshire SL6 8YT
Tel: (01628) 777077

Women's Aid
PO Box 391
Bristol BS99 7WS
Tel: (0345) 023468
Advice and referral to refuges for abused women

Women's Aid (Northern Ireland)
129 University Street
Belfast BT7 1HP
Tel: (01232) 666049/662385

Women's Health Concern (WHC)
93–99 Upper Richmond Road
London SW15 2TG
Information line: 0181-399 9359
(answerphone)
London: 0181-788 2733
Newcastle-upon-Tyne: 0191-213 1672
Peterborough: (01733) 893586
Send sae for further information

Bibliography

Chapter 1 Staying well and beating illness

Adler, M.W. (ed). 1993 (3rd ed). *ABC of AIDS*. London, BMJ Publishing Group

Balarajan, R. 1995. Ethnicity and variations in the nation's health. *Health Trends,* **27**, 114–19

Barker, D.J.B. 1994. *Mothers, Babies and Diseases in Later Life*. London, BMJ Publishing Group

Ben-Shlomo, Y., White, I.R., Marmor, M. 1996. Does the variation in the socioeconomic characteristics of an area affect mortality? *BMJ,* **312**, 1013–14

Charlton, J., Skinner, C. 1995. Fourth national morbidity study. *Br J Gen Pract,* **45**, 565

Cruickshank, J.K. 1989. *Ethnic Factors in Health and Disease*. London, Wright

Davey Smith, G. 1996. Income inequality and mortality: why are they related? *BMJ,* **312**, 987–8

Department of Health. 1991. *Drug Misuse and Dependence*. London, HMSO

Department of Health. 1992. *The Health of the Nation*. London, HMSO

Department of Health. 1993. *HIV/AIDS and Sexual Health key area Handbook*. London, HMSO

Goldberg, D., Huxley, P. 1992. *Common Mental Disorders*. London, Routledge

Graham, H. 1988. Women and smoking in the United Kingdom: The implications for health promotion. *Health Promotion,* **3**, 371-82

Greener, M. 1996. *The Which? Guide to Managing Stress*. London, Which? Books

Hibbard et al. 1994. *Report on Confidential Enquiries into Maternal Deaths in the United Kingdom 1988–1990,* London, HMSO

Hutton, W. 1996. *The state we're in*. London, Vintage

Inter-Departmental Working Group. 1995. *Sensible Drinking*. London, Department of Health

Kassirer, J.P. 1995. The next transformation in the delivery of health care. *N Engl J Med,* **332**, 52–4

Lamont, T. 1993. *Complementary medicine: New approaches to good practice*. Oxford, Oxford University Press

Macfarlane, A., Mugford, M. 1984. *Birth Counts: Statistics of Pregnancy and Childbirth*. London, HMSO

McPherson, A. (ed). 1993. *Women's Problems in General Practice*. Oxford, Oxford University Press

Markowe, H. 1994. Health trends in the past 75 years. *Health Trends,* **26**, 98–99

Pagliuca A., Pawson R., Mufti G.J. 1995. HTLV-1 screening in Britain. *BMJ,* **311**, 1313–14

Patton A. (ed). 1994 (3rd ed). *ABC of Alcohol.* London, BMJ Publishing Group

Oakley, A., Rigby, A.S., Hickey, D. 1994. Life stress, support and class inequality. Explaining the health of women and children. *Eur J Pub Health*, **2**, 81–91

OPCS 1993. *Mortality statistics: cause: review of the Registrar-General on deaths by cause, sex and age in England and Wales 1992.* London, HMSO

Rowlands, B. 1997. *The Which? Guide to Complementary Medicine.* London, Which? Books

Truswell, A.S. (ed). 1992 (2nd ed). *ABC of Nutrition.* London, BMJ Publishing Group

United Nations. 1995. *The world's women 1995: trends and statistics.* New York, UN

Watt, G.C.M. 1996. All together now: why social deprivation matters to everyone. *BMJ*, **312**, 1026–8

White, I. 1996. The cardioprotective effects of moderate alcohol consumption. *BMJ*, **312**, 1179–80

Chapter 2 Emotional and mental well-being

Charlton, J. 1992. Trends in suicide deaths in England and Wales. *Population Trends,* **69**, 10–16

Department of Health. 1994 (2nd ed). *The Health of the Nation. Key area handbook: mental illness.* London, HMSO

Drug and Therapeutics Bulletin. 1992. Managing the premenstrual syndrome. **30**, 69–72

Paykel, E.S., Priest, R.G. 1992. The recognition and management of depression in general practice: consensus statement. *BMJ*, **305**, 1198–202

Pilowsky, I. 1992. Somatic symptoms/somatisation. *Curr Opinion Psych*, **5**, 213–18

Russell, J. 1995. Treating anorexia nervosa. *BMJ*, **311**, 584

Stein, A., Gath, D.H., Bucher, J. 1991. The relationship between postnatal depression and mother-child interaction. *Br J Psychiatry*, **158**, 46–52

The Mental Health Foundation. 1993. *Mental illness: the Fundamental Facts.* London, The Mental Health Foundation

Drug and Therapeutics Bulletin. 1995. The drug treatment of patients with schizophrenia. **33**, 81–6

Chapter 3 Bones and joints

Brooks, P. 1993. Repetitive strain injury. *BMJ*, **307**, 1298

Brown, Dr H. 1996. *The Which? Guide to Managing Back Trouble.* London, Which? Books

Clinical standards advisory group. 1994. *Back Pain.* London, HMSO

Cooper, C., Aihie, A. 1994. Osteoporosis: recent advances in pathogenesis and treatment. *Q J Med,* **87**, 203–9

Johnson, C.G., Slemenda, C.W., Melton, L.J. 1991. Clinical use of bone densitometry. *N Engl J Med,* **324**, 1105–9

Maxwell, R.J. 1993. The osteopath's bill. *BMJ*, **306**, 1556–7

Porter, D.R., McInnes, I., Capell, H.A. 1994. Outcome of second line therapy in rheumatoid arthritis. *Ann Rheum Dis,* **53**, 812–15

Snaith, M.L. (ed). 1996. *ABC of Rheumatology.* London, BMJ Publishing Group

Tan, E.M., Cohen, E.S. 1982. The 1982 revised criteria for the classification of SLE. *Arthritis Rheum,* **25**, 1271–7

Chapter 4 Eyes

Elder, M. 1993. Contact lenses and their complications. *Practitioner*, **237**, 509–12

Elkington, A.R., Khaw, P.T. 1988. *ABC of Eyes.* London, BMJ Publishing Group

Falcon, M. 1991. Glaucoma – managing a growing problem. *MIMS magazine,* **18**, 26–36

Gartry, D.S. 1995. Treating myopia with the excimer laser: the present position. *BMJ,* **310**, 979–985

Roston, C. 1991. Surgery for refractive defects. *Practitioner,* **235**, 115–19

Royal National Institute for the Blind. 1991. *Blind and partially sighted people in Britain – the RNIB survey.* London, HMSO

Sheldrick, J.H. 1993. Management of ophthalmic disease in general practice. *Br J Gen Prac,* **43**, 459–62

Chapter 5 Ear, nose and throat

Drug and Therapeutics Bulletin. 1995. Diagnosis and treatment of streptococcal sore throat. **33**, 9–12

Haddard, J. 1994. Treatment of acute otitis media and its complications. *Otolangol Clin North Am,* **27**, 431–4

Ludman, H. (ed). 1993 (3rd ed). *ABC of Otolaryngology.* London, BMJ Publishing Group

MacKenzie, K. 1994. Diagnosis and treatment of hoarseness. *Practitioner,* **238**, 474–8

Slack, R., Bates, G. 1995. Functional endoscopic sinus surgery. *Practitioner,* **239**, 591–5

Chapter 6 Skin

Bailie, W.T. 1995. Nail problems in practice. *Update.* **50**, 788–90

Buxton, PK. (ed). 1993 (2nd ed). *ABC of Dermatology.* London, BMJ Publishing Group

Champion, R.H. et al (eds) 1992 (5th ed). *Textbook of Dermatology.* Oxford, Blackwell Scientific Publications

Cox, N.H. 1995. Advances in therapy: skin infections. *Update,* **51**, 189–91

Drug and Therapeutics Bulletin. 1996. The management of psoriasis. **34**, 17–19

Marks, R. 1995. An overview of skin cancers: incidence and causation. *Cancer,* **75**, 607–12

Rees, J.L. 1996. The melanoma epidemic: reality and artefact. *BMJ,* **312**, 137–8

Chapter 7 Digestive system

Alberti, K.G.M.M. et al. (eds). 1992. *International Textbook of Diabetes Mellitus.* London, John Wiley

Alberti, K.G.M.M. 1993. Preventing insulin dependent diabetes mellitus. *BMJ,* **307**, 1435–6

Drug and Therapeutics Bulletin. 1994. Managing patients with gallstones. **32**, 33–35

Drug and Therapeutics Bulletin. 1996. The medical management of gastro-oesophageal reflux. **34**, 14

Francis, C.Y., Whorwell, P.J. 1994. Bran and irritable bowel syndrome: time for reappraisal. *Lancet,* **344**, 39–40

Gregory, R. 1996. Oral antidiabetic drugs. *Update,* **52**, 536–7

Jones D.J., Irving, M.H. 1993. *ABC of Colorectal Diseases.* London, BMJ Publishing Group

Lydeard S., Jones, R. 1989. Factors affecting the decision to consult with dyspepsia: a comparison of consulters and non-consulters. Policy statement. *R Coll Gen Pract,* **39**, 495–8

Mandel, J.S., Bond, J.H., Church, T.R., Snover, D.C., Bradley, G.M., Schuman, L.M. et al. 1993. Reducing mortality from colorectal cancer by screening for fecal occult blood. *N Engl J Med,* **328**, 1363–71

Marshall, B.J. 1994. Helicobacter pylori. *Am J Gastroenterol*, **89**, 116–28
McNair A.N.B., Tibbs, C.J., Williams, R. 1995. Recent advances: hepatology. *BMJ*, **311**, 1351–6
Royal College of Physicians of London. 1983. Obesity. *J Roy Coll Phys*, **17**, 3–58
Watkins, P. (ed). 1993 (3rd ed). *ABC of Diabetes*. London, BMJ Publishing Group

Chapter 8 Heart and lungs

Action Asthma. 1991. National asthma survey results
Bennet N., Dodd T., Flatley J., Freeth S., Bolling K. 1995. *Health Survey for England 1993*, London, HMSO
British Heart Foundation. 1993. *Women and the prevention of coronary heart disease. January 1993, Factfile*
British Thoracic Society. 1993. Guidelines on the management of asthma. *Thorax*, **48**, 21–24
Julian, D.G. (ed). 1990. *Current status of clinical cardiology*. London, Kluwer
Khaw, K.T. 1993. Where are the women in studies of coronary heart disease? *BMJ*, **306**, 1145–6
Prentice A., Jebb, S.A. 1995. Obesity in Britain: gluttony or sloth? *BMJ*, **311**, 437–40
Rees, J., Price, J. (eds). 1995 (3rd ed). *ABC of Asthma*. London, BMJ Publishing Group
RITA trial participants. 1993. Coronary angioplasty versus coronary artery bypass surgery: the Randomised Intervention Treatment of Angina (RITA) trial. *Lancet*, **341**, 573–80
Steele, C. 1995. Helping patients to stop smoking. *Practitioner*, **239**, 154–9
Turton, C. 1994. Cardiovascular disability. *Update*, **49**, 452–8

Chapter 9 Head and nervous system

Collins, R., Peto, R., Macmahon, S. 1990. Blood pressure, stroke and CHD. *Lancet*, **335**, 827–38
Drug and Therapeutics Bulletin. 1994. Epilepsy and pregnancy. **32**, 49–51
Graham, J., 1993. *Multiple Sclerosis: a Self Help Guide*. London, Thorsons
Headache classification committee of the International Headache Society. 1988. Classification and diagnostic criteria for headache disorders, cranial neuralgias and facial pain. *Cephalgia*, **8**, 1–96
Manford, M., Hart, Y.M., Sander, J.W.A.S. et al. 1992. The national general practice study of epilepsy. *Arch Neurol*, **49**, 801–8
Manley, P. 1994. Diet in multiple sclerosis. *Practitioner*, **238**, 358–363
McDonald, W.I. 1995. New treatments for multiple sclerosis. *BMJ*, **310**, 345–7
McMichael, A.J. 1996. Bovine spongiform encephalopathy; its wider meaning for population health. *BMJ*, **312**, 1313–14
Olesen, J. 1995. Analgesic headache. *BMJ*, **310**, 479–80
Sandercock, P. 1993. Managing stroke: the way forward. *BMJ*, **307**, 1297–8

Chapter 10 Breasts

Creighton, P.A. 1995. What general practitioners should do about breast screening. *BMJ*, **310**, 204–5
Dixon, J.M. (ed). 1995. *ABC of Breast Diseases*. London, BMJ Publishing Group
Drug and Therapeutics Bulletin. 1992. Cyclical breast pain – what works and what doesn't. **30**, 1–2

Drug and Therapeutics Bulletin. 1992. Following up breast cancer. **30**, 19–21

Drug and Therapeutics Bulletin. 1992. Management of early breast cancer. **30**, 53–6

Duncan, B., Ey, J., Holberg, C.J., Wright, A.L., Martinez, F.D., Taussig, L.M. 1993. Exclusive breastfeeding for at least 4 months protects against otitis media. *Pediatrics,* **91**, 667–9

Early breast cancer trialists' collaborative group. 1992. Systemic treatment of early breast cancer by hormonal, cytotoxic or immune therapy. *Lancet,* **339**, 1–15; 71–85

Field, S., Michell, M.J., Wallis, M.G.W.,Wilson, A.R.M. 1995. What should be done about interval breast cancers? *BMJ,* **310**, 203–4

Fisher, B., Redmond, C.P., Oisson, R. et al. 1989. Eight year results of a randomised clinical trial comparing total mastectomy and lumpectomy with or without irradiation in the treatment of breast cancer. *N Engl J Med,* **320**, 822–8

Hughes, L.E., Mansel, R.E., Webster, D.J.T. 1989. *Benign Disorders and Diseases of the Breast.* London, Baillière Tindall

Inch S., Fisher, C. 1995. Mastitis: infection or inflammation? *Practitioner,* **239**, 472–6

Jordan, V.C. 1993. How safe is tamoxifen? *BMJ,* **307**, 1371–2

Lucas, A., Morley, R., Cole, T.J. 1992. Breastmilk and subsequent IQ in children born preterm. *Lancet,* **339**, 261–4

McPherson, K. 1995. Breast cancer and hormonal supplements in postmenopausal women. *BMJ,* **311**, 699–700

NHS. 1994. Breast screening programme; information folder

OPCS. 1990. *Infant Feeding.* London, HMSO

Sampson, M.A., Rubin, C.M.E. 1996. Breast screening of younger women is futile. *Update,* **52**, 524-8

Szabo, C.I., King, M-C. 1995. Inherited breast and ovarian cancer. *Hum Molec Genet,* **4**, 1811-17

Yates, J.R.W. 1996. Recent advances: medical genetics. *BMJ,* **312**, 1021-6

Chapter 11 Gynaecology

Advanced ovarian cancer trialists' group. 1991. Chemotherapy in advanced ovarian cancer: an overview of randomised clinical trials. *BMJ,* **303**, 884–93

Bewley, S. 1995. In vitro fertilisation is rarely successful in older women. *BMJ,* **310**, 1457

Bosch, F.X., Manos, M.M., Munoz, M., Sherman, M., Jansen, A.M., Peto, J. et al. 1995. Prevalence of human papillomavirus in cervical cancer: a worldwide perspective. *J Natl Cancer Inst,* **87**, 796–802

Bury, J. 1993. Women and HIV infection. *Practitioner,* **237**, 659–66

Clark, A., Black, N., Rowe, P., Mott, S., Howle, K. 1995. Indications for and outcome of total abdominal hysterectomy for benign disease: a prospective cohort study. *J Obstet Gynaecol,* **102**, 611–20

Colvin, D., Lucas, C. 1995. Vulval problems. *Practitioner,* **239**, 547–52

Drug and Therapeutics Bulletin. 1992. Managing the premenstrual syndrome. **30**, 69–72

Drug and Therapeutics Bulletin. 1994. Surgical management of menorrhagia. **32**, 70–2

Dwyer, N., Hutton, J., Stirrat, G.M. 1993. Randomised controlled trial comparing endometrial resection and abdominal hysterectomy for the treatment of menorrhagia. *Br J Obstet Gynaecol,* **100**, 237–43

Havelock, C., Havelock, P. 1994. Towards effective cervical screening. *Practitioner,* **238**, 296–302

Hay, P.E., Lamont, R.F., Taylor et al. 1994. Abnormal bacterial colonisation of the genital tract and subsequent preterm delivery and late miscarriage. *BMJ,* **308**, 295–8

Hines, J.F., Ghim, S-J., Jenson, A.B. 1996. Human papillomavirus infection. *BMJ*, **312**, 522–3

Holland, W.H. 1993. Screening: reasons to be cautious. *BMJ*, **306**, 1222–3

Limb, D.G. 1995. Endometriosis – a gynaecological headache. *Update*, **50**, 499–508

Mahmood, T.A., Templeton, A. 1991. Prevalence and genesis of endometriosis. *Hum Reprod*, **6**, 544–9

Marwood, R.P. 1994. Dysmenorrhoea. *Update*, **48**, 649–657

McPherson, A. (ed). 1993. *Women's Problems in General Practice*. Oxford, Oxford University Press

O'Dowd, T. 1995. Treating bacterial vaginosis. *Practitioner*, **239**, 538–42

OPCS. 1988. *Cancer statistics: registrations 1987 England and Wales*. London, HMSO

Pinion, S.B., Parkin, D.E., Abramovich, D.R., Naji, A., Alexander, D.A., Russell, I.T., et al. 1994. Randomised trial of hysterectomy, endometrial laser ablation, and transcervical endometrial resection for dysfunctional uterine bleeding. *BMJ*, **309**, 979–83

Smith, R., Studd, J. 1994. Gynaecological drugs – an update. *Update*, **49**, 221–33

Smith, S.K. 1996. Gynaecology – medical or surgical? *BMJ*, **312**, 592–3

Uthayakumar, S., Shah, P.N., Smith, J.R. 1994. Vaginal discharge. *Update*, **49**, 155–163

Wiener, J. 1994. Chronic pelvic pain. *Practitioner*, **238**, 352–8

Working group of the British society for Medical Mycology. 1995. Management of genital candidiasis. *BMJ*, **310**, 1241–5

Chapter 12 Fertility

Cates, W.J.R., Stone, K.M. 1992. Family planning, sexually transmitted diseases and contraceptive choice: a literature update part I. *Fam Plann Perspect*, **24**, 75–84

Chantler, E. 1992. Spermicides – some current concerns. *Br J Fam Plann*, **17**, 118–19

Committee on Safety of Medicines. 1995. *Combined oral contraceptives and thromboembolism*. London, CSM

Drug and Therapeutics Bulletin. 1993. Femidom – a condom for women. **31**, 15–16

Guillebaud, J. 1995. Advising women on which pill to take. *BMJ*, **311**, 1111–12

Guillebaud, J. 1994. *Contraception – your questions answered*. Edinburgh, Churchill Livingstone

Hull, M.G.R. et al. 1985. Population study of causes, treatment and outcome of infertility. *BMJ*, **291**, 1693–71

Kirkman, R., Chantler, E. 1993. Contraception and the prevention of sexually transmitted diseases. *Br Med Bull*, **49**, 171–81

MacRae, K., Kay, C. 1995. Third generation oral contraceptive pills. *BMJ*, **311**, 1112–13

Mansour, D. 1996. Oral contraception after the pill scare. *Update*, **52**, 497–9

Paintin, D. (ed). 1995. *The Provision of Emergency Contraception*. London, Royal College of Obstetricians and Gynaecologists Press

Polson, D.W., Adams, J., Wadsworth, J., Franks, S. 1988. Polycystic ovaries – a common finding in normal women. *The Lancet*, **i**, 870–2

Which? Way to Health. 1993. Condoms on test. August 1993, 119–23

Chapter 13 Pregnancy

Chalmers, I., Enkin, M., Kierse, M.J.N.C. 1989. *Effective Care in Pregnancy and Childbirth*. Oxford, Oxford University Press

Chamberlain, G. (ed). 1994 (2nd ed). *ABC of Antenatal Care*. London, BMJ Publishing Group

CLASP (Collaborative low-dose aspirin study in pregnancy) collaborative group. 1994. CLASP: a randomised controlled trial of low-dose aspirin for the prevention and treatment of pre-eclampsia among 9,364 pregnant women. *Lancet*, **343**, 619–29

Connor, M. 1993. Biochemical screening for Down's syndrome. *BMJ*, **306**, 1705–6

Department of Health. 1993. *Changing Childbirth*. London, HMSO

Department of Health. 1994. *Report on confidential enquiries into maternal deaths in the UK 1988–90*. London, HMSO

Drife, J.O. 1995. Assessing the consequences of changing childbirth. *BMJ*, **310**, 144–5

Glazener, C.M.A., MacArthur, C., Garcia, J. 1993. Postnatal care: time for a change. *Obstetrics and Gynaecology*, **5**, 130–6

Lieberman, E. 1995. Low birth weight – not a black and white issue. *N Engl J Med*, **332**, 117–18

MacArthur, C., Lewis, M., Knox, E.G., Crawford, J.S. 1990. Epidural anaesthesia and long-term backache after childbirth. *BMJ*, **301**, 9–12

Noble, T. 1993. The routine six-week postnatal vaginal examination. *BMJ*, **307**, 698–9

Paterson, C.M., Chapple, J.C., Beard, R.W., Joffe, M., Steer, P.J., Wright, C.S.W. 1991. Evaluating the quality of maternity services – a discussion paper. *Br J Obstet Gynaecol*, **98**, 1073–8

Steer, P. 1995. Recent advances: obstetrics. *BMJ*, **311**, 1209–12

Steer, P. 1993. Rituals in antenatal care – do we need them? *BMJ*, **307**, 697–8

Treffers, P.E., Pel, M. 1993. The rising trend for caesarean birth. *BMJ*, **307**, 1017–18

Wilson, A.G., Duff, G.W. 1995. Genetic traits in common diseases. *BMJ*, **310**, 1482–3

Chapter 14 Menopause

Berg, G., Hammer, M. (eds). 1994. *The Modern Management of the Menopause; a Perspective for the 21st century*. London, Parthenon

British Medical Association. 1993. *Complementary Medicine: Good Approaches to Clinical Practice*. Oxford, Oxford University Press

Felson, D.T., Zhang, Y., Hannan, M.T., Kiel, D.P., Wilson, P.W.F., Anderson, J.J. 1993. The effect of postmenopausal estrogen therapy on bone density in elderly women. *N Engl J Med*, **329**, 1141–6

Grady, D., Rubin, S.M., Petitii, D.B., Fox, C.S., Black, D., Ettinger, B. et al. 1992. Hormone therapy to prevent disease and prolong life in postmenopausal women. *Ann Intern Med*, **117**, 1016–37

Daly, E.,Vessy, P., Barlow, D., Gray, A., McPherson, K., Roche, M. 1994. Measuring the impact of menopausal symptoms on quality of life. *BMJ*, **307**, 836–40

McPherson, K. 1995. Breast cancer and hormonal supplements in postmenopausal women. *BMJ*, **311**, 699–700

Meade, T.W., Berra, A. 1992. Hormone replacement therapy and cardiovascular disease. *Br Med Bull*, **48**, 276–308

Studd, J. 1992. Complications of hormone replacement therapy in postmenopausal women. *J R Soc Med*, **85**, 376–8

Studd, J., Whitehead, M. I. (eds). 1988. *The Menopause*. Oxford, Blackwell

Wilson, R.C.D. 1995. *Understanding HRT and the Menopause*. London, Which? Books

Wolman, R.L. 1994. Osteoporosis and exercise. *BMJ*, **309**, 400–3

Chapter 15 Cosmetic surgery

Barry, D. 1996. *Nips and Tucks*. Santa Monica, General Publishing Group

Cooper, C., Dennison, E. 1998. Do silicone implants cause connective tissue disease? *BMJ*, **316**, 403-4

Davies, D., Sadgrove, J. 1996. *Safe Cosmetic Surgery: A Complete Guide*. London, Metro

Goldwyn, R.M. 1998. Breast reduction ad absurdum. *Plastic and Reconstructive Surgery*, **102**, 246

Health Which?. 1997. The surgery sale. October 1997, 154-7

Horlock, N. 1997. Rationing breast reduction surgery. *BMJ*, **314**, 1045-6

McDaniel, D.H. 1990. Cutaneous vascular disorders: advances in laser treatment. *Cutis*, **45**, 339-60

Pape, S. 1997. Laser treatment of skin conditions. *Update*, **54**, 724-8

Index

Page numbers in **bold** indicate where a subject is dealt with in more detail.

candidiasis *see* thrush
cap *see* diaphragm
capillaries, broken 401–2
capsulitis 94
cardiotocographs 358
carpal tunnel syndrome 97
cartilage 79, 101
cataracts 44, **124**
cellulite 398
central nervous system (CNS) 241–2, 243
cervical cancer 21, 41, **303–4**
cervical erosion 302
cervical smear tests 18, 21, 41, **303–4**, 306
cervical spondylosis 244–5
cervix 293, 295, 299, 367–8
chalazions 118
chemical peels 403
chest 216–40
chest drain 235
chest infections 223, 236, 240
chest pain 216, **219–39**
chickenpox 154, 348
chilblains 107
childbirth 200, 310, 311, 317
　see also labour
children
　glue ear 136
　infections 37
　and passive smoking 28
Chinese herbal medicines **157**, 162
chiropodists *see* podiatrists
chiropractic 42, **44–5**, 87, 110
chlamydia 37, 116, 313, **314**, 348
cholecystectomy 209
cholesterol 40, 218, 227, **228**, **229**, 328
chorionic villus sampling (CVS) 356–7
circulatory system 216, 218
cirrhosis 197, 198
clinical ecology 45
clitoris 294, 295
cochlear implants 137
codeine products 190, 192, 220
coeliac disease 22, 189, **191**
coelocentesis 357
coil *see* intra-uterine contraceptive device
　(IUCD)
cold sores **144**, 315
colds **128**, 130, 133, 144, **239**
colic 208
colitis 300
collagen injections 403
colonic irrigation 45
colonoscopies 202, 212
colorectal (bowel) cancer 41, 191, 192, 199,
　201–2, 212
colour therapy 45
colposcope 303
colposuspension 317

complaints procedure
　private medicine 403–5
　National Health Service (NHS) 410–11,
　　412
complementary therapies 15, **42–7**
conception
　assisted 337–40
　attempting to conceive 23, **335–6**
condoms **329–30**, 332
confusion 71–2
conjunctivitis 37, **116**, **118–19**
consciousness, loss of 242, **255–8**
constipation 109, 185, 190, **191–3**, 199, 200,
　210, 213
contact eczema 156, 159
contact lenses 117, 123
contraception **326–33**, 376
contraceptive patches 333
contraceptive pill 165, 167, 188, 189, 196, 226,
　312, 395
　and breast cancer 287
　combined oral contraceptive (COC) 88,
　　246, **327–8**, 332
　and fertility 336
　and hirsutism 177
　mini-pill (progestogen-only pill) 88, 196,
　　246, **328**, 332
　protective benefits 86, 327
　skin condition and 152, 153
contractions 369
cordocentesis 358
corns 106–7, **169**
coronary arteries 218, 226
coronary artery bypass graft (CABG) 232
cosmetic dentistry 400–1
cosmetic surgery 9, 139, 152, **383–405**
　breast augmentation 269, **391–3**
　breast implants 385
　breast reduction 268, 384, 385, **393–4**
　capillaries, broken 401–2
　choosing a clinic or surgeon 386–8
　complaints procedure 403–5
　cosmetic dentistry 400–1
　eyelid reduction 385
　face-lifts 394–7
　GP referral 385
　liposuction 397–9
　on the NHS 385
　nose reshaping 385, **389–90**
　opting for 384
　private medical practice 385–6
　pros and cons 384
　risks 384
　sun spots 402
　tummy tucks 384, 385, **399–400**
　wrinkles 402–3
cosmetics 117, 119, 127, 165
costochondritis **222**, 275, 276, 277

coughing 40, 51, 216, **239–40**
counselling 25, 65
cranial osteopathy 46
Creutzfeldt-Jakob disease (CJD) 67, **69–70**
Crohn's disease 22, 111, 113, 185, 189, 190,
    199, **200–1**, 202, **213**
CT scan 253
cystectomy 310
cystic fibrosis 356, 365
cystitis 186, **214–15**, 319, 321
cystocele 317
cysts 102, 126, 150, 164, 170, 186, **279**
cytology 283, 285
cytomegalovirus 367

D & C (dilation and curettage) 304, 309, 375
dandruff 174–5
deafness *see* hearing loss
death, causes of 38
deep-vein thrombosis (DVT) 103, **224**
dementia 30, **66–71**, 319, 324
dental health **26–8**, 42, 134, 144
    see also cosmetic dentistry
depo-provera (injectable contraceptive) 300,
    328, 332
depression and anxiety 20, 25, 50, **60–6**, 191,
    242
    causes 61–3
    manic depression 63
    phobias and panic attacks 65–6
    postnatal depression 62–3
    seeking professional help 64
    self-help 64–5
    symptoms 61
    treating 65
dermabrasion 402–3
dermatitis *see* eczema
dermatologists 159, 162, 163, 164, 168
deviated nasal septum 141
diabetes 33, 40, 51, 56, 72, 122, 133, 173, 180,
    185, **194–6**, 227, 300, 319, 322
diaphragm 196, **329**, 332
diarrhoea 185, **189–91**, 194, 210
diet and nutrition
    eating habits, changing 34
    food intolerances 45
    healthy eating **22–4**, 25, 40, 229–30
    nutritional supplements 23–4
diets
    elimination diets 45, 86, 213
    vegetarian diet 101
    yo-yo dieting 56, 230
digestive system **183–215**
    abdominal pain 183, 185, 186, **202–15**,
        363–4
    care of 187
    functioning of 183–5
    problems 22, **186–94**

discoid eczema 155
discs and disc pain **79–80**, 107
diuretics 56, 72, 106, 126, 127, 237, 323
diverticulitis 185, **199–200**, 211
dizziness 50, 130, 131, 135, 188, 242, **253–5**
donor insemination 339, 340
dopamine 70, 242
Doppler studies 358
'dowager's hump' 83
Down's syndrome 351, 353, **355–6**, 365
dowsing 45
drug use and dependence **31–2**, 346
dual energy X-ray absorptiometry (DEXA) 84
duct ectasia 279
duodenal ulcers 206
dyskaryosis 303
dysmenorrhoea 296–7

ear 128–30
ear drops 133
ear, nose and throat structure 128–31
ear problems 131–8
earache **131–4**, 145
eardrum, perforated 132, 133, 135, 136
ears, pierced 132
ears, pressure in 133–4
ears, wax in 132, 135, 136
eating disorders 35, **56–60**, 242
    see also anorexia nervosa; bulimia
ECG tests 232
echocardiograms 232
eclampsia 363
ectopic pregnancy 303, **307–8**, 328, 330, 337,
    338, 355, **360–1**
eczema 22, 149, 152, 154, **155–9**, 168, 174,
    318
egg donation 339
elbow pain 95
electrolysis 178, 402
emollients 156
emphysema 28, 72, **238**
encephalitis 252–3
endocarditis 181
endometrial cancer 299, **304**, 327, 381
endometrial sampling 306
endometriosis 186, 211, 213, **296**, 297, 299,
    307, 309, 311, 337
endoscopy 205, 207, 221
entropion/ectropion 118
epidurals 373
epilepsy 242, **255–7**, 324
episiotomy 310, **371–2**
ethnically related factors 18–20, 83, 87, 101,
    196
eustachian tube, blocked 128
evening primrose oil 55, 82, 86, 157, **272**, **274**
exercise **24**, 25, 110, 227–8, 346–7
eye care 117

eye checks 117
eye disease 41–2
eye drops and ointment 116
eye exercises 44
eye problems **116–27**
    bulging eyes 127
    dry eyes 126–7
    puffy eyes 127
    red eyes 112, **116–19**
    visual loss 120–6
    watering eyes 126
eye strain 245
eye, structure of the 114–16
eyelid reduction 385

face-lifts 394–7
factors influencing health **15–22**
    ethnicity factors 18–20
    gender factors 17–18
    regional variations 15, 20–1
    socio-economic factors 15, 16–17
    workplace and environment 21
faints 255
fallopian tubes 293, 295, 314, 360
    blockage 337, 338
family planning, natural **326–7**, 333
feet and foot pain 104–7
fertility **326–40**
    conception 335–40
    contraception 326–33
    male fertility 337
    preparing to have a baby 333–4
    problems 314, **335–7**
fibre, dietary 191, **192**, 193, 212
fibroadenoma **279**, 285
fibroids **298**, 306, 355, **363**
fibromyalgia 50, **91**
fine needle aspiration 283, 285
fits *see* epilepsy
floaters 120
fluid retention 98–9
fluoride 27, 85
foetus 342–3
folic acid 23, **256–7**, 334, **344**, 366
food hygiene 187
food, inhalation of 234
food poisoning 37, **187**, 188, 210, 334
forceps deliveries 371
foreign bodies
    in the ear 136
    in the eye 118
    in the throat 143–4, 146
'frozen shoulder' 93

galactorrhoea 269
gall bladder inflammation 112
gall bladder removal 209
gall stones 56, 93, 185, 197, 204, **208–10**, 275,

276
gamete intra-fallopian transfer (GIFT) 338, 340
ganglions 97
gastric ulcers 206
gastroenteritis 188, **190**, 203, **205**
gastroenterologists 205, 221
gay relationships 52
general practitioners (GPs) 406–7
genetic counselling 334
genetic disorders 8–9, 38, **356–7**
genital herpes 37, **315**
genital warts 37, **316**, 318
genitals 294
genito-urinary medicine (GUM) clinics 37, 311–12
German measles *see* rubella
gestational diabetes 196
glandular fever 145
glaucoma 41, 44, 117, 119, 121, 122, **124–6**
glucose 194, 195
glucose tolerance test 195
'glue ear' 136
gonorrhoea 37, **313**, **314**
good health, maintaining 15, **22–8**
    dental health 26–8
    exercise 24
    healthy eating **22–4**, 229–30
    stress avoidance 24–6
gout 79, 81, 103, **105–6**, 169
groin pain 99
grommets 136
guttate psoriasis 160
gynaecological problems 41, 294, **296–325**

haemorrhoids 192, 198–9, 322, **349**
hair care 175
hair, excess 177–9
hair loss 87, 174, **175–7**
hair problems 149–50, **173–9**
hair structure 173–4
hand and wrist problems 96–9
hay fever 22, 116, 133, 139, 140, 155
head injuries 72
headaches 46, 55, 242, **244–51**, 329
health visitors 374
hearing aids 137
hearing loss 131, **134–8**
hearing tests 137–8
heart 216–18
heart attacks 72, 218, **226**, **231**, 233
heart disease 17, 23, 218, 219, **226–33**
    alcohol and 30
    ethnicity factor 19
    family history 228
    hormone replacement therapy (HRT) and 17, 381
    investigation 232

tranquillisers 66
trans-cervical resection of the endometrium
(TCRE) 299
transient ischaemic attacks (TIAs) 257
tremor 258–9
trichomonas 37, 310, 313, **314**, 316
trigeminal neuralgia 247
tuberculosis (TB) 51, 92, 239, 251–2
tummy tucks 384, 385, **399–400**

ulcerative colitis 111, 113, 185, 189, **190**, 199,
200, 201, 202, 213
ulcers
of cornea 119
leg ulcers 173
mouth ulcers **144**, 183
peptic ulcers 198, 203, 204, **206–7**
rodent ulcers 171–2
stomach ulcers 198, 220
ultrasound scans 84, 285, 306, 347, **352–3**,
354–5, 358
upper arm pain 95–6
ureter 186, 319
urethra 186, 214, 293, 319
urethritis 319
urge incontinence 323, 324, 325
uric acid 105, 169
urinary infections 186, 211, 213, **214–15**, **319**,
321, **322**, **364**
urinary problems 319–25
urinary system 319–20
urination 319, 321–2
urine
blood in the 322
leaking 322–5
urodynamics 325
urticaria 154
uterus *see* womb

vagina 293, 294, 295, 310
vaginal bleeding
during pregnancy 111, **359–62**
erratic 301–6
periods *see* periods
vaginal cones 324
vaginal deliveries 371–2
vaginal discharge **311–12**, 318, 321
vaginal dryness 379
vaginal examination 306
vaginal infections 321, 368
vaginal itch 317–19
vaginal lumps 315, 316
vaginal problems 311–19
vaginal ring 333
vaginismus 52, 311

vaginitis 319
varicose eczema 155, 157
varicose veins 56, 103, 157, 198, **349–50**
vasectomy 331, 332
VDUs, using 41–2
vegetarian diet 101
ventouse 371
verrucas 107, **169**
vertebrae 77, 89, 107
vertebrobasilar insufficiency 257
vertigo 253–4
vitamin A 23, 167, 176, 382
vitamin B6 23, 55
vitamin C 24, 143, 382
vitamin D 85, 101
vitamin E 382
vitamin deficiencies 70
vocal cords 147
voice loss 144
vomiting 185, **186–8**, 198, 221
vulva 294
vulval cancer **305**, 318
vulval itch 317–19
vulval lumps 315

warts 169, **316**, 318
water pills *see* diuretics
waters breaking 369
waxing 178
weakness 260
weight loss, sudden 40, 221
weight reduction 230–1
whiplash injury 46, 89, 92, 97, 134, 244, 245
wind and bloating 193–4
winter blues 48
wisdom teeth, impacted 134
womb 186, 293, 295
obstructions in the 337
retroverted uterus 310
workplace 21, 39
and health 21, 40
pregnant women in the 347, 348
repetitive strain injury (RSI) 95–6
work-related problems 50, 109
wrinkles 402–3
wrist pain *see* hand and wrist problems

X-rays 84, 92, 100, 347

yoga 42, 46

zinc 24
zinc paste bandages 159
zygote intra-fallopian transfer (ZIFT) 339,
340